COLORADO EVIDENCE

2021–2022 Courtroom Manual

ROBERT M. HARDAWAY
Professor of Law
University of Denver Sturm College of Law

GLEN WEISSENBERGER
Professor of Law Emeritus, University of Cincinnati
Former Dean, DePaul University College of Law

QUESTIONS ABOUT THIS PUBLICATION?

For questions about the **Editorial Content** appearing in these volumes or for reprint permission, please call:

James Hardin at	(800) 424-0651
Email:	james.hardin@lexisnexis.com
Outside the United States and Canada, please call	(973) 820-2000

For assistance with replacement pages, shipments, billing or other customer service matters, please call:

Customer Services Department at	(800) 833-9844
Outside the United States and Canada, please call	(518) 487-3385
Fax Number	(800) 828-8341
Customer Service Website	http://www.lexisnexis.com/custserv/

For information on other Matthew Bender publications, please call

Your account manager or	(800) 223-1940
Outside the United States and Canada, please call	(937) 247-0293

ISBN: 978-1-6633-1913-5 (print)
ISSN: 1084-5747

Cite this publication as:

Colorado Evidence Courtroom Manual, § [sec. no.] (2021–2022 ed.) (Matthew Bender)

Because the section you are citing may be revised in a later release, you may wish to photocopy or print out the section for convenient future reference.

This publication is designed to provide authoritative information in regard to the subject matter covered. It is sold with the understanding that the publisher is not engaged in rendering legal, accounting, or other professional services. If legal advice or other expert assistance is required, the services of a competent professional should be sought.

Editorial Office
230 Park Ave., 7th Floor, New York, NY 10169 (800) 543-6862
www.lexisnexis.com

MATTHEW⬥BENDER

Dedication

To the memory of our friend and colleague, Frank Jamison, with appreciation for his scholarly strength and his common sense.

Dedicated to Judy Trejos *R.M.H.*

To My Children *G.W.*

Acknowledgements

This work would not have been possible without the help from my research assistants. I wish to acknowledge with gratitude Alex White and Daniela Masur for their research and contributions to this work.

I would like to extend a special thanks to my senior research assistant, Michael Summers, for his coordination, editing, organization, and management of the research team.

Table of Contents

TABLE OF CONTENTS

TABLE OF CONTENTS

Using This Book

As its title indicates, this book has been designed specifically for courtroom use; its purpose is to provide fast, authoritative answers to the questions which arise in the course of trials and hearings. It accomplishes this through a unique combination of features, which are discussed below.

Locating a Topic

Index—This book's Index is located inside the front cover. It refers the user directly to the evidence rule covering each topic. When you are uncertain which rule covers an issue, this is the place to begin.

Rules—The Colorado Rules of Evidence are reprinted in their entirety in a separate section in the front of the book. They are preceded by a complete Table of Contents.

Section Locator—If you know the rule or article in which your topic is covered and need to review the authors' Analysis, cases, incorporated statutes, or any of the book's other features, the Section Locator on the back cover directs you to the section of the book where this information is found.

Finding an Answer

Rules—If your question can be answered simply by reading the applicable rule, you can find the language of the rule either in the section in the front of the book where all the rules are collected, or at the beginning of the chapter in which the rule is discussed. The Section Locator on the back cover will guide you to either location.

Analysis—Perhaps the most important part of this book, the authors' Analysis provides a quick overview of the rule under discussion, authoritative guidance in interpreting the rule, and pointers for applying the rule in actual practice. In many chapters the Analysis contains special features such as Illustrations, Constitutional Considerations, and Current Trends and New Developments.

Incorporated Statutes—Some rules require reference to sections of the Colorado Code. When this is the case, the incorporated statutes appear in the appropriate chapter.

Authority—Additional authorities are cited following each chapter's Analysis. These give the user a starting point for additional research.

Comparison to Federal Rule—A brief comparison of the Colorado and Federal rules in each chapter provides additional insight.

IMPORTANT NOTE:

On December 1, 2012, the Federal Rules of Evidence were "re-styled" in order to update the rules according to modern syntax without changing the actual substance of the rules. To date, there has been no comparable re-styling of the Colorado Rules. As a result, there are fewer verbatim comparisons of the federal to the Colorado rules, though in terms of substance the federal and state rules remain substantially the same, with exceptions noted in the author's notes to each rule.

Cases—Recent significant cases are summarized at the end of each chapter. These provide support for argument and decisions required during the course of proceedings. LEXIS citations are provided for recent cases which have not been given official *Pacific Reporter* citations. The reader should be aware that until the official citation is given, the case is subject to withdrawal.

Colorado Evidence Courtroom Manual is published annually. This edition contains Rules which are complete through May 2021. The comments and suggestions of users are welcome.

COLORADO RULES OF EVIDENCE AND SELECTED COLORADO REVISED STATUTES

ARTICLE I   GENERAL PROVISIONS

Rule 101. Scope

These rules govern proceedings in all courts in the State of Colorado, to the extent and with the exceptions stated in Rule 1101.

Rule 102. Purpose and construction

These rules shall be construed to secure fairness in administration, elimination of unjustifiable expense and delay, and promotion of growth and development of the law of evidence to the end that the truth may be ascertained and proceedings justly determined.

Rule 103. Rulings on Evidence

(a) Effect of erroneous ruling. Error may not be predicated upon a ruling which admits or excludes evidence unless a substantial right of the party is affected, and

(1) Objection. In case the ruling is one admitting evidence, a timely objection or motion to strike appears of record, stating the specific ground of objection, if the specific ground was not apparent from the context; or

(2) Offer of proof. In case the ruling is one excluding evidence, the substance of the evidence was made known to the Court by offer or was apparent from the context within which questions were asked.

Once the Court makes a definitive ruling on the record admitting or excluding evidence, either at or before trial, a party need not renew an objection or offer of proof to preserve a claim of error for appeal.

(Amended June 20, 2002, effective July 1, 2002.)

(b) Record of offer and ruling. The Court may add any other or further statement which shows the character of evidence, the form in which it was offered, the objection made, and the ruling thereon. It may direct the making of an offer in question and answer form.

(c) Hearing of jury. In jury cases, proceedings shall be conducted, to the extent practicable, so as to prevent inadmissible evidence from being suggested to the jury by any means, such as making statements or offers of proof or asking questions in the hearing of the jury.

(d) Plain error. Nothing in this rule precludes taking notice of plain errors affecting substantial rights although they were not brought to the attention of the Court.

Rule 104. Preliminary Questions

(a) Questions of admissibility generally. Preliminary questions concerning the qualification of a person to be a witness, the existence of a privilege, or the admissibility of evidence shall be determined by the court, subject to the provisions of subdivision (b). In making its determination it is not bound by the rules of evidence except those with respect to privileges.

(b) Relevancy conditioned on fact. When the relevancy of evidence depends upon the fulfillment of a condition of fact, the court shall admit it upon, or subject to, the introduction of evidence sufficient to support a finding of the fulfillment of the condition.

(c) Hearing of jury. Hearings on the admissibility of confessions shall in all cases be conducted out of the hearing of the jury. Hearings on other preliminary matters shall be so conducted when the interests of justice require or, when an accused is a witness, if he so requests.

(d) Testimony by accused. The accused does not, by testifying upon a preliminary matter, subject himself to cross-examination as to other issues in the case.

(e) Weight and credibility. This rule does not limit the right of a party to introduce before the jury evidence relevant to weight or credibility.

Rule 105. Limited Admissibility

When evidence which is admissible as to one party or for one purpose but not admissible as to another party or for another purpose is admitted, the court, upon request, shall restrict the evidence to its proper scope and instruct the jury accordingly.

Rule 106. Remainder of or Related Writings or Recorded Statements

When a writing or recorded statement or part thereof is introduced by a party, an adverse party may require him at that time to introduce any other part or any other writing or recorded statement which ought in fairness to be considered contemporaneously with it.

(Amended March 5, 1981, effective July 1, 1981.)

ARTICLE II　JUDICIAL NOTICE

Rule 201. Judicial Notice of Adjudicative Facts

(a) Scope of rule. This rule governs only judicial notice of adjudicative facts.

(b) Kinds of facts. A judicially noticed fact must be one not subject to reasonable dispute in that it is either (1) generally known within the territorial jurisdiction of the trial court, or (2) capable of accurate and ready determination by resort to sources whose accuracy cannot reasonably be questioned.

(c) When discretionary. A court may take judicial notice, whether requested or not.

(d) When mandatory. A court shall take judicial notice if requested by a party and supplied with the necessary information.

(e) Opportunity to be heard. A party is entitled upon timely request to an opportunity to be heard as to the propriety of taking judicial notice and the tenor of the matter noticed. In the absence of prior notification, the request may be made after judicial notice has been taken.

(f) Time of taking notice. Judicial notice may be taken at any stage of the proceeding.

(g) Instructing jury. In a civil action or proceeding, the court shall instruct the jury to accept as conclusive any fact judicially noticed. In a criminal case, the court shall instruct the jury that it may, but is not required to, accept as conclusive any fact judicially noticed.

Committee Comment

This rule is identical to Rule 201 F.R.E. and generally codifies prior Colorado case law. *See* Nicholls v. Barrick, 27 Colo. 432, 62 P. 202 (1900) [courts take judicial notice of those matters which may be designated as common knowledge]; Finnerty v. Cook, 118 Colo. 310, 195 P.2d 973 (1948) [judicial notice of facts which are universally known]; Israel v. Wood, 93 Colo. 500, 27 P.2d 1024 (1933) [courts take judicial notice of matters of common knowledge in the community where they sit]; Bieser v. Stoddard, 73 Colo. 554, 216 P. 707 (1923) [well recognized natural and physical laws are judicially known and may not be put in issue by denial of their inevitable effect]; Winterberg v. Thomas, 126 Colo. 60, 246 P.2d 1058 (1952) [appellate courts will not hesitate to take judicial notice of the unquestioned laws of mathematics]. However, the mandatory nature of subsection (d) is a departure from existing practice.

In this rule judicial notice is limited to adjunctive facts which are those facts that can be readily determined by resort to accurate sources, such as a calendar date. Sierra Mining Company v. Lucero, 118 Colo. 180, 194 P.2d 302 (1948); term of public office, People, ex rel. Flanders v. Neary, 113 Colo. 12, 154 P.2d 48 (1944); or statistical charts, Good v. A.B. Chance Co., 39 Colo. App. 70, 565 P.2d 217 (1977).

ARTICLE III　PRESUMPTIONS

Rule 301. Presumptions in General in Civil Actions and Proceedings

In all civil actions and proceedings not otherwise provided for by statute or by these rules, a presumption imposes upon the party against whom it is directed the burden of going forward with evidence to rebut or meet the presumption, but does not shift to such party the burden of proof in the sense of the risk of non-persuasion, which remains throughout the trial upon the party on whom it was originally cast.

Committee Comment

This rule is essentially identical to the Federal rule, thus achieving a desirable degree of uniformity and simplicity. The rule gives all of the proper traditional benefits of a presumption, but places no new burdens upon the opposing party. *See* House Report, p. 7; Senate Report, p. 9; Joint Explanatory Statement of the Committee of Conference; *also* 1 Jones, *Evidence* § 3.6 (6th ed.); McCormick, *Evidence*, § 354 (2nd ed. 1972). *Contra, see* Weiss v. Axler, 137 Colo. 544, 328 P.2d 88 (1958).

Rule 302. (No Colorado Rule Codified)

ARTICLE IV　RELEVANCY AND ITS LIMITS

Rule 401. Definition of "Relevant Evidence"

"Relevant evidence" means evidence having any tendency to make the existence of any fact that is of consequence to the determination of the action more probable or less probable than it would be without the evidence.

Rule 402. Relevant Evidence Generally Admissible; Irrelevant Evidence Inadmissible

All relevant evidence is admissible, except as otherwise provided by the Constitution of the United States, by the Constitution of the State of Colorado, by these rules, or by other rules prescribed by the Supreme Court or by the statutes of the State of Colorado. Evidence which is not relevant is not admissible.

Rule 403. Exclusion of Relevant Evidence on Grounds of Prejudice, Confusion, or Waste of Time

Although relevant, evidence may be excluded if its probative value is substantially outweighed by the danger of unfair prejudice, confusion of the issues, or misleading the jury, or by considerations of undue delay, waste of time, or needless presentation of cumulative evidence.

Rule 404. Character Evidence Not Admissible to Prove Conduct; Exceptions; Other Crimes

(a) **Character evidence generally.** Evidence of a person's character or a trait of his character is not admissible for the purpose of proving that he acted in conformity therewith on a particular occasion, except:

(1) Character of accused. Evidence of a pertinent trait of his character offered by an accused, or by the prosecution to rebut the same or if evidence of the alleged victim's character for aggressiveness or violence is offered by an accused and admitted under Rule 404(a)(2), evidence of the same trait of character of the accused offered by the prosecution;

(2) Character of alleged victim. Evidence of a pertinent trait of character of the alleged victim of the crime offered by an accused, or by the prosecution to rebut the same, or evidence of a character trait of peacefulness of the alleged victim offered by the prosecution in a homicide case to rebut evidence that the alleged victim was the first aggressor;

(3) Character of witness. Evidence of the character of a witness as provided in Rules 607, 608, and 13-90-101.

(Amended and effective September 27, 2007.)

(b) **Other crimes, wrongs, or acts.**

(1) **Prohibited uses.** Evidence of any other crime, wrong, or act is not admissible to prove a person's character in order to show that on a particular occasion the person acted in conformity with the character.

(2) **Permitted uses.** This evidence may be admissible for another purpose, such as proving motive, opportunity, intent, preparation, plan, knowledge, identity, absence of mistake, or lack of accident.

(3) **Notice in a criminal case.** In a criminal case, the prosecutor must:

(A) **provide reasonable notice of any such evidence that the prosecutor intends to offer at trial, so that the defendant has a fair opportunity to meet it;**

(B) **articulate in the notice the permitted purpose for which the prosecutor intends to offer the evidence and the reasoning that supports the purpose; and**

(C) **do so in writing before trial—or in any form**

during trial if the court, for good cause, excuses lack of pretrial notice.

((a) amended and adopted June 20, 2002, effective July 1, 2002; (a)(1), (a)(2), and (b) amended and effective September 27, 2007; (b) amended and adopted March 29, 2021, effective July 1, 2021, for cases filed on or after July 1, 2021.)

Committee Comment

See also § 16-10-301, C.R.S. (Volume 8, 1978 Repl. Vol.), adopted by 1975 Legislature, setting forth statute on standards and methods of proof relating to evidence of similar transactions in cases involving charges of unlawful sexual behavior.

Rule 405. Methods of Proving Character

(a) **Reputation or opinion.** In all cases in which evidence of character or a trait of character of a person is admissible, proof may be made by testimony as to reputation or by testimony in the form of an opinion. On cross-examination, inquiry is allowable into relevant specific instances of conduct.

(b) **Specific instances of conduct.** Except as limited by § 16-10-301 and 18-3-407, in cases in which character or a trait of character of a person is an essential element of a charge, claim or defense, proof may also be made of specific instances of that person's conduct.

Rule 406. Habit; Routine Practice

Evidence of the habit of a person or of the routine practice of an organization, whether corroborated or not and regardless of the presence of eyewitnesses, is relevant to prove that the conduct of the person or organization on a particular occasion was in conformity with the habit or routine practice.

Rule 407. Subsequent Remedial Measures

When after an event, measures are taken which, if taken previously, would have made the event less likely to occur, evidence of the subsequent measures is not admissible to prove negligence or culpable conduct in connection with the event. This rule does not require the exclusion of evidence of subsequent measures when offered for another purpose, such as proving ownership, control, or feasibility of precautionary measures, if controverted, or impeachment.

Rule 408. Compromise and Offers to Compromise

(a) **Prohibited uses.** Evidence of the following is not admissible on behalf of any party, when offered to prove liability for, invalidity of, or amount of a claim that was disputed as to validity or amount, or to impeach through a prior inconsistent statement or contradiction:

(1) furnishing or offering or promising to furnish accepting or offering or promising to accept a valuable consideration in compromising or attempting to compromise the claim; and

(2) conduct or statements made in compromise

negotiations regarding the claim, except when offered in a criminal case and the negotiations related to a claim by a public office or agency in the exercise of regulatory, investigative, or enforcement authority.

(b) **Permitted uses.** This rule does not require exclusion if the evidence is offered for purposes not prohibited by subdivision (a). Examples of permissible purposes include proving a witness's bias or prejudice; negating a contention of undue delay; and proving an effort to obstruct a criminal investigation or prosecution.
(Amended and effective September 27, 2007.)

Rule 409. Payment of Medical and Similar Expenses
Evidence of furnishing or offering or promising to pay medical, hospital, or similar expenses occasioned by an injury is not admissible to prove liability for the injury.

Rule 410. Offer to Plead Guilty; Nolo Contendere; Withdrawn Pleas of Guilty
Except as otherwise provided by statutes of the State of Colorado, evidence of a plea of guilty, later withdrawn, or a plea of *nolo contendere*, or of an offer to plead guilty or *nolo contendere* to the crime charged or any other crime, or of statements made in any connection with any of the foregoing pleas or offers, is not admissible in any civil or criminal action, case, or proceeding against the person who made the plea or offer. This rule shall not apply to the introduction of voluntary and reliable statements made in court on the record in connection with any of the foregoing pleas or offers where offered for impeachment purposes or in a subsequent prosecution of the declarant for perjury or false statement.

This rule shall be superseded by any amendment to the Colorado Rules of Criminal Procedure which is inconsistent with this rule, and which takes effect after the effective date of these Colorado Rules of Evidence.

Committee Comment
The Committee wishes to advise the Court of a proposed Federal Amendment to Rule 410 as follows:
Rule 410. Inadmissibility of Pleas, Plea Discussions, and Related Statements
Except as otherwise provided in this rule, evidence of *the following* is not admissible against the person who made the plea or *was a party to the discussions, in any civil or criminal proceeding:*

(1) *a plea of guilty which was later withdrawn;*

(2) *a plea of nolo contendere;*

(3) *plea discussions with the attorney for the government, concerning the crime charged or any other crime, which do not result in a plea of guilty or which result in a plea of guilty later withdrawn; or*

(4) *statements made in the course of or as a consequence of such pleas or plea discussions.*

However, *such* a statement is admissible *in any proceeding*

wherein statements made in the course of or as a consequence of the same plea or plea discussions have been introduced, or in a criminal proceeding for perjury or false statement if the statement was made by the defendant under oath, on the record and in the presence of counsel.

FRE ADVISORY COMMITTEE NOTE: Present Rule 410 conforms to Rule 11(e)(6) of the Federal Rules of Criminal Procedure. A proposed amendment to Rule 11(e)(6) would clarify the circumstances in which pleas, plea discussions and related statements are inadmissible in evidence; *see* Advisory Committee Note thereto. The amendment proposed above would make comparable changes in Rule 410.

Rule 411. Liability Insurance
Evidence that a person was or was not insured against liability is not admissible upon the issue whether he acted negligently or otherwise wrongfully. This rule does not require the exclusion of evidence of insurance against liability when offered for another purpose, such as proof of agency, ownership, or control, or bias or prejudice of a witness.

Rule 412. (No Colorado Rule Codified)

COLO. REV. STAT. § 18-3-407. Victim's and Witness' Prior History—Evidentiary Hearing
(1) Evidence of specific instances of the victim's or a witness's prior or subsequent sexual conduct, opinion evidence of the victim's or a witness's sexual conduct, and reputation evidence of the victim's or a witness's sexual conduct may be admissible only at trial and shall not be admitted in any other proceeding except at a proceeding pursuant to paragraph (c) of subsection (2) of this section. At trial, such evidence shall be presumed to be irrelevant except:

(a) Evidence of the victim's or witness' prior or subsequent sexual conduct with the actor;

(b) Evidence of specific instances of sexual activity showing the source or origin of semen, pregnancy, disease, or any similar evidence of sexual intercourse offered for the purpose of showing that the act or acts charged were or were not committed by the defendant.

(2) In any criminal prosecution for class 4 felony internet luring of a child, as described in section 18-3-306 (3) or under sections 18-3-402 to 18-3-405.5, 18-6-301, 18-6-302, 18-6-403, and 18-6-404, or for attempt or conspiracy to commit any of said crimes, if evidence, that is not excepted under subsection (1) of this section, of specific instances of the victim's or a witness's prior or subsequent sexual conduct, or opinion evidence of the victim's or a witness's sexual conduct, or reputation evidence of the victim's or a witness's sexual conduct, or evidence that the victim or a witness has a history of false reporting of sexual assaults is to be offered at trial, the following procedure shall be followed:

(a) A written motion shall be made at least thirty days

prior to trial, unless later for good cause shown, to the court and to the opposing parties stating that the moving party has an offer of proof of the relevancy and materiality of evidence of specific instances of the victim's or witness' prior or subsequent sexual conduct, or opinion evidence of the victim's or witness' sexual conduct, or reputation evidence of the victim's or witness' sexual conduct, or evidence that the victim or witness has a history of false reporting of sexual assaults that is proposed to be presented.

(b) The written motion shall be accompanied by an affidavit in which the offer of proof shall be stated.

(c) If the court finds that the offer of proof is sufficient, the court shall notify the other party of such. If the prosecution stipulates to the facts contained in the offer of proof, the court shall rule on the motion based upon the offer of proof without an evidentiary hearing. Otherwise, the court shall set a hearing to be held in camera prior to trial. In such hearing, to the extent the facts are in dispute, the court may allow the questioning of the victim or witness regarding the offer of proof made by the moving party or otherwise allow a presentation of the offer of proof, including but not limited to the presentation of witnesses.

(d) An in camera hearing may be held during trial if evidence first becomes available at the time of the trial or for good cause shown.

(e) At the conclusion of the hearing, or by written order if no hearing is held, if the court finds that the evidence proposed to be offered regarding the sexual conduct of the victim or witness is relevant to a material issue to the case, the court shall order that evidence may be introduced and prescribe the nature of the evidence or questions to be permitted. The moving party may then offer evidence pursuant to the order of the court.

(f) All motions and supporting documents filed pursuant to this section shall be filed under seal and may be unsealed only if the court rules the evidence is admissible and the case proceeds to trial. If the court determines that only part of the evidence contained in the motion is admissible, only that portion of the motion and supporting documents pertaining to the admissible portion may be unsealed.

(g) The court shall seal all court transcripts, tape recordings, and records of proceedings, other than minute orders, of a hearing held pursuant to this section. The court may unseal the transcripts, tape recordings, and records only if the court rules the evidence is admissible and the case proceeds to trial. If the court determines that only part of the evidence is admissible, only the portion of the hearing pertaining to the admissible evidence may be unsealed.

(3) (a) In a criminal prosecution including an offense described in subsection (2) of this section, the court may, at any time upon motion of the prosecution or on the court's own motion, issue a protective order pursuant to the Colorado rules of criminal procedure concerning disclosure of information relating to the victim or a witness. The court may punish a violation of a protective order by contempt of court.

(b) The victim who would be the subject of the protective order may object to the motion for a protective order.

ARTICLE V   PRIVILEGES

Rule 501. Privileges Recognized Only as Provided
Except as otherwise required by the Constitution of the United States, the Constitution of the State of Colorado, statutes of the State of Colorado, rules prescribed by the Supreme Court of the State of Colorado pursuant to constitutional authority, or by the principles of the common law as they may be interpreted by the courts of the State of Colorado in light of reason and experience, no person has a privilege to:

(1)   Refuse to be a witness; or

(2)   Refuse to disclose any matter; or

(3)   Refuse to produce any object or writing; or

(4)   Prevent another from being a witness or disclosing any matter or producing any object or writing.

Rule 502. Attorney-Client Privilege and Work Product; Limitations On Waiver
The following provisions apply, in the circumstances set out, to disclosure of a communication or information covered by the attorney-client privilege or work-product protection.

(a) **Disclosure Made in a Colorado Proceeding or to a Colorado Office or Agency; Scope of a Waiver.** When the disclosure is made in a Colorado proceeding or to an office or agency of a Colorado state, county, or local government and waives the attorney-client privilege or work-product protection, the waiver extends to an undisclosed communication or information in a Colorado proceeding only if:

(1)   the waiver is intentional;

(2)   the disclosed and undisclosed communications or information concern the same subject matter; and

(3)   they ought in fairness to be considered together.

(b) **Inadvertent Disclosure.** When made in a Colorado proceeding or to an office or agency of a Colorado state, county, or local government, the disclosure does not operate as a waiver in a Colorado proceeding if:

(1)   the disclosure is inadvertent;

(2)   the holder of the privilege or protection took reasonable steps to prevent disclosure; and

(3)   the holder promptly took reasonable steps to rectify the error, including (if applicable) following C.R.C.P. 26(b)(5)(B).

(c) Disclosure Made in a Federal or other State Proceeding. When the disclosure is made in a proceeding in federal court or the court of another state and is not the subject of a court order concerning waiver, the disclosure does not operate as a waiver in a Colorado proceeding if the disclosure:

(1)   would not be a waiver under this rule if it had been made in a Colorado proceeding; or

(2)   is not a waiver under the law governing the state or federal proceeding where the disclosure occurred.

(d) Controlling Effect of a Court Order. A Colorado court may order that the privilege or protection is not waived by disclosure connected with the litigation pending before the court—in which event the disclosure is also not a waiver in any other proceeding.

(e) Controlling Effect of a Party Agreement. An agreement on the effect of disclosure in a Colorado proceeding is binding only on the parties to the agreement, unless it is incorporated into a court order.

(f) Definitions. In this rule:

(1)   "attorney-client privilege" means the protection that applicable law provides for confidential attorney-client communications; and

(2)   "work-product protection" means the protection that applicable law provides for tangible material (or its intangible equivalent) prepared in anticipation of litigation or for trial.

ARTICLE VI   WITNESSES

Rule 601. General Rule of Competency

Every person is competent to be a witness except as otherwise provided in these rules, or in any statute of the State of Colorado.

Committee Comment

The present rule preserves the general Colorado rule under § 13-90-101, *et seq.*, C.R.S.; and the exceptions listed in §§ 13-90-102 through 13-90-108.

Rule 602. Lack of Personal Knowledge

A witness may not testify to a matter unless evidence is introduced sufficient to support a finding that he has personal knowledge of the matter. Evidence to prove personal knowledge may, but need not, consist of the testimony of the witness himself. This rule is subject to the provisions of Rule 703, relating to opinion testimony by expert witnesses.

Rule 603. Oath or Affirmation

Before testifying, every witness shall be required to declare that he will testify truthfully, by oath or affirmation administered in a form calculated to awaken his con-

science and impress his mind with his duty to do so.

Rule 604. Interpreters

An interpreter is subject to the provisions of these rules relating to qualification as an expert and the administration of an oath or affirmation that he will make a true translation.

Rule 605. Competency of Judge as Witness

The judge presiding at the trial may not testify in that trial as a witness. No objection need be made to preserve the point.

Rule 606. Competency of Juror as Witness

(a) At the trial. A member of the jury may not testify as a witness before that jury in the trial of the case in which he is sitting as a juror. No objection need be made in order to preserve the point.

(b) Inquiry into validity of verdict or indictment. Upon an inquiry into the validity of a verdict or indictment, a juror may not testify as to any matter or statement occurring during the course of the jury's deliberations or to the effect of anything upon his or any other juror's mind or emotions as influencing him to assent to or dissent from the verdict or indictment or concerning his mental processes in connection therewith. But a juror may testify about (1) whether extraneous prejudicial information was improperly brought to the jurors' attention, (2) whether any outside influence was improperly brought to bear upon any juror, or (3) whether there was a mistake in entering the verdict onto the verdict form. A juror's affidavit or evidence of any statement by the juror may not be received on a matter about which the juror would be precluded from testifying.

Rule 607. Who May Impeach

The credibility of a witness may be attacked by any party, including the party calling him. Leading questions may be used for the purpose of attacking such credibility.

Committee Comment

This rule abandons the traditional position against impeaching one's own witness. The additional sentence in the Colorado version of the rule should assist in resolving conflicts now existing between Rule 43(b) of the Colorado Rules of Civil Procedure and § 13-90-116, C.R.S. A minority opinion concerning Rule 607 feels that this rule should be restricted to civil cases since it may be prosecutorial misconduct for a prosecutor to attack the credibility of his own witness without a showing of hostility or surprise. The likelihood of a defendant's being found guilty because of a "coparticipant" hesitation to testify against the defendant may prejudice the jury to such an extent that a fair trial cannot be obtained.

Rule 608. Evidence of Character and Conduct of Witness

(a) Opinion and reputation evidence of character. The credibility of a witness may be attacked or supported by evidence in the form of opinion or reputation, but subject to these limitations: (1) the evidence may refer only to character for truthfulness or untruthfulness, and (2) evidence of truthful character is admissible only after the character of the witness for truthfulness has been attacked by opinion or reputation evidence or otherwise.

(b) Specific instances of conduct. Specific instances of the conduct of a witness, for the purpose of attacking or supporting the witness' character for truthfulness, other than conviction of crime as provided in 13-90-101, C.R.S. 1973, may not be proved by extrinsic evidence. They may, however, in the discretion of the court, if probative of truthfulness or untruthfulness, be inquired into on cross-examination of the witness (1) concerning the witness' character for truthfulness or untruthfulness, or (2) concerning the character for truthfulness or untruthfulness of another witness as to which character the witness being cross-examined has testified.

The giving of testimony, whether by an accused or by any other witness, does not operate as a waiver of the accused's or the witness' privilege against self-incrimination when examined with respect to matters that relate only to character for truthfulness.

(Amended September 29, 2005, effective January 1, 2006.)

Rule 609. (No Colorado Rule Codified)

COLO. REV. STAT. § 13-90-101. Who May Testify—Interest

All persons, without exception, other than those specified in sections 13-90-102 to 13-90-108 may be witnesses. Neither parties nor other persons who have an interest in the event of an action or proceeding shall be excluded; nor those who have been convicted of crime; nor persons on account of their opinions on matters of religious belief. In every case the credibility of the witness may be drawn in question, as now provided by law, but the conviction of any person for any felony may be shown for the purpose of affecting the credibility of such witness. The fact of such conviction may be proved like any other fact, not of record, either by the witness himself, who shall be compelled to testify thereto, or by any other person cognizant of such conviction as impeaching testimony or by any other competent testimony. Evidence of a previous conviction of a felony where the witness testifying was convicted five years prior to the time when the witness testifies shall not be admissible in evidence in any civil action.

Rule 610. Religious Beliefs or Opinions

Evidence of the beliefs or opinions of a witness on matters of religion is not admissible for the purposes of showing that by reason of their nature his credibility is impaired or enhanced.

Rule 611. Mode and Order of Interrogation and Presentation

(a) Control by court. The court shall exercise reasonable control over the mode and order of interrogating witnesses and presenting evidence so as to (1) make the interrogation and presentation effective for the ascertainment of the truth, (2) avoid needless consumption of time, and (3) protect witnesses from harassment or undue embarrassment.

(b) Scope of cross-examination. Cross-examination should be limited to the subject matter of the direct examination and matters affecting the credibility of the witness. The court may, in the exercise of discretion, permit inquiry into additional matters as if on direct examination.

(c) Leading questions. Leading questions should not be used on the direct examination of a witness except as may be necessary to develop his testimony. Leading questions should be permitted on cross-examination. When a party calls a hostile witness, an adverse party, or a witness identified with an adverse party, interrogation may be by leading questions.

Rule 612. Writing Used to Refresh Memory

If a witness uses a writing to refresh his memory for the purpose of testifying, either—

(1) while testifying, or

(2) before testifying, if

the court in its discretion determines it is necessary in the interests of justice, an adverse party is entitled to have the writing produced at the hearing, to inspect it, to cross-examine the witness thereon, and to introduce in evidence those portions which relate to the testimony of the witness. If it is claimed that the writing contains matters not related to the subject matter of the testimony the court shall examine the writing in camera, excise any portions not so related, and order delivery of the remainder to the party entitled thereto. Any portion withheld over objections shall be preserved and made available to the appellate court in the event of an appeal. If a writing is not produced or delivered pursuant to order under this rule, the court shall make any order justice requires, except that in criminal cases when the prosecution elects not to comply, the order shall be one striking the testimony or, if the court in its discretion determines that the interests of justice so require, declaring a mistrial.

Rule 613. Prior Statements of Witnesses

(a) Examining witness concerning prior inconsistent statements for impeachment purposes. Before a witness may be examined for impeachment by prior inconsistent statement the examiner must call the attention of the witness to the particular time and occasion when, the place where, and the person to whom he made the statement. As a part of that foundation, the examiner may refer to the witness statement to bring to the attention of the witness any purported prior inconsistent statement. The exact language of the prior statement may be given.

Where the witness denies or does not remember making the prior statement, extrinsic evidence, such as deposition, proving the utterance of the prior evidence is admissible. However, if a witness admits making the prior statement, additional extrinsic evidence that the prior statement was made is inadmissible.

Denial or failure to remember the prior statement is a prerequisite for the introduction of extrinsic evidence to prove that the prior inconsistent statement was made.

Committee Comment

Concerning prior statements of witnesses, the Colorado Rule of Evidence as it now exists is set forth in Transamerica Insurance Co. v. Pueblo Gas & Fuel Co., 33 Colo. App. 92, 95, 519 P.2d 1201, 1203 (1973).

Rule 614. Calling and Interrogation of Witnesses by Court

(a) Calling by court. The court may, on its own motion or at the suggestion of a party, call witnesses and all parties are entitled to cross-examine witnesses thus called.

(b) Interrogation by court. The court may interrogate witnesses, whether called by itself or by a party.

(c) Objections. Objections to the calling of witnesses by the court or to interrogation by it may be made at the time or at the next available opportunity when the jury is not present.

Rule 615. Exclusion of Witnesses

At the request of a party the court shall order witnesses excluded so that they cannot hear the testimony of other witnesses, and it may make the order of its own motion. This rule does not authorize exclusion of (1) a party who is a natural person, or (2) an officer or employee of a party which is not a natural person designated as its representative by its attorney, or (3) a person whose presence is shown by a party to be essential to the presentation of his cause.

ARTICLE VII   OPINIONS AND EXPERT TESTIMONY

Rule 701. Opinion Testimony by Lay Witnesses

If the witness is not testifying as an expert, the witness' testimony in the form of opinions or inferences is limited to those opinions or inferences which are (a) rationally based on the perception of the witness and (b) helpful to a clear understanding of the witness' testimony or the determination of a fact in issue, and (c) not based on scientific, technical, or other specialized knowledge within the scope of Rule 702.

Committee Comment

This rule does not foreclose an owner from giving an opinion as to the value of his real property. Universal Insurance Company v. Arrigo, 96 Colo. 531, 44 P.2d 1020 (1935).

(Amended June 20, 2002, effective July 1, 2002.)

Rule 702. Testimony by Experts

If scientific, technical, or other specialized knowledge will assist the trier of fact to understand the evidence or to determine a fact in issue, a witness qualified as an expert by knowledge, skill, experience, training, or education, may testify thereto in the form of an opinion or otherwise.

(Amended March 5, 1981, effective July 1, 1981.)

Rule 703. Bases of Opinion Testimony by Experts

The facts or data in the particular case upon which an expert bases an opinion or inference may be those perceived by or made known to the expert at or before the hearing. If of a type reasonably relied upon by experts in the particular field in forming opinions or inferences upon the subject, the facts or data need not be admissible in evidence in order for the opinion or inference to be admitted. Facts or data that are otherwise inadmissible shall not be disclosed to the jury by the proponent of the opinion or inference unless the court determines that their probative value in assisting the jury to evaluate the expert's opinion substantially outweighs their prejudicial effect.

(Amended June 20, 2002, effective July 1, 2002.)

Committee Comment

The Committee believes this rule is a substantial deviation from former Colorado law, but there are former cases lending partial support to the rule. *See:* Hensel Phelps Construction Co. v. U.S., 413 F.2d 701 10 th Cir. (1969); Houser v. Eckhardt, 168 Colo. 226, 450 P.2d 664 (1969); McNelley v. Smith, 149 Colo. 177, 368 P.2d 555 (1962); Ison v. Stewart, 105 Colo. 55, 94 P.2d 701 (1939); Enyart v. Orr, 78 Colo. 6, 248 P.29 (1925); Rio Grande W. Ry. Co. v. Rubenstein, 5 Colo. App. 121, 38 P. 76 (1894). *See also,* Good v. A.B. Chance Co., 39 Colo. App. 70, 565 P.2d 217 (1977). Although not directly in point, we believe the case supports the last sentence of Rule 703. (Amended March 5, 1981, effective July 1, 1981.)

Rule 704. Opinion on Ultimate Issue

Testimony in the form of an opinion or inference otherwise admissible is not objectionable because it embraces an ultimate issue to be decided by the trier of fact.

Committee Comment

The present Federal and Colorado rules may conflict with preceding Colorado case law. (*Compare* Bridges v. Lintz, 140 Colo. 582, 346 P.2d 571 (1959) and McNelley v. Smith, 149 Colo. 177, 368 P.2d 555 (1962).) It is felt that the rule expresses the better alternative. The conflict arises in the area of lay witnesses testifying as to an ultimate issue of fact. In Colorado, case law says that he may testify concerning things which would help the jury to understand the facts, but he may not render an opinion on the ultimate fact in issue. Mogote-Northeastern Consolidated Ditch Co. v. Gallegos, 70 Colo. 550, 203 P. 668 (1922). There are exceptions to the rule, and the law in Colorado can best be stated by quoting the following language: It is reversible error to allow an opinion as to ultimate facts unless the witness testifies as an expert or his testimony invokes a description or estimate of condition, value, etc. or when it is difficult or impossible to state with sufficient exactness the facts and their surroundings. Town of Meeker v. Fairfield, 25 Colo. App. 187, 136 P. 471 (1913).

Rule 705. Disclosure of Facts or Data Underlying Expert Opinion

The expert may testify in terms of opinion or inference and give reasons therefor without first testifying to the underlying facts or data, unless the court requires otherwise. The expert may in any event be required to disclose the underlying facts or data on cross-examination.

(Amended and effective November 16, 1995.)

Committee Comment

Although the present rule is contrary to Colorado case law, the Committee believes it to be the better view. The reasons for the retention of the proposed Federal rule as it is presently written are as follows: First, the rule does not disturb the requirement for a proper foundation for expert opinions. City and County of Denver v. Lyttle, 106 Colo. 157, 103 P.2d 1 (1940). Secondly, the elimination of the requirement for preliminary disclosure of underlying facts or data has the effect of reducing the need for hypothetical questions, a goal which has been sought by a number of states. Thirdly: If the objection is made that leaving it to the cross-examiner to bring out the supporting data is essentially unfair, the answer is that he is under no compulsion to bring out any facts or data except those unfavorable to the opinion. The answer assumes that the cross-examiner has the advance knowledge which is essential for effective cross-examination. This advance knowledge has been afforded, though imperfectly, by the traditional foundations requirement. Advisory Committee's Notes, Proposed Federal Rules. *See also,* Archina v. People, 135 Colo. 8, 307 P.2d 1083 (1957). Finally, it is clear that there is built-in safeguard in the discretionary power of the court to require prior disclosure.

Rule 706. Court Appointed Experts

(a) Appointment. The court may on its own motion or on the motion of any party enter an order to show cause why expert witnesses should not be appointed, and may request the parties to submit nominations. The court may appoint any expert witnesses agreed upon by the parties, and may appoint expert witnesses of its own selection. An expert witness shall not be appointed by the court unless he consents to act. A witness so appointed shall be informed of his duties by the court in writing, a copy of which shall be filed with the clerk, or at a conference in which the parties shall have opportunity to participate. A witness so appointed shall advise the parties of his findings, if any; his deposition may be taken by any party; and he may be called to testify by the court or any party. He shall be subject to cross-examination by each party, including a party calling him as a witness.

(b) Compensation. Expert witnesses so appointed are entitled to reasonable compensation in whatever sum the court may allow. The compensation thus fixed is payable from funds which may be provided by law in criminal cases and civil actions and proceedings involving just compensation under the fifth amendment. In other civil actions and proceedings the compensation shall be paid by the parties in such proportion and at such time as the court directs, and thereafter charged in like manner as other costs.

(c) Disclosure of appointment. In the exercise of its discretion, the court may authorize disclosure to the jury of the fact that the court appointed the expert witness.

(d) Parties' experts of own selection. Nothing in this rule limits the parties in calling expert witnesses of their own selection.

ARTICLE VIII   HEARSAY

Rule 801. Definitions

The following definitions apply under this article:

(a) Statement. A "statement" is (1) an oral or written assertion or (2) nonverbal conduct of a person, if it is intended by him to be communicative.

Committee Comment

The change reflected in the Colorado rule was necessary, in the minds of the Committee members, because the Committee believed that the word assertion was extremely unclear; the change is felt to be more precise.

(b) Declarant. A "declarant" is a person who makes a statement.

(c) Hearsay. "Hearsay" is a statement other than one made by the declarant while testifying at the trial or hearing, offered in evidence to prove the truth of the matter asserted.

(d) Statements which are not hearsay. A statement is not hearsay if—

(1) Prior statement by witness. The declarant testifies at the trial or hearing and is subject to cross-examination concerning the statement, and the statement is (A) inconsistent with his testimony, or (B) consistent with his testimony and is offered to rebut an express or implied charge against him of recent fabrication or improper influence or motive, or (C) one of identification of a person made after perceiving him, or

(2) Admission by party-opponent. The statement is offered against a party and is (A) the party's statement in either an individual or a representative capacity or (B) a statement of which the party has manifested his adoption or belief in its truth; or (C) a statement by a person authorized by the party to make a statement concerning the subject; or (D) a statement by the party's agent or servant concerning a matter within the scope of the agency or employment, made during the existence of the relation-

ship, or (E) a statement by a co-conspirator of a party during the course and in furtherance of the conspiracy. The contents of the statement shall be considered but are not alone sufficient to establish the declarant's authority under subdivision (C), the agency or employment relationship and scope thereof under subdivision (D), or the existence of the conspiracy and the participation therein of the declarant and the party against whom the statement is offered under subdivision (E).

(Amended November 25, 1998, effective January 1, 1999.)

Committee Comment

The last sentence of this Rule was added to track a corresponding change in F.R.E. 801 (d)(2).

Rule 802. Hearsay Rule

Hearsay is not admissible except as provided by these rules or by the civil and criminal procedural rules applicable to the courts of Colorado or by any statutes of the State of Colorado.

Rule 803. Hearsay Exceptions; Availability of Declarant Immaterial

The following are not excluded by the hearsay rule, even though the declarant is available as a witness:

(1) Spontaneous present sense impression. A spontaneous statement describing or explaining an event or condition made while the declarant was perceiving the event or condition.

Committee Comment

The change reflected above was based on the fact that neither immediacy nor spontaneity would be guaranteed by the Federal rule. Colorado case law requires that a present sense impression be instinctive and spontaneous in order to be admissible. *See* Denver City Tramway Co. v. Brumley, 51 Colo. 251, 116 P. 1051 (1911). It was felt that the requirements set forth in that opinion constitute a greater guarantee of trustworthiness than the Federal rule, *i.e.*, spontaneity is the most important factor governing trustworthiness. This is especially true when there is no provision that the declarant be unavailable as a witness.

(2) Excited utterance. A statement relating to a startling event or condition made while the declarant was under the stress of excitement caused by the event or condition.

(3) Then existing mental, emotional, or physical condition. A statement of the declarant's then existing state of mind, emotion, sensation, or physical condition (such as intent, plan, motive, design, mental feeling, pain, and bodily health), but not including a statement of memory or belief to prove the fact remembered or believed unless it relates to the execution, revocation, identification, or terms of declarant's will.

(4) Statements for purposes of medical diagnosis or treatment. Statements made for purposes of medical diagnosis or treatment and describing medical history, or past

or present symptoms, pain, or sensations, or the inception or general character of the cause or external source thereof insofar as reasonably pertinent to diagnosis or treatment.

Committee Comment

See: Houser v. Eckhardt, 168 Colo. 226, 450 P.2d 664 (1969); Ingles v. People, 90 Colo. 51, 6 P.2d 455 (1931); and § 8-53-103(2)(a) & (b), C.R.S. (Workmen's Compensation Act of Colorado).

(5) Recorded recollection. A past recollection recorded when it appears that the witness once had knowledge concerning the matter and; (A) can identify the memorandum or record, (B) adequately recalls the making of it at or near the time of the event, either as recorded by the witness or by another, and (C) can testify to its accuracy. The memorandum or record may be read into evidence but may not itself be received unless offered by an adverse party.

Committee Comment

The change reflected above was made because the Federal rule is more restrictive than the Colorado rule, which does not require absence of a present recollection to be expressly shown as a preliminary to use of recorded recollection. Jordan v. People, 151 Colo. 133, 376 P.2d 699 (1962).

(6) Records of regularly conducted activity. A memorandum report, record, or data compilation, in any form, of acts, events, conditions, opinions, or diagnosis, made at or near the time by, or from information transmitted by, a person with knowledge, if kept in the course of a regularly conducted business activity, and if it was the regular practice of that business activity to make the memorandum, report, record, or data compilation, all as shown by the testimony of the custodian or other qualified witness, or by certification that complies with Rule 902(11), Rule 902(12), or a statute permitting certification, unless the source of information or the method or circumstances of preparation indicate a lack of trustworthiness. The term "business" as used in this paragraph includes business, institution, association, profession, occupation, and calling of every kind, whether or not conducted for profit.

(Amended June 20, 2002, effective July 1, 2002.)

Committee Comment

The rule makes no reference to any objective standard of trustworthiness, *e.g.*, regularity with which records are kept. *See* Colorado cases: Patterson v. Pitoniak, 173 Colo. 454, 480 P.2d 579 (1971); Moseley v. Smith, 170 Colo. 177, 460 P.2d 222 (1969); Seib v. Standley, 164 Colo. 394, 435 P.2d 395 (1967); Rocky Mountain Beverage v. Walter Brewing Company, 107 Colo. 63, 108 P.2d 885 (1941); Hobbs v. Breen, 74 Colo. 277, 230 P. 997 (1923); Powell v. Brady, 30 Colo. App. 406, 496 P.2d 328 (1972).

(7) Absence of entry in records kept in accordance with the provisions of paragraph (6). Evidence that a matter is not included in the memoranda reports, records, or data compilations, in any form, kept in accordance with the provisions of paragraph (6), to prove the nonoccur-

rence or nonexistence of the matter, if the matter was of a kind of which a memorandum, report, record, or data compilation was regularly made and preserved, unless the sources of information or other circumstances indicate lack of trustworthiness.

(8) Public records and reports. Unless the sources of information or other circumstances indicate lack of trust-worthiness, records, reports, statements, or data compilations in any form, of public offices or agencies, setting forth (A) the activities of the office or agency, or (B) matters observed pursuant to duty imposed by law as to which matters there was a duty to report excluding, however, in criminal cases matters observed by police officers and other law enforcement personnel, or (C) in civil actions and proceedings and against the Government in criminal cases, factual findings resulting from an investigation made pursuant to authority granted by law.

(9) Records of vital statistics. Records or data compilations, in any form, of births, fetal deaths, deaths, or marriages, if the report thereof was made to a public office pursuant to requirements of law.

Committee Comment

This rule is somewhat broader than the provisions of § 25-2-117, C.R.S., and respecting marriage records is desirable because the evidentiary use of the book of marriages provided in § 90-1-20, C.R.S. 1963, was repealed in 1973.

(10) Absence of a public record. Testimony—or a certification under Rule 902—that a diligent search failed to disclose a public record or statement if:

(A) the testimony or certification is admitted to prove that

(i) the record or statement does not exist; or

(ii) a matter did not occur or exist, if a public office regularly kept a record or statement for a matter of that kind; and

(B) in a criminal case, a prosecutor who intends to offer a certification provides written notice of that intent at least 14 days before trial, and the defendant does not object in writing within 7 days of receiving the notice— unless the court sets a different time for the notice or the objection.

(Amended February 18, 2014, effective immediately.)

Committee Comment

The Committee recommended adoption of this amended version of C.R.E. 803(10) to follow the identical amendment to F.R.E. 803(10) which took effect on December 1, 2013.

(11) Records of religious organizations. Statements of births, marriages, divorces, deaths, legitimacy, ancestry, relationship by blood or marriage, or other similar facts of personal or family history, contained in a regularly kept record of a religious organization.

(12) Marriage, baptismal, and similar certificates.
Statements of fact contained in a certificate that the maker performed a marriage or other ceremony or administered a sacrament, made by a clergyman, public official, or other person authorized by the rules or practices of a religious organization or by law to perform the act certified, and purporting to have been issued at the time of the act or within a reasonable time thereafter.

(13) Family records. Statements of fact concerning personal or family history contained in family Bibles, genealogies, charts, engravings on rings, inscriptions on family portraits, engravings on urns, crypts, or tomb-stones, or the like.

Committee Comment

The age of the record or regularity of keeping are immaterial to admissibility. The content of fact is not limited to pedigree or genealogy.

(14) Records of documents affecting an interest in property. The record of a document purporting to establish or affect an interest in property, as proof of the content of the original recorded or filed document and its execution and delivery by each person by whom it purports to have been executed, if the record is a record of a public office and an applicable statute authorizes the recording of documents of that kind in that office.

Committee Comment

The generic term "property" used in the Federal rule indicates an intent that the rule apply to documents relating to interests in both real property and personal property. The term "filed" has been added to render the rule applicable to personal property under Colorado law: the Uniform Commercial Code, the Colorado Rules of Civil Procedure, and § 30-10-103, C.R.S., all refer to filing documents affecting an interest in personal property.

(15) Statements in documents affecting an interest in property. A statement contained in a document purporting to establish or affect an interest in property if the matter stated was relevant to the purpose of the document, unless dealings with the property since the document was made have been inconsistent with the truth of the statement or the purport of the document.

Committee Comment

The rule extends admissibility beyond case law and statutes. *E.g.,* McClure v. Board of Commissioners of La Plata County, 19 Colo. 122, 34 P. 763 (1893); Wright v. People in the Interest of Rowe, 131 Colo. 92, 279 P.2d 676 (1955); Michael v. John Hancock Mutual Life Insurance Co., 138 Colo. 450, 334 P.2d 1090 (1959). Statutes more restrictive than the rule are §§ 38-35-102, 38-35-104, 38-35-105, 38-35-107, and 38-35-108, C.R.S.

(16) Statements in ancient documents. A statement in a document that was prepared before January 1, 1998, and whose authenticity is established.

(Amended and adopted March 29, 2021.)

Committee Comment

The rule liberalizes the hearsay exception for ancient documents by eliminating proof of execution (*see* general statement for this principle in 32A C.J.S., *Evidence*, Sec. 744, page 32) and, further, reduces the required age of such document to twenty years from thirty years. For Colorado authorities on the subject, *see* McGary v. Blakeley, 127 Colo. 495, 258 P.2d 770 (1953) and § 38-35-107, C.R.S.

(17) Market reports, commercial publications. Market quotations, tabulations, lists, directories, or other published compilations, generally used and relied upon by the public or by persons in particular occupations.

Committee Comment

Colorado authorities affecting this rule are: 4-2-724, C.R.S.; Continental Divide Mining Investment Company v. Bliley, 23 Colo. 160, 166, 46 P. 633, 635 (1896); Willard v. Mellor, 19 Colo. 534, 36 P. 148 (1894); Kansas Pacific R.R. Company v. Lundin, 3 Colo. 94 (1876); Rio Grande Southern R.R. Company v. Nichols, 52 Colo. 300, 123 P. 318 (1912); Johnson v. Cousins, 110 Colo. 540, 135 P.2d 1021 (1943). (Amended March 5, 1981, effective July 1, 1981.)

(18) Learned treatises. To the extent called to the attention of an expert witness upon cross-examination or relied upon by him in direct examination, statements contained in published treatises, periodicals, or pamphlets on a subject of history, medicine, or other science or art, established as a reliable authority by the testimony or admission of the witness or by other expert testimony or by judicial notice. If admitted, the statements may be read into evidence and may be received as exhibits, as the court permits.

(Amended March 5, 1981, effective July 1, 1981.)

Committee Comment

Unlike the Federal Rule, the Colorado Rule allows the learned treatises to be admitted as exhibits in the discretion of the court. The former Colorado Rule seemed to be that only if such treatise had been relied upon by the witness in forming his opinion might it be admitted. Denver City Tramway v. Gawley, 23 Colo. App. 332, 129 P. 258 (1912); Wall v. Weaver, 145 Colo. 337, 358 P.2d 1009 (1961); Ross v. Colo. Nat'l Bank, 170 Colo. 436, 463 P.2d 882 (1970). (Amended March 5, 1981, effective July 1, 1981.)

(19) Reputation concerning personal or family history. Reputation among members of his family by blood, adoption, or marriage, or among his associates, or in the community, concerning a person's birth, adoption, marriage, divorce, death, legitimacy, relationship by blood, adoption, or marriage, ancestry, or other similar fact of his personal or family history.

(Amended March 5, 1981, effective July 1, 1981.)

Committee Comment

The former Colorado rule limited such evidence to reputation among persons related by blood or marriage to the family in question. Epple v. First Nat'l Bank of Greeley, 143 Colo. 319, 352 P.2d 796 (1960).

(20) Reputation concerning boundaries or general history. Reputation in a community, arising before the controversy, as to boundaries of or customs affecting lands in the community, and reputation as to events of general history important to the community or state or nation in which located.

Committee Comment

This rule is thought consistent with the former Colorado rule. *See* § 38-44-101, C.R.S., reestablishing disputed boundaries.

(21) Reputation as to character. Reputation of a person's character among his associates or in the community.

(22) Judgment of previous conviction. Evidence of a final judgment, entered after a trial or upon a plea of guilty or *nolo contendere*, adjudging a person guilty of a crime punishable by death or imprisonment in excess of one year, to prove any fact essential to sustain the judgment, but not including, when offered by the Government in a criminal prosecution for purposes other than impeachment, judgments against persons other than the accused. The pendency of an appeal may be shown but does not affect admissibility.

Committee Comment

The rule represents Colorado law by its inclusion of a *nolo contendere* plea. § 13-90-101, C.R.S., construed to include a *nolo contendere* plea in Lacey v. People, 166 Colo. 152, 442 P.2d 402 (1968).

(23) Judgment as to personal, family, or general history, or boundaries. Judgments as proof of matters of personal, family or general history, or boundaries, essential to the judgment, if the same would be provable by evidence of reputation.

Committee Comment

A judgment, under the circumstances stated, creates the reputations, and is admissible subject to the limitations applicable to evidence of reputation.

(24) [Transferred to Rule 807] (Amended November 25, 1998, effective January 1, 1999.)

Committee Comment

The contents of Rule 803(24) and Rule 804(b)(5) have been combined and transferred to Rule 807. This was done to facilitate additions to Rules 803 and 804. No change in meaning is intended.

Rule 804. Hearsay Exceptions; Declarant Unavailable

(a) **Definition of unavailability.** "Unavailability as a witness" includes situations in which the declarant—

(1)   is exempted by ruling of the court on the ground of privilege from testifying concerning the subject matter of his statement; or

(2)   persists in refusing to testify concerning the subject matter of his statement despite an order of the court to do so; or

(3)   testifies to a lack of memory of the subject matter of his statement; or

(4)   is unable to be present or to testify at the hearing

because of death or then existing physical or mental illness or infirmity; or

(5) is absent from the hearing and the proponent of a statement has been unable to procure his attendance (or in the case of a hearsay exception under subdivision (b)(3) or (4) his attendance or testimony) by process or other reasonable means.

A declarant is not unavailable as a witness if his exemption, refusal, claim of lack of memory, inability, or absence is due to the procurement or wrongdoing of the proponent of his statement for the purpose of preventing the witness from attending or testifying.

(Amended March 5, 1981, effective July 1, 1981.)

(b) Hearsay exceptions. The following are not excluded by the hearsay rule if the declarant is unavailable as a witness:

(Amended March 5, 1981, effective July 1, 1981.)

(1) Former testimony. Testimony given as a witness at another hearing of the same or a different proceeding, or in a deposition taken in compliance with law in the course of the same or another proceeding, if the party against whom the testimony is now offered, or, in a civil action or proceeding, a predecessor in interest, had an opportunity and similar motive to develop the testimony by direct, cross, or redirect examination.

(Amended March 5, 1981, effective July 1, 1981.)

Committee Comment

The Federal Rule is substantially the same as the Colorado Rule; except there is no reference to subsection (b)(2) in the Colorado Rule, as there is no Colorado subsection (b)(2). As to testimony given at a preliminary hearing, *see* People v. Smith, 198 Colo. 120, 597 P.2d 204 (1979). This rule expands upon the former rule of evidence in Colorado. For authorities on the use of such evidence in Colorado, *see*: Rule 32 of Colorado Rules of Civil Procedure; Emerson v. Burnett, 11 Colo. App. 86, 52 P. 752 (1898); Daniels v. Stock, 23 Colo. App. 529, 130 P. 1031 (1913); Woodworth v. Gorsline, 30 Colo. 186, 69 P. 705 (1902); Henwood v. People, 57 Colo. 544, 143 P. 373 (1914); Gibson v. Gagnon, 82 Colo. 108, 257 P. 348 (1927); Duran v. People, 156 Colo. 385, 399 P.2d 412 (1965); Insul-Wool Insulation Corp. v. Home Insulation, Inc., 176 F.2d 502 (10th Cir. 1949). (Amended March 5, 1981, effective July 1, 1981.)

(2) (No Colorado Rule Codified)

(3) Statement against interest. A statement that:

(A) a reasonable person in the declarant's position would have made only if the person believed it to be true because, when made, it was so contrary to the declarant's proprietary or pecuniary interest or had so great a tendency to invalidate the declarant's claim against someone else or to expose the declarant to civil or criminal liability; and

(B) is supported by corroborating circumstances that clearly indicate its trustworthiness, if it is offered in a criminal case as one that tends to expose the declarant to criminal liability.

(Amended January 13, 2011, effective January 13, 2011.)

Committee Comment

The rule was revised, consistent with recent amendments to FRE 804(b)(3) only to clarify that corroborating circumstances are required regardless of whether a statement is offered to inculpate or exculpate an accused. *See* People v. Newton, 966 P.2d 563 (Colo. 1998) (prosecutors seeking to admit statements against the accused must satisfy the corroborating requirements solely by reference to the circumstances surrounding its making).

(4) Statement of personal or family history. (A) A statement concerning the declarant's own birth, adoption, marriage, divorce, legitimacy, relationship by blood, adoption, or marriage, ancestry, or other similar fact of personal or family history, even though declarant had no means of acquiring personal knowledge of the matter stated; or (B) a statement concerning the foregoing matters, and death also, of another person, if the declarant was related to the other by blood, adoption, or marriage or was so intimately associated with the other's family as to be likely to have accurate information concerning the matter declared.

Committee Comment

This rule expanded the former Colorado rule to admit statements of unrelated associates. Some independent proof of relationship under (B) will continue to be required.

(5) [Transferred to Rule 807] (Amended November 25, 1998, effective January 1, 1999.)

Committee Comment

The contents of Rule 803(24) and Rule 804(b)(5) have been combined and transferred to Rule 807. This was done to facilitate additions to Rules 803 and 804. No change in meaning is intended.

Rule 805. Hearsay Within Hearsay

Hearsay included within hearsay is not excluded under the hearsay rule if each part of the combined statements conforms with an exception to the hearsay rule provided in these rules.

Rule 806. Attacking and Supporting Credibility of Declarant

When a hearsay statement, or a statement defined in Rule 801(d)(2)(C), (D), or (E), has been admitted in evidence, the credibility of the declarant may be attacked, and if attacked may be supported, by any evidence which would be admissible for those purposes if declarant had testified as a witness. Evidence of a statement or conduct by the declarant at any time, inconsistent with his hearsay statement, is not subject to any requirement that he may have been afforded an opportunity to deny or explain. If the party against whom a hearsay statement has been admitted calls the declarant as a witness, the party is entitled to examine him on the statement as if under cross-examination.

Rule 807. Residual Exception

A statement not specifically covered by Rule 803 or 804 but having equivalent circumstantial guarantees of trustworthiness, is not excluded by the hearsay rule, if the court determines that (A) the statement is offered as evidence of a material fact; (B) the statement is more probative on the point for which it is offered than any other evidence which the proponent can procure through reasonable efforts; and (C) the general purposes of these rules and the interests of justice will best be served by admission of the statement into evidence. However, a statement may not be admitted under this exception unless the proponent of it makes known to the adverse party sufficiently in advance of the trial or hearing to provide the adverse party with a fair opportunity to prepare to meet it, the proponent's intention to offer the statement and the particulars of it, including the name and address of the declarant.

(Amended November 25, 1998, effective January 1, 1999.)

ARTICLE IX AUTHENTICATION AND IDENTIFICATION

Rule 901. Requirement of Authentication or Identification

(a) General provision. The requirement of authentication or identification as a condition precedent to admissibility is satisfied by evidence sufficient to support a finding that the matter in question is what its proponent claims.

(b) Illustrations. By way of illustration only, and not by way of limitation, the following are examples of authentication or identification conforming with the requirements of this rule:

(1) Testimony of witness with knowledge. Testimony that a matter is what it is claimed to be.

(2) Non-expert opinion on handwriting. Non-expert opinion as to the genuineness of handwriting, based upon familiarity not acquired for purposes of the litigation.

(Amended March 5, 1981, effective July 1, 1981.)

(3) Comparison by trier or expert witness. Comparison by the trier of fact or by expert witnesses with specimens which have been authenticated.

(4) Distinctive characteristics and the like. Appearance, contents, substance, internal patterns, or other distinctive characteristics, taken in conjunction with circumstances.

(5) Voice identification. Identification of a voice, whether heard firsthand or through mechanical or electronic transmission or recording, by opinion based upon hearing the voice at any time under circumstances connecting it with the alleged speaker.

(6) Telephone conversations. Telephone conversations, by evidence that a call was made to the number assigned at the time by the telephone company to a particular person or business, if (A) in the case of a person, circumstances, including self-identification, show the person answering to be the one called, or (B) in the case of business, the call was made to a place of business and the conversation related to business reasonably transacted over the telephone.

(7) Public records or reports. Evidence that a writing authorized by law to be recorded or filed and in fact recorded or filed in a public office, or a purported public record, report, statement, or data compilation, in any form, is from the public office where items of this nature are kept.

(8) Ancient documents or data compilation. Evidence that a document or data compilation, in any form, (A) is in such condition as to create no suspicion concerning its authenticity, (B) was in a place where it, if authentic, would likely be, and (C) that was prepared before January 1, 1998.

(9) Process or system. Evidence describing a process or system used to produce a result and showing that the process or system produces an accurate result.

(10) Methods provided by statute or rule. Any method of authentication or identification provided by Colorado Rules of Procedure, or by statute of the State of Colorado.

(Amended March 5, 1981, effective July 1, 1981. Subsection (b)(8) amended and adopted, effective March 29, 2021.)

Rule 902. Self-Authentication

Extrinsic evidence of authenticity as a condition precedent to admissibility is not required with respect to the following:

(1) Domestic public documents under seal. A document bearing a seal purporting to be that of the United States, or of any State, district, Commonwealth, territory, or insular possession thereof, or the Panama Canal Zone, or the Trust Territory of the Pacific Islands, or of a political subdivision, department, officer or agency thereof, and a signature purporting to be an attestation or execution.

(2) Domestic public documents not under seal. A document purporting to bear the signature in his official capacity of an officer or employee of any entity included in paragraph (1) hereof, having no seal, if a public officer having a seal and having official duties in the district or political subdivision of the officer or employee certifies under seal that the signer had the official capacity and that the signature is genuine.

(3) Foreign public documents. A document purporting to be executed or attested in his official capacity by a person authorized by the laws of a foreign country to make the execution or attestation, and accompanied by a final

certification as to the genuineness of signature and official position (A) of the executing or attesting person, or (B) of any foreign official whose certificate of genuineness of signature and official position relates to the execution or attestation or is in a chain of certificates of genuineness of signature and official position relating to the execution or attestation. A final certification may be made by a secretary of embassy or legation, consul general, consul, vice consul, or consular agent of the United States, or a diplomatic or consular official of the foreign country assigned or accredited to the United States. If reasonable opportunity has been given to all parties to investigate the authenticity and accuracy of official documents, the court may, for good cause shown, order that they be treated as presumptively authentic without final certification or permit them to be evidenced by an attested summary with or without final certification.

(4) Certified copies of public records. A copy of an official record or report or entry therein, or of a document authorized by law to be recorded or filed and actually recorded or filed in a public office, including data compilations in any form, certified as correct by the custodian or other person authorized to make the certification, by certificate complying with paragraph (1), (2), or (3) of this rule or complying with any Federal or Colorado Rule of Procedure, or with any Act of the United States Congress, or any statute of the State of Colorado.

(5) Official publications. Books, pamphlets, or other publications purporting to be issued by public authority.

(6) Newspapers and periodicals. Printed materials purporting to be newspapers or periodicals.

(7) Trade inscriptions and the like. Inscriptions, signs, tags, or labels purporting to have been affixed in the course of business and indicating ownership, control, or origin.

(8) Acknowledged documents. Documents accompanied by a certificate of acknowledgment executed in the manner provided by law by a notary public or other officer authorized by law to take acknowledgments.

(9) Commercial paper and related documents. Commercial paper, signatures thereon, and documents relating thereto to the extent provided by general commercial law.

(10) Presumptions under legislative Act. Any signature, document, or other matter declared by Act of the Congress of the United States, or by any statute of the State of Colorado to be presumptively or prima facie genuine or authentic.

(11) Certified domestic records of regularly conducted activity. The original or a duplicate of a domestic record of regularly conducted activity that would be admissible under Rule 803(6) if accompanied by an affidavit of its custodian or other qualified person, in a manner complying with any Colorado statute or rule

prescribed by the Colorado Supreme Court, certifying that the record—

(a)   was made at or near the time of the occurrence of the matters set forth by, or from information transmitted by, a person with knowledge of those matters;

(b)   was kept in the course of the regularly conducted activity; and

(c)   was made by the regularly conducted activity as a regular practice.

A party intending to offer a record into evidence under this paragraph must provide written notice of that intention to all adverse parties, and must make the record and affidavit available for inspection sufficiently in advance of their offer into evidence to provide an adverse party with a fair opportunity to challenge them.

(12) Certified foreign records of regularly conducted activity. In a civil case, the original or a duplicate of a foreign record of regularly conducted activity that would be admissible under Rule 803(6) if accompanied by a written declaration by its custodian or other qualified person certifying that the record—

(a)   was made at or near the time of the occurrence of the matters set forth by, or from information transmitted by, a person with knowledge of those matters;

(b)   was kept in the course of the regularly conducted activity; and

(c)   was made by the regularly conducted activity as a regular practice.

The declaration must be signed in a manner that, if falsely made, would subject the maker to criminal penalty under the laws of the country where the declaration is signed. A party intending to offer a record into evidence under this paragraph must provide written notice of that intention to all adverse parties, and must make the record and declaration available for inspection sufficiently in advance of their offer into evidence to provide an adverse party with a fair opportunity to challenge them.

(Amended June 20, 2002, effective July 1, 2002.)

Rule 903. Subscribing Witness' Testimony Unnecessary

The testimony of a subscribing witness is not necessary to authenticate a writing unless required by the laws of the jurisdiction whose laws govern the validity of the writing.

Committee Comment

The Committee finds that the Federal rules in this area are for the most part an accurate representation of Colorado case law, statutes, and the Rules of Procedure. The Committee opinion is that the rules as adopted provide a more flexible guide to evidentiary problems relating to authentication and identification and thereby avoid the necessity of the search for a "case in point."

The rules would cover a number of cases and situations arising in trial, not currently reported in case law.

ARTICLE X   CONTENTS OF WRITINGS, RECORDINGS AND PHOTOGRAPHS

Rule 1001. Definitions
For purposes of this article the following definitions are applicable:

(1) Writings and recordings. "Writings" and "recordings" consist of letters, words, or numbers, or their equivalent, set down by handwriting, typewriting, printing, photostating, photographing, magnetic impulse, mechanical or electronic recording, or other form of data compilation.

(2) Photographs. "Photographs" include still photographs, X-ray films, video tapes, and motion pictures.

(3) Original. An "original" of a writing or recording is the writing or recording itself or any counterpart intended to have the same effect by a person executing or issuing it. An "original" of a photograph includes the negative or any print therefrom. If data are stored in a computer or similar device, any printout or other output readable by sight, shown to reflect the data accurately, is an "original."

(4) Duplicate. A "duplicate" is a counterpart produced by the same impression as the original, or from the same matrix, or by means of photography, including enlargements and miniatures, or by mechanical or electronic re-recording, or by chemical reproduction, or by other equivalent techniques which accurately reproduce the original.

Rule 1002. Requirement of Original
To prove the content of a writing, recording, or photograph, the original writing, recording, or photograph is required, except as otherwise provided in these rules or by statute of the State of Colorado or of the United States.

Rule 1003. Admissibility of Duplicates
A duplicate is admissible to the same extent as an original unless (1) a genuine question is raised as to the authenticity of the original or (2) in the circumstances it would be unfair to admit the duplicate in lieu of the original.

Committee Comment

The Committee notes the desirability of requiring, in pretrial procedures, that any genuine questions as to the authenticity of the original, or of circumstances that it would be unfair to admit the duplicate, be raised, so that the offering party may take appropriate steps under Rule 1004 to obtain the original.

Rule 1004. Admissibility of Other Evidence of Contents
The original is not required, and other evidence of the contents of a writing, recording, or photograph is admissible if:

(1) Originals lost or destroyed. All originals are lost or have been destroyed, unless the proponent lost or destroyed them in bad faith; or

(2) Original not obtainable. No original can be obtained by any available judicial process or procedure; or

(3) Original in possession of opponent. At a time when an original was under the control of the party against whom offered, he was put on notice, by the pleadings or otherwise, that the contents would be a subject of proof at the hearing, and he does not produce the original at the hearing; or

(4) Collateral matters. The writing, recording, or photograph is not closely related to a controlling issue.

Committee Comment

Subparagraph (1) of the rule will be in lieu of Rule 43(g)(1) of the Colorado Rules of Civil Procedure; subparagraph (2) will be in lieu of Rule 43(g)(6); subparagraph (3) will be in lieu of Rule 43(g)(2). With respect to subparagraph (2), the adoption of this provision has a direct correlation with the comments appended to Rule 1003 regarding pretrial procedure. The Committee suggests that subparagraph (2) be viewed in terms of available judicial process or procedure that is reasonable in the circumstances considering time and expense. For example, the FRE Committee's Advisory Notes refer to procedure including subpoena duces tecum as an incident to the taking of a deposition in another jurisdiction. Such time and expense would often appear to be unjustified, and should in part be taken care of by the pretrial procedures recommended in comments under Rule 1003.

Rule 1005. Public Records
The contents of an official record, or of a document authorized to be recorded, or filed and actually recorded or filed, including data compilations in any form, if otherwise admissible, may be proved by copy, certified as correct in accordance with Rule 902 or testified to be correct by a witness who has compared it with the original. If a copy which complies with the foregoing cannot be obtained by the exercise of reasonable diligence, then other evidence of the contents may be given.

Committee Comment

This provision is in lieu of Rule 43(g)(3) of the Colorado Rules of Civil Procedure. The Committee does not recommend any changes in the language, but this is based upon the assumption that Rule 902 would be amended to provide for certification in accordance with Colorado statute.

Rule 1006. Summaries
The contents of voluminous writings, recordings, or photographs which cannot conveniently be examined in court may be presented in the form of a chart, summary, or calculation. The originals or duplicates, shall be made available for examination or copying, or both, by other parties at reasonable time and place. The court may order that they be produced in court.

Committee Comment

This rule will replace Rule 43(g)(5) of the Colorado Rules of Civil Procedure.

Rule 1007. Testimony or Written Admission of Party

Contents of writings, recordings, or photographs may be proved by the testimony or deposition of the party against whom offered or by his written admission, without accounting for the nonproduction of the original.

Rule 1008. Functions of Court and Jury

When the admissibility of other evidence of contents of writings, recordings, or photographs under these rules depends upon the fulfillment of a condition of fact, the question whether the condition has been fulfilled is ordinarily for the court to determine in accordance with the provisions of Rule 104. However, when an issue is raised (a) whether the asserted writing ever existed, or (b) whether another writing, recording, or photograph produced at the trial is the original, or (c) whether other evidence of contents correctly reflects the contents, the issue is for the trier of fact to determine as in the case of other issues of fact.

ARTICLE XI   MISCELLANEOUS RULES

Rule 1101. Applicability of Rules

(a) **Courts.** These rules apply to all courts in the State of Colorado.

(b) **Proceedings generally.** These rules apply generally to civil actions, to criminal proceedings, and to contempt proceedings, except those in which the court may act summarily.

(c) **Rule of privilege.** The rule with respect to privileges applies at all stages of all actions, cases, and proceedings.

(Amended March 5, 1981, effective July 1, 1981.)

(d) **Rules inapplicable.** The rules (other than with respect to privileges) do not apply in the following situations:

(1) Preliminary questions of fact. The determination of questions of fact preliminary to admissibility of evidence when the issue is to be determined by the court under Rule 104.

(2) Grand jury. Proceedings before grand juries.

(3) Miscellaneous proceedings. Proceedings for extradition or rendition; preliminary examinations in criminal cases; sentencing, or granting or revoking probation; issuance of warrants for arrest, criminal summonses, and search warrants; and proceedings with respect to release on bail or otherwise.

(e) **Rules applicable in part.** In any special statutory proceedings, these rules apply to the extent that matters of evidence are not provided for in the statutes which govern procedure therein.

(Amended March 5, 1981, effective July 1, 1981.)

Committee Comment

The Colorado rule is culled from Rule 81 of the Colorado Rules of Civil Procedure and Rule 1101(e) of the Federal Rules of Evidence.

Rule 1102. (No Colorado Rule Codified)

Rule 1103. Title

These rules shall be known and cited as the Colorado Rules of Evidence, or CRE.

FEDERAL RULES OF EVIDENCE

ARTICLE I
GENERAL PROVISIONS

Rule 101. Scope; Definitions

(a) Scope. These rules apply to proceedings in United States courts. The specific courts and proceedings to which the rules apply, along with exceptions, are set out in Rule 1101.

(b) Definitions. In these rules:

(1) "civil case" means a civil action or proceeding;

(2) "criminal case" includes a criminal proceeding;

(3) "public office" includes a public agency;

(4) "record" includes a memorandum, report, or data compilation;

(5) a "rule prescribed by the Supreme Court" means a rule adopted by the Supreme Court under statutory authority; and

(6) a reference to any kind of written material or any other medium includes electronically stored information.

Rule 102. Purpose

These rules should be construed so as to administer every proceeding fairly, eliminate unjustifiable expense and delay, and promote the development of evidence law, to the end of ascertaining the truth and securing a just determination.

Rule 103. Rulings on Evidence

(a) Preserving a Claim of Error. A party may claim error in a ruling to admit or exclude evidence only if the error affects a substantial right of the party and:

(1) if the ruling admits evidence, a party, on the record:

(A) timely objects or moves to strike; and

(B) states the specific ground, unless it was apparent from the context; or

(2) if the ruling excludes evidence, a party informs the court of its substance by an offer of proof, unless the substance was apparent from the context.

(b) Not Needing to Renew an Objection or Offer of Proof. Once the court rules definitively on the record—either before or at trial—a party need not renew an objection or offer of proof to preserve a claim of error for appeal.

(c) Court's Statement About the Ruling; Directing an Offer of Proof. The court may make any statement about the character or form of the evidence, the objection made, and the ruling. The court may direct that an offer of proof be made in question-and-answer form.

(d) Preventing the Jury from Hearing Inadmissible Evidence. To the extent practicable, the court must conduct a jury trial so that inadmissible evidence is not suggested to the jury by any means.

(e) Taking Notice of Plain Error. A court may take notice of a plain error affecting a substantial right, even if the claim of error was not properly preserved.

Rule 104. Preliminary Questions

(a) In General. The court must decide any preliminary question about whether a witness is qualified, a privilege exists, or evidence is admissible. In so deciding, the court is not bound by evidence rules, except those on privilege.

(b) Relevance That Depends on a Fact. When the relevance of evidence depends on whether a fact exists, proof must be introduced sufficient to support a finding that the fact does exist. The court may admit the proposed evidence on the condition that the proof be introduced later.

(c) Conducting a Hearing So That the Jury Cannot Hear It. The court must conduct any hearing on a preliminary question so that the jury cannot hear it if:

(1) the hearing involves the admissibility of a confession;

(2) a defendant in a criminal case is a witness and so requests; or

(3) justice so requires.

(d) Cross-Examining a Defendant in a Criminal Case. By testifying on a preliminary question, a defendant in a criminal case does not become subject to cross-examination on other issues in the case.

(e) Evidence Relevant to Weight and Credibility. This rule does not limit a party's right to introduce before the jury evidence that is relevant to the weight or credibility of other evidence.

Rule 105. Limiting Evidence That Is Not Admissible Against Other Parties or for Other Purposes

If the court admits evidence that is admissible against a party or for a purpose—but not against another party or for another purpose—the court, on timely request, must restrict the evidence to its proper scope and instruct the jury accordingly.

Rule 106. Remainder of or Related Writings or Recorded Statements

If a party introduces all or part of a writing or recorded statement, an adverse party may require the introduction, at that time, of any other part—or any other writing or recorded statement—that in fairness ought to be considered at the same time.

ARTICLE II
JUDICIAL NOTICE

Rule 201. Judicial Notice of Adjudicative Facts

(a) Scope. This rule governs judicial notice of an adjudicative fact only, not a legislative fact.

(b) Kinds of Facts That May Be Judicially Noticed. The court may judicially notice a fact that is not subject to reasonable dispute because it:

(1) is generally known within the trial court's territorial jurisdiction; or

(2) can be accurately and readily determined from sources whose accuracy cannot reasonably be questioned.

(c) Taking Notice. The court:

(1) may take judicial notice on its own; or

(2) must take judicial notice if a party requests it and the court is supplied with the necessary information.

(d) Timing. The court may take judicial notice at any stage of the proceeding.

(e) Opportunity to Be Heard. On timely request, a party is entitled to be heard on the propriety of taking judicial notice and the nature of the fact to be noticed. If the court takes judicial notice before notifying a party, the party, on request, is still entitled to be heard.

(f) Instructing the Jury. In a civil case, the court must instruct the jury to accept the noticed fact as conclusive. In a criminal case, the court must instruct the jury that it may or may not accept the noticed fact as conclusive.

ARTICLE III
PRESUMPTIONS IN CIVIL CASES

Rule 301. Presumptions in Civil Cases Generally

In a civil case, unless a federal statute or these rules provide otherwise, the party against whom a presumption is directed has the burden of producing evidence to rebut the presumption. But this rule does not shift the burden of persuasion, which remains on the party who had it originally.

Rule 302. Applying State Law to Presumptions in Civil Cases

In a civil case, state law governs the effect of a presumption regarding a claim or defense for which state law supplies the rule of decision.

ARTICLE IV
RELEVANCE AND ITS LIMITS

Rule 401. Test for Relevant Evidence

Evidence is relevant if:

(a) it has any tendency to make a fact more or less probable than it would be without the evidence; and

(b) the fact is of consequence in determining the action.

Rule 402. General Admissibility of Relevant Evidence

Relevant evidence is admissible unless any of the following provides otherwise:

- the United States Constitution;
- a federal statute;
- these rules; or
- other rules prescribed by the Supreme Court.

Irrelevant evidence is not admissible.

Rule 403. Excluding Relevant Evidence for Prejudice, Confusion, Waste of Time, or Other Reasons

The court may exclude relevant evidence if its probative value is substantially outweighed by a danger of one or more of the following: unfair prejudice, confusing the issues, misleading the jury, undue delay, wasting time, or needlessly presenting cumulative evidence.

Rule 404. Character Evidence; Other Crimes, Wrongs, or Acts

(a) Character Evidence.

(1) Prohibited Uses. Evidence of a person's character or character trait is not admissible to prove that on a particular occasion the person acted in accordance with the character or trait.

(2) *Exceptions for a Defendant or Victim in a Criminal Case.* The following exceptions apply in a criminal case:

(A) a defendant may offer evidence of the defendant's pertinent trait, and if the evidence is admitted, the prosecutor may offer evidence to rebut it;

(B) subject to the limitations in Rule 412, a defendant may offer evidence of an alleged victim's pertinent trait, and if the evidence is admitted, the prosecutor may:

(i) offer evidence to rebut it; and

(ii) offer evidence of the defendant's same trait; and

(C) in a homicide case, the prosecutor may offer evidence of the alleged victim's trait of peacefulness to rebut evidence that the victim was the first aggressor.

(3) *Exceptions for a Witness.* Evidence of a witness's character may be admitted under Rules 607, 608, and 609.

(b) Other Crimes, Wrongs, or Acts.

(1) *Prohibited Uses.* Evidence of any other crime, wrong, or act is not admissible to prove a person's character in order to show that on a particular occasion the person acted in accordance with the character.

(2) *Permitted Uses.* This evidence may be admissible for another purpose, such as proving motive, opportunity, intent, preparation, plan, knowledge, identity, absence of mistake, or lack of accident.

(3) *Notice in a Criminal Case.* In a criminal case, the prosecutor must:

(A) provide reasonable notice of any such evidence that the prosecutor intends to offer at trial, so that the defendant has a fair opportunity to meet it;

(B) articulate in the notice the permitted purpose for which the prosecutor intends to offer the evidence and the reasoning that supports the purpose; and

(C) do so in writing before trial—or in any form during trial if the court, for good cause, excuses lack of pretrial notice.

Rule 405. Methods of Proving Character

(a) By Reputation or Opinion. When evidence of a person's character or character trait is admissible, it may be proved by testimony about the person's reputation or by testimony in the form of an opinion. On cross-examination of the character witness, the court may allow an inquiry into relevant specific instances of the person's conduct.

(b) By Specific Instances of Conduct. When a person's character or character trait is an essential element of a charge, claim, or defense, the character or trait may also be proved by relevant specific instances of the person's conduct.

Rule 406. Habit; Routine Practice

Evidence of a person's habit or an organization's

routine practice may be admitted to prove that on a particular occasion the person or organization acted in accordance with the habit or routine practice. The court may admit this evidence regardless of whether it is corroborated or whether there was an eyewitness.

Rule 407. Subsequent Remedial Measures

When measures are taken that would have made an earlier injury or harm less likely to occur, evidence of the subsequent measures is not admissible to prove:

- negligence;
- culpable conduct;
- a defect in a product or its design; or
- a need for a warning or instruction.

But the court may admit this evidence for another purpose, such as impeachment or—if disputed—proving ownership, control, or the feasibility of precautionary measures.

Rule 408. Compromise Offers and Negotiations

(a) Prohibited Uses. Evidence of the following is not admissible—on behalf of any party—either to prove or disprove the validity or amount of a disputed claim or to impeach by a prior inconsistent statement or a contradiction:

(1) furnishing, promising, or offering—or accepting, promising to accept, or offering to accept—a valuable consideration in compromising or attempting to compromise the claim; and

(2) conduct or a statement made during compromise negotiations about the claim—except when offered in a criminal case and when the negotiations related to a claim by a public office in the exercise of its regulatory, investigative, or enforcement authority.

(b) Exceptions. The court may admit this evidence for another purpose, such as proving a witness's bias or prejudice, negating a contention of undue delay, or proving an effort to obstruct a criminal investigation or prosecution.

Rule 409. Offers to Pay Medical and Similar Expenses

Evidence of furnishing, promising to pay, or offering to pay medical, hospital, or similar expenses resulting from an injury is not admissible to prove liability for the injury.

Rule 410. Pleas, Plea Discussions, and Related Statements

(a) Prohibited Uses. In a civil or criminal case, evidence of the following is not admissible against the defendant who made the plea or participated in the plea discussions:

(1) a guilty plea that was later withdrawn;

(2) a nolo contendere plea;

(3) a statement made during a proceeding on either of those pleas under Federal Rule of Criminal Procedure 11 or a comparable state procedure; or

(4) a statement made during plea discussions with an attorney for the prosecuting authority if the discussions did not result in a guilty plea or they resulted in a later-withdrawn guilty plea.

(b) Exceptions. The court may admit a statement described in Rule 410(a)(3) or (4):

(1) in any proceeding in which another statement made during the same plea or plea discussions has been introduced, if in fairness the statements ought to be considered together; or

(2) in a criminal proceeding for perjury or false statement, if the defendant made the statement under oath, on the record, and with counsel present.

Rule 411. Liability Insurance

Evidence that a person was or was not insured against liability is not admissible to prove whether the person acted negligently or otherwise wrongfully. But the court may admit this evidence for another purpose, such as proving a witness's bias or prejudice or proving agency, ownership, or control.

Rule 412. Sex-Offense Cases: The Victim's Sexual Behavior or Predisposition

(a) Prohibited Uses. The following evidence is not admissible in a civil or criminal proceeding involving alleged sexual misconduct:

(1) evidence offered to prove that a victim engaged in other sexual behavior; or

(2) evidence offered to prove a victim's sexual predisposition.

(b) Exceptions.

(1) *Criminal Cases.* The court may admit the following evidence in a criminal case:

(A) evidence of specific instances of a victim's sexual behavior, if offered to prove that someone other than the defendant was the source of semen, injury, or other physical evidence;

(B) evidence of specific instances of a victim's sexual behavior with respect to the person accused of the sexual misconduct, if offered by the defendant to prove consent or if offered by the prosecutor; and

(C) evidence whose exclusion would violate the defendant's constitutional rights.

(2) *Civil Cases.* In a civil case, the court may admit evidence offered to prove a victim's sexual behavior or sexual predisposition if its probative value substantially outweighs the danger of harm to any victim and of unfair prejudice to any party. The court may admit evidence of a

victim's reputation only if the victim has placed it in controversy.

(c) Procedure to Determine Admissibility.

(1) *Motion.* If a party intends to offer evidence under Rule 412(b), the party must:

(A) file a motion that specifically describes the evidence and states the purpose for which it is to be offered;

(B) do so at least 14 days before trial unless the court, for good cause, sets a different time;

(C) serve the motion on all parties; and

(D) notify the victim or, when appropriate, the victim's guardian or representative.

(2) *Hearing.* Before admitting evidence under this rule, the court must conduct an in camera hearing and give the victim and parties a right to attend and be heard. Unless the court orders otherwise, the motion, related materials, and the record of the hearing must be and remain sealed.

(d) Definition of "Victim." In this rule, "victim" includes an alleged victim.

Rule 413. Similar Crimes in Sexual-Assault Cases

(a) Permitted Uses. In a criminal case in which a defendant is accused of a sexual assault, the court may admit evidence that the defendant committed any other sexual assault. The evidence may be considered on any matter to which it is relevant.

(b) Disclosure to the Defendant. If the prosecutor intends to offer this evidence, the prosecutor must disclose it to the defendant, including witnesses' statements or a summary of the expected testimony. The prosecutor must do so at least 15 days before trial or at a later time that the court allows for good cause.

(c) Effect on Other Rules. This rule does not limit the admission or consideration of evidence under any other rule.

(d) Definition of "Sexual Assault." In this rule and Rule 415, "sexual assault" means a crime under federal law or under state law (as "state" is defined in 18 U.S.C. § 513) involving:

(1) any conduct prohibited by 18 U.S.C. chapter 109A;

(2) contact, without consent, between any part of the defendant's body—or an object—and another person's genitals or anus;

(3) contact, without consent, between the defendant's genitals or anus and any part of another person's body;

(4) deriving sexual pleasure or gratification from inflicting death, bodily injury, or physical pain on another person; or

(5) an attempt or conspiracy to engage in conduct described in subparagraphs (1)–(4).

Rule 414. Similar Crimes in Child—Molestation Cases

(a) Permitted Uses. In a criminal case in which a defendant is accused of child molestation, the court may admit evidence that the defendant committed any other child molestation. The evidence may be considered on any matter to which it is relevant.

(b) Disclosure to the Defendant. If the prosecutor intends to offer this evidence, the prosecutor must disclose it to the defendant, including witnesses' statements or a summary of the expected testimony. The prosecutor must do so at least 15 days before trial or at a later time that the court allows for good cause.

(c) Effect on Other Rules. This rule does not limit the admission or consideration of evidence under any other rule.

(d) Definition of "Child" and "Child Molestation." In this rule and Rule 415:

(1) "child" means a person below the age of 14; and

(2) "child molestation" means a crime under federal law or under state law (as "state" is defined in 18 U.S.C. § 513) involving:

(A) any conduct prohibited by 18 U.S.C. chapter 109A and committed with a child;

(B) any conduct prohibited by 18 U.S.C. chapter 110;

(C) contact between any part of the defendant's body—or an object—and a child's genitals or anus;

(D) contact between the defendant's genitals or anus and any part of a child's body;

(E) deriving sexual pleasure or gratification from inflicting death, bodily injury, or physical pain on a child; or

(F) an attempt or conspiracy to engage in conduct described in subparagraphs (A)–(E).

Rule 415. Similar Acts in Civil Cases Involving Sexual Assault or Child Molestation

(a) Permitted Uses. In a civil case involving a claim for relief based on a party's alleged sexual assault or child molestation, the court may admit evidence that the party committed any other sexual assault or child molestation. The evidence may be considered as provided in Rules 413 and 414.

(b) Disclosure to the Opponent. If a party intends to offer this evidence, the party must disclose it to the party against whom it will be offered, including witnesses' statements or a summary of the expected testimony. The party must do so at least 15 days before trial or at a later time that the court allows for good cause.

(c) Effect on Other Rules. This rule does not limit the admission or consideration of evidence under any other rule.

ARTICLE V
PRIVILEGES

Rule 501. Privilege in General

The common law—as interpreted by United States courts in the light of reason and experience—governs a claim of privilege unless any of the following provides otherwise:

- the United States Constitution;

- a federal statute; or

- rules prescribed by the Supreme Court.

But in a civil case, state law governs privilege regarding a claim or defense for which state law supplies the rule of decision.

Rule 502. Attorney-Client Privilege and Work Product; Limitations on Waiver

The following provisions apply, in the circumstances set out, to disclosure of a communication or information covered by the attorney-client privilege or work-product protection.

(a) Disclosure Made in a Federal Proceeding or to a Federal Office or Agency; Scope of a Waiver. When the disclosure is made in a federal proceeding or to a federal office or agency and waives the attorney-client privilege or work-product protection, the waiver extends to an undisclosed communication or information in a federal or state proceeding only if:

(1) the waiver is intentional;

(2) the disclosed and undisclosed communications or information concern the same subject matter; and

(3) they ought in fairness to be considered together.

(b) Inadvertent Disclosure. When made in a federal proceeding or to a federal office or agency, the disclosure does not operate as a waiver in a federal or state proceeding if:

(1) the disclosure is inadvertent;

(2) the holder of the privilege or protection took reasonable steps to prevent disclosure; and

(3) the holder promptly took reasonable steps to rectify the error, including (if applicable) following Federal Rule of Civil Procedure 26(b)(5)(B).

(c) Disclosure Made in a State Proceeding. When the disclosure is made in a state proceeding and is not the subject of a state-court order concerning waiver, the disclosure does not operate as a waiver in a federal proceeding if the disclosure:

(1) would not be a waiver under this rule if it had been made in a federal proceeding; or

(2) is not a waiver under the law of the state where the disclosure occurred.

(d) Controlling Effect of a Court Order. A federal court may order that the privilege or protection is not waived by disclosure connected with the litigation pending before the court—in which event the disclosure is also not a waiver in any other federal or state proceeding.

(e) Controlling Effect of a Party Agreement. An agreement on the effect of disclosure in a federal proceeding is binding only on the parties to the agreement, unless it is incorporated into a court order.

(f) Controlling Effect of this Rule. Notwithstanding Rules 101 and 1101, this rule applies to state proceedings and to federal court—annexed and federal court—mandated arbitration proceedings, in the circumstances set out in the rule. And notwithstanding Rule 501, this rule applies even if state law provides the rule of decision.

(g) Definitions. In this rule:

(1) "attorney-client privilege" means the protection that applicable law provides for confidential attorney-client communications; and

(2) "work-product protection" means the protection that applicable law provides for tangible material (or its intangible equivalent) prepared in anticipation of litigation or for trial.

ARTICLE VI
WITNESSES

Rule 601. Competency to Testify in General

Every person is competent to be a witness unless these rules provide otherwise. But in a civil case, state law governs the witness's competency regarding a claim or defense for which state law supplies the rule of decision.

Rule 602. Need for Personal Knowledge

A witness may testify to a matter only if evidence is introduced sufficient to support a finding that the witness has personal knowledge of the matter. Evidence to prove personal knowledge may consist of the witness's own testimony. This rule does not apply to a witness's expert testimony under Rule 703.

Rule 603. Oath or Affirmation to Testify Truthfully

Before testifying, a witness must give an oath or affirmation to testify truthfully. It must be in a form designed to impress that duty on the witness's conscience.

Rule 604. Interpreter

An interpreter must be qualified and must give an oath or affirmation to make a true translation.

Rule 605. Judge's Competency as a Witness

The presiding judge may not testify as a witness at the trial. A party need not object to preserve the issue.

Rule 606. Juror's Competency as a Witness

(a) At the Trial. A juror may not testify as a witness before the other jurors at the trial. If a juror is called to testify, the court must give a party an opportunity to object outside the jury's presence.

(b) During an Inquiry into the Validity of a Verdict or Indictment.

(1) *Prohibited Testimony or Other Evidence.* During an inquiry into the validity of a verdict or indictment, a juror may not testify about any statement made or incident that occurred during the jury's deliberations; the effect of anything on that juror's or another juror's vote; or any juror's mental processes concerning the verdict or indictment. The court may not receive a juror's affidavit or evidence of a juror's statement on these matters.

(2) *Exceptions.* A juror may testify about whether:

(A) extraneous prejudicial information was improperly brought to the jury's attention;

(B) an outside influence was improperly brought to bear on any juror; or

(C) a mistake was made in entering the verdict on the verdict form.

Rule 607. Who May Impeach a Witness

Any party, including the party that called the witness, may attack the witness's credibility.

Rule 608. A Witness's Character for Truthfulness or Untruthfulness

(a) Reputation or Opinion Evidence. A witness's credibility may be attacked or supported by testimony about the witness's reputation for having a character for truthfulness or untruthfulness, or by testimony in the form of an opinion about that character. But evidence of truthful character is admissible only after the witness's character for truthfulness has been attacked.

(b) Specific Instances of Conduct. Except for a criminal conviction under Rule 609, extrinsic evidence is not admissible to prove specific instances of a witness's conduct in order to attack or support the witness's character for truthfulness. But the court may, on cross-examination, allow them to be inquired into if they are probative of the character for truthfulness or untruthfulness of:

(1) the witness; or

(2) another witness whose character the witness being cross-examined has testified about.

By testifying on another matter, a witness does not waive any privilege against self-incrimination for testimony that relates only to the witness's character for truthfulness.

Rule 609. Impeachment by Evidence of a Criminal Conviction

(a) In General. The following rules apply to attacking a witness's character for truthfulness by evidence of a criminal conviction:

(1) for a crime that, in the convicting jurisdiction, was punishable by death or by imprisonment for more than one year, the evidence:

(A) must be admitted, subject to Rule 403, in a civil case or in a criminal case in which the witness is not a defendant; and

(B) must be admitted in a criminal case in which the witness is a defendant, if the probative value of the evidence outweighs its prejudicial effect to that defendant; and

(2) for any crime regardless of the punishment, the evidence must be admitted if the court can readily determine that establishing the elements of the crime required proving—or the witness's admitting—a dishonest act or false statement.

(b) Limit on Using the Evidence After 10 Years. This subdivision (b) applies if more than 10 years have passed since the witness's conviction or release from confinement for it, whichever is later. Evidence of the conviction is admissible only if:

(1) its probative value, supported by specific facts and circumstances, substantially outweighs its prejudicial effect; and

(2) the proponent gives an adverse party reasonable written notice of the intent to use it so that the party has a fair opportunity to contest its use.

(c) Effect of a Pardon, Annulment, or Certificate of Rehabilitation. Evidence of a conviction is not admissible if:

(1) the conviction has been the subject of a pardon, annulment, certificate of rehabilitation, or other equivalent procedure based on a finding that the person has been rehabilitated, and the person has not been convicted of a later crime punishable by death or by imprisonment for more than one year; or

(2) the conviction has been the subject of a pardon, annulment, or other equivalent procedure based on a finding of innocence.

(d) Juvenile Adjudications. Evidence of a juvenile adjudication is admissible under this rule only if:

(1) it is offered in a criminal case;

(2) the adjudication was of a witness other than the defendant;

(3) an adult's conviction for that offense would be admissible to attack the adult's credibility; and

(4) admitting the evidence is necessary to fairly determine guilt or innocence.

(e) Pendency of an Appeal. A conviction that satisfies

this rule is admissible even if an appeal is pending. Evidence of the pendency is also admissible.

Rule 610. Religious Beliefs or Opinions

Evidence of a witness's religious beliefs or opinions is not admissible to attack or support the witness's credibility.

Rule 611. Mode and Order of Examining Witnesses and Presenting Evidence

(a) Control by the Court; Purposes. The court should exercise reasonable control over the mode and order of examining witnesses and presenting evidence so as to:

(1) make those procedures effective for determining the truth;

(2) avoid wasting time; and

(3) protect witnesses from harassment or undue embarrassment.

(b) Scope of Cross-Examination. Cross-examination should not go beyond the subject matter of the direct examination and matters affecting the witness's credibility. The court may allow inquiry into additional matters as if on direct examination.

(c) Leading Questions. Leading questions should not be used on direct examination except as necessary to develop the witness's testimony. Ordinarily, the court should allow leading questions:

(1) on cross-examination; and

(2) when a party calls a hostile witness, an adverse party, or a witness identified with an adverse party.

Rule 612. Writing Used to Refresh a Witness's Memory

(a) Scope. This rule gives an adverse party certain options when a witness uses a writing to refresh memory:

(1) while testifying; or

(2) before testifying, if the court decides that justice requires the party to have those options.

(b) Adverse Party's Options; Deleting Unrelated Matter. Unless 18 U.S.C. § 3500 provides otherwise in a criminal case, an adverse party is entitled to have the writing produced at the hearing, to inspect it, to cross-examine the witness about it, and to introduce in evidence any portion that relates to the witness's testimony. If the producing party claims that the writing includes unrelated matter, the court must examine the writing in camera, delete any unrelated portion, and order that the rest be delivered to the adverse party. Any portion deleted over objection must be preserved for the record.

(c) Failure to Produce or Deliver the Writing. If a writing is not produced or is not delivered as ordered, the court may issue any appropriate order. But if the prosecution does not comply in a criminal case, the court must

strike the witness's testimony or—if justice so requires—declare a mistrial.

Rule 613. Witness's Prior Statement

(a) Showing or Disclosing the Statement During Examination. When examining a witness about the witness's prior statement, a party need not show it or disclose its contents to the witness. But the party must, on request, show it or disclose its contents to an adverse party's attorney.

(b) Extrinsic Evidence of a Prior Inconsistent Statement. Extrinsic evidence of a witness's prior inconsistent statement is admissible only if the witness is given an opportunity to explain or deny the statement and an adverse party is given an opportunity to examine the witness about it, or if justice so requires. This subdivision (b) does not apply to an opposing party's statement under Rule 801(d)(2).

Rule 614. Court's Calling or Examining a Witness

(a) Calling. The court may call a witness on its own or at a party's request. Each party is entitled to cross-examine the witness.

(b) Examining. The court may examine a witness regardless of who calls the witness.

(c) Objections. A party may object to the court's calling or examining a witness either at that time or at the next opportunity when the jury is not present.

Rule 615. Excluding Witnesses

At a party's request, the court must order witnesses excluded so that they cannot hear other witnesses' testimony. Or the court may do so on its own. But this rule does not authorize excluding:

(a) a party who is a natural person;

(b) an officer or employee of a party that is not a natural person, after being designated as the party's representative by its attorney;

(c) a person whose presence a party shows to be essential to presenting the party's claim or defense; or

(d) a person authorized by statute to be present.

ARTICLE VII
OPINIONS AND EXPERT TESTIMONY

Rule 701. Opinion Testimony by Lay Witnesses

If a witness is not testifying as an expert, testimony in the form of an opinion is limited to one that is:

(a) rationally based on the witness's perception;

(b) helpful to clearly understanding the witness's testimony or to determining a fact in issue; and

(c) not based on scientific, technical, or other specialized knowledge within the scope of Rule 702.

Rule 702. Testimony by Expert Witnesses

A witness who is qualified as an expert by knowledge, skill, experience, training, or education may testify in the form of an opinion or otherwise if:

(a) the expert's scientific, technical, or other specialized knowledge will help the trier of fact to understand the evidence or to determine a fact in issue;

(b) the testimony is based on sufficient facts or data;

(c) the testimony is the product of reliable principles and methods; and

(d) the expert has reliably applied the principles and methods to the facts of the case.

Rule 703. Bases of an Expert's Opinion Testimony

An expert may base an opinion on facts or data in the case that the expert has been made aware of or personally observed. If experts in the particular field would reasonably rely on those kinds of facts or data in forming an opinion on the subject, they need not be admissible for the opinion to be admitted. But if the facts or data would otherwise be inadmissible, the proponent of the opinion may disclose them to the jury only if their probative value in helping the jury evaluate the opinion substantially outweighs their prejudicial effect.

Rule 704. Opinion on an Ultimate Issue

(a) In General—Not Automatically Objectionable. An opinion is not objectionable just because it embraces an ultimate issue.

(b) Exception. In a criminal case, an expert witness must not state an opinion about whether the defendant did or did not have a mental state or condition that constitutes an element of the crime charged or of a defense. Those matters are for the trier of fact alone.

Rule 705. Disclosing the Facts or Data Underlying an Expert's Opinion

Unless the court orders otherwise, an expert may state an opinion—and give the reasons for it—without first testifying to the underlying facts or data. But the expert may be required to disclose those facts or data on cross-examination.

Rule 706. Court-Appointed Expert Witnesses

(a) Appointment Process. On a party's motion or on its own, the court may order the parties to show cause why expert witnesses should not be appointed and may ask the parties to submit nominations. The court may appoint any expert that the parties agree on and any of its own choosing. But the court may only appoint someone who consents to act.

(b) Expert's Role. The court must inform the expert of the expert's duties. The court may do so in writing and have a copy filed with the clerk or may do so orally at a conference in which the parties have an opportunity to participate. The expert:

(1) must advise the parties of any findings the expert makes;

(2) may be deposed by any party;

(3) may be called to testify by the court or any party; and

(4) may be cross-examined by any party, including the party that called the expert.

(c) Compensation. The expert is entitled to a reasonable compensation, as set by the court. The compensation is payable as follows:

(1) in a criminal case or in a civil case involving just compensation under the Fifth Amendment, from any funds that are provided by law; and

(2) in any other civil case, by the parties in the proportion and at the time that the court directs—and the compensation is then charged like other costs.

(d) Disclosing the Appointment to the Jury. The court may authorize disclosure to the jury that the court appointed the expert.

(e) Parties' Choice of Their Own Experts. This rule does not limit a party in calling its own experts.

ARTICLE VIII
HEARSAY

Rule 801. Definitions That Apply to This Article; Exclusions from Hearsay

(a) Statement. "Statement" means a person's oral assertion, written assertion, or nonverbal conduct, if the person intended it as an assertion.

(b) Declarant. "Declarant" means the person who made the statement.

(c) Hearsay. "Hearsay" means a statement that:

(1) the declarant does not make while testifying at the current trial or hearing; and

(2) a party offers in evidence to prove the truth of the matter asserted in the statement.

(d) Statements That Are Not Hearsay. A statement that meets the following conditions is not hearsay:

(1) A Declarant-Witness's Prior Statement. The declarant testifies and is subject to cross-examination about a prior statement, and the statement:

(A) is inconsistent with the declarant's testimony and was given under penalty of perjury at a trial, hearing, or other proceeding or in a deposition;

(B) is consistent with the declarant's testimony and is offered:

(i) to rebut an express or implied charge that the declarant recently fabricated it or acted from a recent improper influence or motive in so testifying; or

(ii) to rehabilitate the declarant's credibility as a witness when attacked on another ground; or

(C) identifies a person as someone the declarant perceived earlier.

(2) *An Opposing Party's Statement.* The statement is offered against an opposing party and:

(A) was made by the party in an individual or representative capacity;

(B) is one the party manifested that it adopted or believed to be true;

(C) was made by a person whom the party authorized to make a statement on the subject;

(D) was made by the party's agent or employee on a matter within the scope of that relationship and while it existed; or

(E) was made by the party's coconspirator during and in furtherance of the conspiracy.

The statement must be considered but does not by itself establish the declarant's authority under (C); the existence or scope of the relationship under (D); or the existence of the conspiracy or participation in it under (E).

Rule 802. The Rule Against Hearsay

Hearsay is not admissible unless any of the following provides otherwise:

- a federal statute;
- these rules; or
- other rules prescribed by the Supreme Court.

Rule 803. Exceptions to the Rule Against Hearsay—Regardless of Whether the Declarant Is Available as a Witness

The following are not excluded by the rule against hearsay, regardless of whether the declarant is available as a witness:

(1) *Present Sense Impression.* A statement describing or explaining an event or condition, made while or immediately after the declarant perceived it.

(2) *Excited Utterance.* A statement relating to a startling event or condition, made while the declarant was under the stress of excitement that it caused.

(3) *Then-Existing Mental, Emotional, or Physical Condition.* A statement of the declarant's then-existing state of mind (such as motive, intent, or plan) or emotional, sensory, or physical condition (such as mental feeling, pain, or bodily health), but not including a statement of memory or belief to prove the fact remembered or believed unless it relates to the validity or terms of the declarant's will.

(4) *Statement Made for Medical Diagnosis or Treatment.* A statement that:

(A) is made for—and is reasonably pertinent to—medical diagnosis or treatment; and

(B) describes medical history; past or present symptoms or sensations; their inception; or their general cause.

(5) *Recorded Recollection.* A record that:

(A) is on a matter the witness once knew about but now cannot recall well enough to testify fully and accurately;

(B) was made or adopted by the witness when the matter was fresh in the witness's memory; and

(C) accurately reflects the witness's knowledge.

If admitted, the record may be read into evidence but may be received as an exhibit only if offered by an adverse party.

(6) *Records of a Regularly Conducted Activity.* A record of an act, event, condition, opinion, or diagnosis if:

(A) the record was made at or near the time by—or from information transmitted by—someone with knowledge;

(B) the record was kept in the course of a regularly conducted activity of a business, organization, occupation, or calling, whether or not for profit;

(C) making the record was a regular practice of that activity;

(D) all these conditions are shown by the testimony of the custodian or another qualified witness, or by a certification that complies with Rule 902(11) or (12) or with a statute permitting certification; and

(E) the opponent does not show that the source of information or the method or circumstances of preparation indicate a lack of trustworthiness.

(7) *Absence of a Record of a Regularly Conducted Activity.* Evidence that a matter is not included in a record described in paragraph (6) if:

(A) the evidence is admitted to prove that the matter did not occur or exist;

(B) a record was regularly kept for a matter of that kind; and

(C) the opponent does not show that the possible source of the information or other circumstances indicate a lack of trustworthiness.

(8) *Public Records.* A record or statement of a public office if:

(A) it sets out:

(i) the office's activities;

(ii) a matter observed while under a legal duty to report, but not including, in a criminal case, a matter observed by law-enforcement personnel; or

(iii) in a civil case or against the government in a

criminal case, factual findings from a legally authorized investigation; and

(B) the opponent does not show that the source of information or other circumstances indicate a lack of trustworthiness.

(9) *Public Records of Vital Statistics.* A record of a birth, death, or marriage, if reported to a public office in accordance with a legal duty.

(10) *Absence of a Public Record.* Testimony—or a certification under Rule 902—that a diligent search failed to disclose a public record or statement if:

(A) the testimony or certification is admitted to prove that

(i) the record or statement does not exist; or

(ii) a matter did not occur or exist, if a public office regularly kept a record or statement for a matter of that kind; and

(B) in a criminal case, a prosecutor who intends to offer a certification provides written notice of that intent at least 14 days before trial, and the defendant does not object in writing within 7 days of receiving the notice—unless the court sets a different time for the notice or the objection.

(11) *Records of Religious Organizations Concerning Personal or Family History.* A statement of birth, legitimacy, ancestry, marriage, divorce, death, relationship by blood or marriage, or similar facts of personal or family history, contained in a regularly kept record of a religious organization.

(12) *Certificates of Marriage, Baptism, and Similar Ceremonies.* A statement of fact contained in a certificate:

(A) made by a person who is authorized by a religious organization or by law to perform the act certified;

(B) attesting that the person performed a marriage or similar ceremony or administered a sacrament; and

(C) purporting to have been issued at the time of the act or within a reasonable time after it.

(13) *Family Records.* A statement of fact about personal or family history contained in a family record, such as a Bible, genealogy, chart, engraving on a ring, inscription on a portrait, or engraving on an urn or burial marker.

(14) *Records of Documents That Affect an Interest in Property.* The record of a document that purports to establish or affect an interest in property if:

(A) the record is admitted to prove the content of the original recorded document, along with its signing and its delivery by each person who purports to have signed it;

(B) the record is kept in a public office; and

(C) a statute authorizes recording documents of that kind in that office.

(15) *Statements in Documents That Affect an Interest in Property.* A statement contained in a document that purports to establish or affect an interest in property if the matter stated was relevant to the document's purpose—unless later dealings with the property are inconsistent with the truth of the statement or the purport of the document.

(16) *Statements in Ancient Documents.* A statement in a document that was prepared before January 1, 1998, and whose authenticity is established.

(17) *Market Reports and Similar Commercial Publications.* Market quotations, lists, directories, or other compilations that are generally relied on by the public or by persons in particular occupations.

(18) *Statements in Learned Treatises, Periodicals, or Pamphlets.* A statement contained in a treatise, periodical, or pamphlet if:

(A) the statement is called to the attention of an expert witness on cross—examination or relied on by the expert on direct examination; and

(B) the publication is established as a reliable authority by the expert's admission or testimony, by another expert's testimony, or by judicial notice.

If admitted, the statement may be read into evidence but not received as an exhibit.

(19) *Reputation Concerning Personal or Family History.* A reputation among a person's family by blood, adoption, or marriage—or among a person's associates or in the community—concerning the person's birth, adoption, legitimacy, ancestry, marriage, divorce, death, relationship by blood, adoption, or marriage, or similar facts of personal or family history.

(20) *Reputation Concerning Boundaries or General History.* A reputation in a community—arising before the controversy—concerning boundaries of land in the community or customs that affect the land, or concerning general historical events important to that community, state, or nation.

(21) *Reputation Concerning Character.* A reputation among a person's associates or in the community concerning a person's character.

(22) *Judgment of a Previous Conviction.* Evidence of a final judgment of conviction if:

(A) the judgment was entered after a trial or guilty plea, but not a nolo contendere plea;

(B) the conviction was for a crime punishable by death or by imprisonment for more than a year;

(C) the evidence is admitted to prove any fact essential to the judgment; and

(D) when offered by the prosecutor in a criminal case for a purpose other than impeachment, the judgment was against the defendant.

The pendency of an appeal may be shown but does not affect admissibility.

(23) *Judgments Involving Personal, Family, or General History, or a Boundary.* A judgment that is admitted to prove a matter of personal, family, or general history, or boundaries, if the matter:

(A) was essential to the judgment; and

(B) could be proved by evidence of reputation.

(24) *[Other Exceptions.]* [Transferred to Rule 807.]

Rule 804. Exceptions to the Rule Against Hearsay—When the Declarant Is Unavailable as a Witness

(a) Criteria for Being Unavailable. A declarant is considered to be unavailable as a witness if the declarant:

(1) is exempted from testifying about the subject matter of the declarant's statement because the court rules that a privilege applies;

(2) refuses to testify about the subject matter despite a court order to do so;

(3) testifies to not remembering the subject matter;

(4) cannot be present or testify at the trial or hearing because of death or a then—existing infirmity, physical illness, or mental illness; or

(5) is absent from the trial or hearing and the statement's proponent has not been able, by process or other reasonable means, to procure:

(A) the declarant's attendance, in the case of a hearsay exception under Rule 804(b)(1) or (6); or

(B) the declarant's attendance or testimony, in the case of a hearsay exception under Rule 804(b)(2), (3), or (4).

But this subdivision (a) does not apply if the statement's proponent procured or wrongfully caused the declarant's unavailability as a witness in order to prevent the declarant from attending or testifying.

(b) The Exceptions. The following are not excluded by the rule against hearsay if the declarant is unavailable as a witness:

(1) *Former Testimony.* Testimony that:

(A) was given as a witness at a trial, hearing, or lawful deposition, whether given during the current proceeding or a different one; and

(B) is now offered against a party who had—or, in a civil case, whose predecessor in interest had—an opportunity and similar motive to develop it by direct, cross-, or redirect examination.

(2) *Statement Under the Belief of Imminent Death.* In a prosecution for homicide or in a civil case, a statement that the declarant, while believing the declarant's death to be imminent, made about its cause or circumstances.

(3) *Statement Against Interest.* A statement that:

(A) a reasonable person in the declarant's position would have made only if the person believed it to be true because, when made, it was so contrary to the declarant's proprietary or pecuniary interest or had so great a tendency to invalidate the declarant's claim against someone else or to expose the declarant to civil or criminal liability; and

(B) is supported by corroborating circumstances that clearly indicate its trustworthiness, if it is offered in a criminal case as one that tends to expose the declarant to criminal liability.

(4) *Statement of Personal or Family History.* A statement about:

(A) the declarant's own birth, adoption, legitimacy, ancestry, marriage, divorce, relationship by blood, adoption, or marriage, or similar facts of personal or family history, even though the declarant had no way of acquiring personal knowledge about that fact; or

(B) another person concerning any of these facts, as well as death, if the declarant was related to the person by blood, adoption, or marriage or was so intimately associated with the person's family that the declarant's information is likely to be accurate.

(5) *[Other Exceptions.]* [Transferred to Rule 807.]

(6) *Statement Offered Against a Party That Wrongfully Caused the Declarant's Unavailability.* A statement offered against a party that wrongfully caused—or acquiesced in wrongfully causing—the declarant's unavailability as a witness, and did so intending that result.

Rule 805. Hearsay Within Hearsay

Hearsay within hearsay is not excluded by the rule against hearsay if each part of the combined statements conforms with an exception to the rule.

Rule 806. Attacking and Supporting the Declarant's Credibility

When a hearsay statement—or a statement described in Rule 801(d)(2)(C), (D), or (E)—has been admitted in evidence, the declarant's credibility may be attacked, and then supported, by any evidence that would be admissible for those purposes if the declarant had testified as a witness. The court may admit evidence of the declarant's inconsistent statement or conduct, regardless of when it occurred or whether the declarant had an opportunity to explain or deny it. If the party against whom the statement was admitted calls the declarant as a witness, the party may examine the declarant on the statement as if on cross-examination.

Rule 807. Residual Exception

(a) In General. Under the following conditions, a hearsay statement is not excluded by the rule against hearsay even if the statement is not admissible under a hearsay exception in Rule 803 or 804:

(1) the statement is supported by sufficient guarantees of trustworthiness—after considering the totality of circumstances under which it was made and evidence, if any, corroborating the statement; and

(2) it is more probative on the point for which it is offered than any other evidence that the proponent can obtain through reasonable efforts.

(b) Notice. The statement is admissible only if the proponent gives an adverse party reasonable notice of the intent to offer the statement—including its substance and the declarant's name—so that the party has a fair opportunity to meet it. The notice must be provided in writing before the trial or hearing—or in any form during the trial or hearing if the court, for good cause, excuses a lack of earlier notice.

ARTICLE IX
AUTHENTICATION AND IDENTIFICATION

Rule 901. Authenticating or Identifying Evidence

(a) In General. To satisfy the requirement of authenticating or identifying an item of evidence, the proponent must produce evidence sufficient to support a finding that the item is what the proponent claims it is.

(b) Examples. The following are examples only—not a complete list—of evidence that satisfies the requirement:

(1) *Testimony of a Witness with Knowledge.* Testimony that an item is what it is claimed to be.

(2) *Nonexpert Opinion About Handwriting.* A nonexpert's opinion that handwriting is genuine, based on a familiarity with it that was not acquired for the current litigation.

(3) *Comparison by an Expert Witness or the Trier of Fact.* A comparison with an authenticated specimen by an expert witness or the trier of fact.

(4) *Distinctive Characteristics and the Like.* The appearance, contents, substance, internal patterns, or other distinctive characteristics of the item, taken together with all the circumstances.

(5) *Opinion About a Voice.* An opinion identifying a person's voice—whether heard firsthand or through mechanical or electronic transmission or recording—based on hearing the voice at any time under circumstances that connect it with the alleged speaker.

(6) *Evidence About a Telephone Conversation.* For a telephone conversation, evidence that a call was made to the number assigned at the time to:

(A) a particular person, if circumstances, including self-identification, show that the person answering was the one called; or

(B) a particular business, if the call was made to a business and the call related to business reasonably transacted over the telephone.

(7) *Evidence About Public Records.* Evidence that:

(A) a document was recorded or filed in a public office as authorized by law; or

(B) a purported public record or statement is from the office where items of this kind are kept.

(8) *Evidence About Ancient Documents or Data Compilations.* For a document or data compilation, evidence that it:

(A) is in a condition that creates no suspicion about its authenticity;

(B) was in a place where, if authentic, it would likely be; and

(C) is at least 20 years old when offered.

(9) *Evidence About a Process or System.* Evidence describing a process or system and showing that it produces an accurate result.

(10) *Methods Provided by a Statute or Rule.* Any method of authentication or identification allowed by a federal statute or a rule prescribed by the Supreme Court.

Rule 902. Evidence That Is Self-Authenticating

The following items of evidence are self-authenticating; they require no extrinsic evidence of authenticity in order to be admitted:

(1) *Domestic Public Documents That Are Sealed and Signed.* A document that bears:

(A) a seal purporting to be that of the United States; any state, district, commonwealth, territory, or insular possession of the United States; the former Panama Canal Zone; the Trust Territory of the Pacific Islands; a political subdivision of any of these entities; or a department, agency, or officer of any entity named above; and

(B) a signature purporting to be an execution or attestation.

(2) *Domestic Public Documents That Are Not Sealed but Are Signed and Certified.* A document that bears no seal if:

(A) it bears the signature of an officer or employee of an entity named in Rule 902(1)(A); and

(B) another public officer who has a seal and official duties within that same entity certifies under seal—or its equivalent—that the signer has the official capacity and that the signature is genuine.

(3) *Foreign Public Documents.* A document that purports to be signed or attested by a person who is

authorized by a foreign country's law to do so. The document must be accompanied by a final certification that certifies the genuineness of the signature and official position of the signer or attester—or of any foreign official whose certificate of genuineness relates to the signature or attestation or is in a chain of certificates of genuineness relating to the signature or attestation. The certification may be made by a secretary of a United States embassy or legation; by a consul general, vice consul, or consular agent of the United States; or by a diplomatic or consular official of the foreign country assigned or accredited to the United States. If all parties have been given a reasonable opportunity to investigate the document's authenticity and accuracy, the court may, for good cause, either:

(A) order that it be treated as presumptively authentic without final certification; or

(B) allow it to be evidenced by an attested summary with or without final certification.

(4) *Certified Copies of Public Records.* A copy of an official record—or a copy of a document that was recorded or filed in a public office as authorized by law—if the copy is certified as correct by:

(A) the custodian or another person authorized to make the certification; or

(B) a certificate that complies with Rule 902(1), (2), or (3), a federal statute, or a rule prescribed by the Supreme Court.

(5) *Official Publications.* A book, pamphlet, or other publication purporting to be issued by a public authority.

(6) *Newspapers and Periodicals.* Printed material purporting to be a newspaper or periodical.

(7) *Trade Inscriptions and the Like.* An inscription, sign, tag, or label purporting to have been affixed in the course of business and indicating origin, ownership, or control.

(8) *Acknowledged Documents.* A document accompanied by a certificate of acknowledgment that is lawfully executed by a notary public or another officer who is authorized to take acknowledgments.

(9) *Commercial Paper and Related Documents.* Commercial paper, a signature on it, and related documents, to the extent allowed by general commercial law.

(10) *Presumptions Under a Federal Statute.* A signature, document, or anything else that a federal statute declares to be presumptively or prima facie genuine or authentic.

(11) *Certified Domestic Records of a Regularly Conducted Activity.* The original or a copy of a domestic record that meets the requirements of Rule 803(6)(A)–(C), as shown by a certification of the custodian or another qualified person that complies with a federal statute or a

rule prescribed by the Supreme Court. Before the trial or hearing, the proponent must give an adverse party reasonable written notice of the intent to offer the record—and must make the record and certification available for inspection—so that the party has a fair opportunity to challenge them.

(12) *Certified Foreign Records of a Regularly Conducted Activity.* In a civil case, the original or a copy of a foreign record that meets the requirements of Rule 902(11), modified as follows: the certification, rather than complying with a federal statute or Supreme Court rule, must be signed in a manner that, if falsely made, would subject the maker to a criminal penalty in the country where the certification is signed. The proponent must also meet the notice requirements of Rule 902(11).

(13) *Certified Records Generated by an Electronic Process or System.* A record generated by an electronic process or system that produces an accurate result, as shown by a certification of a qualified person that complies with the certification requirements of Rule 902(11) or (12). The proponent must also meet the notice requirements of 902(11). (On track to become effective December 1, 2017).

Rule 903. Subscribing Witness's Testimony

A subscribing witness's testimony is necessary to authenticate a writing only if required by the law of the jurisdiction that governs its validity.

ARTICLE X
CONTENTS OF WRITINGS, RECORDINGS, AND PHOTOGRAPHS

Rule 1001. Definitions That Apply to This Article
In this article:

(a) A "writing" consists of letters, words, numbers, or their equivalent set down in any form.

(b) A "recording" consists of letters, words, numbers, or their equivalent recorded in any manner.

(c) A "photograph" means a photographic image or its equivalent stored in any form.

(d) An "original" of a writing or recording means the writing or recording itself or any counterpart intended to have the same effect by the person who executed or issued it. For electronically stored information, "original" means any printout—or other output readable by sight—if it accurately reflects the information. An "original" of a photograph includes the negative or a print from it.

(e) A "duplicate" means a counterpart produced by a mechanical, photographic, chemical, electronic, or other equivalent process or technique that accurately reproduces the original.

Rule 1002. Requirement of the Original
An original writing, recording, or photograph is re-

quired in order to prove its content unless these rules or a federal statute provides otherwise.

Rule 1003. Admissibility of Duplicates

A duplicate is admissible to the same extent as the original unless a genuine question is raised about the original's authenticity or the circumstances make it unfair to admit the duplicate.

Rule 1004. Admissibility of Other Evidence of Content

An original is not required and other evidence of the content of a writing, recording, or photograph is admissible if:

(a) all the originals are lost or destroyed, and not by the proponent acting in bad faith;

(b) an original cannot be obtained by any available judicial process;

(c) the party against whom the original would be offered had control of the original; was at that time put on notice, by pleadings or otherwise, that the original would be a subject of proof at the trial or hearing; and fails to produce it at the trial or hearing; or

(d) the writing, recording, or photograph is not closely related to a controlling issue.

Rule 1005. Copies of Public Records to Prove Content

The proponent may use a copy to prove the content of an official record—or of a document that was recorded or filed in a public office as authorized by law—if these conditions are met: the record or document is otherwise admissible; and the copy is certified as correct in accordance with Rule 902(4) or is testified to be correct by a witness who has compared it with the original. If no such copy can be obtained by reasonable diligence, then the proponent may use other evidence to prove the content.

Rule 1006. Summaries to Prove Content

The proponent may use a summary, chart, or calculation to prove the content of voluminous writings, recordings, or photographs that cannot be conveniently examined in court. The proponent must make the originals or duplicates available for examination or copying, or both, by other parties at a reasonable time and place. And the court may order the proponent to produce them in court.

Rule 1007. Testimony or Statement of a Party to Prove Content

The proponent may prove the content of a writing, recording, or photograph by the testimony, deposition, or written statement of the party against whom the evidence is offered. The proponent need not account for the original.

Rule 1008. Functions of the Court and Jury

Ordinarily, the court determines whether the proponent has fulfilled the factual conditions for admitting other evidence of the content of a writing, recording, or photograph under Rule 1004 or 1005. But in a jury trial, the jury determines—in accordance with Rule 104(b)—any issue about whether:

(a) an asserted writing, recording, or photograph ever existed;

(b) another one produced at the trial or hearing is the original; or

(c) other evidence of content accurately reflects the content.

ARTICLE XI
MISCELLANEOUS RULES

Rule 1101. Applicability of the Rules

(a) To Courts and Judges. These rules apply to proceedings before:

- United States district courts;
- United States bankruptcy and magistrate judges;
- United States courts of appeals;
- the United States Court of Federal Claims; and
- the district courts of Guam, the Virgin Islands, and the Northern Mariana Islands.

(b) To Cases and Proceedings. These rules apply in:

- civil cases and proceedings, including bankruptcy, admiralty, and maritime cases;
- criminal cases and proceedings; and
- contempt proceedings, except those in which the court may act summarily.

(c) Rules on Privilege. The rules on privilege apply to all stages of a case or proceeding.

(d) Exceptions. These rules—except for those on privilege—do not apply to the following:

(1) the court's determination, under Rule 104(a), on a preliminary question of fact governing admissibility;

(2) grand-jury proceedings; and

(3) miscellaneous proceedings such as:

- extradition or rendition;
- issuing an arrest warrant, criminal summons, or search warrant;
- a preliminary examination in a criminal case;
- sentencing;
- granting or revoking probation or supervised release; and
- considering whether to release on bail or otherwise.

(e) Other Statutes and Rules. A federal statute or a rule prescribed by the Supreme Court may provide for admitting or excluding evidence independently from these rules.

Rule 1102. Amendments

These rules may be amended as provided in 28 U.S.C. § 2072.

Rule 1103. Title

These rules may be cited as the Federal Rules of Evidence.

I
GENERAL PROVISIONS

Chapter 101

Rule 101. Scope

Rule 101 reads as follows:

> These rules govern proceedings in all courts in the State of Colorado, to the extent and with the exceptions stated in Rule 1101.

ANALYSIS

Rule 101 identifies the proceedings in which the Evidence Rules apply. Functionally, the Rule directs that the Rules are applicable to all proceedings, subject to the exceptions set forth in Rule 1101.

The Rules provide for a unitary system of evidence. Accordingly, the Rules apply to all proceedings, civil and criminal, regardless of whether the matter is tried to the court or to a jury. In certain instances, however, the Rules draw distinctions between certain types of cases. For example, under Rule 404 certain applications of character evidence are available only in criminal cases. Other examples may be found in Rules 104(c), 803(8) and 804(b)(3).

Exceptions. Rule 1101 identifies proceedings in which the Rules of Evidence are inapplicable. The following proceedings are not subject to the Rules of Evidence:

1. Grand juries
2. Preliminary questions of fact
3. Extradition or rendition
4. Preliminary examinations in criminal cases
5. Sentencing
6. Probation
7. Warrants for arrest, criminal summons, and search warrants
8. Bail

AUTHORITY

WEISSENBERGER'S FEDERAL EVIDENCE § 1

1 WEINSTEIN 2d §§ 101.01–.03

1 MUELLER & KIRKPATRICK § 1

COMPARISON TO FEDERAL RULE

The Colorado Rule is culled from Rule 81 of the Colorado Rules of Civil Procedure and Rule

1101(e) of the Federal Rules of Evidence.

SIGNIFICANT CASES

Lovato v. Johnson, 617 P.2d 1203, 1204 (Colo. 1980) (judicial notice may be taken at any stage of a proceeding, whether in the trial court or on appeal).

Loomis v. Seely, 677 P.2d 400, 402 (Colo. App. 1983) (if a litigant, for whatever reason, presents his own case to the court, he is bound by the same rules of procedure and evidence as bind those who are admitted to practice law before the courts of this state. A judge may not become a surrogate attorney for a pro se litigant).

The following cases all follow the rule in *Loomis, supra*:

Manka v. Martin, 200 Colo. 260, 614 P.2d 875 (1980).

Viles v. Scofield, 128 Colo. 185, 261 P.2d 148 (1953).

Knapp v. Fleming, 127 Colo. 414, 258 P.2d 489 (1953).

Deason v. Lewis, 706 P.2d 1283 (Colo. App. 1985).

In re Marriage of Snyder, 701 P.2d 153 (Colo. App. 1985).

Richardson v. White, 497 P.2d 348 (Colo. App. 1972).

Sims v. Great American Life Ins. Co., 469 F.3d 870 (10th Cir. 2006) (Although Congress may prescribe housekeeping rules for federal courts even though some of those rules will inevitably differ from comparable state rules, the Federal Rules of Evidence are an act of Congress and therefore subject neither to the dictate of the *Erie* doctrine nor to the Rules of Enabling Act or Rules of Decision Act).

Chapter 102

Rule 102. Purpose and Construction

Rule 102 reads as follows:

> These rules shall be construed to secure fairness in administration, elimination of unjustifiable expense and delay, and promotion of growth and development of the law of evidence to the end that the truth may be ascertained and proceedings justly determined.

ANALYSIS

The purpose of Rule 102 is to establish the spirit within which the Rules should be applied and construed. While the Rule imparts discretion to the trial judge, it is not intended to be applied in a manner which subverts the express requirements or limitations of other specific Rules of Evidence.

AUTHORITY

WEISSENBERGER'S FEDERAL EVIDENCE § 102.1

1 WEINSTEIN 2d §§ 102.01–.06

1 MUELLER & KIRKPATRICK §§ 2–3

COMPARISON TO FEDERAL RULE

In substance, Colorado Rule 102 is identical to Federal Rule 102. However, on Dec. 1, 2011 Federal Rule 102 was restyled. Please see Federal Rule 102 in the appendix for comparison.

SIGNIFICANT CASES

Berger v. Coon, 199 Colo. 133, 606 P.2d 68 (1980) (the policy underlying the Colorado Rules of Evidence is to guarantee each party an opportunity to present the testimony of the adverse witnesses and to favor admissibility of their testimony so as to ascertain the truth within the bounds of fairness).

Maloney v. Brassfield, 251 P.3d 1097 (Colo. App. 2010) (in a personal injury action arising from an automobile accident the trial court set a seven-day trial and imposed rigid time limits, this was not error and did not deny the plaintiff's due process rights).

Chapter 103

Rule 103. Rulings on Evidence

Rule 103 reads as follows:

> **(a) Effect of erroneous ruling.** Error may not be predicated upon a ruling which admits or excludes evidence unless a substantial right of the party is affected, and
>
> *(1) Objection.* In case the ruling is one admitting evidence, a timely objection or motion to strike appears of record, stating the specific ground of objection, if the specific ground was not apparent from the context; or
>
> *(2) Offer of proof.* In case the ruling is one excluding evidence, the substance of the evidence was made known to the Court by offer or was apparent from the context within which questions were asked.
>
> Once the Court makes a definitive ruling on the record admitting or excluding evidence, either at or before trial, a party need not renew an objection or offer of proof to preserve a claim of error for appeal.
>
> **(b) Record of offer and ruling.** The Court may add any other or further statement which shows the character of evidence, the form in which it was offered, the objection made, and the ruling thereon. It may direct the making of an offer in question and answer form.
>
> **(c) Hearing of jury.** In jury cases, proceedings shall be conducted, to the extent practicable, so as to prevent inadmissible evidence from being suggested to the jury by any means, such as making statements or offers of proof or asking questions in the hearing of the jury.
>
> **(d) Plain error.** Nothing in this rule precludes taking notice of plain errors affecting substantial rights although they were not brought to the attention of the Court.

ANALYSIS

Rule 103 establishes the trial procedures necessary to preserve errors for appellate review. The Rule does not purport to provide substantive standards under which a reversal is required.

There are two circumstances in which the record must clearly reflect the alleged error:

(1) Error predicated on improper admission of evidence (objection overruled improperly).

(2) Error predicated on improper exclusion of evidence (objection sustained improperly).

In the first instance, stating the basis of the objection or motion to strike easily preserves error. If the basis of the objection is not stated, error is waived unless the reason for the objection is

7

apparent from the context of the testimony. Even if the court rules before hearing the basis of the objection, counsel should state the reason for the record. The reason may be abbreviated.

If the objection to admissibility of the evidence is sustained, the proponent should make an offer of proof of the evidence that he expected to elicit from the witness. The offer of proof permits the reviewing court to determine whether the ruling was prejudicial error. An offer of proof is simply a statement on the record, outside the hearing of the jury, summarizing the import of the offered evidence.

Illustration

Counsel:	And then what did defendant tell you?
Objection:	Hearsay.
Court:	Sustained.
Counsel:	Your Honor, I wish to make a[n] offer of proof.
Court:	Proceed.
Counsel:	*(Out of hearing of the jury)* This witness would have testified that the defendant said to her, "I should have seen that traffic signal."
	The better procedure would be to have the witness state in the record, "I should have seen that traffic signal."

Rule 103(c) provides that, whenever practical, discussions concerning rulings on evidence should be conducted outside the hearing of the jury. Obviously, the purpose of the procedure set forth in Rule 103(a) and (b) would be wholly defeated if the jury were permitted to hear a proffer of excluded evidence or to hear a lengthy explanation on the highly prejudicial nature of evidence sought to be admitted over objection.

It should be noted that in order for evidentiary error to operate as the basis for appeal, a substantial right must be affected. Moreover, it should be noted that under Rule 103(d) error may be reviewed on appeal even if it has not been preserved where it falls within the category of "plain error."

AUTHORITY

WEISSENBERGER'S FEDERAL EVIDENCE §§ 103.1–.5

McCORMICK §§ 51–52, 54–55

1 WEINSTEIN 2d §§ 103.01–.43

1 MUELLER & KIRKPATRICK §§ 4–23

1 WIGMORE §§ 17, 18

Poulos, *The Trial of Celebrated Criminal Cases: An Analysis of Evidentiary Objections*, 56 TUL. L. REV. 602 (1982)

Note, *Harmful Use of Harmless Error in Criminal Cases*, 64 CORNELL L. REV. 538 (1979)

Note, *Harmless Error: The Need for a Uniform Standard*, 53 ST. JOHN'S L. REV. 541 (1979)

COMPARISON TO FEDERAL RULE

In substance, Colorado Rule 103 is identical to Federal Rule 103. However, on Dec. 1, 2011

Federal Rule 103 was restyled. Please see Federal Rule 103 in the appendix for comparison.

SIGNIFICANT CASES

Campbell v. People, 443 P.3d 72 (Colo. 2019) (allowing a police officer to testify as a lay witness, instead of an expert witness, was not unconstitutional and, furthermore, harmless. It did not affect defendant's substantial rights because the majority of the evidence, even absent the portion of the officer's testimony which should have been qualified as expert testimony, supported a finding that defendant was guilty).

Bly v. Story, 241 P.3d 529 (Colo. 2010) (in a private condemnation case trial court was in error to not allow expert witness to testify as to value based on cost of construction appraisal).

Am. Family Mut. Ins. Co. v. DeWitt, 218 P.3d 318 (Colo. 2009) (where basis of objection is not apparent from context, and it is not specifically stated, objection may nevertheless preserve issue for appeal if the objection uses arguments or includes terms that draw the trial judge's attention to the error).

Medina v. People, 114 P.3d 845 (Colo. 2005) (jury questioning of witnesses, or juror overhearing bench discussion of whether or not to ask a witness a question submitted by a juror, does not create a per se violation of a defendant's right to a fair trial; juror questions deemed improper are subject to review for harmless error).

People v. Welsh, 80 P.3d 296 (Colo. 2003) (court commits a harmful error when the court admits evidence which should have been excluded and compounds the error by failing to provide a limiting instruction regarding the weight a jury should give to the evidence, especially when the wrongfully admitted evidence may impact substantial rights of the defendant).

People v. Saiz, 32 P.3d 441 (Colo. 2001) (trial court did not abuse its discretion by excluding videotaped statements from an interview of defendant's minor son, since defense counsel merely offered to impeach the child by showing his prior inconsistent statements on videotape without making any contention of probative value beyond that of extrinsic evidence already admitted from a detective who conceded that the child had made the conflicting statements).

Itin v. Bertrand T. Ungar, P.C., 17 P.3d 129 (Colo. 2000) (although a party seeking to impeach a witness failed to state the pertinent rule of evidence, Rule 608(b), as the basis for admissibility, that party could raise the issue on appeal, since the context of the question at trial made clear that impeachment was intended).

People v. Kruse, 839 P.2d 1 (Colo. 1992) (the admission of service worker's testimony during the prosecution's case-in-chief, and not as rebuttal testimony, did not rise to the level of plain error).

Lanari v. People, 827 P.2d 495 (Colo. 1992) (where the trial court questioned defense counsel about expert witness's testimony on offer of proof, it was "incumbent" upon the trial court to obtain sufficient information concerning the content of the doctor's testimony to permit the exercise of discretion).

People v. Fuller, 788 P.2d 741 (Colo. 1990) (the proper inquiry in determining a harmless error question is whether the error substantially influenced the verdict or affected the fairness of the trial proceedings).

Hancock v. State, Dep't of Revenue, Motor Vehicle Div., 758 P.2d 1372 (Colo. 1988) (district court review of an agency decision is limited to the record before it).

Williams v. People, 724 P.2d 1279 (Colo. 1986) (the defendant did not, at any time during the trial before a jury, object as irrelevant an exhibit of evidence as a prior inconsistent statement, therefore, on appeal, the defendant's objection may only be reviewed under the plain error standard).

Uptain v. Huntington Lab, 723 P.2d 1322 (Colo. 1986) (motion *in limine* was deemed to be a timely objection for preservation of error; distinguished from *Higgs* because the motion *in limine* was for specific evidence where *Higgs* was for broad array of evidence).

Higgs v. District Court, 713 P.2d 840 (Colo. 1985) (denial of *in limine* motion to exclude evidence does not waive requirement of contemporaneous objection when the evidence is offered to the court).

People v. Shannon, 683 P.2d 792 (Colo. 1984) (a trial court is justified in requiring an *in camera* offer of proof as a prophylactic device to prevent inadmissible evidence from being suggested to the jury).

People v. Mattas, 645 P.2d 254 (Colo. 1982) (preservation of a defendant's right to challenge a trial court's evidentiary rulings requires a pretrial motion to suppress the evidence or an objection at trial to its introduction).

Schlesselman v. Gouge, 163 Colo. 312, 431 P.2d 35 (1967) (where the trial court's ruling is one excluding evidence offered, the substance of the evidence must be made known via an offer of proof unless its substance was "apparent").

Baker Metro Water Dist. v. Baca, 138 Colo. 239, 331 P.2d 511 (1958) (allowing the daughter of the landowner to give her opinion of land value was error).

Graham v. Swift, 123 Colo. 309, 228 P.2d 969 (1951) (the court may notice questions, not raised by the assignments of error, that appear on the face of the record when such consideration is necessary to do justice).

Bernache v. Brown, 471 P.3d 1234 (Colo. App. 2020) (in a car accident case, the plaintiff/appellant neither relinquished his right to appeal nor invited error by submitting the statement of the witness's testimony because the court had already admitted the witness's statement and defendant had relied on it when addressing the court at trial).

People v. Marx, 2019 Colo. App. LEXIS 1336 (Colo. App. 2019) (defendant's offer of proof that his accuser had a history of making prior false reports of sexual assault, through an affidavit by an investigator claiming such, was sufficient under the Rape Shield Statute to establish by "a preponderance of the evidence" that a court would find at an evidentiary hearing the alleged victim has made multiple false accusations of sexual assault).

People v. Martin, 338 P.3d 1106 (Colo. App. 2014). When it decides whether to reopen the evidence in a criminal case to allow a defendant to testify after the defendant has waived the right to do so, a trial court should consider the motion's timeliness, the character of the proposed testimony, the effect of granting the motion, the reasonableness of the defendant's explanation for not moving sooner, the circumstances of the waiver, and the reasons why the defendant did not testify originally.

People v. Harmon, 2011 Colo. App. LEXIS 1635 (Colo. App. 2011) (In child abuse case, court determined it was within discretion of trial judge to allow pictures to be displayed during opening argument prior to being admitted, case reversed on other grounds).

People v. Rosa, 928 P.2d 1365 (Colo. App. 1996) (the admission of evidence at a suppression hearing where a trial court's statement may have confused the defendant about his Fourth Amendment rights at the suppression hearing was harmless error because the evidence in question did not affect a substantial right of the defendant; there was independent and overwhelming evidence of guilt).

Locke v. Vanderark, 843 P.2d 27 (Colo. App. 1992) (where expert witness was cross-examined about previous medical malpractice actions unrelated to the current trial, the court held that although the cross-examination was not relevant to the witness's bias or credibility, it did not constitute reversible error. The jury was not prejudiced by the cross-examination and the expert witness was effectively impeached by other means).

Melton v. Larrabee, 832 P.2d 1069 (Colo. App. 1992) (where plaintiff claims that negligent construction of addition to residence caused a fire, the plaintiff must show a causal link between the claimed negligent act and the resulting fire to constitute reversible error).

People v. Watson, 668 P.2d 965 (Colo. App. 1983); *People v. Lucero*, 724 P.2d 1374 (Colo. App. 1986) (on appeal, a party must argue the objection made at the trial court on the same grounds asserted at the trial court or he is deemed to have waived the objection).

Chapter 104

Rule 104. Preliminary Questions

Rule 104 reads as follows:

> **(a) Questions of admissibility generally.** Preliminary questions concerning the qualification of a person to be a witness, the existence of a privilege, or the admissibility of evidence shall be determined by the court, subject to the provisions of subdivision (b). In making its determination it is not bound by the rules of evidence except those with respect to privileges.
>
> **(b) Relevancy conditioned on fact.** When the relevancy of evidence depends upon the fulfillment of a condition of fact, the court shall admit it upon, or subject to, the introduction of evidence sufficient to support a finding of the fulfillment of the condition.
>
> **(c) Hearing of jury.** Hearings on the admissibility of confessions shall in all cases be conducted out of the hearing of the jury. Hearings on other preliminary matters shall be so conducted when the interests of justice require or, when an accused is a witness, if he so requests.
>
> **(d) Testimony by accused.** The accused does not, by testifying upon a preliminary matter, subject himself to cross-examination as to other issues in the case.
>
> **(e) Weight and credibility.** This rule does not limit the right of a party to introduce before the jury evidence relevant to weight or credibility.

ANALYSIS

Rule 104 governs the allocation responsibility between judge and jury for determining questions of admissibility.

The primary focus of the Rule is on situations where a prerequisite showing must be made in order for certain evidence to be properly admitted. This procedure is commonly referred to as "laying a foundation" for the admission of evidence. The necessity of a foundation may be indicated by the Rules of Evidence or by substantive case law or statutes.

Rule 104(a) provides that preliminary questions regarding the admissibility of evidence shall be determined by the trial judge. Where the trial judge considers the foundation to be sufficient, the primary evidence will be admitted to the jury or trier of fact.

As the Rule specifies, preliminary questions may involve the qualifications of a person to be a witness (e.g., whether a person is qualified to testify as an expert, or whether a lay witness is competent or incompetent by virtue of the exclusionary provisions of Rule 601); the existence of a privilege (i.e., whether the criteria exist for invocation of a privilege); and questions of admissibility of the evidence itself. This latter category includes a broad range of questions such as, for example, whether the prerequisites for applicability of an exception to the hearsay exclusionary rule have been met.

Rule 104(a) contains a significant principle relating to foundational evidence. Foundational evidence which is directed exclusively to the trial judge need not be "admissible" evidence under the Rules. For example, foundational evidence directed exclusively to the trial judge may consist of inadmissible hearsay or unauthenticated documents. The only limitation is that privileged information may not be utilized.

Illustration

Q: Did he say anything to you regarding his condition?

A: Yes—he said, "I know I haven't long to live. The doctor told me I have about five minutes left."

[*Note:* Objections based on hearsay or even multiple hearsay as to what the doctor told the victim would not be appropriate because the Rules of Evidence do not apply in admissibility determinations.]

Q: Did the victim say anything to you after that?

A: Yes, he told me who shot him.

Opposing counsel: Objection—hearsay.

Court: Overruled—I find the elements of a foundation for a dying declaration to have been met.

Rule 104(a) is qualified in certain situations by Rule 104(b) which pertains to conditional relevancy. Where conditional relevancy applies, both the foundation and the primary evidence is considered by the jury in reaching its verdict. The standard of Rule 104(b) applies whenever the existence of one fact is necessary for the relevance of some connected fact. Whenever this is the case, the first fact must be proven in satisfaction of the standard of Rule 104(b) in order to enable the trier of fact to use the second fact as evidence. Authentication under Article IX, where authenticating testimony is conditional to the admission of a document or objects, represents a clear example of conditional relevancy.

Illustration

Q: I am handing you now what has been marked as Plaintiff's Exhibit Number 5. Please look at the last line of the document?

A: Yes.

Q: Please describe what you see?

A: I see the signature of the defendant, Ralph Jackson.

Q: Please state the basis for your testimony that this is Mr. Jackson's signature?

> **A:** I was present when he wrote his name on this document, and I recognize both the document and Mr. Jackson's signature.
>
> **Counsel:** *(After showing document to opposing counsel)* I would now like to offer Plaintiff's Exhibit Number 5 into evidence.

In the foregoing illustration, the evidence is subject to Rule 104(b) because the trier of fact would be required to believe the foundational testimony in order to attach relevancy to the document.

Another example of conditional relevancy is the determination of factual competency of a witness.

Illustration

Q: Where were you at about 8:00 a.m., November 16, last year?

A: At the corner of Eighth and Walnut.

Q: Did you observe anything at that time?

A: Yes, an automobile accident at that intersection.

Q: Was there a traffic signal at that intersection?

A: Yes.

Q: How far were you from the signal?

A: About 50 feet.

Q: Did you see what color the traffic light was at the moment of collision?

A: Yes.

Q: What color was the light?

Opposing counsel: Objection. The court should not believe this witness because he is totally biased and I can prove it.

Court: Overruled. He is a competent witness under Rule 602. You may show his bias on cross-examination.

Rule 104(c) identifies situations in which testimony on preliminary matters should be conducted outside the hearing of the jury.

Rule 104(d) contains a provision applicable only in criminal cases in providing that the accused does not, by testifying on preliminary matters subject himself to cross-examination on other issues in the case. Finally, Rule 104(e) clarifies the effect of the Rule in not limiting the right of a party to introduce evidence to affect the weight or credibility of any evidence.

AUTHORITY

WEISSENBERGER'S FEDERAL EVIDENCE §§ 104.1–.14

McCORMICK § 53 at 124

1 WEINSTEIN 2d §§ 104.01–.60

1 MUELLER & KIRKPATRICK §§ 24–37

9 WIGMORE § 2550

Garland & Schmitz, *Of Judges and Juries: A Proposed Revision of Federal Rule of Evidence 104*, 23 U.C. DAVIS L. REV. 77 (1989)

Ball, *The Myth of Conditional Relevancy*, 14 GA. L. REV. 435 (1980)

COMPARISON TO FEDERAL RULE

In substance, Federal Rule 104 and Colorado Rule 104 are identical. However, on Dec. 1, 2011 Federal Rule 104 was restyled. Please see Federal Rule 104 in the appendix for comparison.

SIGNIFICANT CASES

Huddleston v. United States, 485 U.S. 681 (1988) (in theft case involving stolen videotapes, evidence of defendant's prior television sales was admissible in accordance with Federal Rule 104(b), where jury could have reasonably concluded that televisions were stolen from the low price, large quantity offered for sale, and defendant's inability to produce bill of sale).

Jackson v. Denno, 378 U.S. 368 (1964) (the Court held as unconstitutional New York's procedure of allowing the jury alone to determine the voluntariness of a confession).

Moore v. People, 318 P.3d 511 (Colo. 2014). A defendant is not precluded from introducing off-the-record evidence in a post-conviction proceeding to demonstrate the invalidity of his waiver on the right to testify. A successful challenge to the validity of a waiver will likely involve off-the-record evidence demonstrating that the waiver was not knowing, voluntary, and intelligent.

People v. Wittrein, 221 P.3d 1076 (Colo. 2009) (if competency hearing for child witness is held within the presence of the jury, prejudice may rise to the level of reversible error; though it is the "better practice to hold this hearing outside the presence of the jury, there is no per se requirement to do so").

People v. Garner, 806 P.2d 366 (Colo. 1991) (decisions to include other crime evidence must be determined as a preliminary matter by the trial court under CRE 104(a) and not CRE 104(b)).

Bd. of Assessment App. v. Colorado Arlberg Club, 762 P.2d 146 (Colo. 1988) (the board improperly refused to accept witness as an expert in the field of appraising).

People v. Montoya, 753 P.2d 729 (Colo. 1988) (to determine whether a statement is admissible under the coconspirator exception, a trial court must find by a preponderance of the evidence that a conspiracy exists).

Deeds v. People, 747 P.2d 1266 (Colo. 1987) (in determining whether the defendant's confession of sexual assault was voluntary or not, the hearing of admissibility should be conducted *in camera*. The question of credibility of the witness and the weight of the testimony is for the jury).

People v. Gay, 24 P.3d 624 (Colo. App. 2000) (Rule 104(a) requires that prior to determining whether a defendant's statement made to the police was made voluntarily, a trial court must consider the preliminary question of whether the statement was in fact ever made).

People v. Lesslie, 939 P.2d 443 (Colo. App. 1996) (testing by the CBI on a listening device used as evidence in a criminal eavesdropping prosecution which included inserting a paper clip in the back of the device to cause an electrical connection did not alter the character of the device nor did it constitute destruction of the device or failure to preserve evidence. The jury is allowed to consider such testing in determining the weight to be given to the evidence).

People v. Robinson, 874 P.2d 453 (Colo. App. 1994) (an evidentiary ruling by the trial court in front of the jury does not mandate reversible error).

People v. Lewis, 710 P.2d 1110 (Colo. App. 1985) (where evidence shows prima facie case of conspiracy the question of admissibility of a coconspirator's statement is one for the trial court).

People v. Dunham, 381 P.3d 415 (Colo. App. 2016) (in an attempted-murder trial in which the defendant raised a self-defense claim, the court should have allowed for cross examination of the victims' statements to medical personnel about methamphetamine use because a jury could reasonably find by a preponderance of the evidence that a conditional fact (methamphetamine use that night) has been established).

Chapter 105

Rule 105. Limited Admissibility

Rule 105 reads as follows:

> When evidence which is admissible as to one party or for one purpose but not admissible as to another party or for another purpose is admitted, the court, upon request, shall restrict the evidence to its proper scope and instruct the jury accordingly.

ANALYSIS

Rule 105 provides for the "limiting instruction" or "admonition." A party is entitled to a limiting instruction by the trial judge directed to the jury whenever evidence might be misapplied by the jury in reaching its final determination.

The following Rules illustrate that evidence may be admissible for one purpose while at the same time remaining inadmissible for another purpose:

- Rule 407, Subsequent Remedial Measures
- Rule 408, Compromise and Offers to Compromise
- Rule 411, Liability Insurance
- Rule 609, Impeachment by Evidence of Conviction of Crime

Evidence admitted under any of these Rules is subject to limiting instruction upon the request of opposing counsel.

Trial counsel may request a limiting instruction when appropriate during the course of trial. Where anticipated prior to trial, a pretrial request for a limiting instruction is also appropriate. Where trial counsel wishes to suggest the tenor of the limiting instruction to the trial judge during the course of trial, counsel should ask to approach the bench for a side bar conference.

A limiting instruction is often used as a second line of defense after an attorney has unsuccessfully attempted to exclude evidence. For example, if a party seeks to impeach a witness with a prior conviction under C.R.S. § 13-90-101, the opponent may, as a second line of defense, ask the judge for an instruction which limits the jury's use of the prior conviction to the evaluation of the witness's credibility.

Where appropriate, a limiting instruction is mandatory on request. Likewise, a court may provide a limiting instruction in the absence of a request.

AUTHORITY

Weissenberger's Federal Evidence §§ 105.1–.3

McCORMICK §§ 56, 59

1 WEINSTEIN 2d §§ 105.01–.07

1 MUELLER & KIRKPATRICK §§ 38–41

1 WIGMORE §§ 13.215, 216.5

Note, *Co-defendant's Confessions*, 3 COLUM. L.J. & SOC. PROBS. 80 (1967)

Note, *The Limiting Instruction—Its Effectiveness and Effect*, 51 MINN. L. REV. 264 (1966)

Note, *Evidence Admissible for a Limited Purpose—The Risk of Confusion Upsetting the Balance of Advantage*, 16 SYRACUSE L. REV. 81 (1964)

COMPARISON TO FEDERAL RULE

In substance, Colorado Rule 105 is identical to Federal Rule 105. However, on Dec. 1, 2011 Federal Rule 105 was restyled. Please see Federal Rule 105 in the appendix for comparison.

SIGNIFICANT CASES

Cruz v. New York, 481 U.S. 186 (1987) (the "interlocking" nature of the co-defendant's statement may be considered on appeal in assessing whether a violation of the confrontation clause was harmless).

People v. Robinson, 226 P.3d 1145 (Colo. App. 2009) (trial court's failure to include a limiting instruction *sua sponte* is not reversible error).

Hansen v. Lederman, 759 P.2d 810 (Colo. App. 1988) (when evidence is admissible for one purpose, but not for another, the trial court, upon request, must restrict the evidence to its proper scope and instruct the jury accordingly).

O'Neal v. Reliance Mortgage Corp., 721 P.2d 1230 (Colo. App. 1986) (it is incumbent upon counsel to request an instruction that the jury not consider the "similar transaction" evidence in evaluating a plaintiff's claim for negligence).

People v. Moore, 693 P.2d 388 (Colo. App. 1984) (since the defendant did not request an instruction that rebuttal evidence be considered only as it related to defendant's credibility and not as evidence of any past crime or tendency toward criminal acts, the failure to so instruct is not reversible error).

People v. Walker, 44 Colo. App. 249, 615 P.2d 57 (1980) (the court held that it was not reversible error to refuse to instruct the jury on prior convictions where the defense was entrapment because the defendant's predisposition to commit the crime is a relevant factor in determining whether there was entrapment).

Chapter 106

Rule 106. Remainder of or Related Writings or Recorded Statements

Rule 106 reads as follows:

> When a writing or recorded statement or part thereof is introduced by a party, an adverse party may require him at that time to introduce any other part or any other writing or recorded statement which ought in fairness to be considered contemporaneously with it.

ANALYSIS

Rule 106 codifies the common law of Colorado which provides that when a party introduces a writing or recording in whole or in part into evidence at trial, the adverse party may require him to introduce any other recording or writing, or the remainder of the evidence introduced, which in fairness should be considered contemporaneously with the admitted evidence.

The Rule is procedural in nature, requiring only that the complementary evidence be introduced at a time when it is needed to place the primary writing or recording into proper context or perspective. The Rule is limited to writings and recordings and does not include conversations.

In practice, Rule 106 operates to avoid the need for an adverse party to wait until cross-examination or rebuttal to introduce the writing or recording. Accordingly, it is intended to prevent consideration of matters out of context.

Obviously, the Rule contemplates a very high degree of discretion to be exercised by the trial judge.

AUTHORITY

WEISSENBERGER'S FEDERAL EVIDENCE § 106.1

McCORMICK § 56

1 MUELLER & KIRKPATRICK §§ 42–46

7 WIGMORE §§ 2094–2125

COMPARISON TO FEDERAL RULE

In substance, Colorado Rule 106 is identical to Federal Rule 106. However, on Dec. 1, 2011 Federal Rule 106 was restyled. Please see Federal Rule 106 in the appendix for comparison.

SIGNIFICANT CASES

People v. A.W., 982 P.2d 842 (Colo. 1999) (trial court erred in holding that the rule of completeness required exclusion of a statement made by a juvenile to a detective because to explain that statement the juvenile would be forced to refer to other inadmissible statements; the rule of completeness does not favor suppression but rather favors admission of a defendant's entire statement).

McLaughlin v. BNSF Railway Co., 300 P.3d 925 (Colo. App. 2012) (the entire transcript of the plaintiff's interview with a claims investigator employed by the defendant was properly admitted as a response to a general charge of fabrication, and also to provide context for the plaintiff's testimony during cross-examination).

People v. Davis, 218 P.3d 718 (Colo. App. 2008) (where excluded statements only include defendant's self-serving hearsay, lacking in independent guarantees of trustworthiness, trial court is not required to admit the entire statement).

People v. Medina, 72 P.3d 405 (Colo. App. 2003) (where prosecution introduced a partial transcript of a co-defendant's statement, CRE 106, which gives an adverse party the right to introduce any other part of the transcript, was satisfied where defendant was permitted to introduce any or all of the transcript from the videotape on cross-examination).

People v. Wilson, 841 P.2d 337 (Colo. App. 1992) (defendant had made statements about the origin of cuts on his fingers. The police officers subsequently testified as to the existence of the cuts but did not testify in regard to the defendant's statements as to the origin of his injuries. The court ruled that to the extent that the "rule of completeness" allowed for the admission of exculpatory statements, it was not applicable in this case).

Kedar v. Pub. Serv. Co. of Colorado, 709 P.2d 15 (Colo. App. 1985) (in personal injury action, against the owner of an electric power line which came into contact with copper pipe being carried by construction worker, trial court's denying admission of entire 1961 electric safety code, after receiving into evidence a photographic enlargement of one page, would be presumed to be correct where no offer of proof of relevancy of other portions of code was made).

People v. Short, 425 P.3d 1208 (Colo. App. 2018) (a defendants otherwise inadmissible self-serving hearsay is admissible under rule of completeness to place into context the evidence offered by prosecution, but it should not subject the defendant to impeachment because of his prior conviction).

People v. Murray, 452 P.3d 101, 2018 Colo. App. LEXIS 1035 (Colo, App. 2018) (a defendant convicted of assault and burglary cannot, under the doctrine of completeness, introduce statements that were recorded when the victim visited the defendant in jail, even though the defendant may have preferred that the jurors hear his response; the statements made are inadmissible as self-serving hearsay because he likely knew he was being recorded).

II
JUDICIAL NOTICE

NOTICE

Chapter 201

Rule 201. Judicial Notice of Adjudicative Facts

Rule 201 reads as follows:

> **(a) Scope of rule.** This rule governs only judicial notice of adjudicative facts.
>
> **(b) Kinds of facts.** A judicially noticed fact must be one not subject to reasonable dispute in that it is either (1) generally known within the territorial jurisdiction of the trial court, or (2) capable of accurate and ready determination by resort to sources whose accuracy cannot reasonably be questioned.
>
> **(c) When discretionary.** A court may take judicial notice, whether requested or not.
>
> **(d) When mandatory.** A court shall take judicial notice if requested by a party and supplied with the necessary information.
>
> **(e) Opportunity to be heard.** A party is entitled upon timely request to an opportunity to be heard as to the propriety of taking judicial notice and the tenor of the matter noticed. In the absence of prior notification, the request may be made after judicial notice has been taken.
>
> **(f) Time of taking notice.** Judicial notice may be taken at any stage of the proceeding.
>
> **(g) Instructing jury.** In a civil action or proceeding, the court shall instruct the jury to accept as conclusive any fact judicially noticed. In a criminal case, the court shall instruct the jury that it may, but is not required to, accept as conclusive any fact judicially noticed.

ANALYSIS

Judicial notice is the process by which a court takes recognition of a fact in the absence of any formal proof. Judicial notice is a substitute for formal proof where the facts sought to be proved are reasonably beyond dispute.

The principles of judicial notice are employed by the trial judge at numerous points during the course of the trial, often without the awareness of the participants in the courtroom. Judicial notice is taken of the English language and of the many human qualities that permit a conclusion that testimony is relevant and material. It is virtually impossible to identify all the occasions on which judicial notice is appropriate.

Rule 201 provides for the judicial notice of adjudicative facts. Where a fact is judicially noticed, it must be reasonably indisputable according to the standards set forth in Rule 201(b). It should be noted that Rule 201(b) applies to so-called adjudicative facts and not legislative facts. Simply

23

stated, adjudicative facts are those facts which concern the immediate parties and which are determinative of the outcome of the case. Adjudicative facts are customarily established through formal proof and only through judicial notice pursuant to the conditions identified in Rule 201.

By comparison, legislative facts are those facts which are used by the court in the decisional process of a case, in the expansion of the law, or in the interpretation or construction of legislative enactments. Accordingly, when a court makes new law, it "legislates." Inevitably, this lawmaking function relies upon factual assumptions as to the way in which the world operates. In *Conrad v. City and Cnty. of Denver*, 724 P.2d 1309 (Colo. 1986), the Colorado Supreme Court adopted the doctrine of legislative judicial notice.

In accordance with subdivision (a) of Rule 201, the conditions precedent to a court taking judicial notice are that the subject must be well known within the jurisdiction or, in the alternative, subject to verification by resort to a reasonably reliable source. The judge determines what a reasonably well informed person within the jurisdiction would know to be true beyond reasonable dispute. Otherwise, resort to an authoritative source is necessary. Representative authoritative sources for verification include such reference materials as historical works, science and art books, language and medical journals and dictionaries, calendars, encyclopedias, commercial lists and directories, maps and charts, statutes and legislative reports.

Illustration

Counsel: Your honor, may I approach the bench? *(At the bench)* Your honor, I would like the court to take judicial notice of the fact that January 19, 1989 occurred on a Thursday.

Judge: Are you suggesting that the day of the week on which January 19 occurred is a matter of common knowledge?

Counsel: No, your honor, I am providing you with an almanac as well as a calendar which will conclusively demonstrate that January 19 fell on a Thursday in 1989.

Judge: Does opposing counsel have any objection?

Opposing Counsel: Your honor, it would appear that this should be a matter of testimony from a witness sworn under oath. Consequently, I object to your taking judicial notice of this fact.

Judge: I will overrule the objection. These sources are essentially beyond dispute as to the day of the week on which January 19 occurred in 1989. Regardless of what a witness's memory may indicate, these sources are sufficient bases for judicial notice, and I will so instruct the jury. No formal evidence will be necessary.

Judicial notice is appropriate if requested by a party where the party supplies necessary information, or in the alternative the court may take judicial notice on its own initiative. In any event, a party is entitled to an opportunity to be heard in opposition to the taking of judicial notice or in support of the taking of judicial notice. Moreover, judicial notice may be taken at any time at any stage of the proceeding. Accordingly, judicial notice may be taken by the trial court or by any reviewing court.

Rule 201(g) provides once a fact has been judicially noticed in a civil action, it is conclusively established and the adverse party may not introduce evidence to contradict the noticed fact. In a criminal case, however, the Rule respects the principle that a conviction may only rest upon a finding that each element of the charged offense has been proved beyond a reasonable doubt. In accordance with this doctrine, the Rule provides that where judicially noticed facts represent an element of the charged crime, the jury may be instructed that the taking of the judicial notice raises a permissible inference as to the truth of the fact. Effectively, the jury may, but is not required to, accept as conclusive any fact judicially noticed in a criminal case.

It should be noted here, that C.R.S. 18-3-106 (5) covers judicial notice as it pertains to vehicular homicide. In relevant part the statute reads as follows: "In all actions, suits, and judicial proceedings in any court of this state concerning alcohol-related or drug related traffic offenses, the court shall take judicial notice of methods of testing a person's alcohol or drug level and of the design and operation of devices, as certified by the department of public health and environment, for testing a person's blood, breath, saliva, or urine to determined his alcohol or drug level. This subsection (5) shall not prevent the necessity of establishing during a trial that the testing devices used were working properly and that such testing devices were properly operated. Nothing in this subsection (5) shall preclude a defendant from offering evidence concerning the accuracy of testing devices."

AUTHORITY

WEISSENBERGER'S FEDERAL EVIDENCE §§ 201.1–.9

McCORMICK §§ 328–335

1 WEINSTEIN 2d §§ 201.01–.52

1 MUELLER & KIRKPATRICK §§ 47–60

9 WIGMORE §§ 2565–2583

Comment, *The Presently Expanding Concept of Judicial Notice*, 13 VILL. L. REV. 528, 530 (1969)

Roberts, *Preliminary Notes Toward a Study of Judicial Notice*, 52 CORNELL L.Q. 210 (1967)

See generally Morgen, *Judicial Notice*, 36 HARV. L. REV. 269 (1944)

COMPARISON TO FEDERAL RULE

In substance, Colorado Rule 201 is identical to Federal Rule 201. However, on Dec. 1, 2011 Federal Rule 201 was restyled. Please see Federal Rule 201 in the appendix for comparison.

SIGNIFICANT CASES

People in Interest of T.T., 442 P.3d 851 (Colo. 2019) (it is proper to take judicial notice of ICON, the record-keeping system used by Colorado courts, in order to preserve judicial resources and avoid the necessity of having to present the same evidence by testimony).

Doyle v. People, 343 P.3d 961 (Colo. 2015). (a factual matter at issue in a prior judicial proceeding does not become an indisputable fact within the contemplation of CRE 201 merely because it was reflected in a prior court record; the trial court erred in taking judicial notice that the defendant had failed to appear in court as required by a condition of his bond).

Mountain States Mutual Casualty Company v. Roinestad, 296 P.3d 1020 (Colo. 2013) (the court took judicial notice of a city's ordinances in effect at the time of disputed conduct, because they were a matter of public record).

Mun. Subdistrict v. OXY USA, Inc., 990 P.2d 701, 711 (Colo. 1999) (where the activities of a non-party entity at a particular time were relevant and were known to a Water Judge from another case, the judge erred in taking judicial notice of those activities, since the parties in interest were not the same in the current case as in the prior case, and because judicial notice in general is not permitted "on the very issue the parties are litigating").

People v. Brockelman, 933 P.2d 1315 (Colo. 1997) (pursuant to court records, the court took judicial notice of the fact that defendant's probation terminated on a specific date).

In re Interrogatory Propounded by Romer etc., 814 P.2d 875 (Colo. 1991) (the Court declined to take judicial notice of the existence and terms of a proposed intergovernmental agreement between the state and Denver relating to a proposal by United Airlines to build a maintenance facility in Colorado).

Prestige Homes Inc. v. Legouffe, 658 P.2d 850 (Colo. 1983), *appeal after remand Legouffe v. Prestige Homes Inc.*, 689 P.2d 697 (Colo. 1984) (the fact that two medical experts have a reasonable dispute over the cause of respondent's heart attack, whether caused by an electrical shock or not, indicates that the court of appeal's decision to disregard the findings of the referee was clearly erroneous).

People v. Walker, 199 Colo. 475, 610 P.2d 496 (1980) (the Court took judicial notice of scientific principles involved in the use of radar to determine vehicular speed).

Chavez v. People of City of Lakewood, 193 Colo. 50, 561 P.2d 1270 (1977) (where a municipal ordinance was properly the subject of judicial notice in the municipal court, and the case is then before a district court on appeal on the record, the district court may also take judicial notice of the municipal ordinance).

Winterberg v. Thomas, 126 Colo. 60, 246 P.2d 1058 (1952) (courts cannot indulge in deductions from scientific laws as applied to evidence except where the conclusions reached are so irrefutable that no room is left for the entertainment by reasonable minds of any other conclusion).

Sosa v. Indus. Claim Appeals Office, 259 P.3d 558 (Colo. App. 2011) (in appeal of award of unemployment compensation benefits where employment was terminated because employee failed drug test, court reversed because employer's failure to prove laboratory conducting drug test was licensed or certified was unnecessary and no need for judicial notice).

In re of C.A.B.L., 221 P.3d 433 (Colo. App. 2009) (where a previous case involved same parties and same issue, a court may take judicial notice of its own records and factual findings).

Sinclair Mktg. v. City of Commerce City, 226 P.3d 1239 (Colo. App. 2009) (in railroad and right-of-way annexation dispute, City's motives are not so well known and understood so as to be judicially noticed fact).

People v. Stanley, 170 P.3d 782 (Colo. App. 2007) (judicial notice was taken of the dates of a judge's oath of office and contract of employment).

Quintana v. City of Westminster, 56 P.3d 1193 (Colo. App. 2002), *cert. denied* (Rule 201 does not allow judicial notice of mathematical principles that are refutable).

Timm v. Reitz, 39 P.3d 1252 (Colo. App. 2001) (in action involving constitutionality of random drug testing for racing dog trainers, "facts" that drug impairment of dog trainers would inevitably cause harm to the trainers or to the animals in their care were not subject to judicial notice because they are not the kind of commonly known facts that are beyond dispute).

One Hour Cleaners v. Industrial Claim Appeals Office, 914 P.2d 501 (Colo. App. 1996) (where a dispute turned on the issue of whether thermography was a reasonable and necessary treatment for a claimant's injury and a federal agency the Health Care Financing Administration gave notice in the Federal Register that Medicare funding had been withdrawn for thermography, for all indications, an administrative law judge properly refused to take judicial notice of the ineffectiveness of thermography for the treatment of the claimant's injury, because such a finding was not determinative of the issue whether thermography was reasonable and necessary for the claimant).

Weingarten v. Bd. of Assessment Appeals, 876 P.2d 118 (Colo. App. 1994) (Board of Assessment Appeals has the authority to take the requested notice of its previous decisions).

Martinez v. RTD, 832 P.2d 1060 (Colo. App. 1992) (a tribunal is not required to take judicial notice unless it has been supplied with the specific facts, records, or documents that are the subject of the request).

Larsen v. Archdiocese of Denver, 631 P.2d 1163 (Colo. App. 1981) (whether certain conditions in a negligence action present more than an ordinary risk of harm depends upon the circumstances of each case, and thus, are not adjudicative facts).

People ex rel. I.S., 415 P.3d 869 (Colo. App. 2017) The court may take judicial notice of the procedural effects (but not the adjudicative effects) of a prior court's findings on appeal, including appendices to briefs, even when they are not part of the record.

Scott R. Larson, P.C. v. Grinnan, ___P.3d___, 2017 Colo. App. LEXIS 766 (Colo. App. 2017) When the court expressly takes judicial notice of a fact that may be subject to reasonable dispute, a timely objection is required to preserve the issue for appeal, even when the taking of notice occurred in a seemingly "toss-away" manner.

People ex rel. A.D., 413 P.3d 290 (Colo. App. 2017) The court taking judicial notice of a prior proceeding does not satisfy requirement of "continuing inquiries" as set forth in § 19-1-126(1)(a), which requires that the party petitioning or filing for termination of parental rights "make continuing inquiries to determine whether the child who is the subject of the proceeding is an Indian child."

NOTICE

III
PRESUMPTIONS

PRESUMPTIONS

Chapter 301

Rule 301. Presumptions in General in Civil Actions and Proceedings

Rule 301 reads as follows:

In all civil actions and proceedings not otherwise provided for by statute or by these rules, a presumption imposes upon the party against whom it is directed the burden of going forward with evidence to rebut or meet the presumption, but does not shift to such party the burden of proof in the sense of the risk of non-persuasion, which remains throughout the trial upon the party on whom it was originally cast.

ANALYSIS

Rule 301 governs the effect of presumptions on the allocation of the burden of proof in civil actions and other civil proceedings. Its scope is thus somewhat limited, leaving to case law the resolution of corollary issues that are raised by the invocation of a presumption.

Under the Rule, a presumption is a procedural device that operates to shift the evidentiary burden of producing evidence, i.e., the burden of going forward, to the party against whom the presumption is directed. The burden of producing evidence operates generally to expose a party to an adverse result where evidence on the issue has not been advanced. The burden of proof, i.e., the risk of non-persuasion, is not affected under the Rule and it remains on the party on whom it was originally cast by the law and the pleadings. The Rule provides that the burden of proof, i.e., the risk of non-persuasion, may not be shifted from one party to another during the course of an action. The Rule, of course, creates no presumption. It merely governs the operation and effect of presumptions.

At the outset, a clarification of terms is helpful in identifying the appropriate occasion for the use of any evidentiary presumption.

Inference: An inference is a conclusion that may be drawn from facts admitted in evidence as to a matter material to the case. An inference exists as a matter of common experience and logic, and while it may be recognized or even specifically authorized as a matter of law, its function is limited to permitting the trier of fact to find the facts sought to be established. An inference is the basic ingredient of all circumstantial evidence.

Conclusive presumption: A conclusive presumption is in reality a rule of substantive law, not a rule of evidence. It is, by definition, not rebuttable. Once the facts giving rise to the conclusive presumption are established, there is no further evidentiary function involved. It is, in effect, a policy determination that removes an issue from factual contest. For example, a conclusive presumption that a child under a specified age is incapable of committing a felony precludes any attempt to prove that such a child committed a felony, once the child's age has been established.

Rebuttable presumption: A rebuttable presumption exists only as a matter of law established either by common law, rule of court, or statute. If underlying facts giving rise to a presumption are offered into evidence, the presumption, as a matter of law, imposes on the party against whom it is directed the burden of going forward with evidence to rebut the presumption. It does not shift to such party the burden of proof in the sense of the risk of non-persuasion.

Presumptions in criminal cases: Presumptions in criminal cases raise difficult constitutional issues. On the one hand, the burden of production may not be placed upon the defendant such as to impose the risk of a directed or instructed verdict on an element of the case, and the burden of persuasion may not be shifted to the defendant on an element necessary for conviction.

Limitation of the use of presumptions in criminal cases is established by case law construing constitutional and statutory provisions relating to the burden of proof in criminal cases. These cases require the prosecution to prove each and every element of the case beyond a reasonable doubt, including those elements subject to a presumption. In Colorado, presumptions are generally treated as permissible inferences. Even with statutory presumptions the courts should only treat presumed facts as permissible inferences, unless the legislature has clearly required a mandatory presumption.

AUTHORITY

WEISSENBERGER'S FEDERAL EVIDENCE §§ 301.1–.4

McCORMICK §§ 336–348

1 WEINSTEIN 2d §§ 301.01–.30

1 MUELLER & KIRKPATRICK §§ 61–72, 77–81

9 WIGMORE §§ 2483–2493

Zavadil, *Rule 301: Overcoming Presumptions*, 27 COLO. LAW. 55 (1998)

Allen, *Presumptions, Inferences and Burden of Proof in Federal Civil Actions—An Anatomy of Unnecessary Ambiguity and a Proposal for Reform*, 75 NW. U. L. REV. 892 (1983)

Note, *Res Ipsa Loquitur—The Effect of Comparative Negligence*, 53 U. COLO. L. REV. 777 (1982)

Allen, *Presumptions in Civil Actions Reconsidered*, 66 IOWA L. REV. 843 (1981)

Gordon & Tenebaum, *Conclusive Presumption Analysis: The Principle of Individual Opportunity*, 71 NW. U. L. REV. 579 (1977)

Louisell, *Construing Rule 301: Instructing the Jury on Presumptions in Civil Actions and Proceedings*, 63 VA. L. REV. 28 (1977)

COMPARISON TO FEDERAL RULE

Colorado Rule 301 is substantially the same as the Federal Rule 301. However, on Dec. 1, 2011 Federal Rule 301 was restyled. Please see Federal Rule 301 in the appendix for comparison.

SIGNIFICANT CASES

Wolfe v. Jim Hutton Educ. Foundations, 344 P.3d 855 (Colo. 2015) (when engineers prove that a water right holder has not used the decreed point of diversion for ten years or more, this triggers a rebuttable presumption of abandonment and the burden shifts to the water rights holder to demonstrate a lack of intent to abandon the water right).

Chapman v. Harner, 339 P.3d 519 (Colo. 2014) (in *res ipsa loquitur* cases the CRE 301 shift of the production burden applies, overruling prior cases that treated the presumption as shifting the persuasion burden).

Krueger v. Ary, 205 P.3d 1150 (Colo. 2009) (applying the rebuttable presumptions of undue influence and unfairness, the party seeking to void a conveyance may raise the presumptions by proving the grantee was in a fiduciary and confidential relationship with the grantor; if the party seeking to uphold the conveyance offers sufficient rebutting evidence, the questions of the grantee's influence and the transaction's fairness must be resolved as questions of fact and the rebuttable presumption has no further role in the case).

Roaring Fork Club, L.P. v. St. Jude's Co., 36 P.3d 1229 (Colo. 2001) (in dicta, court explained that in a dispute over alterations to real property covered by an easement, the burdened owner would present to the court a prima facie case that the alteration would cause no damage to the benefited owner, and that this showing would create a presumption that would shift the burden of production to the benefited owner to establish damage).

United Blood Servs. v. Quintana, 827 P.2d 509 (Colo. 1992) (the presumption that adherence to the applicable standard of care adopted by a profession constitutes due care for those practicing that profession is a rebuttable presumption and the burden is on the one challenging the standard of care to rebut the presumption by competent evidence).

Colorado Dog Fanciers, Inc. v. City and Cnty. of Denver, 820 P.2d 644 (Colo. 1991) (a Denver ordinance was found unconstitutional because the ordinance failed to include a standard of proof).

Barnes v. People, 735 P.2d 869 (Colo. 1987) (statutory presumption that person with 0.10 or more grams of alcohol per 210 liters of breath is under the influence of alcohol is to be construed to authorize only a permissive inference that the defendant was under the influence of alcohol).

People v. Gallegos, 692 P.2d 1074 (Colo. 1984) (the presumption of regularity which attaches to administrative acts requires that defendant must produce some evidence of the grounds of his objection before the prosecution will be required to demonstrate statutory compliance).

Holmes v. Gamble, 655 P.2d 405 (Colo. 1982) (to withstand a defense motion for a directed verdict on a cause of action premised on *res ipsa loquitur*, a plaintiff must adduce evidence, which, when viewed in a light most favorable to the plaintiff, establishes that the existence of each element of that doctrine is more probable than not).

People in Interest of S.P.B., 651 P.2d 1213 (Colo. 1982) (a statutory presumption can be invalidated only when a two-pronged test is met: when the presumption is not necessarily or universally true and when the state has a reasonable alternative means of making the crucial determination).

Montgomery Elevator Co. v. Gordon, 619 P.2d 66 (Colo. 1980) (if the elements of *res ipsa loquitur* are established, a jury is permitted to presume that the defendant was negligent. This presumption may be rebutted by evidence showing that the event resulting in the plaintiff's injuries was not due to any negligence on defendant's part).

City of Littleton v. Industrial Claim Appeals Office, 370 P.3d 157 (Colo. 2016) (Colo. Rev. Stat. Ann. section 8-41-209(2)(b) allows an employer or insurer to overcome the presumption of job-relatedness in section 8-41-209(2)(a) by showing, by a preponderance of the medical evidence, that the firefighter's condition or health impairment caused by a listed cancer "did not occur on the job; this is a burden of proof-shifting presumption that differs from the shift in the production burden provided in CRE 301).

Rome v. HEI Res., Inc., 2014 COA 160 (Colo. App. 2014) (On the issue of whether a general partnership interest is a security, the Court declined to recognize a presumption against such a finding. Rather, the court held that an economic realities test should apply to consider all relevant factors that show the substantive economic realities underlying the transaction, including but not limited to, pre-investment activity, how investors were solicited, whether the partners expected to rely solely on the efforts of others, and the expectations at the time the interest was sold.).

Campbell v. IBM Corp., 867 P.2d 77 (Colo. App. 1993) (when evidence of whether a letter was actually mailed is conflicting, the presumption does not arise and the conflict must be resolved by the trier of fact).

Martin v. Minnard, 862 P.2d 1014 (Colo. App. 1993) (*res ipsa loquitur* is a rule of evidence which allows, in a proper case, an inference of a breach of duty and causation and requires the defendant to then prove there was no negligence).

Bodah v. Montgomery Ward & Co., 724 P.2d 102 (Colo. App. 1986) (where the evidence showed no inspection of premises by a public official, the defendant was not entitled to any instruction by which the jury would be told to presume there was no code violation).

Hartford Fire Ins. Co. v. Public Serv. Co. of Colorado, 676 P.2d 25 (Colo. App. 1983) (because of CRE 301, the doctrine of *res ipsa loquitur* now only shifts a burden of going forward with evidence to rebut the presumed fact of negligence).

Sours v. Goodrich, 674 P.2d 995 (Colo. App. 1983) (where the effects of the injury have persisted for a number of years, a jury should reasonably infer that those effects are permanent).

Motor Crane Serv. v. Barker Constr. Co., 650 P.2d 1329 (Colo. App. 1982) (once plaintiff established the fact that her property was returned in a damaged condition, the presumption arose that the damage occurred as a result of bailee's negligence. Bailee then had the burden of rebutting the presumption to avoid liability).

Zimmer v. Celebrities, Inc., 615 P.2d 76 (Colo. App. 1980) (the plaintiff had the burden of proof to show the four elements of *res ipsa loquitur*).

City of Littleton Colo. v. Industrial Claim App. Office, 370 P.3d 157 (Colo. 2016) (when a firefighter diagnosed with cancer seeks workers' compensation benefits under the "firefighter statute," § 8-41-209, C.R.S. (2015), of the Workers Compensation Act of Colorado, §§ 8-40-101 to -47-209, C.R.S. (2015), the statute "creates a substantive, "Morgan"-type presumption that shifts the burden of persuasion to the employer regarding the job-relatedness of the firefighter's condition or health impairment" which can be overcome by a preponderance of the medical evidence).

People v. Ortiz, 381 P.3d 410 (Colo. 2016) (in the sentencing phase of a vehicular eluding case, the district court did not err in allowing the state patrol to seek restitution; therefore, there is no need to consider whether there was plain error).

Chapter 302

Rule 302. *(No Colorado Rule Codified)*

IV
RELEVANCY AND ITS LIMITS

RELEVANCY

Chapter 401

Rule 401. Definition of "Relevant Evidence"

Rule 401 reads as follows:

> "Relevant evidence" means evidence having any tendency to make the existence of any fact that is of consequence to the determination of the action more probable or less probable than it would be without the evidence.

ANALYSIS

Considered in conjunction with Rule 402, Rule 401 constitutes the cornerstone of Colorado's evidentiary system. In essence, Rule 401 provides that in order for evidence to qualify for admissibility, the evidence must meet the threshold of relevancy. Once relevancy is established, however, evidence may be excludable for affirmative reasons identified in Rule 402. Accordingly, relevant evidence is presumptively admissible. The proponent of evidence must establish its relevancy, and the opponent of the evidence must seek to establish its inadmissibility predicated on one of the bases cited in Rule 402.

Evidence may be relevant because it is direct evidence of the event sought to be proved, e.g., the eyewitness account of the murder or the exhibit establishing an element of the case, such as the executed contract or the letter constituting libel.

Alternatively, evidence may be relevant because it is of a quality that leads to an inference that a provable event did or did not occur. This is called circumstantial evidence.

Determining whether evidence is relevant is ordinarily not a question of law, but one of common experience and logic. Under Rule 401 the definition of relevance requires only that the evidence has any tendency to make the fact to be proved more or less likely than if the evidence was not introduced. The term "any" indicates that the merest tendency will suffice. This broad definition is tempered, however, by Rule 403, which excludes relevant evidence which is remote, misleading, or unfairly prejudicial.

No listing of all relevant evidence or irrelevant evidence would be complete, possible, or helpful. Cases on the subject of relevancy are generally legal limitations on the definition or the verbalized logic of the court deciding the case. The reasoning of the court in the latter instance is often of little authoritative value since it is so intimately related to the facts peculiar to the case.

By its terms, Rule 401 does not purport to deal with the concept of "conditional relevancy." Where evidence is conditionally relevant, its probative value depends upon not only satisfying the basic requirement of relevancy, but also upon establishing the existence of some other fact. Under conditional relevancy, one item of evidence is relevant only if another item of evidence is established. The discussion of conditional relevancy appears in connection with Rule 104, which

RELEVANCY

specifically addresses the concept.

AUTHORITY

WEISSENBERGER'S FEDERAL EVIDENCE §§ 401.1–.9

McCORMICK § 185 at 541–48

2 WEINSTEIN 2d §§ 401.01–.08

1 MUELLER & KIRKPATRICK §§ 82–89

1 WIGMORE §§ 24–43

Kaye, *The Numbers Game: Statistical Inference in Discrimination Cases*, 80 MICH. L. REV. 833 (1982)

Lempert, *Modeling Relevancy*, 75 MICH. L. REV. 1021 (1977)

COMPARISON TO FEDERAL RULE

In substance, Federal Rule 401 and Colorado Rule 401 are identical. However, on Dec. 1, 2011 Federal Rule 401 was restyled. Please see Federal Rule 401 in the appendix for comparison.

SIGNIFICANT CASES

Yeager v. United States, 557 U.S. 110 (2009) (jury's hung counts are not relevant to the record and should not be considered under the issue-preclusion analysis of the Double Jeopardy Clause of the Fifth Amendment).

Pennsylvania v. Muniz, 496 U.S. 582 (1990) (videotaped evidence of the defendant's slurred speech and lack of muscular coordination obtained without *Miranda* warnings is not testimonial and is admissible; defendant's videotaped response when asked if he knew the date of his sixth birthday also obtained without *Miranda* warnings is testimonial and is not admissible).

Scott v. Matlack, Inc., 39 P.3d 1160 (Colo. 2002) (evidence related to Occupational Safety and Health (OSH) regulations was properly admitted in negligence action by independent contractor against trucking company and refinery as non-conclusive evidence of the standard of care in the industry; although the statute bars the use of OSH regulations to establish a negligence per se claim, and although the plaintiff was not an employee and arguably fell outside the class of persons protected by the Act, the OSH statute was relevant to show whether defendants complied with the industry standard regarding fall protection).

Salcedo v. People, 999 P.2d 833 (Colo. 2000) (trial court erred in allowing the prosecution to use a narcotics detective's testimony about drug courier profiles as substantive evidence of a defendant's guilt; the profile was unwritten and apparently quite general, and there was no showing that the attributes relied upon are "relatively unique to drug couriers").

People v. Carlson, 712 P.2d 1018 (Colo. 1986) (testimony of the insurance company's denial to pay defendant's claim because the insurer believed it had a provable arson defense to the claim, failed to meet the relevancy requirement of Rule 401).

Callis v. People, 692 P.2d 1045 (Colo. 1984) (statements within a confession dealing with prior criminality are admissible only if they have independent relevance to the charges).

People v. Quintana, 665 P.2d 605 (Colo. 1983) (where the probative value of evidence of post-arrest silence is so remotely related to an issue as to afford only conjectural inferences, the evidence should not be admitted).

People v. Loscutoff, 661 P.2d 274 (Colo. 1983) (defense counsel sought to establish a witness's possible bias by inquiring about an instance where defendant rejected an offer of sex from this witness, the court found the testimony irrelevant since the witness's hostility toward defendant had already been made evident).

People v. Ferrell, 613 P.2d 324 (Colo. 1980) (a defendant in a homicide case must meet three requirements to be entitled to present evidence of a prior violent act of the victim: (1) the defendant contends that he acted in self-defense and there is competent evidence to support that contention; (2) either the act occurred or defendant became aware of its occurrence within a reasonable time of the homicide; and (3) the defendant knew of the victim's prior violent act at the time of the homicide).

People v. Corbett, 611 P.2d 965 (Colo. 1980) (the court admitted a conversation that helped to establish the defendant's motive in killing the victim and as a motive is a circumstance which tends to show criminal intent, the testimony was probative of one of the material elements of the crime charged).

People v. Mulligan, 568 P.2d 449 (Colo. 1977) (defendant must first offer proof directly connecting the third person with the crime before evidence of that person's opportunity or motive to commit the crime becomes admissible).

People v. Tun, 486 P.3d 490 (Colo. App. 2021) (in a DUI case, the defendant's prior receipt of his driving record was relevant to question of whether defendant knew his license was suspended). Not selected for final or official publication as of June 1, 2021.

People v. Cardenas, 338 P.3d 430 (Colo. App. 2014) (in a sex trafficking case, a defendant's tattoo depicting the letters "MOB" which stood for "money over bitches" was relevant to show the defendant's intent and motive to sexually exploit the victim, and a *res gestae* evidence to provide the jury with a full and complete understanding of the events surrounding the crime and its context).

People v. Morales, 298 P.3d 1000 (Colo. App. 2012) (even though the defendant had offered to stipulate that DNA found at a crime scene matched the defendant's DNA, the prosecution was entitled to present testimony to establish that fact).

People v. Herrera, 272 P.3d 1158 (Colo. App. 2012) (in a prosecution for sexual assault on a child, the trial court acted within its discretion in admitting first communion photographs of the alleged victims, even though the age of the victims was not disputed).

Silva v. Wilcox, 223 P.3d 127 (Colo. App. 2009) (immigration status of injured driver requesting damages for future lost earnings is relevant if the injured driver violated the IRCA and will not be in the United States for the requested damages period).

People v. Tucker, 232 P.3d 194 (Colo. App. 2009) (proposed expert opinion on the Montana Rules of Professional Conduct concerning attorney-client relationships is irrelevant unless the defense puts forth evidence showing defendant was familiar with the rules and relied on them when he sent his attorney a letter he wrote pretending to be District Attorney for the 12th Judicial District of Colorado).

People v. Cauley, 32 P.3d 602 (Colo. App. 2001) (in trial for criminally negligent child abuse, court was within its discretion in admitting a computer animation video demonstrating injuries that can occur when a baby is shaken as relevant to an expert's opinion regarding the manner in which shaken baby syndrome injuries occur).

Loza v. State Farm Ins. Co., 970 P.2d 478 (Colo. App. 1997) (where the insurer sought to enter into evidence previous payments made to the insured under the no-fault automobile insurance laws, the court did not allow admission of such payments for the purpose of disproving bad faith for non-payment of other required payments; such evidence was irrelevant and any potential relevancy was outweighed by prejudice).

People v. Dooley, 944 P.2d 590 (Colo. App. 1997) (in a first degree murder case, where the defendant asserted heat of passion as a defense the trial court properly excluded evidence of an undelivered sealed package from a women's clothing store believed to contain clothing allegedly intended as a gift for the victim, as irrelevant).

People v. Metcalf, 926 P.2d 133 (Colo. App. 1996) (in a prosecution for kidnapping and violation of child custody, the trial court acted within its discretion when it limited the introduction of evidence by the defendant of his care of the child in the years subsequent to the abduction; the defendant's care of the child was relevant only to his state of mind when he abducted the child).

People v. Mendoza, 876 P.2d 98 (Colo. App. 1994) (evidence that defendant was affiliated with a gang was relevant to prove the existence of a motive to kill the victim).

People v. Reaud, 821 P.2d 870 (Colo. App. 1991) (the defendant's discharge by the victim was relevant as tending to establish a motive for him to retaliate against the victim).

RELEVANCY

Martinez v. W.R. Grace Co., 782 P.2d 827 (Colo. App. 1989) (a model of a speed bump at issue in trial was properly verified and the opposing party had ample opportunity to point out differences with the actual speed bump, therefore the model was admitted).

People v. Trefethen, 751 P.2d 657 (Colo. App. 1987) (remoteness in time affects the weight to be given evidence, not its admissibility).

People v. Avery, 736 P.2d 1233 (Colo. App. 1986) (the law and policy governing admissibility of photographs and motion pictures applies to videotapes).

People v. Durre, 713 P.2d 1344 (Colo. App. 1985) (the history of the defendant's accomplice as having previously robbed homosexuals was irrelevant in the case against the defendant).

Myers v. Beem, 712 P.2d 1092 (Colo. App. 1985) (evidence of compensation from a collateral source is inadmissible because it is irrelevant).

Swartwood v. Burlington Northern, Inc., 669 P.2d 1051 (Colo. App. 1983) (in a wrongful death action the remarriage of the surviving spouse is irrelevant because the damages are measured at the time of the spouse's death).

Phillips v. Monarch Recreation Corp., 668 P.2d 982 (Colo. App. 1983) (the threshold determination of admissibility of a statute is one of relevancy).

Goodboe v. Gabriella, 663 P.2d 1051 (Colo. App. 1983) (the trial court properly admitted evidence of a government psychiatric disability pension to prove the plaintiff's mental state immediately prior to hospitalization).

People v. August, 375 P.3d 140 (Colo. 2016) (in a criminal case where the defendant makes a motion for a mistrial, "the defendant has the burden of establishing that the prosecutor acted with the intent to provoke the defense into obtaining a mistrial.").

Nicholls v. People, 396 P.3d 675 (Colo. 2017) (when a mother is a defendant in a homicide trial, evidence showing that she grieved in different ways to each child is relevant).

People v. Trujillo, 433 P.3d 78 (Colo. App. 2018) (evidence of prior foreclosure showed interactions between the defendant and the bank making it more probable that the defendant had intent to commit the theft and is relevant).

Herrera v. Lerma, 2018 COA 141 (Colo. App. 2018) (the probative value of the expert witness's testimony that the plaintiff suffered 15% bodily impairment under the AMA guidelines was not substantially outweighed by the danger of unfair prejudice).

People v. Gwinn, 428 P.3d 727 (Colo. App. 2018) (in a DUI case, defendant's evidence regarding the ineffectiveness of a breathalyzer is irrelevant if the defendant at the time of being stopped by the police did not state that the ineffectiveness of the breathalyzer was the reason for his refusal to take the test).

Zapata v. People, 428 P.3d 517 (Colo. 2018) (although the CRE makes no reference to the common law term "res gestae", the Supreme Court of Colorado continues to apply the common law doctrine of "res gestae" which it defines as including "evidence of another offense, which is related to the charge on trial, that helps to 'provide the fact-finder with a full and complete understanding of the events surrounding the crime and the context in which the charged crime occurred' ").

People ex rel. M.H-K. v. S.K., 433 P.3d 627 (Colo. App. 2018) (in a child welfare case, evidence that a mother refused to subject her child to drug testing is relevant only if: 1) the mother had a duty to so subject the child; or 2) the court finds that the "normal reaction" of a parent would be to subject the child to drug testing).

People v. Wakefield, 428 P.3d 639 (Colo. App. 2018) (in a homicide case, the probative value of photographs of marijuana plants allegedly belonging to defendant was substantially outweighed by the danger of unfair prejudice where the defendant's possession of marijuana had no bearing on the defendant's defense of self-defense).

Danko v. Conyers, 432 P.3d 958 (Colo. App. 2018) (in a medical malpractice case where there was no evidence demonstrating a superseding cause of the patient's injury, evidence of another doctor's negligence is substantially outweighed by the danger of confusing the jury).

RELEVANCY

Chapter 402

Rule 402. Relevant Evidence Generally Admissible; Irrelevant Evidence Inadmissible

Rule 402 reads as follows:

> All relevant evidence is admissible, except as otherwise provided by the Constitution of the United States, by the Constitution of the State of Colorado, by these rules, or by other rules prescribed by the Supreme Court or by the statutes of the State of Colorado. Evidence, which is not relevant is not admissible.

ANALYSIS

This Rule is central to all evidence law. Evidence which is relevant is admissible unless there are express reasons invoked justifying exclusion. Policy reasons of exclusion are sometimes paramount to the accurate determination of facts in a lawsuit. Obvious examples of values of greater import are those associated with privileges, conclusive presumptions, subsequent repairs and compromise negotiations.

Other limitations on relevancy arise from concerns over trustworthiness such as those found in the hearsay rule and best evidence rule.

Rule 402 implicitly indicates that no attempt is made within the Colorado Rules of Evidence to codify constitutional principles of exclusion. Evidence which is relevant may appear to be admissible because no specific Rule within the Colorado Rules of Evidence would require its exclusion. Nevertheless, the evidence may be subject to exclusion in order to protect the constitutional rights of a litigant. Consequently, constitutional inadmissibility may be a distinct basis for precluding the admission of evidence. Like other bases, the opponent of the evidence generally must assert the constitutional doctrine in an effort to exclude the evidence in question. While there is no embodiment within the Rules of constitutional doctrines such as unlawful search, seizure or incriminating statements, or the right of confrontation, such doctrines of constitutional inadmissibility may be the basis for excluding evidence.

AUTHORITY

WEISSENBERGER'S FEDERAL EVIDENCE §§ 402.1–.5

2 WEINSTEIN 2d §§ 402.01–.06

1 MUELLER & KIRKPATRICK §§ 90–91

Martin, *Inherent Judicial Power, Flexibility Congress Did Not Write Into the Federal Rules of Evidence*, 57 TEX. L. REV. 167 (1979)

A Deposition Primer Part II: At the Deposition, 11 COLO. LAW. 1215 (1982)

The Admissibility of Hypnotically Refreshed Testimony in Criminal Cases, 12 COLO. LAW. 600 (1983)

COMPARISON TO FEDERAL RULE

Colorado Rule 402 is modeled after Federal Rule 402 and is substantially the same. However, on Dec. 1, 2011 Federal Rule 402 was restyled. Please see Federal Rule 402 in the appendix for comparison.

SIGNIFICANT CASES

Northstar Project Management, Inc. v. DLR Group, Inc., 295 P.3d 956 (Colo. 2013) (all of the testimony admitted at a trial of a contract dispute is presumed to have been relevant to that dispute, and was therefore required to be designated for appellate review under the sufficiency of the evidence examination).

Bly v. Story, 241 P.3d 529 (Colo. 2010)substantially outweighed by the prejudicial effect o

People v. Nuanez, 973 P.2d 1260 (Colo. 1999) (the CRE require a four-part analysis to determine the admissibility of evidence of prior acts. According to this test the court inquires whether: (1) the evidence relates to a material fact, (2) the evidence has any tendency to make the existence of the material fact more or less probable, (3) the evidence is subject to any of the specific prohibitions set forth in 404(b), and (4) the probative value is substantially outweighed by the danger of unfair prejudice).

People v. Martinez, 486 P.3d 412 (Colo. App. 2020) (in a sexual assault case, the State's evidence of victim's depression and "close suicide scare" following the assault was irrelevant and thus improperly admitted; however the court's error was harmless). Not selected for final or official publication as of June 1, 2021.

Weingarten v. Bd. of Assessment Appeals, 876 P.2d 118 (Colo. App. 1994) (evidence of property tax valuations of subject property for prior tax years is relevant to valuation issues concerning subsequent tax year).

Simon v. Coppola, 876 P.2d 10 (Colo. App. 1993) (evidence of other incidents admissible to impeach if proponent first shows similarity to product at issue).

Coffee v. Inman, 728 P.2d 376 (Colo. App. 1986) (it was a harmless error to allow an attorney to testify as to how his firm disbursed fees on withdrawal of a partner in an unrelated matter. The testimony was irrelevant).

People v. Galang, 382 P.3d 1241 (Colo. Ct. App. 2016) (in a case against a defendant for criminal stalking and harassment, evidence that the defendant had asked the victim for naked photos may have had some prospect for unfair prejudice, but it did not substantially outweigh the probative value of the evidence).

People v. Gwinn, 428 P.3d 727 (Colo. App. 2018) (in a DUI case, defendant's evidence regarding the ineffectiveness of a breathalyzer is irrelevant if the defendant at the time of being stopped by the police did not state that the ineffectiveness of the breathalyzer was the reason for his refusal to take the test).

People ex rel. M.H-K. v. S.K., 433 P.3d 627 (Colo. App. 2018) (in a child welfare case, evidence that a mother refused to subject her child to drug testing is relevant only if: 1) the mother had a duty to so subject the child; or 2) the court finds that the "normal reaction" of a parent would be to subject the child to drug testing).

People v. Wakefield, 428 P.3d 639 (Colo. App. 2018) (in a homicide case, the probative value of photographs of marijuana plants allegedly belonging to defendant was substantially outweighed by the danger of unfair prejudice where the defendant's possession of marijuana had no bearing on the defendant's defense of self-defense).

Danko v. Conyers, 432 P.3d 958 (Colo. App. 2018) (in a medical malpractice case where there was no evidence demonstrating a superseding cause of the patient's injury, evidence of another doctor's negligence is substantially outweighed by the danger of confusing the jury).

Chapter 403

Rule 403. Exclusion of Relevant Evidence on Grounds of Prejudice, Confusion, or Waste of Time

Rule 403 reads as follows:

> Although relevant, evidence may be excluded if its probative value is substantially outweighed by the danger of unfair prejudice, confusion of the issues, or misleading the jury, or by considerations of undue delay, waste of time, or needless presentation of cumulative evidence.

ANALYSIS

Rule 403 provides that relevant evidence may be excluded where the probative value is substantially outweighed by the danger of unfair prejudice, confusion of the issues, misleading the jury, undue delay, waste of time or needless presentation of cumulative evidence.

In applying Rule 403, the trial judge should consider alternate means by which the facts sought to be proven can be established. Obviously, if the same facts can be proven by evidence unattended by the risk of prejudice, confusion or inefficiency, the trial judge should exercise his or her inherent power under Rule 403 to compel the use of the alternate method of proof. A trial judge should also consider whether a limiting instruction pursuant to Rule 105 will sufficiently diminish the danger of prejudice, confusion or inefficiency.

Rule 403 provides that the trial judge may exclude evidence that is excessively prejudicial. Accordingly, if the evidence arouses the jury's emotional sympathies, evokes a sense of horror, or appeals to an instinct to punish, the evidence may be unfairly prejudicial under Rule 403. Usually, although not always, unfairly prejudicial evidence appeals to the jury's emotions rather than intellect.

Confusion of the issues and misleading the jury may be bases for exclusion of evidence in instances where evidence is partially inadmissible or where evidence is admissible for one purpose and not for another. Exclusion based upon confusion is usually justified where the offered evidence would require the trier of fact to engage in intricate, extraordinary, or impossible mental gymnastics in order to comprehend the import of the evidence or to evaluate its weight. Likewise, if the jury is likely to ascribe excessive, unwarranted importance or weight to the evidence, the offered evidence is susceptible to exclusion under Rule 403.

RELEVANCY

Highlights

Old Chief v. United States, 519 U.S. 172 (1997), is the Court's most definitive analysis of how easily the requirement of relevance may be satisfied. In the case, the defendant was convicted of violating 18 U.S.C. § 922(g)(1), which prohibits possession of a firearm by anyone with a prior felony conviction. Prior to trial, defendant offered to stipulate to the prior conviction element. Defendant argued that the nature of his prior offense, assault causing serious bodily injury, was unfairly prejudicial under Rule 403. The prosecution refused defendant's offer, insisting that it had the right to present the evidence on this prior offense at trial.

Defendant argued on appeal that the trial court erred in permitting the prosecution to refuse the defendant's offer of stipulation. The Supreme Court of the United States held that the trial court abused its discretion in refusing the defendant's offer to stipulate to the prior offense and instead admitting evidence concerning the nature of that offense, because the nature of the offense raised the danger of prejudice to defendant. The Court noted that the details of the conviction were absolutely relevant. However, it found that, in this case, the sole purpose for the admission of evidence regarding the nature of the prior offense was to prove the element of prior conviction. Consequently, the Court held that the trial court abused its discretion in admitting the conviction record when the defendant's admission was available.

AUTHORITY

WEISSENBERGER'S FEDERAL EVIDENCE §§ 403.1–.7

MCCORMICK § 180

2 WEINSTEIN 2d §§ 403.01–.07

1 MUELLER & KIRKPATRICK §§ 92–98

2 WIGMORE §§ 443–44

6 WIGMORE §§ 1904–1907

Lewis, *Proof and Prejudice: A Constitutional Challenge to the Treatment of Prejudicial Evidence in Federal Criminal Cases*, 64 WASH. L. REV. 289 (1989)

Tanford, *A Political Choice Approach to Limiting Prejudicial Evidence*, 64 IND. L.J. 831 (1989)

Imwinkelried, *The Meaning of Probative Value and Prejudice in Federal Rule of Evidence 403: Can 403 Be Used to Resurrect the Common Law of Evidence?*, 41 VAND. L. REV. 879 (1988)

Wellborn, *The Federal Rules of Evidence and the Application of State Law in Federal Courts*, 55 TEX. L. REV. 3 (1977)

Travers, *An Essay on the Determination of Relevancy Under the Federal Rules of Evidence*, 1977 ARIZ. ST. L.J. 327 (1977)

Weinstein & Berger, *Basic Rules of Relevancy in the Proposed Rules of Evidence*, 4 GA. L. REV. 43 (1969)

Admissibility of Governmental Studies to Prove Causation, 11 COLO. LAW. 1822 (1982)

COMPARISON TO FEDERAL RULE

In substance, Federal Rule 403 is identical to Colorado Rule 403. However, on Dec. 1, 2011 Federal Rule 403 was restyled. Please see Federal Rule 403 in the appendix for comparison.

SIGNIFICANT CASES

Old Chief v. United States, 519 U.S. 172 (1997) (where the Court rejected the defendant's offer to admit into evidence a prior conviction which was an element of the crime charged, and allowed the prosecution to admit the entire record of the prior conviction, the court abused its discretion; the risk of unfair prejudice substantially outweighed the probative value of the record of the prior conviction).

Kutzly v. People, 442 P.3d 838 (Colo. 2019) (it was proper to deny a defendant's motion for a Shreck hearing to determine reliability of a social worker's testimony, where the court made sufficient specific findings by disagreeing with the defendant that the testimony was inadmissible and emphasizing the witness's experience in its finding).

Wal-Mart Stores, Inc. v. Crossgrove, 276 P.3d 562 (Colo. 2012) (the common law collateral source rule reflects the requirements of Rule 403 since it requires exclusion of evidence that has a substantial likelihood of juror misuse).

Glustrom v. Colorado Public Utilities Commission, 280 P.3d 662 (Colo. 2012) (applying CRE 403, the Public Utilities Commission acted properly in excluding testimony, for reasons of undue delay or needless presentation of cumulative evidence, that was substantially identical to testimony that a party had presented previously).

People v. Greenlee, 200 P.3d 363 (Colo. 2009) (claim that witnesses who reported a defendant's out-of-court statement were unreliable and that therefore the statement should have been excluded because of the risk of unfair prejudice was rejected, because the reliability of lay witness testimony goes to its weight and not to its admissibility).

Fletcher v. People, 179 P.3d 969 (Colo. 2007) (evidence that the adult victim of sexual assault was a virgin at the time of the assault should not have been admitted; it may have evoked jurors' sympathy and moral judgment in a way that could cause unfair prejudice).

People v. Welsh, 80 P.3d 296 (Colo. 2003) (in a case for first degree murder where the defendant raised the defense of not guilty by reason of insanity, the defendant's silence several hours after the killing "had virtually no probative value as rebuttal testimony" regarding her sanity at the time of the killing).

People v. Martinez, 74 P.3d 316 (Colo. 2003) (in a case against the defendant for murder in the first degree for knowingly killing a child under 12 years old, expert's testimony of an accident scenario was inadmissible under a 703 and 403 analysis as to the question of defendant's *mens rea* because the expert "did not show how the accident scenarios relate to shaken-impact syndrome." However, such testimony is admissible "as the basis of [the expert's] opinion that a subdural hematoma results from massive, violent force").

Leaffer v. Zarlengo, 44 P.3d 1072 (Colo. 2002) (Rule 403 requirements have no bearing on standards of discovery pursuant to CRCP 26 which permits discovery of all material that may *lead to* admissible evidence).

Masters v. People, 58 P.3d 979 (Colo. 2002) (in case against defendant for murder involving sexual mutilation, defendant's writings and drawings depicting sexual mutilation were properly admitted in the context of admission of expert testimony relating to characteristics of perpetrators of sexual homicide; probative value of evidence outweighed prejudicial effect and was admissible under CRE 403).

People v. Melillo, 25 P.3d 769 (Colo. 2001) (at defendant's trial for sexual assault of his stepdaughter, trial court properly excluded defendant's statement to an investigator explaining his odd behavior upon being discovered by the victim's mother alone in a bedroom with the victim as due to a "big deal in the house" because of the victim's sexual abuse by a babysitter when she was three years old, even though the court admitted a portion of the statement in which the defendant said he had acted suspiciously because he realized "how it must look," since the probative value of the proffered evidence was substantially outweighed by the risk of prejudice to the victim, and no further offer of proof as to the probative value of the proffered evidence was submitted by defendant).

People v. Shreck, 22 P.3d 68 (Colo. 2001) (reversing a trial court's exclusion of DNA evidence, the court held that Rules 702 and 403, rather than the *Frye* test or *Daubert* factors, govern admissibility of all novel and non-novel scientific evidence).

Bonser v. Shainholtz, 3 P.3d 422 (Colo. 2000) (evidence that expert witness in dental malpractice case was insured by the same entity that insured defendant is admissible when offered to show that the witness is biased if there is a substantial connection between the expert witness and the insurance entity; witness's possible financial losses if defendant lost case were significant, since insurance group had only about 1,500 members, and additional evidence showed that witness was a founder of the insurance group).

People v. Nuanez, 973 P.2d 1260 (Colo. 1999) (trial court properly admitted evidence of the defendant's prior act where the prejudicial effect of the defendant's deferred judgment for burglary did not substantially outweigh its probative effect).

People v. Gibbens, 905 P.2d 604 (Colo. 1995) (when evidence has a close relationship to the event charged, the balance between probative value and prejudicial effect should generally be struck in favor of admission).

People v. Quintana, 882 P.2d 1366 (Colo. 1994) (court of appeals erred in determining that murder defendant's statements expressing intent to kill other people, were more prejudicial than probative, given these statements were accompanied before and after by limiting instructions and that none of the statements were given undue emphasis).

People v. Snyder, 874 P.2d 1076 (Colo. 1994) (trial courts are accorded considerable discretion in determining whether the probative value of the similar transaction evidence was substantially outweighed by the danger of unfair prejudice).

Campbell v. People, 814 P.2d 1 (Colo. 1991) (the trial court is in a superior position to judge the advisability of allowing testimony and the decision to admit the testimony is best left to the trial court's discretion).

People v. Pronovost, 773 P.2d 555 (Colo. 1989) (the limitations on a trial court's discretion to exclude an expert witness are equivalent to the limitations on the court's discretion to exclude alibi evidence since both are derived from the same protections found in the Sixth and Fourteenth Amendments).

People v. Hampton, 758 P.2d 1344 (Colo. 1988) (the trial court's discretion to exclude relevant and competent defense evidence must be exercised in consideration of the circumstances underlying the defendant's case).

People v. Rowerdink, 756 P.2d 986 (Colo. 1988) (competent evidence which explains, refutes, counteracts, or disproves the other party's evidence, may be introduced as rebuttal testimony even if such evidence tends to support that party's case in chief. The admission of rebuttal testimony is within the discretion of the trial court).

I.M.A. Inc. v. Rocky Mountain Airways, Inc., 713 P.2d 882 (Colo. 1986) (evidence was relevant to show the intent of the parties to proceed with the contract terms and was admissible since the evidence was neither unfairly prejudicial nor confusing to the jury).

People v. Randall, 711 P.2d 689 (Colo. 1985) (the trial court properly admitted the testimony that defendant viewed obscene magazines immediately prior to sexual abuse of child since the prejudicial effect of the magazines did not substantially outweigh their probative value).

Palmer v. A. H. Robins Co., 684 P.2d 187 (Colo. 1984) (evidence of intent is only relevant if the terms of the agreement are ambiguous).

People v. De Herrera, 680 P.2d 848 (Colo. 1984) (the defendant's possession of driver's licenses bearing names other than his own is not probative of his guilt concerning aggravated robbery).

People v. Freeman, 668 P.2d 1371 (Colo. 1983) (the court declared that evidence of other crimes that occur as part of the *res gestae* of the offense is admissible so long as it is relevant and its probative value is not substantially outweighed by the probability of unfair prejudice to the accused).

People v. Walker, 666 P.2d 113 (Colo. 1983) (cross-examination by questions which focus on the motive of a witness is liberally permitted. The scope and limits of cross-examination for impeachment and general credibility are within the discretion of the trial court and will not be disturbed absent an abuse of the discretion).

People v. Forgette, 2021 Colo. App. LEXIS 270 (Colo. App. 2021) (in a burglary case, prosecution evidence of three photos of defendant while in custody were probative of defendant's identity, and not substantially outweighed by the prejudicial effect of showing a defendant's custodial status). Not selected for final or official publication as of June 1, 2021.

People v. Forgette, 2021 Colo. App. LEXIS 270 (Colo. App. 2021) (testimony related to defendant's evasive and obstreperous conduct during a traffic stop that occurred after a charged burglary was probative of defendant's consciousness of guilt and not substantially outweighed by its prejudicial effect). Not selected for final or official publication as of June 1, 2021.

People v. Rodriguez, 2021 Colo. App. LEXIS 548 (Colo. App. 2021) (in a domestic violence assault case, evidence of victim's pregnancy was not substantially outweighed by the danger of unfair prejudice and thus admissible). Not selected for final or official publication as of June 1, 2021.

People v. Rojas, 2020 Colo. App. LEXIS 733 (Colo. App. 2020) (evidence of criminal intent as set forth in a defendant's application for food stamps was admissible as part of the res gestae). *Cert. granted. Rojas v. People*, Colo. LEXIS 916 (Colo. Oct. 6, 2020).

Trujillo v. Vail Clinic, Inc., 480 P.3d 721 (Colo. App. 2020) (in a medical malpractice suit, testimony of Plaintiff's expert setting forth the theory of cranial compression ischemic encephalopathy was improperly excluded because the concepts underlying the theory were widely accepted, and because it was reasonably reliable, bore on causation, and was helpful to the jury).

People In Interest of D.F.A.E., 482 P.3d 489 (Colo. App. 2020) (in sexual assault case, State's evidence of the victim's virginity, even if improperly admitted, was harmless; defendant's evidence that the victim was seeking to lose her virginity was properly excluded because the defendant did not overcome the presumption prohibited by the Rape Shield Statute § 18-3-407).

People v. Dominguez, 454 P.3d 364 (Colo. App. 2019) (in a drug case, text messages on the defendant's cellphone asking whether the recipient could "do 2 for 1500 if I got all of it" and "do 2 for 1600" were properly admitted into evidence and not considered unfairly prejudicial because they were not designed to incite an emotional response from the jury).

People v. McClelland, 350 P.3d 976 (Colo. App. 2015) (trial court should have excluded "in life" photographs of the victim in a manslaughter case, since they showed only that he had been alive prior to the defendant's conduct, and they were used at trial in a way that likely caused extreme unfair prejudice to the defendant, since they were repeatedly referred to as showing the victim in wholesome family circumstances).

People v. Clark, 370 P.3d 197 (Colo. App. 2015) (evidence showing a defendant's gang affiliation was properly admitted, because it had probative value to show the defendant's motive for an act, and that probative value exceeded the risks of unfair prejudice associated with the evidence).

Lombard v. Colorado Outdoor Ed. Ctr., Inc., 266 P.3d 412 (Colo. App. 2011) (in personal injury case, third expert on same topic excluded because evidence was cumulative and evidence of building plan drawn up eight years after building was built was relevant but inadmissible under 403).

Haralampopoulos v. Kelly, 2011 Colo. App. LEXIS 1890 (Colo. App. 2011) (in medical malpractice case; evidence of cocaine use two years prior to injury was not relevant because too far removed).

People v. Schreiber, 226 P.3d 1221 (Colo. App. 2009) (defendant's *res gestae* statement to the victim, "do you have problems with women masturbating in the bathroom" was not so inflammatory as to require exclusion under CRE 403).

People v. Asberry, 172 P.3d 927 (Colo. App. 2007) (testimony about the basis for a police stop was properly admitted under 404(b) because it gave the jury an understanding of why defendant was stopped and thus formed a natural and integral part of an account of the crime; because there was no testimony about the nature of the area restriction, the testimony was not unfairly prejudicial).

People v. Mintz, 165 P.3d 829 (Colo. App. 2007) (testimony that the defendant had a court-appointed counselor and a court-appointed therapist did not violate the rule against introduction of evidence of

RELEVANCY

past crimes to show bad character; because testimony showed that the defendant was involved in a divorce, the jury could have concluded that the court appointments had been made in the context of the divorce case, not in the context of criminal activity).

People v. St. James, 75 P.3d 1122 (Colo. App. 2002) (in a sexual assault case, where the defendant had offered to stipulate to a fact and the People's case thereby has not been weakened, the prosecution may be required to accept the stipulation where the probative value of offered evidence was substantially outweighed by the danger of unfair prejudice).

People v. Fry, 74 P.3d 360 (Colo. App. 2002) (in assault case where defendant set his girlfriend on fire, evidence of other acts of domestic violence was admissible to show defendant's intent, malice, and the absence of mistake pursuant to 404(b); the probative value of the evidence was not substantially outweighed by the danger of unfair prejudice).

People v. Hall, 60 P.3d 728 (Colo. App. 2002) (in a homicide case, prosecution evidence that defendant had made a statement concerning her multiple personality disorder in order to explain the inconsistency of her prior statements was not admissible under 404(b) which permits only evidence of "crimes, wrongs or acts"; nevertheless evidence was admissible under 403 absent showing of abuse of discretion).

People v. White, 55 P.3d 220 (Colo. App. 2002) (in trial for illegal discharge of a firearm, the court held that the probative value of the following pieces of evidence exceeded the prejudicial effect: (1) a handgun seized at the scene not used in the offense, (2) a witness's use of defendant's nickname when referring to him in her testimony, and (3) evidence that a SWAT team responded to the scene).

City of Englewood v. Denver Waste Transfer, 55 P.3d 191 (Colo. App. 2002) (in condemnation proceeding where defendant introduced evidence of plaintiff-city's efforts to block defendant's unit development application, Court did not abuse its discretion under 403 in admitting evidence for limited purpose of showing background of defendant's application).

People v. Balkey, 53 P.3d 788 (Colo. App. 2002) (where trial judge in response to a jury's request provided a transcript of testimony by the State's chief witness, said transcript did not improperly bolster that witness's testimony, nor was it unduly prejudicial since the request for the transcript was not "needless" and was therefore within the discretion of the trial court to grant; the jury's request was specific and well focused, and the instructions to the jury with regard to the transcript reduced danger that undue emphasis would be placed on the transcript).

People v. Underwood, 53 P.3d 765 (Colo. App. 2002) (in a sexual assault case, the probative value of evidence that the victim experienced a miscarriage after the assault but prior to reporting of the crime exceeded the unfair prejudice and the evidence was therefore admissible under 403).

City of Boulder v. Fowler Irrevocable Trust 1992-1, 53 P.3d 725 (Colo. App. 2002), *cert. denied* (trial court's exclusion of testimony from a surrebuttal witness was proper under CRE 403 where appellant had already given similar testimony from two witnesses, and the third request came at 5 p.m. on the third day of a three-day trial).

People v. James, 40 P.3d 36 (Colo. App. 2001) (statements of witness that defendant asked her to participate in a check-cashing scheme, defendant gave her a false birth certificate to obtain a false identification card, and that it was defendant's idea to cut her index finger with a razor blade to disguise her fingerprint when obtaining the identification card were admissible, even though they did not relate to any charge of theft or forgery against the defendant, because they were integral to charges of conspiracy and contributing to the delinquency of a minor, and there was a large body of similar evidence against the defendant).

People v. Webster, 987 P.2d 836 (Colo. App. 1998) (defendant's statement that he was a member of a gang was not unfairly prejudicial to the defendant since it was relevant to proving a motive for the crime).

People v. Parga, 964 P.2d 571 (Colo. App. 1998) (the defendant's driving record and previous traffic offenses were relevant and not unfairly prejudicial, where the prosecution was entitled to attempt to establish his habitual offender status).

People v. Anderson, 954 P.2d 627 (Colo. App. 1997) (the defendant in a vehicular homicide case objected to the entry into evidence of photographic transparencies (slides) showing the bodies of the victims inside the damaged vehicle on grounds that showing slides on a large screen would be unduly prejudicial and irrelevant because he had already conceded the death of the victims; the court upheld the trial court's entry of the slides into evidence to illustrate the testimony of fire and emergency medical personnel present at the scene of the crime).

People v. Thompson, 950 P.2d 608 (Colo. App. 1997) (where the prosecution used a knife as demonstrative evidence, even though the actual murder weapon was never found, the likelihood of prejudice did not outweigh the relevancy of the evidence).

People v. Burgess, 946 P.2d 565 (Colo. App. 1997) (trial court allowed a videotaped police interview of the victim into evidence in addition to testimony of the victim at trial; the admission of the videotaped interview was not unfairly prejudicial).

Peiffer v. State Farm Mut. Auto. Ins. Co., 940 P.2d 967 (Colo. App. 1996) (in an action for breach of contract and bad faith, expert testimony that the insurer violated the Unfair Claims Settlement Act in denying further no-fault payments was relevant so long as the testimony concerned the contention that the insurer acted in bad faith within the purview of the Act).

People v. Woods, 931 P.2d 530 (Colo. App. 1996) (evidence that the victim's loss of job was due to the victim discussing with customers her problems with the defendant, after having been warned not to do so, was properly excluded when offered for impeachment, because its value was outweighed by the prejudicial impact on the jury and because it raised collateral issues).

People v. Kemp, 885 P.2d 260 (Colo. App. 1994) (expert testimony regarding impairment of memory is less probative where more than one eyewitness is used and is outweighed by the risk of confusing issues, misleading jurors, and wasting time).

Simon v. Coppola, 876 P.2d 10 (Colo. App. 1993) (evidence of other thermostat failures of similar circumstances and conditions as the one at issue is admissible since the judge has discretion to weigh its probative value against its prejudicial effects).

Voight v. Colorado Mountain Club, 819 P.2d 1088 (Colo. App. 1991) (the trial court correctly excluded the cross-examination of an economist concerning the present value of specific issues because this examination would prejudice or confuse the jury).

In re Marriage of Blake, 807 P.2d 1211 (Colo. App. 1990) (cumulative evidence can be excluded under Rule 403).

People v. Vazquez, 768 P.2d 721 (Colo. App. 1988), *cert. denied*, 787 P.2d 174 (Colo. 1990) (photocopies of law book found in defendant's possession were allowed to show the defendant's knowledge and intent relevant to distribution of controlled substance).

People v. King, 765 P.2d 608 (Colo. App. 1988), *aff'd*, 785 P.2d 596 (Colo. 1990) (statements allowed under other rules of evidence may be excluded by Rule 403).

People v. Auldridge, 724 P.2d 87 (Colo. App. 1986) (the minimal probative value of the defendant's knowledge that carrying a concealed weapon was illegal was substantially outweighed by the danger of unfair prejudice, and thus, the trial court abused its discretion in admitting this evidence).

Lamont v. Union Pac. R. Co., 714 P.2d 1341 (Colo. App. 1986) (the testimony of defendant's motives for early retirement were excluded because the trial court found that the probative value was substantially outweighed by the danger of unfair prejudice).

People v. Myers, 714 P.2d 513 (Colo. App. 1985) (the mother's testimony that the victim had undergone counseling at the suggestion of Social Services is relevant to the occurrence of the sexual assault and was not unduly prejudicial).

People v. Wafai, 713 P.2d 1354 (Colo. App. 1985), *aff'd*, 750 P.2d 37 (Colo. App. 1988) (in admitting a translation of a letter from Arabic to English the court held that there is no abuse of discretion where the evidence has probative value in that it is indicative of defendant's intent, and such probativeness outweighs any prejudicial effect).

People v. Robinson, 713 P.2d 1333 (Colo. App. 1985) (the unfair portion of testimony may be excised from relevant testimony to avoid any unfair prejudice).

People v. Evans, 710 P.2d 1167 (Colo. App. 1985) (the trial court did not abuse its discretion in refusing to allow defendant's testimony that marijuana was his "religious food").

People v. Fernandez, 687 P.2d 502 (Colo. App. 1984) (death threat evidence is admissible to show a defendant's consciousness of guilt).

Marlow v. Atchison, T. & S. F. R. Co., 671 P.2d 438 (Colo. App. 1983) (the trial court correctly refused defendant's offer of proof concerning the effect of taxes on the amount of damages to be awarded since the testimony had very little relevance to the actual effect of taxes on plaintiff's future earnings and would have confused the issues to the jury).

People v. Perez, 656 P.2d 44 (Colo. App. 1982) (where defendant fled because he recognized an officer as a narcotics agent, inference of prior criminal activity was not sufficiently strong to require exclusion of the evidence since knowledge is a necessary element of the crime charged).

Venalonzo v. People, 388 P.3d 868 (Colo. 2017) (in a child assault case, testimony by an interviewing witness that another witness is credible "is especially problematic where the outcome of the case turns on that witness's credibility).

Danko v. Conyers, 432 P.3d 958 (Colo. App. 2018) (where a plaintiff offers testimony to prove negligence in a medical malpractice case and defendant offers evidence that other doctors contributed to plaintiff's injuries, the plaintiff is entitled to exclude defendant's evidence under 403 because such evidence would confuse jurors).

People v. Palacios, ___ P.3d ___, 2018 Colo. App. LEXIS 219 (Colo. App. 2018) (prosecution's full-size mockup of garage was not misleading or prejudicial since the mockup had only minor inconsistencies with the actual garage).

People v. Folsom, 431 P.3d 652 (Colo. App. 2017) (Cert Denied) (where the defendant offers alternate suspect evidence as part of a misidentification defense, defendant's evidence that the alternate suspects had criminal records should have been admitted over prosecution's 403 objection).

People v. Tardif, 433 P.3d 60 (Colo. App. 2017) (the prejudicial effect of prosecution's slow-motion recording of a shooting substantially exceeds its probative value, and therefore violates 403 since it can give false ideas concerning the defendant's state of mind).

People v. Trujillo, 433 P.3d 78 (Colo. App. 2018) (when evidence of prior foreclosures in a criminal mischief case alleging that defendant destroyed his property before a foreclosure sale are only mentioned in passing, and no details are revealed the danger of unfair prejudice does not substantially outweigh its probative value).

Herrera v. Lerma, 2018 COA 141 (Colo. App. 2018) (the probative value of the expert witness's testimony that the plaintiff suffered 15% bodily impairment under the AMA guidelines was not substantially outweighed by the danger of unfair prejudice).

People v. Gwinn, 428 P.3d 727 (Colo. App. 2018) (in a DUI case, defendant's evidence regarding the ineffectiveness of a breathalyzer is irrelevant if the defendant at the time of being stopped by the police did not state that the ineffectiveness of the breathalyzer was the reason for his refusal to take the test).

Zapata v. People, 428 P.3d 517 (Colo. 2018) (although the CRE makes no reference to the common law term "res gestae", the Supreme Court of Colorado continues to apply the common law doctrine of "res gestae" which it defines as including "evidence of another offense, which is related to the charge on trial, that helps to 'provide the fact-finder with a full and complete understanding of the events surrounding the crime and the context in which the charged crime occurred' ").

People v. Wakefield, 428 P.3d 639 (Colo. App. 2018) (in a homicide case, the probative value of photographs of marijuana plants allegedly belonging to defendant was substantially outweighed by the danger of unfair prejudice where the defendant's possession of marijuana had no bearing on the defendant's defense of self-defense).

Danko v. Conyers, 432 P.3d 958 (Colo. App. 2018) (in a medical malpractice case where there was no evidence demonstrating a superseding cause of the patient's injury, evidence of another doctor's negligence is substantially outweighed by the danger of confusing the jury).

Perez v. Archuleta, 737 Fed. Appx. 419 (10 Cir. 2018) (evidence of other suspects actions were not relevant because there was no connection between the plaintiff's conduct and the suspects conduct, the suspects testimony was too remote in time to be relevant, and other evidence attempting to link the suspects to the plaintiff's case was already admitted).

People v. Cohen, 440 P.3d 1256 (Colo. App. 2019) (In a theft case, the court held that the "opening the door" doctrine is limited to "otherwise inadmissible rebuttal evidence . . . ' "only to the extent necessary to remove any unfair prejudice which might otherwise have ensued from the original evidence," ' " citing *United States v. Martinez*, 988 F.2d 685, 702 (7th Cir. 1993) quoting *United States v. Winston*, 447 F.2d 1236, 1240 (D.C. Cir. 1971)).

RELEVANCY

Chapter 404

Rule 404. Character Evidence Not Admissible to Prove Conduct; Exceptions; Other Crimes

Rule 404 reads as follows:

(a) **Character evidence generally.** Evidence of a person's character or a trait of his character is not admissible for the purpose of proving that he acted in conformity therewith on a particular occasion, except:

(1) Character of accused. Evidence of a pertinent trait of his character offered by an accused, or by the prosecution to rebut the same or if evidence of the alleged victim's character for aggressiveness or violence is offered by an accused and admitted under Rule 404(a)(2), evidence of the same trait of character of the accused offered by the prosecution;

(2) Character of alleged victim. Evidence of a pertinent trait of character of the alleged victim of the crime offered by an accused, or by the prosecution to rebut the same, or evidence of a character trait of peacefulness of the alleged victim offered by the prosecution in a homicide case to rebut evidence that the alleged victim was the first aggressor;

(3) Character of witness. Evidence of the character of a witness as provided in Rules 607, 608, and 13-90-101.

(b) **Other crimes, wrongs, or acts.**

(1) **Prohibited uses.** Evidence of any other crime, wrong, or act is not admissible to prove a person's character in order to show that on a particular occasion the person acted in conformity with the character.

(2) **Permitted uses.** This evidence may be admissible for another purpose, such as proving motive, opportunity, intent, preparation, plan, knowledge, identity, absence of mistake, or lack of accident.

(3) **Notice in a criminal case.** In a criminal case, the prosecutor must:

(A) **provide reasonable notice of any such evidence that the prosecutor intends to offer at trial, so that the defendant has a fair opportunity to meet it;**

(B) **articulate in the notice the permitted purpose for which the prosecutor intends to offer the evidence and the reasoning that supports the purpose; and**

(C) **do so in writing before trial - or in any form during trial if the court, for good cause, excuses lack of pretrial notice.**

Editor's Note: Revised subsection (b) was amended and adopted March 29, 2021, effective July 1, 2021, for cases filed on or after July 1, 2021.

ANALYSIS

Evidence of a person's character or character traits tends to distract the trier of fact from the primary issues of the case. Such evidence creates a substantial risk that a finding will be predicated on the trier's attitude toward a person's character, rather than upon an objective determination of the facts. Consequently, specialized rules have developed to limit the use of character evidence in order to protect the integrity of the fact-finding process. Rule 404(a) codifies the basic rule that evidence of a person's character or character traits is not admissible for the purpose of proving that such a person acted in conformity with his character on a particular occasion. This basic prohibition is often called the "propensity rule." Essentially, the fundamental exclusionary rule creates a forbidden inferential pattern. Under the Rule, a person's character or propensity to act in a certain way may not be offered as a basis for the inference that on a specific occasion he acted in conformity with the propensity or the character trait. The basic exclusionary rule applies both in civil and criminal cases, but it most frequently will be applied to exclude evidence in a criminal case. For example, a negative character trait of an accused may not be established by the prosecution as evidence of the propensity of the accused to commit the crime in question.

Illustration

In a prosecution for murder, the State cannot seek to show the violent character or the violent propensity of the accused in order to establish that, in connection with the operative facts of the case, the accused acted in conformity with his propensity and murdered the victim in question. Such evidence of the accused's character trait or propensity would be relevant under Rule 401. It would tend to alter the probabilities that the accused committed the murder in question, i.e., as a matter of common experience, murders are more frequently committed by those with violent propensities than by those who lack such propensities. Nevertheless, such evidence is rejected under Rule 404(a) because evidence of a person's character may unduly excite the emotions and prejudices of the trier of fact; the trier might seek to penalize the accused for his violent propensities rather than making a dispassionate and objective evaluation of the facts of the case.

It should be noted that the basic exclusionary principle of Rule 404(a) prohibits the use of a specific type of inference. It does not forbid the use of character evidence generally. Consequently, when character evidence is used to establish something other than conforming conduct, such character evidence is not within the forbidden inferential pattern prohibited by Rule 404(a). Such situations where character evidence is used in a manner other than to prove conforming conduct will generally fall into the application of character evidence known as "character in issue." Where character is "in issue," character evidence itself forms an essential element of a charge, claim, or a defense. Character is "in issue" where it is not used as a basis for a further inference, but it is a terminal point of proof.

Illustration

In a libel or slander case involving certain alleged character traits, the character traits may constitute an element of a defense. Accordingly, if the substantive law dictates that character or a character trait is an element of a defense, character then is "in issue," and it is outside the basic prohibition of 404(a). Consequently, if P charged D with slander claiming that D said, "P is dishonest," and D pleads truth as a defense, D must prove P's dishonesty to prevail. P's character trait of dishonesty is a terminal point of proof. It is not used as the basis for a further inference. Consequently, P's trait is "in issue," and such use of character evidence is not prohibited by Rule 404(a).

Rule 404(a) sets forth three exceptions where the exclusionary rule will not apply to character used to prove conforming conduct. First, the accused in a criminal case may seek to introduce pertinent evidence of his good character in order to raise the inference that on a particular occasion involving the crime for which he is charged, he acted in conformity with his good character and did not commit the operative facts of the crime. It should be noted that this exception applies only to an accused in a criminal proceeding.

Illustration

Where an accused is charged with murder, he may introduce evidence of his character trait for peacefulness in the hope that the jury will make the inference that he acted in conformity with his peaceful character on the particular occasion and did not commit the murder. Such application of character evidence is particularly useful where the prosecution's case is based on circumstantial evidence. Character evidence is often used by the accused in this situation to establish reasonable doubt as to whether or not he committed the crime.

The second exception to the exclusionary rule provides that an accused may introduce pertinent evidence of the character of a victim of the charged crime.

A third exception to Rule 404(a) provides that the character of a witness may be explored as to the witness's traits of veracity or truth-telling. This exception to the basic exclusionary rule is more specifically codified in Rules 607, 608, and C.R.S. § 13-90-101. *See* Analysis to Rules 607, 608, and C.R.S. § 13-90-101. It is important to note that the exception relating to the character of witnesses will apply to the accused if he takes the stand on his own behalf. Consequently, if the accused elects to be a witness in his own case, certain aspects of his character may be explored by the prosecution pursuant to Rules 608 and C.R.S. § 13-90-101.

Another basic exclusionary principle is codified in Rule 404(b). Rule 404(b) provides that evidence of other crimes, wrongs, or acts is not admissible to prove the character of a person in order to show that such person acted in conformity with his character on a particular occasion. It should be evident that this exclusionary principle is merely an extension of the basic exclusionary rule contained in Rule 404(a). Here the prohibition relates to the establishment of prior acts as a basis for the inference that the individual acted in conformity with his prior action and his propensity. The exclusionary rule applies in both civil and criminal cases, but it most frequently

RELEVANCY

will arise in a criminal case. For example, the exclusionary rule generally prohibits the prosecution from offering evidence of prior anti-social acts of the accused where the prosecution is seeking to establish that the accused acted in conformity with his prior behavior and committed the anti-social act for which he is charged. The policy for Rule 404(b) is essentially the same as that supporting Rule 404(a). The evidence of the prior act is excluded because it is thought that the jury might seek to punish the accused for his prior anti-social behavior rather than weigh the evidence relevant to the specific occurrence in question.

Certain prior acts of an individual, including prior crimes, can be relevant for a purpose other than showing the character or propensity of a person to commit a similar act. Such prior acts would not be subject to the exclusionary principle of Rule 404(b). Accordingly, the Rule specifically authorizes the use of prior acts where the evidence is offered to prove a relevant fact in the case other than conforming conduct.

Illustration 1

A prior act may be utilized to show the motive of the accused rather than to show the accused's propensity to commit anti-social acts. For example, if the defendant is charged with stealing an expensive diamond cutting device, the prosecution may seek to offer evidence that the month prior to the alleged theft of the diamond cutting device, the defendant stole a bag of uncut diamonds. Proof of the prior act would give rise to the inference that the defendant had a motive for stealing the diamond cutting machine.

Illustration 2

Often, prior acts of an accused are offered by the prosecution to establish the identity of the perpetrator of the crime which is charged. For example, where the defendant is charged with armed robbery and the defendant denies that he is the perpetrator, the prosecution may seek to establish his identity through the accused's unique *modus operandi* of committing crimes. If the robbery in question was committed by a man wearing a Halloween mask who claimed to have dynamite wired to his body, and the accused has committed robberies on three prior occasions using the same method of operation, evidence of the accused's prior acts would tend to identify him as the perpetrator of the crime. The prosecution would argue that the prior acts of the defendant are outside the exclusionary rule because they are not offered to establish character or criminal propensity.

Highlights

The leading case, *Huddleston v. United States*, 485 U.S. 681 (1988), is one in which the government sought to prove that the defendant knowingly sold stolen property. In support of its case, the government offered evidence of prior acts. The defense contended that prior act evidence could not be submitted to the jury unless the trial court made a preliminary finding that the government had proven the prior act by a preponderance of the evidence. The United

States Supreme Court found such a requirement to be inconsistent with both the plain language and the legislative history of the Federal Rules of Evidence. According to *Huddleston*, under Federal Rule 404(b), evidence of prior acts is admissible where there is "sufficient evidence to support a finding . . . that the defendant committed the similar act." *See* Federal Rule 104(b).

Subsequently, the United States Supreme Court determined that the double jeopardy clause of the Constitution did not prohibit testimony regarding a previous robbery of which the defendant had been acquitted. *See Dowling v. United States*, 493 U.S. 342 (1990). The Court noted that the acquittal did not determine the ultimate issue in the case at bar. Further, the jury could "reasonably conclude" that the defendant committed the previous robbery even if it did not believe so beyond a reasonable doubt.

The doctrine of *res gestae* is sometimes used as an exception to the prohibition against the admission of evidence under 404(b), and is most often referred to in connection with evidence of past crimes committed by a person who is charged with another crime. It may also be used as a means for admitting statements that would otherwise be barred by the hearsay exclusionary rule. Courts have admitted statements under the doctrine of *res gestae* where the statements lack the specific requirements for admission under specific exceptions to the hearsay rule. (*See* Chapter 803 for additional information on the doctrine of *res gestae*.)

In any case in which the court accepts the proponent's theory of the admissibility of evidence of a prior act and proceeds to admit the prior act, the judge should be asked to provide the jury with a limiting instruction. Such an instruction would advise the jury that the evidence of the prior act may not be considered as a basis for an inference that the individual in question acted in conformity with his prior conduct or with his indicated propensity. *See* Analysis to Rule 105.

RELEVANCY

SPOTO FACTORS: ORIGINS OF 404(b)

Spoto is the leading case for all of Colorado evidence admissibility under 404(b), understanding the nature of this case and its importance is important in understanding the determination of evidence admissibility. Before a trial court may admit acts evidence under CRE 404(b) and section §16-10-301 it must analyze the admissibility of the evidence under the four part Spoto test. *People v. Snyder*, 874 P.2d 1076 (Colo. 1994). The test started out as mere factors, but over time the Supreme Court has required the test to be analyzed by the trial court in determining whether evidence is suitable for 404(b) or § 16-10-301 admittance, of similar acts under Colorado rules of evidence.

The 4-part test analysis requires trial courts to determine that;
(1) The evidence related to a material fact
(2) The evidence is logically relevant
(3) The logical evidence is independent of the intermediate inference that the defendant was acting in conformity with this bad character
(4) The evidence has probative value that is not substantially out weighed by the danger of unfair prejudice.

Factors 2 and 3 relate to 401 while 1 and 2 relate to the prohibition against the propensity inference.

The statutes below modify subsections (a) and (b) of CRE 404.

STATUTES

§ 16-10-301. Evidence of similar transactions—legislative declaration

(1) The general assembly hereby finds and declares that sexual offenses are a matter of grave statewide concern. These frequently occurring offenses are aggressive and assaultive violations of the well-being, privacy, and security of the victims, are severely contrary to common notions of proper behavior between people, and result in serious and long-lasting harm to individuals and society. These offenses often are not reported or are reported long after the offense for many reasons, including: The frequency with which the victims are vulnerable, such as young children who may be related to the perpetrator; the personal indignity, humiliation, and embarrassment involved in the offenses themselves; and the fear of further personal indignity, humiliation, and embarrassment in connection with investigation and prosecution. These offenses usually occur under circumstances in which there are no witnesses except for the accused and the victim, and, because of this and the frequent delays in reporting, there is often no evidence except for the conflicting testimony. Moreover, there is frequently a reluctance on the part of others to believe that the offenses occurred because of the inequality between the victim and the perpetrator, such as between the child victim and the adult accused, or because of the deviant and distasteful nature of the charges. In addition, it is recognized that some sex offenders cannot or will not respond to treatment or otherwise resist the impulses which motivate such conduct and that sex offenders are extremely habituated. As a result, such offenders often commit numerous offenses involving sexual deviance over many years, with the same or different victims, and often, but not necessarily, through similar methods or by common design. The general assembly reaffirms and reemphasizes that, in the prosecution of sexual offenses, including in proving the corpus delicti of such offenses, there is a greater need and propriety for consideration by the fact finder of evidence of other relevant acts of the accused, including any actions, crimes, wrongs, or transactions, whether isolated acts or ongoing actions and whether occurring prior to or after the charged offense. The general assembly finds that such evidence of other sexual acts is typically relevant and highly probative, and it is expected that normally the probative value of such evidence will outweigh any danger of unfair prejudice, even when incidents are remote from one another in time.

(2) This section applies to prosecution for any offense involving unlawful sexual behavior as defined in section 18-3-412.5(1), C.R.S., or first degree murder, as defined in section 18-3-102(1)(d), C.R.S., in which the underlying felony on which the first degree murder charge is based is the commission or attempted commission of sexual assault in the first or second degree as defined in sections 18-3-402 and 18-3-403, C.R.S., or the commission of a class 3 felony for sexual assault on a child as defined in section 18-3-405(2), C.R.S.

(3) The prosecution may introduce evidence of other acts of the defendant to prove the commission of the offense as charged for any purpose other than propensity, including: Refuting defenses, such as consent or recent fabrication; showing a common plan, scheme, design, or *modus operandi*, regardless of whether identity is at issue and regardless of

whether the charged offense has a close nexus as part of a unified transaction to the other act; showing motive, opportunity, intent, preparation, including grooming of a victim, knowledge, identity, or absence of mistake or accident; or for any other matter for which it is relevant. The prosecution may use such evidence either as proof in its case in chief or in rebuttal, including in response to evidence of the defendant's good character.

(4) If the prosecution intends to introduce evidence of other acts of the defendant pursuant to this section, the following procedures shall apply:

(a) The prosecution shall advise the trial court and the defendant in advance of trial of the other act or acts and the purpose or purposes for which the evidence is offered.

(b) The trial court shall determine by a preponderance of the evidence whether the other act occurred and whether the purpose is proper under the broad inclusionary expectations of this section.

(c) The evidence of other acts may not be admitted until the trial court finds that the prosecution has by evidence or offer of proof established a prima facie case for the charged offense.

(d) The trial court shall, at the time of the reception into evidence of other acts and again in the general charge to the jury, direct the jury as to the limited purpose or purposes for which the evidence is admitted and for which the jury may consider it.

(e) The court in instructing the jury, and the parties when making statements in the presence of the jury, shall use the words "other act or transaction" and at no time shall refer to "other offense", "other crime", or other terms with a similar connotation.

(5) The procedural requirements of this section shall not apply when the other acts are presented to prove that the offense was committed as part of a pattern of sexual abuse under section 18-3-405(2)(d), C.R.S.

Repealed and reenacted by Laws 1996, H.B.96-1181, s. 1, effective July 1, 1996.

§ 18-3-407.   Victim's and witness' prior history—evidentiary hearing—victim's identity—protective order

(1) Evidence of specific instances of the victim's or a witness's prior or subsequent sexual conduct, opinion evidence of the victim's or a witness's sexual conduct, and reputation evidence of the victim's or a witness's sexual conduct may be admissible only at trial and shall not be admitted in any other proceeding except at a proceeding pursuant to paragraph (c) of subsection (2) of this section. At trial, such evidence shall be presumed to be irrelevant except:

(a) Evidence of the victim's or witness' prior or subsequent sexual conduct with the actor;

(b) Evidence of specific instances of sexual activity showing the source or origin of semen, pregnancy, disease, or any similar evidence of sexual intercourse offered for the purpose of showing that the act or acts charged were or were not committed by the defendant.

(2) In any criminal prosecution for class 4 felony internet luring of a child, as described in section 18-3-306 (3) or under sections 18-3-402 to 18-3-405.5, 18-6-301, 18-6-302, 18-6-403, and 18-6-404, or for attempt or conspiracy to commit any of said crimes, if evidence, that is not excepted under subsection (1) of this section, of specific instances of the victim's or a witness's prior or subsequent sexual conduct, or opinion evidence of the

victim's or a witness's sexual conduct, or reputation evidence of the victim's or a witness's sexual conduct, or evidence that the victim or a witness has a history of false reporting of sexual assaults is to be offered at trial, the following procedure shall be followed:

(a) A written motion shall be made at least thirty-five days prior to trial, unless later for good cause shown, to the court and to the opposing parties stating that the moving party has an offer of proof of the relevancy and materiality of evidence of specific instances of the victim's or witness' prior or subsequent sexual conduct, or opinion evidence of the victim's or witness' sexual conduct, or reputation evidence of the victim's or witness' sexual conduct, or evidence that the victim or witness has a history of false reporting of sexual assaults that is proposed to be presented.

(b) The written motion shall be accompanied by an affidavit in which the offer of proof shall be stated.

(c) If the court finds that the offer of proof is sufficient, the court shall notify the other party of such. If the prosecution stipulates to the facts contained in the offer of proof, the court shall rule on the motion based upon the offer of proof without an evidentiary hearing. Otherwise, the court shall set a hearing to be held in camera prior to trial. In such hearing, to the extent the facts are in dispute, the court may allow the questioning of the victim or witness regarding the offer of proof made by the moving party or otherwise allow a presentation of the offer of proof, including but not limited to the presentation of witnesses.

(d) An in camera hearing may be held during trial if evidence first becomes available at the time of the trial or for good cause shown.

(e) At the conclusion of the hearing, or by written order if no hearing is held, if the court finds that the evidence proposed to be offered regarding the sexual conduct of the victim or witness is relevant to a material issue to the case, the court shall order that evidence may be introduced and prescribe the nature of the evidence or questions to be permitted. The moving party may then offer evidence pursuant to the order of the court.

(f) All motions and supporting documents filed pursuant to this section shall be filed under seal and may be unsealed only if the court rules the evidence is admissible and the case proceeds to trial. If the court determines that only part of the evidence contained in the motion is admissible, only that portion of the motion and supporting documents pertaining to the admissible portion may be unsealed.

(g) The court shall seal all court transcripts, tape recordings, and records of proceedings, other than minute orders, of a hearing held pursuant to this section. The court may unseal the transcripts, tape recordings, and records only if the court rules the evidence is admissible and the case proceeds to trial. If the court determines that only part of the evidence is admissible, only the portion of the hearing pertaining to the admissible evidence may be unsealed.

(3) (a) In a criminal prosecution including an offense described in subsection (2) of this section, the court may, at any time upon motion of the prosecution or on the court's own motion, issue a protective order pursuant to the Colorado rules of criminal procedure concerning disclosure of information relating to the victim or a witness. The court may punish a violation of a protective order by contempt of court.

(b) The victim who would be the subject of the protective order may object to the motion for a protective order.

§ 18-6-801.5.   Domestic violence—evidence of similar transactions

(1) The general assembly hereby finds that domestic violence is frequently cyclical in nature, involves patterns of abuse, and can consist of harm with escalating levels of seriousness. The general assembly therefore declares that evidence of similar transactions can be helpful and is necessary in some situations in prosecuting crimes involving domestic violence.

(2) In criminal prosecutions involving domestic violence in which the defendant and the victim named in the information have engaged in an intimate relationship as of the time alleged in the information, evidence of any other acts of domestic violence between the defendant and the victim named in the information, and between the defendant and other persons, constitute other acts or transactions for the purposes of this section, and the court may authorize the admission of evidence as provided in subsection (3) of this section.

(3) The proponent of evidence of other acts or transactions under this section shall advise the trial court by offer of proof of such evidence and shall specify whether the evidence is offered to show a common plan, scheme, design, identity, modus operandi, motive, or guilty knowledge or for some other purpose.

(4) Upon the offer of proof under subsection (3) of this section, the trial court shall determine whether the probative value of the evidence of similar acts or transactions is substantially outweighed by the danger of unfair prejudice to the defendant, confusion of the issues, or misleading of the jury if the evidence is allowed or by considerations of undue delay, waste of time, or needless presentation of cumulative evidence.

(5) Upon admitting evidence of other acts or transactions into evidence pursuant to this section and again in the general charge to the jury, the trial court shall direct the jury as to the limited purpose for which the evidence is admitted and for which the jury may consider it.

AUTHORITY

McCormick §§ 186–193 at 539–74

2 Weinstein 2d §§ 404.01–.23

1 Mueller & Kirkpatrick §§ 99–118

1 Wigmore §§ 52–81

Dopke, *Evidence: Sexual Assault and Child Molestation Cases*, 75 Denv. U. L. Rev. 929 (1998)

Larsen, *Of Propensity, Prejudice, and Plain Meaning: The Accused's Use of Exculpatory Specific Acts Evidence and the Need to Amend Rule 404(b)*, 87 Nw. U. L. Rev. 651 (1993)

Kaloyanides, *The Depraved Sexual Instinct Theory: An Example of the Propensity for Aberrant Application of Federal Rule of Evidence 404(b)*, 25 Loy. L.A. L. Rev. 1297 (1992)

Ledgerwood, *Evidence of Prior Acquitted Conduct Under Rule 404(b); Why Collateral Estoppel is No Bar in Unrelated Criminal Trial*, 44 Okla. L. Rev. 161 (1991)

Hutton, *Commentary: Prior Bad Acts Evidence in Cases of Sexual Contact with a Child*, 34 S.D. L. Rev. 604 (1989)

Ordover, *Balancing the Presumptions of Guilt and Innocence: Rules 404(B), 608(B) & 609(A)*, 38 Emory L.J. 135 (1989)

Tuerkheimer, *A Reassessment and Redefinition of Rape Shield Laws*, 50 Ohio St. L.J. 1245 (1989)

Myers, *Uncharged Misconduct Evidence in Child Abuse Litigation*, 1988 Utah L. Rev. 479 (1988)

RELEVANCY

Hearsay in Criminal Cases Under the Colorado Rules of Evidence: An Overview, 50 U. COLO. L. REV. 277 (1979)

Carroll E. Multz, *Cross-Examination in Criminal Cases*, 7 COLO. LAW. 1727 (Oct. 1978)

COMPARISON TO FEDERAL RULE

Colorado Rule 404 is substantially the same as Federal Rule 404. However, the Colorado rule includes statutory references and a notice provision that are absent from the Federal rule. Also, the Federal rule allows a prosecutor to respond to a defendant's character evidence about the victim by introducing character evidence about the defendant's same character trait, a provision not included in the Colorado rule. Please note that on Dec. 1, 2011 Federal Rule 404 was restyled. Please see Federal Rule 404 in the appendix for comparison.

On December 1, 2020, the new Federal Rule 404(b), which governs the admissibility of other crimes, wrongs, or acts of a defendant came into effect. Similarly, Colorado changed its 404(b) Rule to align directly with the new federal rule, which became effective July 1, 2021. Subsection (b) is effective July 1, 2021, for cases filed on or after July 1, 2021.

This rule is amended to provide additional notice requirements on the prosecution. The prosecution must now not only identify the evidence that it intends to offer pursuant to the rule but also articulate in the notice the permitted purpose for which the prosecutor intends to offer the evidence and the reasoning that supports the purpose. The notice must be in writing, and must be provided before trial in such time as to allow the defendant a fair opportunity to meet the evidence.

SIGNIFICANT CASES

Old Chief v. United States, 519 U.S. 172 (1997) (the court referred to the traditional rule prohibiting the inference that because a deponent committed a past crime, he is likely to have committed the charged crime).

Dowling v. United States, 493 U.S. 342 (1990) (testimony regarding a robbery of which defendant had been acquitted was admissible under FRE 404(b) in a trial for a second, unrelated robbery because the jury could "reasonably conclude" that the defendant committed the crime even if the jury did not believe so beyond a reasonable doubt; consequently, there was no violation of the double jeopardy clause).

Huddleston v. United States, 485 U.S. 681 (1988) (under FRE 404(b), the court need not make a preliminary finding that the Government has proved defendant's "other acts" consistent with Rule 104(b) before submitting the evidence to the jury).

Buell v. People, 439 P.3d 857 (Colo. 2019) (it was proper for a trial court to consolidate aggravated robbery and attempted aggravated robbery charges, since they were similar in nature and contained cross-admissible evidence. Whether these two incidents were part of a common scheme or plan was immaterial).

Bondsteel v. People, 439 P.3d 847 (Colo. 2019) (it was proper for a trial court to consolidate two charges of sexual offenses, since the evidence was cross-admissible and the facts were of the same or similar character).

People v. Elmarr, 351 P.3d 431 (Colo. 2015) (in considering the admissibility of alternative suspect evidence, the trial court must consider both relevance and probative value; "the touchstone of relevance in this context is whether the alternate suspect evidence establishes a non-speculative connection or nexus between the alternate suspect and the crime charged. Where the evidence concerns other acts by the alternate suspect, a court must look to whether all the similar acts and circumstances, taken together, support a finding that the same person probably was involved in both the other act and the charged crime.").

Perez v. People, 351 P.3d 397 (Colo. 2015) (trial court error in admitting past bad acts of the defendant with regard to one of three counts was not harmless error, because of the extreme prejudice associated with the improperly admitted evidence; proof that the defendant had four years earlier stalked a forty-two-year-old married woman was wrongly admitted to show intent in connection with a charge of enticement of a fourteen-year-old girl).

People v. Jones, 311 P.3d 274 (Colo. 2013) (in applying the *Spoto* factors, a trial court need not use the doctrine of chances; in this case two past acts of sexual assault were properly admitted because their attributes were adequately similar—they involved assaults on white women who had been drinking and who suffered facial injuries during the assaults).

People v. Luna-Solis, 298 P.3d 927 (Colo. 2013) (recognizing that sexual offences are a matter of grave state wide concern §16-10-301(1), the general assembly has specifically delineated the CRE 404(b) admissibility requirements for other acts, evidence of other acts of defendant to prove the commission of the offense as charged for any purpose other than propensity. §16-10-301(3).

Davis v. People, 310 P.3d 58 (Colo. 2013) (trial court properly allowed testimony from investigating detectives that they "didn't believe" one witness, felt another "obviously hadn't been entirely truthful," and that another's information was "true," on the theory that the testimony was offered for the limited purpose of providing "context for the detective's interrogation tactics and investigative decisions").

People v. Williams, 297 P.3d 1011 (Colo. 2012) (a single reference to a defendant's past criminality, such as a reference to the defendant's having threatened to murder someone, does not necessitate a mistrial per se).

People v. Salazar, 272 P.3d 1067 (Colo. 2012) (defendant charged with sexual assault on a child sought to show that the child's grandfather had committed the crime by introducing evidence that he had committed a similar crime against the child's mother when the mother was the age at which the victim in the current case was abused; on review of a trial court decision to allow this evidence, the Supreme Court reversed, holding that its probative value was substantially outweighed by the risk that the evidence would mislead the jury).

Kaufman v. People, 202 P.3d 542 (Colo. 2009) (trial court erroneously admitted evidence of murder defendant's possession of weapons other than the one used to kill the victim, the defendant's possession of a Kung-Fu manual, a drawing made by the defendant and captioned "kill," and the defendant's participation in two prior fights in bars, because proper application of the *Spoto/Garner* test would have shown that under the facts of the case each of these items of evidence had no allowable relevance and each had the significant risk of inviting an inference of bad character).

Yusem v. People, 210 P.3d 458 (Colo. 2009) (defendant's prior bad act of carrying a gun in a hip holster while arguing with his apartment manager did not show "a specific tendency" that could be separated from the prohibited inference that the defendant bullied before and therefore menaced in this case).

People v. Greenlee, 200 P.3d 363 (Colo. 2009) (defendant's statement of a plan to commit a crime could be admitted without violating Rule 404(b) because their relevance did not depend on an inference about the defendant's character).

Kinney v. People, 187 P.3d 548 (Colo. 2008) (when evidence is introduced showing that a defendant committed a past criminal act, evidence that the defendant had been acquitted of charges related to that act is relevant because it would make it less probable that the prior act occurred as the testifying witness has alleged that it did).

People v. Skufca, 176 P.3d 83 (Colo. 2008) (evidence of prior drug transactions the defendant had been involved in a number of hours prior to his arrest for the charged crime was properly admitted as *res gestae* evidence, since it helped the jury to understand how the defendant might have come into possession of drugs and three $100 bills).

Masters v. People, 58 P.3d 979 (Colo. 2002) (reaffirming the required four-part analysis of *Spoto* to determine admissibility of other crimes evidence).

People v. Ziglar, 45 P.3d 1266 (Colo. 2002) (because sentencing under the Habitual Criminal Statute, § 16-13-101 to 103, 6 C.R.S. (2001), was bifurcated from the trial, evidence in the sentencing phase of a second degree assault conviction was not governed by CRE 404(b)).

People v. Rath, 44 P.3d 1033 (Colo. 2002) (in case against defendant for sexual assault, prosecution

RELEVANCY

evidence of prior instances of defendant's sexual misconduct was properly admitted pursuant to CRE 404(b)).

Douglas v. People, 969 P.2d 1201 (Colo. 1998) (evidence that the defendant on prior occasions threatened people with a gun was properly admitted to show the defendant's state of mind in connection with his claim of self-defense).

People v. Cobb, 962 P.2d 944 (Colo. 1998) (testimony from a police officer that victim was seen in a parked car nine days before alleged sexual assault was relevant to impeach victim's testimony rather than to show that she was engaged in an act of prostitution).

People v. Dist. Court, 953 P.2d 184 (Colo. 1998) (where the Possession of a Weapon by a Prior Offender (POWPO) statute (C.R.S. § 18-12-108) requires the prosecution to prove the fact of a prior felony conviction, and where such evidence is so prejudicial that the jury will unlikely be able to erase it from their minds, the only remedy available to the defendant or the trial court is the trial court's cautionary instruction to the jury, irrespective of the standards set forth in CRE 403 or CRE 404(b)).

People v. Rollins, 892 P.2d 866 (Colo. 1995) (it was error to admit under a *"res gestae"* rationale evidence of uncharged sexual assaults by the defendant against a victim committed prior to the offense against that same victim for which the defendant was charged).

People v. Miller, 890 P.2d 84 (Colo. 1995) (defendant should not be allowed to introduce character evidence about his own truthfulness since "truthfulness" was not "pertinent" to the drug offense he was being tried for).

People v. Quintana, 882 P.2d 1366 (Colo. 1994) (although trial court erroneously admitted evidence under 404(b), the possibility that the evidence could have been admitted as *res gestae* would allow admission of the evidence anyway).

Hock v. New York Life Ins. Co., 876 P.2d 1242 (Colo. 1994) (evidence of fraudulent misrepresentation by insured was inadmissible. It did not show intent or plan to defraud the insurer in this case because the other insurers may have had different qualifications for disclosure).

People v. Ibarra, 849 P.2d 33 (Colo. 1993) (when a witness testified that he had no personal knowledge of the events of the night in question, it was proper for the court to limit the witness's testimony to general knowledge of the suspect's reputation for peacefulness in the community).

Harper v. People, 817 P.2d 77 (Colo. 1991) (in a trial for sexual assault on a child, an unsubstantiated newspaper report containing information about the defendant's prior conviction for sexual assault was highly prejudicial, and precluding questions in voir dire regarding potential jurors' exposure to the article constituted reversible error).

Harper v. People, 817 P.2d 77 (Colo. 1991) (in criminal case, it was error for trial court to refuse to poll jurors regarding exposure to newspaper article potentially prejudicial to the defendant; court should follow a three-step process to establish prejudice: (1) determination of the potential for unfair prejudice, (2) whether jurors had actually learned of the potentially prejudicial information, and (3) an examination of the jurors to determine if it affected their ability to decide the case fairly).

People v. Garner, 806 P.2d 366 (Colo. 1991) (prior to admission of other crimes evidence, the court must be satisfied by a preponderance of the evidence that the defendant committed the other crime).

People v. Spoto, 795 P.2d 1314 (Colo. 1990) (there is a four-part analysis to determine the admissibility of other crimes evidence: (1) whether the proffered evidence relates to a material fact; (2) whether the evidence is logically relevant; (3) whether the logical relevance of the evidence is independent of an intermediate inference that the defendant has a bad character which would be employed to suggest a probability that the defendant committed the present crime; (4) whether the probative value of the evidence is substantially outweighed by the danger of unfair prejudice).

Adrian v. People, 770 P.2d 1243 (Colo. 1989) (the statute of limitations does not govern introduction of prior incidents of sexual abuse, when it is introduced to show evidence of a plan, scheme, design, or *modus operandi* in a current sexual abuse case).

People v. Yaklich, 744 P.2d 504 (Colo. 1987) (evidence of an attorney's prior misconduct was admissible in a disciplinary proceeding to refute his testimony claiming that he regularly attended to his client's needs).

People v. Ray, 626 P.2d 167 (Colo. 1981) (evidence of burglaries committed after the charged burglary was admissible to show that all three crimes were committed as part of a continuing plan).

People v. Ferrell, 613 P.2d 324 (Colo. 1980) (defendant in a homicide case may present evidence of prior violent act of the victim if he is claiming self-defense, and there is other competent evidence to establish that the defendant knew of the victim's prior violent acts when he killed him). *See also People v. Lucero*, 714 P.2d 498 (Colo. App. 1985).

Trujillo v. People, 372 P.2d 86 (Colo. 1962) (in an insanity hearing which is held separately from the trial for the substantive offense, evidence which tends to show that a defendant was sane at the time of the offense is admissible, even if it brings with it evidence of the defendant's prior criminality, because the prejudice of this type of evidence is lessened by the separate trials). *See also People v. Bieber*, 835 P.2d 542 (Colo. App. 1992).

People v. Hamilton, 452 P.3d 184 (Colo. App. 2019) (in a sexual assault case, prior charges were admissible as evidence of modus operandi because of the similar behavior in the cases).

People v. A.W., 363 P.3d 784 (Colo. App. 2015) (Rule 404(b) does not apply to consideration of evidence showing a mother's prior dependency and neglect cases in a proceeding to determine whether a child was dependent or neglected; when relevant to the issue of whether a child would be exposed to a dangerous environment, the past conduct relates to potential parental care, not the mother's character or her conduct at any particular time).

People v. Weeks, 369 P.3d 699 (Colo. App. 2015) (to show that the defendant's daughter's death was caused by the defendant and not by an accidental contact with a stove, evidence was properly admitted showing that the defendant had in the past administered harsh discipline to another child and to pets, when that child and those pets had had urination accidents).

People v. Brown, 342 P.3d 564 (Colo. App. 2014) (in a case involving unlawful voycuristic conduct, the admission of an allegation of nonconsensual sexual contact by a witness violated the fourth prong of the *Spoto* analysis as being unfairly prejudicial to the defendant. This was due to the fact that the allegation was uncharged, it was more serious than the charged offense, and it was distinct in nature from the charged offense).

People v. Delsordo, 2014 COA 174 (Colo. App. 2014) (in an arson case, the trial court abused its discretion by admitting evidence of the defendant's prior false reports of sexual assault to show the defendant's motive to portray herself as a victim and to get attention. The court found that the defendant's prior allegations were too distinct from the arson to support the alleged motive).

People v. Trujillo, 338 P.3d 1039 (Colo. App. 2014) (In a kidnapping case, evidence related to defendant's gang affiliation involving a separate and distinct episode was admissible under the CRE 404(b) prior act standard. Court cautioned that because evidence of gang affiliation contains strong potential for bias and disfavor, evidence must be admitted with care and comply with four prong test articulated in *People v. Spoto*. Appellate court found such evidence in this case failed third prong of test, and reversed and remanded for new trial).

People v. Lahr, 316 P.3d 74 (Colo. App. 2013) (robberies committed by the defendant only hours prior to a charged robbery and a charged vehicle theft were admissible as proof of identity; adequate similarities were shown, since the perpetrator of each robbery was around six feet tall, wore a black beanie hat and longer black coat, and showed a black-handled gun near his left chest area when demanding money).

People v. Osorio-Bahena, 312 P.3d 247 (Colo. App. 2013) (the trial court abused its discretion in finding that evidence of an alleged child victim's prior sexual conduct was not relevant to show an alternative source of his sexual knowledge; the child's limited mental capacity may give rise to an inference of a lack of sexual knowledge and evidence of prior incidents may show an alternative source of sexual knowledge, regardless of whether the prosecution injects the issue into the trial).

People v. Pollard, 307 P.3d 1124 (Colo. App. 2013) (evidence of illegal drug possession after the time of the charged offense was properly admitted to show the defendant's knowledge of crack cocaine at the time of the charged offense).

People v. Everett, 250 P.3d 649 (Colo. App. 2010) (single prior incident met logical relevance prong of the *Spoto* test where evidence of a prior sexual assault fell into the same "general category" as the charged sexual assault and the frequency of two women, separated by great geographical distance, describing similar sexual incidents involving the same defendant exceeds the general population's frequency rate for such incidents).

People v. Mosley, 167 P.3d 157 (Colo. App. 2007) (trial court acted within its discretion in admitting evidence of defendant's past crimes; they demonstrated a pattern of preying upon young females in his household).

People v. Fry, 74 P.3d 360 (Colo. App. 2002) (in assault case where defendant set his girlfriend on fire evidence of other acts of domestic violence was admissible to show defendant's intent, malice, and the absence of mistake pursuant to 404(b); the probative value of the evidence was not substantially outweighed by the danger of unfair prejudice).

People v. Rivers, 70 P.3d 531 (Colo. App. 2002) (*res gestae* evidence is not subject to the procedural requirement of CRE 404(b)).

People v. Apodaca, 58 P. 3d 1126 (Colo. App. 2002) (in case against defendant for sexual assault on a child where prosecution presented evidence that defendant committed prior similar acts involving sexual assault on a child, evidence was properly admitted to establish identity, *modus operandi* and absence of mistake or accident pursuant to CRE 404(b), provided that the evidence was tested by the trial judge in compliance with the requirements set forth in *People v. Spoto*, 795 P.2d 1314, *above*).

People v. Mata, 56 P.3d 1169 (Colo. App. 2002) (pursuant to CRE 404(b) and § 16-10-301(3), C.R.S. 2002, trial judge properly allowed defendant's daughter's testimony that the defendant had sexually assaulted the daughter several times while she was a child).

People v. Warren, 55 P.3d 809 (Colo. App. 2002) (although Federal Rule 404 has been changed to require pretrial notice of intent to introduce bad act testimony, Colorado's rule has not been changed; therefore nothing in CRE 404(b) requires a pretrial notice for admission of evidence that the defendant in a drug possession trial had previously given her housemate methamphetamine).

People v. Campbell, 58 P.3d 1148 (Colo. App. 2002) (in case against defendant for securities fraud, defendant's prior convictions for theft and securities fraud were properly admitted to show "motive, intent and lack of mistake" pursuant to 404(b), and not to prove conformity with conduct; evidence of these prior convictions was also generally relevant as showing deception, which is an element of securities fraud).

People v. James, 40 P.3d 36 (Colo. App. 2001) (statements of witness that defendant asked her to participate in a check-cashing scheme, defendant gave her a false birth certificate to obtain a false identification card, and that it was defendant's idea to cut her index finger with a razor blade to disguise her fingerprint when obtaining the identification card were admissible as *res gestae* evidence since they were integral to the charges of conspiracy and contributing to the delinquency of a minor).

People v. Martinez, 36 P.3d 154 (Colo. App. 2001) (in trial for sexual assault and related crimes, trial court erred by ruling C.R.S. § 16-10-301 superseded the requirement of a *Spoto/Garner* analysis under CRE 404(b); nonetheless, because the record supported admission, trial court did not abuse its discretion by admitting evidence of defendant's two sexual assaults that had resulted in convictions and in admitting letters and an interview transcript in which he said he had committed nine instances of sexual misconduct, because they were used to counter defendant's assertion that the victim had consented or had recently fabricated her version of the events, they demonstrated that defendant knew the difference between consensual sex and "forced intercourse" or "rape," the evidence showed that defendant knew from the victim's behavior that she did not want to have sex, and the probative value was not substantially outweighed by the danger of unfair prejudice).

People v. Mack, 33 P.3d 1211 (Colo. App. 2001) (in trial for narcotics possession, admission of cash and pager was not abuse of discretion, despite suggestion defendant was a drug dealer, where trial court ruled before trial that prosecution witnesses could not testify that the items were tools of drug dealers or that the money was suspected narcotics proceeds, the challenged evidence was mentioned only twice during trial, the evidence was interwoven with the facts of the defendant's arrest and was relevant to the jury's full understanding of the events surrounding the defendant's search and arrest, the evidence reduced the likelihood that the officers had planted the cocaine on the defendant, and the evidence against the defendant was overwhelming).

People v. Masters, 33 P.3d 1191 (Colo. App. 2001) (in a sexual assault and murder case, the trial court properly admitted the defendant's narratives and drawings depicting sexually violent scenes under Rule 404(b) to show the defendant's intent, motive, knowledge, preparation, planning, identification, and opportunity to commit the crime).

People v. Duncan, 33 P.3d 1180 (Colo. App. 2001) (prior similar acts of sexual assault on a child are admissible pursuant to C.R.S. § 16-10-301 to show intent and to refute the defense of recent fabrication, and pursuant to CRE 404(b) to prove intent and absence of mistake or accident; through C.R.S. § 16-10-301, the General Assembly has delineated a policy judgment that favors admission of prior similar acts of sexual assault on a child).

People v. Cauley, 32 P.3d 602 (Colo. App. 2001) (in trial for criminally negligent child abuse, testimony of coroner and pediatrician regarding rib fractures found during the autopsy was admissible since the pediatrician used it as the basis of her opinion that the child had died as a result of shaken baby syndrome, the testimony was relevant to provide context to the coroner's observations, the evidence was not prior bad acts evidence, the experts' opinions were based upon facts reasonably relied on by experts in the medical field, and the trial court gave a limiting instruction; even though the coroner stated that he did not rely on the evidence in reaching his conclusion that the daughter had suffered from shaken baby syndrome, if the admission was erroneous it was harmless error).

People v. Davalos, 30 P.3d 841 (Colo. App. 2001) (in prosecution for theft for failing to inform the AFDC program that the defendant had inherited his mother's home, in which the defendant advanced an affirmative defense of ignorance of the need to inform the AFDC of the Florida property, the defendant's applications to the Low-income Energy Assistance Program in which he also denied receiving an inheritance were admissible as *res gestae* evidence).

People v. McGraw, 30 P.3d 835 (Colo. App. 2001) (in trial for burning vehicles of ex-girlfriend and ex-girlfriend's new boyfriend, evidence that defendant asked his new girlfriend to tell his ex-girlfriend that "she has been warned and her mother is next" was admissible to show motive to commit the crimes; finding that the defendant committed the act of making the statement was implied in the trial court's finding of admissibility).

People v. Cook, 22 P.3d 947 (Colo. App. 2000) (in a felony murder and robbery case involving robbery and killing of an individual who went to a home to provide a service, evidence of the defendant's prior similar acts, calling a massage therapist to his home and subsequently robbing and strangling her, was admissible to show intent, identity, motive, preparation or plan, and *modus operandi*).

People v. Lucas, 992 P.2d 619 (Colo. App. 1999) (evidence that murder defendant committed a burglary three days before the murder was properly admitted under the *res gestae* doctrine, since the theft was related to a plan to commit crimes to finance a trip).

People v. Silva, 987 P.2d 909 (Colo. App. 1999) (evidence that defendant, charged with reckless manslaughter in a stabbing death, had been convicted previously of stabbing a person was wrongly admitted where prosecution sought its admission on the theory that it showed the defendant had knowledge of the likely consequences of stabbing someone; the defendant was willing to stipulate to his knowledge that stabbing someone in the chest is likely to cause death, and this willingness to stipulate reduced the probative value of the past crime).

Bennett v. Greeley Gas Co., 969 P.2d 754 (Colo. App. 1998) (in a case involving a 1994 explosion, evidence of the defendant's 1987 non-compliance with a 1982 statute was not material to any of the plaintiff's injuries, and therefore not admissible).

People v. Agado, 964 P.2d 565 (Colo. App. 1998) (evidence of defendant's prior conduct during an argument the day before, and firing a weapon in the air earlier on the same night of the alleged commission of a crime, was held admissible as *res gestae* evidence; since such evidence need not meet the procedural requirements of CRE 404(b), the trial court need only find that the probative value of such evidence is not substantially outweighed by the danger of unfair prejudice).

People v. Fears, 962 P.2d 272 (Colo. App. 1997) (the defendant appealed a conviction on two counts of first degree murder arising from an effort to keep one of the murder victims from testifying against the defendant in a trial for the robbery of a cafe; the defendant sought to exclude evidence of the cafe robbery as other act evidence, and the court of appeals denied the motion because the evidence of the robbery, while separated in time from the murders by several months, was inextricably intertwined to the defendant's participation in the robbery and was part of the criminal episode and was admissible as *res gestae* evidence).

People v. Mendez, 948 P.2d 105 (Colo. App. 1997) (the arresting officer's opinion testimony regarding "track marks" (from drug use) on the defendant's arms was admitted as *res gestae* evidence and was not subject to the general rule that evidence of prior criminality is excluded absent a showing of unfair prejudice to the defendant).

Walter v. Hall, 940 P.2d 991 (Colo. App. 1996) (in a deceptive trade action subject to the provisions of the Colorado Consumer Protection Act, where the landowners disputed public access across their property, material evidence of prior acts to demonstrate the absence of mistake or accident on the part of subdivision developers was admissible).

People v. Williams, 899 P.2d 306 (Colo. App. 1995) (where defendant was originally charged in two separate cases, concerning two separate victims, but was later consolidated for trial, evidence drawn from two cases is admissible so long as it would have been admissible in separate trials).

People v. Harris, 892 P.2d 378 (Colo. App. 1994) (evidence of prior liquor store robbery committed by defendant's coconspirator is admissible against defendant to prove he possessed the knowledge and intent to rob a separate liquor store, despite the fact that it was not his past actions).

People v. Workman, 885 P.2d 298 (Colo. App. 1994) (evidence that assault car had been vandalized the night before the assault and personal belongings stolen the morning after the assault were admissible as *res gestae* evidence since these events were close enough to make them "inextricably intertwined").

People v. Leonard, 872 P.2d 1325 (Colo. App. 1993) (in sexual assault cases, evidence of prior uncharged bad acts was admissible under CRE 404(b) and C.R.S.A. 16-10-301(2) to establish motive even though the defendant claimed the motive was sexual gratification).

People v. Vega, 870 P.2d 549 (Colo. App. 1993) (even though the special offender statute, C.R.S.A. 18-18-107 (repealed), does not explicitly require a bifurcated trial, in order to avoid the prejudice associated with prior bad acts, the trial for the substantive charge and the trial to establish special offender status should be separated).

Knowles v. Bd. of Education, 857 P.2d 553 (Colo. App. 1993) (evidence of other crimes is admissible in administrative proceedings, provided that it meets the requirements set forth in CRE 404(a)).

People v. Rodriguez, 849 P.2d 799 (Colo. App. 1992) (portions of DMV records relating to the revocation of the defendant's license were admissible when they were offered to prove elements of the charge of driving on a suspended license, not bad character, and the trial court excised the portions relating to the defendant's alcohol offenses, so that the jury would not be prejudiced).

Munson v. Boettcher & Co., 832 P.2d 967 (Colo. App. 1992) (CRE 404(b) applies to civil cases as well as criminal cases).

People v. Hulsing, 825 P.2d 1027 (Colo. App. 1991) (in homicide cases involving spouses, anything relating to the ill-feelings, jealousy, violence, or threats, or any similar conduct is relevant to show motive and malice. However, it cannot be overly prejudicial).

Southerland v. Argonaut Ins. Co., 794 P.2d 1102 (Colo. App. 1990) (evidence of an insurer's regular late payment of checks was admissible for the purpose of demonstrating an ongoing pattern of purposeful delays in a suit for breach of good faith in processing a claim against the insurer).

People v. Duncan, 754 P.2d 796 (Colo. App. 1988) (the fact that the defendant committed the prior act must be shown by clear and convincing evidence before prior acts evidence is admissible).

People v. Fulton, 754 P.2d 398 (Colo. App. 1987) (evidence that one week prior to the charged offense of felony child abuse, the defendant had forced a sock into the mouth of the crying infant was admissible as showing lack of accident in the present case).

People v. Jackson, 748 P.2d 1326 (Colo. App. 1987) (prior insufficient funds checks were admissible to show lack of mistake in a trial for theft by writing insufficient funds checks).

O'Neal v. Reliance Mortg. Corp., 721 P.2d 1230 (Colo. App. 1986) (successive testimony of housing loan applicants, whose actions were joined to challenge a delay in processing, was inadmissible similar transaction evidence, which is not permissible to show negligence. It was, however, admissible to show the defendant's intent to defraud).

People v. Lucero, 720 P.2d 604 (Colo. App. 1985) (evidence of the defendant's drug addiction and evidence of his possession of drugs similar to those taken in the burglary in question was admissible to show identity and motive).

People v. Manners, 713 P.2d 1348 (Colo. App. 1985) (prior crimes evidence was inadmissible as irrelevant to establish motive or intent when offered to show that another party's guilt excluded the defendant's guilt, when the defendant was an accomplice or accessory).

People v. Holder, 687 P.2d 462 (Colo. App. 1984) (the fact that similar transactions followed rather than preceded the charged offenses did not render it inadmissible, provided that the court properly instructed the jury as to the limited purpose for which the evidence was admitted).

People v. Marin, 686 P.2d 1351 (Colo. App. 1983) (defendant was precluded from asking prosecution witness about what kind of person the defendant was when the questioning was outside the scope of the direct examination. However, the defense could have called this witness as their own, so the defendant was not denied his right to present evidence in his own defense).

People v. Lucero, 677 P.2d 370 (Colo. App. 1983) (once a pertinent character trait has been raised by the defense on direct, it is subject to cross-examination by the prosecution, even if the evidence would be considered inadmissible character evidence).

People v. Curtis, 657 P.2d 990 (Colo. App. 1982) (in an assault case, a prior attack by the defendant on the victim was admissible as evidence of intent because it showed malice and ill-will toward the victim).

People v. Alward, 654 P.2d 327 (Colo. App. 1982) (when an expert testifies as to the defendant's mental state, and bases his decision on the defendant's conduct, it is permissible for the prosecution to ask whether that opinion is affected by other examples of the defendant's conduct not previously known by the expert).

People v. Casper, 631 P.2d 1134 (Colo. App. 1981) (in a robbery trial, evidence of another robbery committed by the defendant a few days earlier, at the same time of day, was admissible for the express purpose of proving identity. The fact that there was not an unbroken sequence of acts between the two crimes was immaterial).

People v. Sasson, 628 P.2d 120 (Colo. App. 1980) (a defendant who chooses to testify may be impeached through the introduction of prior felony convictions, but not prior misdemeanor convictions, nor may his general character be attacked).

People v. Heredia-Cobos, 415 P.3d 860 (Colo. App. 2017) (in a sexual assault case when applying the Spoto test for admissibility of similar crime evidence under 404(b) the age differences of past victims was overcome by other similarities in the past and current acts such as all victims were family members and all acts happened in the defendants' home).

People v. Stewart, 417 P.3d 882 (Colo. App. 2017) (evidence that the defendant hid from the police in a past incident amounted to impermissible character evidence when used to determine if the defendant knew the police were chasing him in the present case).

People v. Salas, 405 P.3d 446 (Colo. App. 2017) (admission of inadmissible testimony of ambiguous reference to past criminal activity of the defendant was harmless error).

People v. Fortson, 421 P.3d 1236, 2018 Colo. App. LEXIS 484 (Colo. App. 2018) (failure of a prosecutor in a sexual assault case to give notice of intent to submit evidence of defendant's prior sexual assaults is a violation of CRS 16-10-301, and is grounds for reversal).

Zapata v. People, 428 P.3d 517 (Colo. 2018) although the CRE makes no reference to the common law term "res gestae", the Supreme Court of Colorado continues to apply the common law doctrine of "res gestae" which it defines as including "evidence of another offense, which is related to the charge on trial, that helps to 'provide the fact-finder with a full and complete understanding of the events surrounding the crime and the context in which the charged crime occurred' ").

Chapter 405

Rule 405. Methods of Proving Character

Rule 405 reads as follows:

> **(a) Reputation or opinion.** In all cases in which evidence of character or a trait of character of a person is admissible, proof may be made by testimony as to reputation or by testimony in the form of an opinion. On cross-examination, inquiry is allowable into relevant specific instances of conduct.
>
> **(b) Specific instances of conduct.** Except as limited by §§ 16-10-301 and 18-3-407, in cases in which character or a trait of character of a person is an essential element of a charge, claim or defense, proof may also be made of specific instances of that person's conduct.

ANALYSIS

Rule 405 provides the methodology for proving character where it is determined that character evidence is admissible under Rule 404. Rule 405 recognizes three devices for proving a person's character or character trait. First, reputation within a pertinent community may be used to establish circumstantially the character of an individual. Second, a person familiar with the character of an individual may provide opinion testimony as to the character in question. Third, specific instances of conduct may be offered to establish the character of an individual.

The use of a particular methodology depends upon the way in which character is used in conjunction with the issues of a case. Where character is "in issue," all methodologies of proving character are available. Where character is used circumstantially to establish conforming conduct, only reputation and opinion evidence are available. Where, however, character evidence is utilized to impeach the credibility of a witness, methodology of proof is governed by Rule 608 and C.R.S. § 13-90-101.

Character or character traits are established through a character witness. A person qualifies as a character witness where he is a member of some pertinent community in which the person characterized is known, and where the character witness has been a member of that community for a reasonably extensive period of time. Both of these elements must be established through a foundation in the course of the preliminary examination of the character witness. The character witness must also know the reputation of the person characterized and be prepared to testify to such reputation within the pertinent community. Reputation is the collective opinion of persons within the pertinent community. Rule 405 also provides that the character witness may respond to questions as to the character witness's personal opinion of the individual who is characterized.

Consistent with Rule 701, the character witness is permitted to testify to his personal opinion of the existence of the pertinent trait.

Illustration

Embezzlement trial.

Q: Are you acquainted with the defendant, Mr. Bowman?

A: Yes.

Q: Please state the basis for your acquaintance.

A: I have worked with him at the downtown branch of the Mega Bank Corp. for twelve years.

Q: And during that time, have you had an opportunity to become familiar with Mr. Bowman's reputation for trustworthiness in the downtown banking community?

A: I have.

Q: What is his reputation?

A: He is known to be an honest and trustworthy person.

Q: During the twelve years you have known Mr. Bowman, have you had an opportunity to observe him in situations in which you would be able to determine his trustworthiness?

A: I have.

Q: And as a consequence, have you developed a personal opinion as to Mr. Bowman's trustworthiness?

A: Yes.

Q: What is that opinion?

A: It is my opinion that Mr. Bowman is honest and trustworthy.

It should be noted that in the rare situation where character is "in issue," specific instances of conduct of the person characterized may be proven in order to establish the person's character or character traits. Character is in issue when it constitutes an element of a claim, charge or defense. Specific instances of conduct may be proven through a character witness or through the testimony of any person who has first-hand knowledge of the relevant specific acts of the person characterized.

Rule 405(a) also governs the cross-examination of the character witness. On cross-examination of a character witness, the witness may be asked about specific instances of conduct of the person characterized which are pertinent to the trait being considered. The question on cross-examination may be asked in the traditional form which provides that the cross-examiner may ask: "Have you heard that Mr. X was terminated from his job in May of 1989 because of embezzlement?" Alternately, the cross-examiner may use the more contemporary form: "Do you know that Mr. X was terminated from his job in May of 1989 because of embezzlement?"

Take Notice

Both C.R.S. 18-3-407 and 16-10-301 which govern victim's and witness's prior history and evidence of similar transaction, respectfully, also apply to the methods of proving character C.R.E. 405. These rules govern character evidence that is not admissible and can be referenced under Rule 404.

AUTHORITY

WEISSENBERGER'S FEDERAL EVIDENCE §§ 405.1–.6

MCCORMICK § 191 at 566

2 WEINSTEIN 2d §§ 405.01–.05

1 MUELLER & KIRKPATRICK §§ 119–122

7 WIGMORE §§ 1981–86

Slough, *Relevancy Unraveled—Part II, Character and Habit Evidence*, 5 U. KAN. L. REV. 404, 415–20 (1957)

Curran, *Expert Psychiatric Evidence of Personality Traits*, 103 U. PA. L. REV. 999 (1955)

Hearsay in Criminal Cases Under the Colorado Rules of Evidence: An Overview, 50 U. COLO. L. REV. 277 (1979)

COMPARISON TO FEDERAL RULE

In substance, Colorado Rule 405 is identical to Federal Rule 405 except for statutory limitation. However, on Dec. 1, 2011 Federal Rule 405 was restyled. Please see Federal Rule 405 in the appendix for comparison.

SIGNIFICANT CASES

Lombardi v. Graham, 794 P.2d 610 (Colo. 1990) (opinion evidence of character under Rule 405(a) is not a conduit through which otherwise inadmissible specific instances of misconduct may be brought before the jury).

People v. Ferrell, 613 P.2d 324 (Colo. 1980) (evidence of prior violent acts by the victim was admissible only if the defendant knew of the victim's prior violence at the time of the homicide).

People v. Miller, 981 P.2d 654 (Colo. App. 1998) (evidence regarding a victim's homosexuality can be introduced through reputation or opinion evidence to prove a pertinent character trait if that trait is an essential element of a charge, claim, or defense; however, specific acts of the victim's sexual orientation were not admissible where they did not prove an element of the defendant's self-defense claim).

People v. Erickson, 883 P.2d 511 (Colo. App. 1994) (trial court's refusal to admit evidence of victim's rumored sexual orientation was not reversible error since rumor, unlike reputation, does not constitute competent evidence).

People v. Hardy, 677 P.2d 429 (Colo. App. 1983) (when a defendant testifies, the trial court may not foreclose the use of the name, date, or nature of his prior felony convictions for impeachment purposes. Further details of prior convictions are within the trial court's discretion.).

People v. Johnson, 671 P.2d 1017 (Colo. App. 1983) (evidence of victim's prior virginity in rape case was not improper).

People v. Renstrom, 657 P.2d 461 (Colo. App. 1982) (it is permissible for the district attorney to prove prior felony convictions as bearing upon a witness's credibility).

Chapter 406

Rule 406. Habit; Routine Practice

Rule 406 reads as follows:

> Evidence of the habit of a person or of the routine practice of an organization, whether corroborated or not and regardless of the presence of eyewitnesses, is relevant to prove that the conduct of the person or organization on a particular occasion was in conformity with the habit or routine practice.

ANALYSIS

Rule 406 governs the admissibility of the habit of a natural person and the routine practice of a business or organization. Habits of persons and the routine practices of businesses are equivalent in concept for the operation of Rule 406.

Rule 406 essentially serves two functions. First, the Rule confirms the relevancy of habit or routine practice when used to establish conduct which conforms with the habit or routine practice. In this regard, Rule 406 is dissimilar from most other evidentiary Rules in Article IV. It is essentially a rule of admissibility rather than inadmissibility. Its function is declaratory in light of any confusion that might have been engendered by pre-Rule case law. The second function of Rule 406 is to confirm that the admissibility of habit or routine practice is not affected by the absence of eyewitnesses or corroboration. Again, the Rule is declaratory.

Habit evidence is normally used in the stimulus-response format. The proponent of habit evidence usually seeks to establish that a habitual response occurred on a particular occasion. In order to establish such a conclusion, the proponent must first establish that the habit, in fact, exists.

Proof of the existence of a habit is normally effected through the testimony of a person who has first-hand knowledge of the individual or business whose habit is sought to be proven. The witness must testify that he is familiar with the person or business, and that practice of meeting a particular kind of situation with a response that approaches invariability. Alternately and additionally, the witness may testify that he has observed the person or business conform to the habit on several occasions.

Illustration

A party might seek to establish that an individual punched a time clock on a particular day. The proponent of such a consequential fact could offer testimony from the individual or other witnesses that the individual punched the time clock on the day in question. Such testimony would be based upon the first-hand knowledge of these witnesses. In addition, however, the proponent may wish to offer habit evidence to reinforce the testimony of the witnesses. In order to establish the conclusion indicated by the habit evidence, the proponent would first have to establish the existence of the habit of the individual to invariably punch the time clock when he or she arrived at work. Then the proponent of the evidence would establish that the individual in fact arrived at work on the particular day in question. The evidence having established that the individual arrived on the day in question, the operation of the habit rule would permit the inference that the individual punched the time clock on the particular day in question. The use of habit evidence creates a permissible, but not a mandatory inference that the habitual conduct occurred. In other words, the trier of fact may find that the habitual response occurred, but it is not required to make such a finding.

After establishing the existence of the habit, the proponent of the evidence then submits evidence that would prove that the stimulus for the response occurred on a particular occasion. Such stimulus can be established through any witness possessing first-hand knowledge as required by Rule 602. Having established the habit and the stimulus, the response will be inferentially indicated by the habit rule.

AUTHORITY

WEISSENBERGER'S FEDERAL EVIDENCE §§ 406.1–406.4

MCCORMICK § 195

2 WEINSTEIN 2d §§ 406.01–.06

2 MUELLER & KIRKPATRICK §§ 123–126

1 WIGMORE §§ 92–97

Lewan, *Rationale of Habit Evidence*, 16 SYRACUSE L. REV. 39 (1964)

Slough, *Relevancy Unraveled*, 5 U. KAN. L. REV. 404, 444–5 (1957)

Note, *Relevancy and its Limits in the Proposed Rules of Evidence*, 16 WAYNE L. REV. 167, 179–182 (1969)

COMPARISON TO FEDERAL RULE

In substance, Colorado Rule 406 and Federal 406 are identical. However, on Dec. 1, 2011 Federal Rule 406 was restyled. Please see Federal Rule 406 in the appendix for comparison.

SIGNIFICANT CASES

Columbia Sav. v. Zelinger, 794 P.2d 231 (Colo. 1990) (the normal business practice of the bank was allowed to show the intent of the parties not to cancel a note but that it was rolled over into a larger loan).

Denver Tramway Co. v. Owens, 20 Colo. 107, 36 P. 848 (1894) (recognized the admissibility of evidence of habit to show an individual probably acted in a certain way).

People v. Trujillo, 369 P.3d 693 (Colo. App. 2015) (testimony that an alleged victim never gave others her credit card was properly admitted as evidence of her habitual conduct in the circumstance of having others make purchases for her, and was not improper character evidence showing a general trait such as carefulness).

Great Western Sugar Co. v. Northern Natural Gas Co., 661 P.2d 684 (Colo. App. 1982) (evidence of course of dealing and course of performance is admissible if it does not directly contradict the terms of a written agreement, but merely explains or supplements it).

Chapter 407

Rule 407. Subsequent Remedial Measures

Rule 407 reads as follows:

> When after an event, measures are taken which, if taken previously, would have made the event less likely to occur, evidence of the subsequent measures is not admissible to prove negligence or culpable conduct in connection with the event. This rule does not require the exclusion of evidence of subsequent measures when offered for another purpose, such as proving ownership, control, or feasibility of precautionary measures, if controverted, or impeachment.

ANALYSIS

Rule 407 excludes evidence of subsequent remedial actions where such actions would be offered to prove negligence or any type of culpable conduct in connection with the event which caused the injury. Virtually any kind of subsequent corrective action is within the scope of Rule 407. The Rule is not directed only to the repair of a mechanical device after that device causes personal injury. The Rule is sufficiently broad to apply to the discharge of an employee subsequent to an accident or to a change in product design. As a basic principle, the Rule will apply to any measure, which if taken prior to the accident, would have made the injury less likely to occur.

As the second sentence of Rule 407 indicates, exclusion of evidence of subsequent remedial measures is only required where the evidence is offered to prove negligence or culpable conduct. The Colorado Supreme Court has specifically held that CRE 407, unlike Federal Rule 407, does not apply to strict liability claims based on design defects. This means that under CRE 407, evidence of subsequent remedial measures may be admitted to show a design defect in strict liability cases. Evidence of subsequent remedial action may be offered to establish other relevant issues within a case, such as ownership, control, or feasibility of precautionary measures. In order for such corrective actions to be admissible, the issue must be generally controverted in the case and the remedial action must be probative of the controverted consequential fact.

Illustration
Subsequent to an accident at a construction site, one of the subcontractors erects a barrier around the instrumentality of the injury. Where there is a dispute as to which subcontractor was responsible for the instrumentality of the injury, such action by a particular subcontractor would be probative of ownership or control. Under these facts, the subsequent remedial

measure may be admissible on a theory other than to show negligence or culpability.

Where the subsequent remedial action is only minimally probative of an issue other than negligence or culpability, the trial judge possesses discretion to exclude the evidence of the corrective action on the basis of prejudice, confusion of the issues, or misleading the jury. *See* Rule 403. The trial judge should provide a limiting instruction pursuant to Rule 105 where evidence of remedial action is admitted on a theory of relevance outside the forbidden inferential pattern prohibited by the first sentence of Rule 407.

STATUTES

§ 13-21-404.   Inadmissible evidence

In any product liability action, evidence of any scientific advancements in technical or other knowledge or techniques, or in design theory or philosophy, or in manufacturing or testing knowledge, techniques, or processes, or in labeling, warnings of risks or hazards, or instructions for the use of such product, where such advancements were discovered subsequent to the time the product in issue was sold by the manufacturer, shall not be admissible for any purpose other than to show a duty to warn.

AUTHORITY

WEISSENBERGER'S FEDERAL EVIDENCE §§ 407.1–.5

McCORMICK § 275 at 815–18

2 WEINSTEIN 2d §§ 407.01–.10

2 MUELLER & KIRKPATRICK §§ 127–133

2 WIGMORE § 283

Gonzalez, *Rule 407: Evidence of Subsequent Remedial Measures in Strict Liability Cases*, 28 COLO. LAW. 47 (1999)

Fincham, *Federal Rule of Evidence 407 and Its State Variations: The Courts Perform Some Subsequent Remedial Measures of Their Own in Products Liability Cases*, 49 UMKC L. REV. 388 (1981)

Twerski, *Post-Accident Design Modification Evidence in Manufacturing Defect Setting: Strict Liability and Beyond*, 4 J. PROD. LIAB. 143 (1981)

Kaminsky, *Post Transaction Evidence in Securities Litigation*, 19 B.C. L. REV. 617 (1978)

Comment, *Chart v. General Motors Corp.: Did It Chart the Way for Admission of Evidence of Subsequent Remedial Measures in Products Liability Actions?*, 41 OHIO ST. L.J. 211 (1980)

COMPARISON TO FEDERAL RULE

Colorado Rule 407 and Federal Rule 407 are similar, but differ in one important aspect. Federal Rule 407 bars evidence of subsequent remedial measures if offered to prove "negligence, culpable conduct, a defect in a product, a defect in a product's design, or a need for a warning or instruction," but Colorado Rule 407 only bars that type of evidence when it is offered to prove "negligence or culpable conduct." Please note that on Dec. 1, 2011 Federal Rule 407 was restyled. Please see Federal Rule 407 in the appendix for comparison.

SIGNIFICANT CASES

Rimkus v. Nw. Colorado Ski Corp., 706 F.2d 1060 (10th Cir. 1983) (if defendant alleges contributory negligence on the part of plaintiff, evidence of subsequent remedial measures may be admissible on the issue of contributory negligence).

Forma Scientific v. Biosera, 960 P.2d 108 (Colo. 1998) (in a strict liability products case, evidence of defendant's subsequent remedial actions to modify an on/off switch to their freezers in order to protect medical contents from being destroyed is admissible; the evidence was relevant to understanding the nature of the challenged design, and its probative value outweighed possible unfair prejudice to defendant).

White v. Caterpillar, Inc., 867 P.2d 100 (Colo. App. 1993) (evidence of the defendant's subsequent remedial measure did not create danger of unfair prejudice sufficient to outweigh the probative value; it was admissible impeachment evidence where the defense at trial was that a safety device would have a hazard).

Martinez v. W.R. Grace Co., 782 P.2d 827 (Colo. App. 1989) (evidence that defendant painted the bump shortly after plaintiff's accident was admissible, not as an admission of negligence on defendant's part, but as relevant upon the issue of the difference in color at the time of the accident and to impeach the testimony of the defendant's safety manager upon this issue).

Vallejo v. Eldridge, 764 P.2d 417 (Colo. App. 1988) (evidence was admissible as to subsequent remedial measures when offered for purposes of impeachment).

Martinez v. Atlas Bolt & Screw Co., 636 P.2d 1287 (Colo. App. 1981) (evidence of subsequent repairs is generally inadmissible to prove negligence, except in product liability context. Evidence of subsequent repairs is allowed in products liability cases).

RELEVANCY

Chapter 408

Rule 408. Compromise and Offers to Compromise

Rule 408 reads as follows:

> **(a) Prohibited uses.** Evidence of the following is not admissible on behalf of any party, when offered to prove liability for, invalidity of, or amount of a claim that was disputed as to validity or amount, or to impeach through a prior inconsistent statement or contradiction:
>
> *(1)* furnishing or offering or promising to furnish accepting or offering or promising to accept a valuable consideration in compromising or attempting to compromise the claim; and
>
> *(2)* conduct or statements made in compromise negotiations regarding the claim, except when offered in a criminal case and the negotiations related to a claim by a public office or agency in the exercise of regulatory, investigative, or enforcement authority.
>
> **(b) Permitted uses.** This rule does not require exclusion if the evidence is offered for purposes not prohibited by subdivision (a). Examples of permissible purposes include proving a witness's bias or prejudice; negating a contention of undue delay; and proving an effort to obstruct a criminal investigation or prosecution.

RELEVANCY

ANALYSIS

Rule 408 operates to exclude evidence relating to an offer of compromise or to a completed compromise. Rule 408 also excludes evidence of conduct or statements made during the course of compromise negotiations. It should be noted that the exclusionary principle of Rule 408 does not apply where a dispute does not exist as to liability or the amount of the claim. The Rule cannot be invoked where settlement discussions relate to an amount that is admittedly due. The amount of the claim must be in dispute, or alternatively, liability for the claim must be contested in order for the exclusionary principle to apply.

Rule 408 excludes evidence of compromise negotiations only where such evidence is offered to establish liability for, or invalidity of a claim or its amount. The principle of exclusion does not operate when compromise-related evidence is used to establish some other fact of consequence in the litigation. For example, evidence of statements during the course of settlement discussions are not made inadmissible by Rule 408 where the statements are offered to establish bias or prejudice of a witness, or where offered to show an effort to obstruct a criminal investigation or prosecution.

AUTHORITY

WEISSENBERGER'S FEDERAL EVIDENCE §§ 408.1–.6

McCORMICK § 274

2 WEINSTEIN 2d §§ 408.01–.10

2 MUELLER & KIRKPATRICK §§ 134–138

4 WIGMORE § 1061

Michaels, *Rule 408: A Litigation Minefield*, 19 LITIG. 34 (1992)

Brazil, *Protecting the Confidentiality of Settlement Negotiations*, 39 HASTINGS L.J. 955 (1988)

Note, *Rule 408 and Erie: The Latent Conflict*, 12 GA. L. REV. 275 (1978)

Slough, *Relevancy Unraveled—Part III: Remote and Prejudicial Evidence*, 5 U. KAN. L. REV. 657 (1957)

Falknor, *Extrinsic Policies Affecting Admissibility*, 10 RUTGERS L. REV. 574 (1956)

COMPARISON TO FEDERAL RULE

In substance, Colorado Rule 408 is the same as Federal Rule 408. However, on Dec. 1, 2011 Federal Rule 408 was restyled. Please see Federal Rule 408 in the appendix for comparison.

SIGNIFICANT CASES

Kritikos v. Palmer Johnson, Inc., 821 F.2d 418 (7th Cir. 1987) (trial court erred in admitting letters by one party proposing a compromise solution).

City of Aurora v. ACJ P'ship (In re Application for Water Rights of the City of Aurora), 209 P.3d 1076 (Colo. 2009) (evidence of potential negotiations of a joint agreement to use disputed water storage sites is prohibited to support the inference that an adversary party can and will gain access by way of an agreement).

American Guar. & Liab. Ins. Co. v. King, 97 P.3d 161 (Colo. App. 2003) (mediation communications enjoy greater protections than settlement communications under CRE 408, but opinion of mediator was admissible for limited purpose of establishing prior knowledge).

Genova v. Longs Peak Emergency Physicians, P.C., 72 P.3d 454 (Colo. App. 2003) (in a case about wrongful discharge, breach of contract and breach of fiduciary duty, where defense introduced testimony to certain portions of a settlement letter that trial court excluded under 408, the trial court determination "that the purpose of the testimony was to rebut a contention that defendants acted in a willful and wanton manner with regard to terminating plaintiff, which was relevant to plaintiff's request for punitive damages" and that such testimony was in " 'passing reference' on the sixth day of trial" and "did not create sufficient prejudice to warrant a mistrial" "was neither manifestly arbitrary, unreasonable or unfair, and thus, will not be disturbed on review").

H & H Distributors, Inc. v. BBC Int'l, Inc., 812 P.2d 659 (Colo. App. 1990) (even where letter may constitute an admission of fact, it is excludable if the admission was made in a letter offering to settle the dispute).

Aaron v. Marcove, 685 P.2d 268 (Colo. App. 1984) (the court found that the statement in contention was not made during settlement negotiations and the statement was properly admitted).

People v. Butson, 410 P.3d 744 (Colo. App. 2017) (statements made to a detective by a defendant in a criminal case providing information concerning the crime in hopes for leniency for his co-defendant sons are not protected from disclosure at trial under CRE 408).

Chapter 409

Rule 409. Payment of Medical and Similar Expenses

Rule 409 reads as follows:

> Evidence of furnishing or offering or promising to pay medical, hospital, or similar expenses occasioned by an injury is not admissible to prove liability for the injury.

ANALYSIS

Rule 409 functions to exclude evidence of the furnishing, or the offering, or the promising to pay medical, hospital or similar expenses occasioned by an injury where the evidence is offered to establish liability for the injury or harm. Rule 409 does not, however, render inadmissible conduct or statements, which are part of the act of furnishing, or offering, or promising to pay expenses.

Whenever an express admission of liability arises in conjunction with an offer to pay medical expenses, the trial judge should make an effort to sever any aspect of the statement, which relates to the payment of medical expenses. The express admission of liability is admissible, whereas any offers to pay medical expenses would be insulated from admissibility by Rule 409.

Unlike Rule 408 relating to compromises, Rule 409 does not expressly address the question of whether evidence relating to the payment of medical expenses is admissible to establish issues other than liability. Nevertheless, it is clear that Rule 409 only limits admissibility where the evidence of the payment or offer of payment is directed to liability. Such evidence may be used to establish other consequential facts.

AUTHORITY

Weissenberger's Federal Evidence §§ 409.1–409.4

McCormick § 275 at 815–19

2 Weinstein 2d §§ 409.01–.03

2 Mueller & Kirkpatrick §§ 139–141

2 Wigmore § 283(a) at 159–60

Annotation, *Admissibility of Evidence Showing Payment, or Offer or Promise of Payment, of Medical, Hospital, and Similar Expenses of Injured Party by Opposing Party*, 65 A.L.R.3d 932 (1975)

COMPARISON TO FEDERAL RULE

In substance, Colorado Rule 409 is identical to Federal Rule 409. However, on Dec. 1, 2011 Federal Rule 409 was restyled. Please see Federal Rule 409 in the appendix for comparison.

SIGNIFICANT CASES

Pennington v. Sears, Roebuck & Co., 878 P.2d 152 (Colo. App. 1994) (offers to pay medical expenses cannot be entered into court as proof of mental anguish or aggravation of an injury).

Chapter 410

Rule 410. Offer to Plead Guilty; Nolo Contendere; Withdrawn Pleas of Guilty

Rule 410 reads as follows:

> Except as otherwise provided by statutes of the State of Colorado, evidence of a plea of guilty, later withdrawn, or a plea of *nolo contendere*, or of an offer to plead guilty or *nolo contendere* to the crime charged or any other crime, or of statements made in any connection with any of the foregoing pleas or offers, is not admissible in any civil or criminal action, case, or proceeding against the person who made the plea or offer. This rule shall not apply to the introduction of voluntary and reliable statements made in court on the record in connection with any of the foregoing pleas or offers where offered for impeachment purposes or in a subsequent prosecution of the declarant for perjury or false statement.
>
> This rule shall be superseded by any amendment to the Colorado Rules of Criminal Procedure which is inconsistent with this rule, and which takes effect after the effective date of these Colorado Rules of Evidence.

ANALYSIS

Rule 410 insulates from admissibility certain pleas and certain statements made in conjunction with the plea bargaining process. Rule 410 renders inadmissible any evidence of the following in any criminal or civil proceedings when offered against the person who made the plea or offer: (1) a plea of guilty that was later withdrawn; (2) an admission of the charge that was later withdrawn; (3) a plea of *nolo contendere*; (4) an offer to make such a plea to the crime charged or any other crime; (5) any statements made in the course of the foregoing pleas or offers.

Rule 410 further provides that statements otherwise rendered inadmissible under the Rule are nevertheless admissible when offered in a criminal proceeding for perjury or false statement if the statement was made by the defendant under oath, on the record, and in the presence of counsel.

AUTHORITY

WEISSENBERGER'S FEDERAL EVIDENCE §§ 410.1–.5

McCORMICK § 265

2 WEINSTEIN 2d §§ 410.01–.11

2 MUELLER & KIRKPATRICK §§ 142–151

4 WIGMORE §§ 1066–67

Note, *Evidence—Guilty Plea Not Admissible in Subsequent Civil Suit Based Upon the Same Occurrences*, 24 KAN. L. REV. 193 (1975)

Hearsay in Criminal Cases Under the Colorado Rules of Evidence: An Overview, 50 U. COLO. L. REV. 277 (1979)

COMPARISON TO FEDERAL RULE

Colorado Rule 410 is modeled after Federal Rule 410. The Colorado rule makes explicit provision for use of statements for impeachment purposes, thus allowing greater use of such statements than would be permissible under the Federal rule. Please note that on Dec. 1, 2011 Federal Rule 410 was restyled. Please see Federal Rule 410 in the appendix for comparison.

SIGNIFICANT CASES

United States v. Mezzanatto, 513 U.S. 196 (1995) (an agreement to waive the exclusionary provisions of Rule 410 and Federal Rule of Criminal Procedure 11(c)(6) held valid and enforceable absent some affirmative indication that defendant entered the agreement unknowingly or involuntarily).

People v. Rios, 338 P.3d 495 (Colo. App. 2014) (a court's instruction that a witness had "entered into an agreement to testify as a condition of a guilty plea related to his conduct in this case" was error because the guilty plea of a codefendant may not be used as substantive evidence of a defendant's guilt. The court further erred by not instructing the jury to limit the testimony for impeachment purposes).

People v. Rabes, 258 P.3d 937 (Colo. App. 2010) (defendant pled guilty in Federal Court to charges of child pornography. In State Court trial of sexual child assault charges, it was proper to admit statements made during sentencing in Federal Court.).

People v. Garcia, 169 P.3d 223 (Colo. App. 2007) (where a defendant underwent a polygraph examination because a prosecutor had stated that on the basis of the examination it would be determined what type of plea might be accepted, the examination was in the context of plea negotiations, and Rule 410 prohibits introduction of statements made during the examination).

People v. Martinez, 36 P.3d 154 (Colo. App. 2001) (where defendant requested consideration for his pending charges in another county in exchange for the information he was providing to an officer, but the officer refused to discuss the charges and told him that any consideration would be up to defendant, his attorney, and the prosecuting attorney, defendant's subsequent statements to officers were admissible; defendant's unilateral choice to provide information to those who had no authority to conduct plea negotiations failed to transform his statements into disclosures made "in any connection with" any offers to plead guilty).

People v. Copenhaver, 21 P.3d 413 (Colo. App. 2000) (defendant's written statements regarding a rejected plea agreement, found to have been voluntary and reliable, were properly allowed to be used by the prosecution for impeachment purposes).

People v. Butler, 929 P.2d 36 (Colo. App. 1996) (a defendant's statements to a prosecutor and police investigator, made after his guilty plea had been accepted, were admissible in a subsequent trial after the defendant moved to withdraw his plea; the plea agreement did not bar such use, and the statements were voluntary when made).

People v. Flores, 902 P.2d 417 (Colo. App. 1994) (defendant's pro se letter to county court stating his desire not to contest the charges against him, while unartfully drafted, constituted an offer to plead *nolo contendere*, and therefore was improperly admitted).

People v. Rollins, 759 P.2d 816 (Colo. App. 1988) (spontaneous statements made by an arrestee to an officer other than a prosecuting attorney are not inadmissible "plea negotiations").

Chapter 411

Rule 411. Liability Insurance

Rule 411 reads as follows:

> Evidence that a person was or was not insured against liability is not admissible upon the issue whether he acted negligently or otherwise wrongfully. This rule does not require the exclusion of evidence of insurance against liability when offered for another purpose, such as proof of agency, ownership, or control, or bias or prejudice of a witness.

ANALYSIS

Rule 411 provides that the fact that a person was or was not insured against liability is not admissible in order to establish negligent or wrongful conduct by the individual. The Rule is designed to minimize unfair prejudice relating to the consideration of liability insurance. On one hand, the probative value of liability insurance is exceedingly low regarding issues of liability. On the other hand, the risks of prejudice are extremely high.

The exclusionary principle of Rule 411 applies by its express terms to the fault of a defendant and to the possible contributory negligence or other fault of a plaintiff. Also, it should be noted that Rule 411 specifically excludes evidence of not only the existence, but also the non-existence of insurance where such evidence is offered to establish negligence or wrongful conduct.

The exclusionary operation of Rule 411 applies only where liability insurance is offered to establish negligence or culpability. Where liability insurance is offered to establish some other consequential fact, the exclusionary principle will not prevent the admissibility of the evidence. As the second sentence to Rule 411 confirms, evidence of liability insurance is admissible where offered to prove some other fact such as agency, ownership or control, or to establish the bias or prejudice of a witness.

> *Illustration*
>
> Where a defendant claims that he is not the owner of a vehicle that was involved in an automobile accident, evidence that the defendant had purchased insurance for that vehicle may be admissible as tending to establish the fact that he owned the vehicle or had sufficient control over it to be liable for its use. If such evidence were admitted, it would be subject to a limiting instruction under Rule 105.

RELEVANCY

AUTHORITY

WEISSENBERGER'S FEDERAL EVIDENCE §§ 411.1–.4

MCCORMICK § 201

2 WEINSTEIN 2d §§ 411.01–.06

2 MUELLER & KIRKPATRICK §§ 152–154

2 WIGMORE § 282

Fournier, *Pre-Trial Discovery of Insurance Coverage and Limits*, 28 FORDHAM L. REV. 215 (1959)

Laverci, *Disclosure of Insurance Policy Limits*, 1957 INS. L.J. 505 (1957)

Slough, *Relevancy Unraveled, Part III—Remote and Prejudicial Evidence*, 5 U. KAN. L. REV. 675, 710–18 (1957)

Stopher, *Should a Change be Made in Discovery Rules to Permit Inquiry as to Limits of Liability Insurance?*, 35 INS. COUNSEL J. 53 (1968)

COMPARISON TO FEDERAL RULE

In substance, Colorado Rule 411 and Federal Rule 411 are identical, except for the gender pronoun. However, on Dec. 1, 2011 Federal Rule 411 was restyled. Please see Federal Rule 411 in the appendix for comparison.

SIGNIFICANT CASES

Bonser v. Shainholtz, 3 P.3d 422 (Colo. 2000) (evidence that expert witness in dental malpractice case was insured by the same entity that insured defendant is admissible when offered to show that the witness is biased if there is a substantial connection between the expert witness and the insurance entity; witness's possible financial losses if defendant lost case were significant, since insurance group had only about 1,500 members, and additional evidence showed that witness was a founder of the insurance group).

Prudential Prop. & Cas. Ins. Co. v. Dist. Court, 617 P.2d 556 (Colo. 1980) (evidence of a party's liability insurance is irrelevant to the question of whether he acted negligently or otherwise, and as such, any allusion to insurance coverage is improper).

Chapter 412

Rule 412. *(No Colorado Rule Codified)*
The topic of proof of an alleged sex crime victim's past sexual conduct is treated under Rule 404. The applicable statute governing this type of evidence and its admissibility, C.R.S. 18-3-407, is provided is full under Rule 404

ANALYSIS

Although there is no Colorado Rule 412, C.R.S. § 18-3-407 roughly tracks Federal Rule 412, and is therefore considered here.

C.R.S. § 18-3-407 provides that opinion and reputation evidence of a victim's and witness' prior or subsequent sexual conduct shall be presumed to be irrelevant except for evidence of the victim's and witness' prior or subsequent sexual conduct with the alleged actor and evidence of specific instances of sexual activity offered for the purpose of showing the source of the semen or pregnancy.

The Colorado Supreme Court has held that the basic purpose of the statute is to protect sexual assault victims from embarrassing and humiliating "fishing expeditions" into their past sexual conduct without a particularized showing of relevancy at a preliminary *in camera* hearing. Evidence that the victim has a past history of false reporting of sexual assaults may also be shown. A motion to introduce evidence of past sexual history under the statute must be filed 30 days prior to trial unless good cause is shown for a waiver of this requirement.

Unlike Federal Rule 412, C.R.S. § 18-3-407 has no "savings" provision for a subsequent finding of unconstitutionality. Thus far, however, the statute has withstood constitutional attack under the confrontation clause and under the Colorado Constitution.

In 1992, the Committee on Rules of Practice and Procedure of the Judicial Conference of the United States circulated a proposed revision of Federal Rule 412. This revision purports to promote clarity in the rule, as well as extend its provisions to all criminal and civil cases. In May of 1994, Congress considered the enactment of additional Federal Rules 413, 414, and 415 which would permit the introduction in certain circumstances of the past sexual history of a defendant in sexual assault cases. These proposed rules have triggered considerable controversy.

To date, however, no similar proposals have yet been enacted under Colorado law. It should be noted, however, that C.R.S. § 16-10-301 (see Statutes, below) provides that in sexual assault cases, the prosecution may under certain circumstances introduce evidence of similar acts of the defendant for the purpose of showing a common plan, scheme, design, identity, *modus operandi*, motive, guilty knowledge, or intent. *See* Chapter 404.

AUTHORITY

WEISSENBERGER'S FEDERAL EVIDENCE §§ 412.1–412.7

2 WEINSTEIN 2d §§ 412.01–.05

Boyce & McCloskey, *Legal Application of Standard Laboratory Test for the Identification of Seminal Fluid*, 7 J. CONTEMP. L. 1 (1982)

Churchwell, *The Constitutional Right To Present Evidence: Progeny of Chambers v. Mississippi*, 19 CRIM. L. BUL. 131 (1983)

Tanford v. Bocchino, *Rape, Victim Shield Laws and the Sixth Amendment*, 128 U. PA. L. REV. 244 (1980)

Comment, *Federal Rule of Evidence 412: Was the Change an Improvement?*, 49 U. CIN. L. REV. 244 (1980)

Annotation, *Constitutionality of "Rape Shield" Statute, Restricting Use of Evidence of Victim's Sexual Experience*, 1 A.L.R.4th 283 (1980)

Hearsay in Criminal Cases Under the Colorado Rules of Evidence: An Overview, 50 U. COLO. L. REV. 277 (1979)

SIGNIFICANT CASES

Olden v. Kentucky, 488 U.S. 227 (1988) (where consent was the issue in a rape case, court erred in not admitting a black defendant's evidence that the white victim was living with a black man, and that the rape claim may have been an attempt to protect that relationship).

Pierson v. People, 279 P.3d 1217 (Colo. 2012) (evidence that an eight-year-old alleged victim of sexual abuse had been abused by someone other than the defendant was outside the coverage of § 407(1)(b) even though it was characterized by the defendant as a source of precocious knowledge; it was also outside the coverage of § 407(2)(e) because the defendant failed to introduce evidence about the sexual sophistication of the alleged victim or other children of her age).

People v. MacLeod, 176 P.3d 75 (Colo. 2008) (rape shield statute precludes introduction of evidence that mother of alleged victim had stated she had suffered sexual abuse as a child, even though the proponent of the evidence argued that it would be introduced only to show that the mother had made the claim and not to show that she had actually been the victim of abuse).

People v. Weiss, 133 P.3d 1180 (Colo. 2006) (the exception in the rape shield law for proof of prior false reports applies only when the proponent of evidence shows that the prior reports were in fact false; evidence that charges did not result from an alleged victim's prior reports is not sufficient to establish that they were false).

People v. Melillo, 25 P.3d 769 (Colo. 2001) (during trial of defendant for sexual assault of his stepdaughter, trial court did not abuse its discretion by excluding a portion of defendant's statement to an investigator explaining his odd behavior upon being discovered by the victim's mother alone in a bedroom with the victim as due to a "big deal in the house" because of the victim's sexual abuse by a babysitter when she was three years old, even though the court admitted a portion of the statement in which the defendant said he had acted suspiciously because he realized "how it must look"; the probative value of the proffered evidence was substantially outweighed by the risk of prejudice to the victim).

People ex rel. K.N., 977 P.2d 868 (Colo. 1999) (rape shield statute requires exclusion of testimony showing that alleged victim had a reputation for sexual promiscuity, despite claim by rape defendant that his knowledge of that reputation was relevant to his belief that she had consented to sexual intercourse; statute also bars admission of evidence that alleged victim had had sexual intercourse with individuals other than the defendant prior to the time of the alleged rape, even if she had lied about that prior conduct, since her past sexual conduct is collateral to the relevant issues at trial).

People v. Martinez, 634 P.2d 26 (Colo. 1981) (evidence of specific instances of sexual activity offered to show source of semen is not precluded by the statutory presumption of irrelevance or by the provision for an *in camera* hearing).

People v. McKenna, 585 P.2d 275 (Colo. 1978), *accord*, *People v. Johnson*, 671 P.2d 1017 (Colo. App. 1983) (statute does not violate Confrontation Clause or the Colorado Constitution since there is no constitutional right to introduce irrelevant and highly inflammatory evidence).

People v. Garcia, 179 P.3d 250 (Colo. App. 2007) (prior sexual contact with the actor exception in the rape shield statute should have been interpreted to allow admission of evidence that the alleged victim and defendant had engaged in bondage and acted out a rape fantasy prior to the defendant's alleged assault of the victim, particularly because evidence was admitted showing that the defendant had threatened the victim with a knife and then bound her hands and feet).

People v. Strean, 74 P.3d 387 (Colo. App. 2002) (pursuant to § 13-25-129, C.R.S. 2002, which permits child hearsay statements in sexual offense cases if the court finds sufficient safeguards of reliability, court's decision in sexual assault case to admit child hearsay statements was not an abuse of discretion where court applied all the standards under the statute for determining reliability).

People v. Gholston, 26 P.3d 1 (Colo. App. 2000) (rape shield statute, C.R.S. § 18-3-407, disallows evidence of prior or subsequent illegal sexual conduct perpetrated by an alleged victim of such conduct).

People v. Aldrich, 849 P.2d 821 (Colo. App. 1992) ("prior sexual conduct" includes prior sexual assaults; *applied in People v. Meis*, 837 P.2d 258 (Colo. App. 1992)).

People v. Vialpando, 804 P.2d 219 (Colo. App. 1990) (defendant held not to have established right to obtain name of person with whom sexual assault victim had sexual relations days before the date of alleged sexual assault).

People v. Moreno, 739 P.2d 866 (Colo. App. 1987) (evidence of past sexual history of victim not relevant to show defendant's state of mind at time of alleged attack).

People v. Wilson, 678 P.2d 1024 (Colo. App. 1984) (credibility of a victim may be attacked by a showing of past history of making false accusations; reference to past sexual history in a victim's diary may be deleted after victim relies on diary to pinpoint the date of the alleged offense; *see also* denial of certiorari in *Wilson v. Sly*, 469 U.S. 843 (1984)).

RELEVANCY

V
PRIVILEGES

PRIVILEGES

Chapter 501

Rule 501. Privileges Recognized Only as Provided

Rule 501 reads as follows:

Except as otherwise required by the Constitution of the United States, the Constitution of the State of Colorado, statutes of the State of Colorado, rules prescribed by the Supreme Court of the State of Colorado pursuant to constitutional authority, or by the principles of the common law as they may be interpreted by the courts of the State of Colorado in light of reason and experience, no person has a privilege to:

(1) Refuse to be a witness; or

(2) Refuse to disclose any matter; or

(3) Refuse to produce any object or writing; or

(4) Prevent another from being a witness or disclosing any matter or producing any object or writing.

ANALYSIS

Rule 501 recognizes privileges provided by constitution, statute, court rules and common law. In addition to Rule 501, other Evidence Rules are pertinent to privileges. Rules 104 and 1101 relate to procedural aspects of the application of privilege laws. Rule 1101 sets forth the broad applicability of privilege law by providing in subsection (c) that "The rule with respect to privileges applies at all stages of all actions, cases and proceedings." Rule 104 provides that the question as to whether a privilege exists in a given situation is a preliminary question to be determined by the trial court. In making its determination, as well as making the determination as to all preliminary questions of admissibility, the court remains bound by the rules and statutes with respect to privilege even though it is not bound at this stage by other evidentiary rules.

In understanding privilege law, it should be appreciated that a privilege is essentially a personal right to preserve the confidentiality of certain private communications. Inadmissibility is an incidental and derivative ramification of this right. Consequently, privilege law is anchored in considerations of policy that exist independently of the usual evidentiary concerns with accuracy and reliability of evidence.

A privilege may involve a refusal to testify, a refusal to disclose a matter during the discovery stage of litigation, a refusal to produce real proof, or the right to prevent other persons from doing any of these things. A privilege permits a person to resist any judicial or governmental process aimed at eliciting protected information. As such, it is the only right that relieves an individual from the duty of revealing facts in response to governmental or judicial process and from the corollary risk of contempt for failure to respond.

Privileges generally only apply to privileged communications. In this regard, the protected status applies to oral or written communications. It may additionally extend in certain instances to nonverbal actions and to knowledge gained by means of observation. As a further qualification, privileges generally attach only to communications made in confidence. Consequently, a privilege will not apply where confidentiality is compromised by a showing that the communication was made in the presence of a third person who was not essential to the transaction or communication. Nevertheless, presence of third persons who were essential to the communication will not destroy confidentiality.

The basic elements of Colorado's privilege law are set forth in a statute defining "particular relations in which it is the policy of the law to encourage confidence and to preserve it inviolate." C.R.S. § 13-90-107. The statute shields certain communications made within specified confidential relationships. The main relationships it covers are: husband and wife; attorney and client; clergyman and individual communicating in the course of the religious body's expected discipline; medical personnel and patient; public officer and individual communicating in a context in which the public interest is served by confidentiality; certified public accountant and client; psychologist, counselor, therapist or social worker and client; victim's advocate and victim. It should be noted that while C.R.S. § 13-90-107, provides for relationships that prohibit admittance of certain types of testimony, there are some statutes that express the importance of when certain privileges will not attach to certain communications. One such example is C.R.S. § 13-21-117, which discusses the duty warn and provides for an exception to physician-patient privilege. A newsperson's privilege is provided for in C.R.S. § 13-90-119. The full texts of these statutes are shown below.

Rules of privilege should be distinguished from two other doctrines. The first of these is Rule 601 governing competency. While both privilege and competency involve limitations on who may testify and the subject matter of testimony, these distinct concepts approach the subject from entirely different policies. Competency, on one hand, generally concerns the reliability of witnesses. Privilege, on the other hand, precludes the introduction of possibly reliable testimony due to extrinsic policy considerations directed toward protecting certain confidential relationships. Privilege should also be distinguished from the work product doctrine set forth in Civil Procedure Rule 26(b)(3) and Criminal Procedure Rule 16(I)(e)(1). This doctrine may operate to shield from discovery the attorney's work product generated in anticipation of litigation. Its design is to preserve the adversary nature of our judicial system, a policy distinguishable from that supporting the protection of confidential relationships.

SELECTED INCORPORATED STATUTES

§ 13-90-107.   Who may not testify without consent

(1)   There are particular relations in which it is the policy of the law to encourage confidence and to preserve it inviolate; therefore, a person shall not be examined as a witness in the following cases:

(a) (I) Except as otherwise provided in section 14-13-310(4), C.R.S., a husband shall not be examined for or against his wife without her consent nor a wife for or against her husband without his consent; nor during the marriage or afterward shall either be examined without the consent of the other as to any communications made by one to the other during the marriage; but this exception does not apply to a civil action or proceeding by one against the other, a criminal action or proceeding for a crime committed by one against the other, or a criminal action or proceeding against one or both spouses when the alleged offense occurred prior to the date of the parties' marriage. However, this exception shall not attach if the otherwise privileged information is communicated after the marriage.

(II) The privilege described in this paragraph (a) does not apply to class 1, 2, or 3 felonies as described in section 18-1.3-401(1)(a)(IV) and (1)(a)(V), C.R.S. In this instance, during the marriage or afterward, a husband shall not be examined for or against his wife as to any communications intended to be made in confidence and made by one to the other during the marriage without his consent, and a wife shall not be examined for or against her husband as to any communications intended to be made in confidence and made by one to the other without her consent.

(III) Communications between a husband and wife are not privileged pursuant to this paragraph (a) if such communications are made for the purpose of aiding the commission of a future crime or of a present continuing crime.

(IV) The burden of proving the existence of a marriage for the purposes of this paragraph (a) shall be on the party asserting the claim.

(V) Notice of the assertion of the marital privilege shall be given as soon as practicable but not less than ten days prior to assertion at any hearing.

(a.5) (I) Except as otherwise provided in section 14-13-310(5), C.R.S., a partner in a civil union shall not be examined for or against the other partner in the civil union without the other partner's consent, nor during the civil union or afterward shall either be examined without the consent of the other as to any communications made by one to the other during the civil union; except that this exception does not apply to a civil action or proceeding by one against the other, a criminal action or proceeding for a crime committed by one against the other, or a criminal action or proceeding against one or both partners when the alleged offense occurred prior to the date of the parties' certification of the civil union. However, this exception shall not attach if the otherwise privileged information is communicated after the certification of the civil union.

(II) The privilege described in this paragraph (a.5) does not apply to class 1, 2, or 3 felonies as described in section 18-1.3-401(1)(a)(IV) and (1)(a)(V), C.R.S. In this instance, during the civil union or afterward, a partner in a civil union shall not be examined for or against the other partner in the civil union as to any communications intended to be made in confidence and made by one to the other during the civil union without the other partner's consent.

(III) Communications between partners in a civil union are not privileged pursuant to this paragraph (a.5) if such communications are made for the purpose of aiding the commission of a future crime or of a present continuing crime.

(IV) The burden of proving the existence of a civil union for the purposes of this paragraph (a.5) shall be on the party asserting the claim.

(V) Notice of the assertion of the privilege described in this paragraph (a.5) shall be given as soon as practicable but not less than ten days prior to assertion at any hearing.

(VI) For the purposes of this paragraph (a.5), "partner in a civil union" means a person who has entered into a civil union established in accordance with the requirements of article 15 of title 14, C.R.S.

(b) An attorney shall not be examined without the consent of his client as to any communication made by the client to him or his advice given thereon in the course of professional employment; nor shall an attorney's secretary, paralegal, legal assistant, stenographer, or clerk be examined without the consent of his employer concerning any fact, the knowledge of which he has acquired in such capacity.

(c) A clergy member, minister, priest, or rabbi shall not be examined without both his or her consent and also the consent of the person making the confidential communication as to any confidential communication made to him or her in his or her professional capacity in the course of discipline expected by the religious body to which he or she belongs.

(d) A physician, surgeon, or registered professional nurse duly authorized to practice his profession pursuant to the laws of this state or any other state shall not be examined without the consent of his patient as to any information acquired in attending the patient which was necessary to enable him to prescribe or act for the patient, but this paragraph (d) shall not apply to:

(I) A physician, surgeon, or registered professional nurse who is sued by or on behalf of a patient or by or on behalf of the heirs, executors, or administrators of a patient on any cause of action arising out of or connected with the physician's or nurse's care or treatment of such patient;

(II) A physician, surgeon, or registered professional nurse who was in consultation with a physician, surgeon, or registered professional nurse being sued as provided in subparagraph (I) of this paragraph (d) on the case out of which said suit arises;

(III) A review of a physician's or registered professional nurse's services by any of the following:

(A) The governing board of a hospital licensed pursuant to part 1 of article 3 of title 25, C.R.S., where said physician or registered professional nurse practices or the medical staff of such hospital if the medical staff operates pursuant to written bylaws approved by the governing board of such hospital;

(B) An organization authorized by federal or state law or contract to review physicians' or registered professional nurses' services or an organization which reviews the cost or quality of physicians' or registered professional nurses' services under a contract with the sponsor of a nongovernment group health care program;

(C) The Colorado medical board, the state board of nursing, or a person or group authorized by such board to make an investigation in its behalf;

(D) A peer review committee of a society or association of physicians or registered professional nurses whose membership includes not less than one-third of the medical doctors or doctors of osteopathy or registered professional nurses licensed to practice in this state and only if the physician or registered professional nurse whose services are the subject of review is a member of such society or association and said physician or registered professional nurse has signed a release authorizing such review;

(E) A committee, board, agency, government official, or court to which appeal may be taken from any of the organizations or groups listed in this subparagraph (III);

(IV) A physician or any health care provider who was in consultation with the physician who may have acquired any information or records relating to the services performed by the physician specified in subparagraph (III) of this paragraph (d);

(V) A registered professional nurse who is subject to any claim or the nurse's employer subject to any claim therein based on a nurse's actions, which claims are required to be defended and indemnified by any insurance company or trust obligated by contract;

(VI) A physician, surgeon, or registered professional nurse who is being examined as a witness as a result of his consultation for medical care or genetic counseling or screening pursuant to section 13-64-502 in connection with a civil action to which section 13-64-502 applies.

(e) A public officer shall not be examined as to communications made to him in official confidence, when the public interests, in the judgment of the court, would suffer by the disclosure.

(f) (I) A certified public accountant shall not be examined without the consent of his or her client as to any communication made by the client to him or her in person or through the media of books of account and financial records or his or her advice, reports, or working papers given or made thereon in the course of professional employment; nor shall a secretary, stenographer, clerk, or assistant of a certified public accountant be examined without the consent of the client concerned concerning any fact, the knowledge of which he or she has acquired in such capacity.

(II) No certified public accountant in the employ of the state auditor's office shall be examined as to any communication made in the course of professional service to the legislative audit committee either in person or through the media of books of account and financial records or advice, reports, or working papers given or made thereon; nor shall a secretary, clerk, or assistant of a certified public accountant who is in the employ of the state auditor's office be examined concerning any fact, the knowledge of which such secretary, clerk, or assistant acquired in such capacity, unless such information has been made open to public inspection by a majority vote of the members of the legislative audit committee.

(III) (A) Subpoena powers for public entity audit and reviews. Subparagraph (I) of this paragraph (f) shall not apply to the Colorado state board of accountancy, nor to a person or group authorized by the board to make an investigation on the board's behalf, concerning an accountant's reports, working papers, or advice to a public entity that relate to audit or review accounting activities of the certified public accountant or certified public accounting firm being investigated.

(B) For the purposes of this subparagraph (III), a "public entity" shall include a governmental agency or entity; quasi-governmental entity; nonprofit entity; or public company that is considered an "issuer", as defined in section 2 of the federal "Sarbanes-Oxley Act of 2002", 15 U.S.C. sec. 7201.

(IV) (A) Subpoena powers for private entity audit and reviews. Subparagraph (I) of this paragraph (f) shall not apply to the Colorado state board of accountancy, nor to a person or group authorized by the board to make an investigation on the board's behalf, concerning an accountant's reports or working papers of a private entity that is not publicly traded and relate to audit or review attest activities of the certified public accountant or certified public accounting firm being investigated. This subparagraph (IV) shall not be construed to authorize the Colorado state

PRIVILEGES

board of accountancy or its agent to subpoena or examine income tax returns.

(B)   At the request of either the client of the certified public accountant or certified public accounting firm or the certified public accountant or certified public accounting firm subject to the subpoena pursuant to this subparagraph (IV), a second certified public accounting firm or certified public accountant with no interest in the matter may review the report or working papers for compliance with the provisions of article 2 of title 12, C.R.S. The second certified public accounting firm or certified public accountant conducting the review must be approved by the board prior to beginning its review. The approval of the second certified public accounting firm or certified public accountant shall be in good faith. The written report issued by a second certified public accounting firm or certified public accountant shall be in lieu of a review by the board. Such report shall be limited to matters directly related to the work performed by the certified public accountant or certified public accounting firm being investigated and should exclude specific references to client financial information. The party requesting that a second certified public accounting firm or certified public accountant review the reports and working papers shall pay any additional expenses related to retaining the second certified public accounting firm or certified public accountant by the party who made the request. The written report of the second certified public accounting firm or certified public accountant shall be submitted to the board. The board may use the findings of the second certified public accounting firm or certified public accountant as grounds for discipline pursuant to article 2 of title 12, C.R.S.

(V) Disclosure of information under subparagraph (III) or (IV) of this paragraph (f) shall not waive or otherwise limit the confidentiality and privilege of such information nor relieve any certified public accountant, any certified public accounting firm, the Colorado state board of accountancy, or a person or group authorized by such board of the obligation of confidentiality. Disclosure which is not in good faith of such information shall subject the board, a member thereof, or its agent to civil liability pursuant to section 12-2-103(6), C.R.S.

(VI) Any certified public accountant or certified public accounting firm that receives a subpoena for reports or accountant's working papers related to the audit or review attest activities of the accountant or accounting firm pursuant to subparagraph (III) or (IV) of this paragraph (f) shall notify his or her client of the subpoena within three business days after the date of service of the subpoena.

(VII) Subparagraph (III) or (IV) of this paragraph (f) shall not operate as a waiver, on behalf of any third party or the certified public accountant or certified public accounting firm, of due process remedies available under the "State Administrative Procedure Act", article 4 of title 24, C.R.S., the open records laws, article 72 of title 24, C.R.S., or any other provision of law.

(VIII) Prior to the disclosure of information pursuant to subparagraph (III) or (IV) of this paragraph (f), the certified public accountant, certified public accounting firm, or client thereof shall have the opportunity to designate reports or working papers related to the attest function under subpoena as privileged and confidential pursuant to this paragraph (f) or the open records laws, article 72 of title 24, C.R.S., in order to assure that the report or working papers shall not be disseminated or otherwise republished and shall only be reviewed pursuant to limited authority granted to the board under subparagraph (III) or (IV) of this paragraph (f).

(IX) No later than thirty days after the board of accountancy completes the investigation for which records or working papers are subpoenaed pursuant to subparagraph (III) or (IV) of this paragraph (f), the board shall return all original records, working papers, or copies thereof to the certified public accountant or certified public accounting firm.

(X) Nothing in subparagraphs (III) and (IV) of this paragraph (f) shall cause the accountant-client privilege to be waived as to customer financial and account information of depository institutions or to the regulatory examinations and other regulatory information relating to depository institutions.

(XI) For the purposes of subparagraphs (III) to (X) of this paragraph (f), "entity" shall have the same meaning as in section 7-90-102(20), C.R.S.

(g) A licensed psychologist, professional counselor, marriage and family therapist, social worker, or addiction counselor, a registered psychotherapist, or a certified addiction counselor shall not be examined without the consent of the licensee's, certificate holder's, or registrant's client as to any communication made by the client to the licensee, certificate holder, or registrant or the licensee's, certificate holder's, or registrant's advice given in the course of professional employment; nor shall any secretary, stenographer, or clerk employed by a licensed psychologist, professional counselor, marriage and family therapist, social worker, or addiction counselor, a registered psychotherapist, or a certified addiction counselor be examined without the consent of the employer of the secretary, stenographer, or clerk concerning any fact, the knowledge of which the employee has acquired in such capacity; nor shall any person who has participated in any psychotherapy, conducted under the supervision of a person authorized by law to conduct such therapy, including group therapy sessions, be examined concerning any knowledge gained during the course of such therapy without the consent of the person to whom the testimony sought relates.

(h) A qualified interpreter, pursuant to section 13-90-202, who is called upon to testify concerning the communications he interpreted between a hearing-impaired person and another person, one of whom holds a privilege pursuant to this subsection (1), shall not be examined without the written consent of the person who holds the privilege.

(i) A confidential intermediary, as defined in section 19-1-103 (26), C.R.S., shall not be examined as to communications made to him or her in official confidence when the public interests, in the judgment of the court, would suffer by the disclosure of such communications.

(j) (I) (A) If any person or entity performs a voluntary self-evaluation, the person, any officer or employee of the entity or person involved with the voluntary self-evaluation, if a specific responsibility of such employee was the performance of or participation in the voluntary self-evaluation or the preparation of the environmental audit report, or any consultant who is hired for the purpose of performing the voluntary self-evaluation for the person or entity may not be examined as to the voluntary self-evaluation or environmental audit report without the consent of the person or entity or unless ordered to do so by any court of record, or, pursuant to section 24-4-105, C.R.S., by an administrative law judge.

For the purposes of this paragraph (j), "voluntary self-evaluation" and "environmental audit report" have the meanings provided for the terms in section 13-25-126.5 (2).

(B) This paragraph (j) does not apply if the voluntary self-evaluation is subject to an exception allowing admission into evidence or discovery pursuant to the provisions of section 13-25-126.5 (3) or (4).

(II) This paragraph (j) applies to voluntary self-evaluations that are performed on or after June 1, 1994.

(k) (I) A victim's advocate shall not be examined as to any communication made to such victim's advocate by a victim of domestic violence, as defined in section 18-6-800.3(1), C.R.S., or a victim of sexual assault, as described in sections 18-3-401 to 18-3-405.5, 18-6-301, and 18-6-302, C.R.S., in person or through the media of written records or reports without the consent of the victim.

(II) For purposes of this paragraph (k), a "victim's advocate" means a person at a battered women's shelter or rape crisis organization or a comparable community-based advocacy program for victims of domestic violence or sexual assault and does not include an advocate employed by any law enforcement agency:

(A) Whose primary function is to render advice, counsel, or assist victims of domestic or family violence or sexual assault; and

(B) Who has undergone not less than fifteen hours of training as a victim's advocate or, with respect to an advocate who assists victims of sexual assault, not less than thirty hours of training as a sexual assault victim's advocate; and

(C) Who supervises employees of the program, administers the program, or works under the direction of a supervisor of the program.

(l) (I) A parent may not be examined as to any communication made in confidence by the parent's minor child to the parent when the minor child and the parent were in the presence of an attorney representing the minor child, or in the presence of a physician who has a confidential relationship with the minor child pursuant to paragraph (d) of this subsection (1), or in the presence of a mental health professional who has a confidential relationship with the minor child pursuant to paragraph (g) of this subsection (1), or in the presence of a clergy member, minister, priest, or rabbi who has a confidential relationship with the minor child pursuant to paragraph (c) of this subsection (1). The exception may be waived by express consent to disclosure by the minor child who made the communication or by failure of the minor child to object when the contents of the communication are demanded. This exception does not relieve any physician, mental health professional, or clergy member, minister, priest, or rabbi from any statutory reporting requirements.

(II) This exception does not apply to:

(A) Any civil action or proceeding by one parent against the other or by a parent or minor child against the other;

(B) Any proceeding to commit either the minor child or parent, pursuant to title 27, C.R.S., to whom the communication was made;

(C) Any guardianship or conservatorship action to place the person or property or both under the control of another because of an alleged mental or physical condition of the minor child or the minor child's parent;

(D) Any criminal action or proceeding in which a minor's parent is charged with a crime committed against the communicating minor child, the parent's spouse, the parent's partner in a civil union, or a minor child of either the parent or the parent's spouse or the parent's partner in a civil union;

(E) Any action or proceeding for termination of the parent-child legal relationship;

(F) Any action or proceeding for voluntary relinquishment of the parent-child legal relationship; or

(G) Any action or proceeding on a petition alleging child abuse, dependency or neglect, abandonment, or non-support by a parent.

(III) For purposes of this paragraph (l):

(A) "Minor child" means any person under the age of eighteen years.

(B) "Parent" includes the legal guardian or legal custodian of a minor child as well as adoptive parents.

(C) "Partner in a civil union" means a person who has entered into a civil union in accordance with the requirements of article 15 of title 14, C.R.S.

(m) (I) A law enforcement or firefighter peer support team member shall not be examined without the consent of the person to whom peer support services have been provided as to any communication made by the person to the peer support team member under the circumstances described in subparagraph (III) of this paragraph (m); nor shall a recipient of individual peer support services be examined as to any such communication without the recipient's consent.

(II) For purposes of this paragraph (m):

(A) "Communication" means an oral statement, written statement, note, record, report, or document, made during, or arising out of, a meeting with a peer support team member.

(A.5) "Emergency medical service provider or rescue unit peer support team member" means an emergency medical service provider, as defined in section 25-3.5-103(8), C.R.S., a regular or volunteer member of a rescue unit, as defined in section 25-3.5-103(11), C.R.S., or other person who has been trained in peer support skills and who is officially designated by the supervisor of an emergency medical service agency as defined in section 25-3.5-103(11.5), C.R.S., or a chief of a rescue unit as a member of an emergency medical service provider's peer support team or rescue unit's peer support team.

(B) "Law enforcement or firefighter peer support team member" means a peace officer, civilian employee, or volunteer member of a law enforcement agency or a regular or volunteer member of a fire department or other person who has been trained in peer support skills and who is officially designated by a police chief, the chief of the Colorado state patrol, a sheriff, or a fire chief as a member of a law enforcement agency's peer support team or a fire department's peer support team.

(III) The provisions of this paragraph (m) shall apply only to communications made during individual interactions conducted by a peer support team member:

(A) Acting in the person's official capacity as a law enforcement or firefighter peer support team member; and

(B) Functioning within the written peer support guidelines that are in effect for the person's respective law enforcement agency or fire department.

(IV) This paragraph (m) shall not apply in cases in which:

(A) A law enforcement or firefighter peer support team member was a witness or a party to an incident which prompted the delivery of peer support services;

(B) Information received by a peer support team member is indicative of actual or suspected child abuse, as described in section 18-6-401, C.R.S., or actual or suspected child neglect, as described in section 19-3-102, C.R.S.;

(C) Due to alcohol or other substance intoxication or abuse, as described in sections 25-1-310 and 25-1-1106, C.R.S., the person receiving peer support is a clear and immediate danger to the person's self or others;

(D) There is reasonable cause to believe that the person receiving peer support has a mental illness and, due to the mental illness, is an imminent threat to himself or herself or others or is gravely disabled as defined in section 27-10-102, C.R.S.; or

(E) There is information indicative of any criminal conduct.

(2) The medical records produced for use in the review provided for in subparagraphs (III), (IV), and (V) of paragraph (d) of subsection (1) of this section shall not become public records by virtue of such use. The identity of any patient whose records are so reviewed shall not be disclosed to any person not directly involved in such review process, and procedures shall be adopted by the state board of medical examiners or state board of nursing to ensure that the identity of the patient shall be concealed during the review process itself.

(3) The provisions of paragraph (d) of subsection (1) of this section shall not apply to physicians required to make reports in accordance with section 12-36-135, C.R.S. In addition, the provisions of paragraphs (d) and (g) of subsection (1) of this section shall not apply to physicians or psychologists eligible to testify concerning a criminal defendant's mental condition pursuant to section 16-8-103.6, C.R.S. Physicians and psychologists testifying concerning a criminal defendant's mental condition pursuant to section 16-8-103.6, C.R.S., do not fall under the attorney-client privilege in paragraph (b) of subsection (1) of this section.

§ 13-21-117.   Civil Liability-mental health providers-duty to warn

(1) As used in this section, unless the context otherwise requires:

(a) "Mental health provider" means a physician, social worker, psychiatric nurse, psychologist, or other mental health professional, or mental health hospital, community mental health center or clinic, institution, or their staff

(b) "Psychiatric nurse" means a registered professional nurse as defined in section 12-38-103(11), C.R.S., who by virtue of post graduate education and additional nursing preparation has gained knowledge, judgment, and skill in psychiatric or mental health nursing.

(2) (a) A mental health provider is not liable for damages in any civil action for failure to warn or protect a specific person or persons, including those identifiable by their association with a specific location or entity, against the violent behavior of a person

receiving treatment from the mental health provider, and any such mental health provider must not be held civilly liable for failure to predict such violent behavior except where the patient has communicated to the mental health provider a serious threat of imminent physical violence against a specific person or persons, including those identifiable by their association with a specific location or entity.

(b) When there is a duty to warn and protect under the provisions of paragraph (a) of this subsection (2), the mental health provider shall make reasonable and timely efforts to notify the person or persons, or the person or persons responsible for a specific location or entity, that is specifically threatened, as well as to notify an appropriate law enforcement agency or to take other appropriate action, including but not limited to hospitalizing the patient. A mental health provider is not liable for damages in any civil action for warning a specific person or persons, or a person or persons responsible for a specific location or entity, against or predicting the violent behavior of a person receiving treatment from the mental health provider.

(c) A mental health provider must not be subject to professional discipline when there is a duty to warn and protect pursuant to this section.

(3) The provisions of this section do not apply to the negligent release of a patient from any mental health hospital or ward or to the negligent failure to initiate involuntary seventy-two-hour treatment and evaluation after a personal patient evaluation determining that the person appears to have a mental illness and, as a result of the mental illness, appears to be an imminent danger to others.

§ 13-90-119.   Privilege for newsperson

(1) As used in this section, unless the context otherwise requires:

(a) "Mass medium" means any publisher of a newspaper or periodical; wire service; radio or television station or network; news or feature syndicate; or cable television system.

(b) "News information" means any knowledge, observation, notes, documents, photographs, films, recordings, videotapes, audiotapes, and reports, and the contents and sources thereof, obtained by a newsperson while engaged as such, regardless of whether such items have been provided to or obtained by such newsperson in confidence.

(c) "Newsperson" means any member of the mass media and any employee or independent contractor of a member of the mass media who is engaged to gather, receive, observe, process, prepare, write, or edit news information for dissemination to the public through the mass media.

(d) "Press conference" means any meeting or event called for the purpose of issuing a public statement to members of the mass media, and to which members of the mass media are invited in advance.

(e) "Proceeding" means any civil or criminal investigation, discovery procedure, hearing, trial, or other process for obtaining information conducted by, before, or under the authority of any judicial body of the state of Colorado. Such term shall not include any investigation, hearing, or other process for obtaining information conducted by, before, or under the authority of the general assembly.

(f) "Source" means any person from whom or any means by or through which news information is received or procured by a newsperson, while engaged as such, regardless of whether such newsperson was requested to hold confidential the identity of such person or means.

(2) Notwithstanding any other provision of law to the contrary and except as provided in subsection (3) of this section, no newsperson shall, without such newsperson's express consent, be compelled to disclose, be examined concerning refusal to disclose, be subjected to any legal presumption of any kind, or be cited, held in contempt, punished, or subjected to any sanction in any judicial proceedings for refusal to disclose any news information received, observed, procured, processed, prepared, written, or edited by a newsperson, while acting in the capacity of a newsperson; except that the privilege of nondisclosure shall not apply to the following:

(a) News information received at a press conference;

(b) News information which has actually been published or broadcast through a medium of mass communication;

(c) News information based on a newsperson's personal observation of the commission of a crime if substantially similar news information cannot reasonably be obtained by any other means;

(d) News information based on a newsperson's personal observation of the commission of a class 1, 2, or 3 felony.

(3) Notwithstanding the privilege of nondisclosure granted in subsection (2) of this section, any party to a proceeding who is otherwise authorized by law to issue or obtain subpoenas may subpoena a newsperson in order to obtain news information by establishing by a preponderance of the evidence, in opposition to a newsperson's motion to quash such subpoena:

(a) That the news information is directly relevant to a substantial issue involved in the proceeding;

(b) That the news information cannot be obtained by any other reasonable means; and

(c) That a strong interest of the party seeking to subpoena the newsperson outweighs the interests under the first amendment to the United States constitution of such newsperson in not responding to a subpoena and of the general public in receiving news information.

(4) The privilege of nondisclosure established by subsection (2) of this section may be waived only by the voluntary testimony or disclosure of a newsperson that directly addresses the news information or identifies the source of such news information sought. A publication or broadcast of a news report through the mass media concerning the subject area of the news information sought, but which does not directly address the specific news information sought, shall not be deemed a waiver of the privilege of nondisclosure as to such specific news information.

(5) In any trial to a jury in an action in which a newsperson is a party as a result of such person's activities as a newsperson and in which the newsperson has invoked the privilege created by subsection (2) of this section, the jury shall be neither informed nor allowed to learn that such newsperson invoked such privilege or has thereby declined to disclose any news information.

(6)   Nothing in this section shall preclude the issuance of a search warrant in compliance with the federal "Privacy Protection Act of 1980", 42 U.S.C. sec. 2000aa.

For other applicable statutes, see C.R.S. §§ 12-36.5-104.4 (medical peer review and quality assurance records and communications); 13-22-307 (dispute resolution proceedings and records); 14-12-105 (domestic relations and marriage counseling communications and records); 16-15.7-101 (crime stopper organization records); 24-72.5-103 (newsperson's privilege outside of judicial proceedings); 25-3-204 (maternity hospital records); 25-4-1404 (AIDS and HIV information); 42-4-1410 (traffic accident reports).

Highlights

Communication between a patient and social worker, occurring in the course of psychotherapy sessions, is privileged under Rule 501, according to the Supreme Court in *Jaffee v. Redmond*, 518 U.S. 1 (1996). The Court noted that Rule 501 allows federal courts to define new evidentiary privileges as dictated by interpretation of the principles of common law and by reason and experience. In that light, it found that a psychotherapist privilege is supported both by private and public interests. The privilege serves private interests by promoting the confidence and trust necessary for effective psychotherapy. The Court recognized that the possibility that confidential information shared with a psychotherapist could be disclosed "may impede development of the confidential relationship needed for successful treatment." The privilege also serves the public interest in that, by facilitating effective treatment, it promotes the mental and emotional health of the citizenry.

The psychotherapist privilege extends not only to psychiatrists and psychologists, but also to social workers performing psychotherapy. Recognizing that a significant amount of mental health treatment is provided by social workers, the Court saw no reason to distinguish between professionals whose counseling services further the same public goals.

AUTHORITY

WEISSENBERGER'S FEDERAL EVIDENCE §§ 501.1–.8

MCCORMICK §§ 72–76.1

3 WEINSTEIN 2d §§ 501.01–.05

2 MUELLER & KIRKPATRICK §§ 169–231

8 WIGMORE §§ 2201–2396

James, *The Use of Mental Health Treatment Records to Impeach Credibility*, 23 COLO. LAW. 839 (1994)

Note, *Making Sense of Rules of Privilege Under the Structural (Il)logic of the Federal Rules of Evidence*, 105 HARV. L. REV. 1339 (1992)

Note, *The Ohio Physician-Patient Privilege: Modified, Revised and Defined*, 49 OHIO ST. L.J. 1147 (1989)

Medine, *The Adverse Testimony Privilege: Time to Dispose of a "Sentimental Relic,"* 67 OR. L. REV. 519 (1988)

Reporter's Privilege: Pankratz v. District Court, 58 DEN. L.J. 681 (1981)

Weissenberger, *Toward Precision in the Attorney-Client Privilege of Corporations*, 65 IOWA L. REV. 899 (1980)

Erickson, *Perjurious Defendant: Defense Lawyer's Conflicting Ethical Obligations to the Court and to His Client*, 59 DEN. L.J. 75 (1981)

Comment, *The Spousal Testimonial Privilege After* Trammel v. United States, 58 DEN. L.J. 357 (1981)

Fregant, *Confidentiality of Personnel Files in the Private Sector*, U.C.D. L. REV. 473 (1981)

Hill, *Testimonial Privileges and Fair Trial*, 80 COLUM. L. REV. 1173 (1980)

COMPARISON TO FEDERAL RULE

Colorado Rule 501 is modeled after Federal Rule 501, which provides that privileges are governed by common law principles as interpreted by the federal courts, or, in civil actions in which state law supplies the rule of decision as to an element of a claim or defense, by principles of state law. Please note that on Dec. 1, 2011 Federal Rule 501 was restyled. Please see Federal Rule 501 in the appendix for comparison.

SIGNIFICANT CASES

Attorney-Client Privilege

Swidler & Berlin v. United States, 524 U.S. 399 (1998) (attorney-client privilege applies to preserve confidential communications even after the death of a client, in order to promote "broader public interests in the observance of law and administration of justice").

People v. Trujillo, 144 P.3d 539 (Colo. 2006) (when a potential defendant entered into a plea agreement that contained a promise to provide truthful testimony, that action did not waive her attorney-client privilege).

People v. Madera, 112 P.3d 688 (Colo. 2005) (a claim of ineffective assistance of counsel does not necessarily waive attorney-client privilege; a finding of waiver requires consideration of whether assertion of the privilege was a result of some affirmative act, such as filing suit, by the asserting party, whether the asserting party put the protected information at issue by making it relevant to the case, and whether applying the privilege would have denied the opposing party access to vital information).

Stone v. Satriana, 41 P.3d 705 (Colo. 2002) (trial court's designation of legal malpractice plaintiff's lawyers as nonparties at fault was erroneous for a number of reasons, including the harmful impact that the designation would have on lawyer-client confidentiality; to protect against liability as nonparties, the plaintiff's lawyers would have been permitted to disclose confidential communications from the plaintiff).

Wesp v. Everson, 33 P.3d 191 (Colo. 2001) (client's description of lawyer-client communications that occurred in the presence of a third party did not waive any privilege, because the presence of the third party prevented any privilege from arising to cover those communications; describing those communications therefore could not have any effect on privilege that might otherwise have applied to different communications between that client and lawyer).

Gordon v. Boyles, 9 P.3d 1106 (Colo. 2000) (where the employer of a newsperson learned the identities of the newsperson's sources in the context of confidential attorney-client communications with a co-defendant and joint counsel, attorney-client privilege protects the employer from being required to reveal those identities; the privilege applies to communications between co-defendants and joint counsel concerning matters of common interest to their joint defense).

Gray v. Dist. Court of the Eleventh Judicial Dist., 884 P.2d 286 (Colo. 1994) (attorney-client privilege does not shield statements made to experts retained to evaluate criminal defendant's possible defenses based on mental condition).

D.A.S. v. People, 863 P.2d 291 (Colo. 1993) (attorney-client privilege cannot bar testimony by medical expert who examined client at request of attorney, when expert's report was widely circulated prior to trial and client's children were with client and expert during examination).

Lanari v. People, 827 P.2d 495 (Colo. 1992) (speaker must have a reasonable expectation of confidentiality, based on circumstances, for attorney-client privilege to apply).

Kay Laboratories, Inc. v. Dist. Court, 653 P.2d 721 (Colo. 1982) (report prepared by hospital personnel about a patient's injury was not shielded by attorney-client privilege despite claim that it was prepared in anticipation of litigation; it was prepared close to the time of the injury and well before a notice of claim was received).

Denver Tramway Co. v. Owens, 36 P. 848 (Colo. 1894) (a bystander who overhears a lawyer-client conversation may testify as to its substance).

Genova v. Longs Peak Emergency Physicians, P.C., 72 P.3d 454 (Colo. Ct. App. 2003) (when a former director of a company/corporation seeks to compel corporation to produce documents created during his tenure with the company that bear upon the case, defendant corporation may assert privilege against the former director for documents that are protected by attorney-client privilege).

In re 2015–2016 Jefferson County Grand Jury, 410 P.3d 53 (Colo. 2018) (documents that were generated by defendant and their attorney after police had thwarted any further criminal activity do not fall within the crime-fraud exception, and a court must review the attorney-client documents of privilege and make a probable cause determination as to each prior to a blanket revocation of attorney-client privileges under the crime-fraud exception; citing Colo. Rev. Stat. § 13-90-107(1)).

Physician-Patient Privilege

Jaffee v. Redmond, 518 U.S. 1 (1996) (under Rule 501, federal law recognizes a privilege protecting confidential communications between patient and psychotherapist, including communications between a patient and social worker in the course of psychotherapy; failure to recognize this privilege may chill the "frank and complete disclosure of facts, emotions, memories and fears" which are necessary for effective treatment).

People v. Kailey, 333 P.3d 89 (Colo. 2014) (The psychologist-patient privilege in Colo. Rev. Stat 13-90-107(1)(a) does not preclude testimony regarding a psychologist's duty warn. Barring admissibility of a therapist's testimony that a patient made threats of imminent physical harm against a specific person was inconsistent with legislative intent because it undermines the legislative intent because it undermines the legislative objective animating the duty to warn without increasing the effectiveness of mental health treatment).

L.A.N. v. L.M.B., 292 P.3d 942 (Colo. 2013) (although part of the Children's Code, specifically § 19-3-311, specifically abrogates the psychotherapist-patient privilege with respect to communications between a client and a licensed mental health professional that form the basis of a report of child abuse or neglect, if communications between a child-patient and his or her psychotherapist do not form the basis of a report of child abuse or neglect as described in § 19-3-304, then the psychotherapist-patient privilege applies to those communications in a dependency and neglect proceeding).

Hartmann v. Nordin, 147 P.3d 43 (Colo. 2006) (the plaintiff impliedly waived her physician-patient privilege by claiming that her stroke was caused by the defendants' malpractice).

Weil v. Dillon Cos., 109 P.3d 127 (Colo. 2005) (plaintiff in a personal injury action made claims for pain, suffering and loss of quality of life; Supreme Court ruled he did *not* waive patient-physician privilege for *all* medical records, only those pertaining to claimed injuries in this law suit).

People v. Palomo, 31 P.3d 879 (Colo. 2001) (in prosecution of defendant for murder of coworker, drug screening and physical ability test results contained in defendant's and coworker's personnel files did not fall under the physician-patient privilege since the tests were not performed in order to enable a physician to treat the defendant or the coworker; in regard to the other medical information contained in the coworker's employment records, the defendant had no standing to assert the coworker's physician-patient privilege since the privilege is personal to the patient or her estate).

People v. Covington, 19 P.3d 15 (Colo. 2001) (photographs of a victim's injuries taken by a physician assistant at the request of an investigating officer fell within the physician-patient privilege, but the privilege was abrogated by C.R.S. § 12-36-135(3) because the injuries resulted from an incident involving gunshot wounds; in cases where a physician has a duty to report an injury to the police, the physician-patient privilege is abrogated with regard to testimony about the information received from the physician's observations of the patient).

Gray v. Dist. Court of the Eleventh Judicial Dist., 884 P.2d 286 (Colo. 1994) (physician-patient privilege does not shield statements made to physician who evaluates criminal defendant's possible defenses based on mental condition).

Belle Bonfils Mem'l Blood Ctr. v. Dist. Court of Denver, 763 P.2d 1003 (Colo. 1988) (physician-patient privilege did not bar disclosure of blood donor's name to recipient of tainted blood, since the technician who had interviewed the donor was not a physician or professional nurse, and no physician, surgeon, or registered nurse was present at the time of the interview).

Bond v. Dist. Court of Cnty. of Denver, 682 P.2d 33 (Colo. 1984) (plaintiffs who sought damages for mental suffering in tort suit waived their psychotherapist-patient privilege as to written notes and records made by their therapists during evaluation and treatment necessitated by the defendant's alleged negligent conduct).

People in Interest of G., 630 P.2d 89 (Colo. 1981) (physician-patient privilege could not apply to statement made by patient to physician in the presence of a police officer).

People v. Moon, 411 P.3d 130 (Colo. 2015) (a doctor's unaltered prescription order for controlled substancesis admissible under the exception to doctor-patient privilege provided in Colo. Rev. Stat. § 18-18-415(1)(d), when it was used by a defendant in a wrongful effort to procure controlled substances).

People v. Bowman, 812 P.2d 725 (Colo. Ct. App. 1991) (the psychologist-patient testimonial privilege did not preclude use of any information therapist obtained related to sexual abuse of a minor, since the purpose of the Child Protection Act, the facilitation of investigation and prosecution of child abusers, could not be fulfilled if disclosure of a child abuse report was prevented).

Bailey v. Hermacinski, 413 P.3d 157 (Colo. 2018) (Colo. Rev. Stat. § 13-90-107(1)(d)(I)–the consultation exception, which provides that the physician-patient privilege does not cover communications between a defendant doctor and a non-party physician in a medical malpractice suit, does not apply when the non-party physician was not in consultation with the defendant physician; however an implied waiver of the physician-patient privilege may constitute consent for waiver of physician-patient privilege for purposes of Colo. Rev. Stat. § 13-90-107(1)(d)).

Crow v. Penrose-St. Francis Healthcare Sys., 292 P.3d 1018 (Colo. App. 2012) (records for the Surgical Peer Review Committee are not subject to subpoena or discovery, unless they fall under one of the statutory exceptions, such as in "any appeal or de novo proceeding" . . . "by a physician seeking judicial review").

Newspersons Privilege

Brokers' Choice of Am., Inc. v. NBC Universal, Inc., 861 F.3d 1081 (10th Cir. 2017) (a defendant may choose to waive their newspersons privilege through disclosure, such as filing the privileged material as an exhibit in support of its motion to dismiss; citing Colo. Rev. Stat. § 13-90-119(4)).

Spousal Privilege

Burlington N. R. Co. v. Hood, 802 P.2d 458 (Colo. 1990) (defendant should have been permitted to question plaintiff's wife about admissions of fraud plaintiff allegedly made to his wife in a private conversation, because plaintiff had called wife as a witness and thus lost the spousal disqualification privilege, and because plaintiff had failed to object to statements by the wife about the conversation during a deposition and had raised a closely related topic in direct examination of the wife).

People v. Buhrle, 744 P.2d 747 (Colo. 1987) (out-of-court statement by defendant's husband concerning age of defendant, admissible under an exception to the hearsay exclusion, would not be barred by the marital communications privilege absent a showing that the husband learned the information from his spouse in confidence).

Balltrip v. People, 401 P.2d 259 (Colo. 1965) (spouse's murder of other spouse's child is properly treated as a crime against the parent spouse, to deny application of the husband-wife privilege).

People v. James, 40 P.3d 36 (Colo. Ct. App. 2001) (trial court did not err in allowing defendant's wife to testify despite his assertion of spousal immunity where, even though the defendant told his wife about certain past crimes, the testimony concerned statements made when the two of them were actively engaged in an ongoing pattern of criminal activity, and the defendant made the statements for the purpose of obtaining his wife's aid in the commission of check forgery and theft schemes that were then ongoing).

People v. Fox, 862 P.2d 1000 (Colo. Ct. App. 1993) (marital communications privilege does not apply to statements made to aid the commission of a crime; portions of defendant-husband's letters to his wife were properly admitted against him).

People v. McGregor, 635 P.2d 912 (Colo. Ct. App. 1981) (wife may testify against husband in trial for crimes allegedly committed against her and another person by her husband).

Other Privileges

University of Pennsylvania v. E.E.O.C., 493 U.S. 182 (1990) (the Supreme Court declined to recognize a privilege against disclosure of peer review information).

Simpson v. Cedar Springs Hosp., Inc., 336 P.3d 180 (Colo. 2014). Documents sought by a patient were covered by the quality management privilege as defined by Colo. Rev. Stat. §25-3-109 (2014), because they were created as part of a quality management program approved by CDPHE.

Yaekle v. Andrews, 195 P.3d 1101 (Colo. 2008) (C.R.S. § 13-22-307 (2008) protects as confidential certain "mediation communications," and thus bars the use of communications made in the presence or at the behest of the mediator as evidence of a binding contract, but it does not prohibit introduction into evidence of other communications parties may make in connection with a mediated dispute).

Gordon v. Boyles, 9 P.3d 1106 (Colo. 2000) (newsperson's privilege is qualified not absolute; to reject the operation of this privilege, a trial court must find that the three statutory conditions of section 5 C.R.S. § 13-90-119(3)(a)–(c) are satisfied, and in a defamation case must make a preliminary determination of whether the plaintiff has made a satisfactory showing of the probable falsity of the defendant's allegedly defamatory statements at the time the statements were made).

Milburn v. Haworth, 108 P. 155 (Colo. 1910) (privilege for communications made to a clergyman does not apply to a communication made to a clergyman outside of his professional character and outside of the scope of any church discipline).

Hunt v. Ortiz, 84 Fed. Appx. 34 (10th Cir. 2003) (the mere fact that a prisoner refused to take a medical test for HIV does not constitute confidential information protected by C.R.S. § 25-4-1404, despite the court acknowledging the unnecessary sharing of such information may cause ridicule).

People v. Turner, 109 P.3d 639 (Colo. 2005) (the victim-advocate privilege, which covers communications between victim-advocates and victims, extends to services or assistance provided by the agency to the victim, such as communications to secure housing).

GSL of ILL, LLC v. Kroskob, ___P.3d___, 2012 U.S. Dist. LEXIS 266 (D. Colo. 2012) (When parties come to a full and complete meeting of the minds over the essential terms of their contract to resolve the litigation between them, the recorded terms of the agreement are admissible and probative of contract formation and interpretation).

Chapter 502

Rule 502. Attorney-Client Privilege and Work Product; Limitations On Waiver

Rule 502 reads as follows:

The following provisions apply, in the circumstances set out, to disclosure of a communication or information covered by the attorney-client privilege or work-product protection.

(a) **Disclosure Made in a Colorado Proceeding or to a Colorado Office or Agency; Scope of a Waiver.** When the disclosure is made in a Colorado proceeding or to an office or agency of a Colorado state, county, or local government and waives the attorney-client privilege or work-product protection, the waiver extends to an undisclosed communication or information in a Colorado proceeding only if:

(1) the waiver is intentional;

(2) the disclosed and undisclosed communications or information concern the same subject matter; and

(3) they ought in fairness to be considered together.

(b) **Inadvertent Disclosure.** When made in a Colorado proceeding or to an office or agency of a Colorado state, county, or local government, the disclosure does not operate as a waiver in a Colorado proceeding if:

(1) the disclosure is inadvertent;

(2) the holder of the privilege or protection took reasonable steps to prevent disclosure; and

(3) the holder promptly took reasonable steps to rectify the error, including (if applicable) following C.R.C.P. 26(b)(5)(B).

(c) **Disclosure Made in a Federal or other State Proceeding.** When the disclosure is made in a proceeding in federal court or the court of another state and is not the subject of a court order concerning waiver, the disclosure does not operate as a waiver in a Colorado proceeding if the disclosure:

(1) would not be a waiver under this rule if it had been made in a Colorado proceeding; or

(2) is not a waiver under the law governing the state or federal proceeding where the disclosure occurred.

(d) **Controlling Effect of a Court Order.** A Colorado court may order that the privilege or protection is not waived by disclosure connected with the litigation pending before the court—in which event the disclosure is also not a waiver in any other proceeding.

(e) Controlling Effect of a Party Agreement. An agreement on the effect of disclosure in a Colorado proceeding is binding only on the parties to the agreement, unless it is incorporated into a court order.

(f) Definitions. In this rule:

(1) "attorney-client privilege" means the protection that applicable law provides for confidential attorney-client communications; and

(2) "work-product protection" means the protection that applicable law provides for tangible material (or its intangible equivalent) prepared in anticipation of litigation or for trial.

ANALYSIS

Rule 502 addresses waiver of attorney-client privilege and work-produce protection in the context of documents and information disclosed in legal proceedings or investigations. The Rule provides that an intentional disclosure of protected information in a Colorado proceeding or to state and local government agencies results in a waiver extending to other protected information concerning the same subject matter that should in fairness be considered with the disclosed information. With regard to inadvertent disclosures, the Rule provides that there is no waiver if the holder of the privilege or protection took reasonable steps to prevent disclosure and promptly to reasonable steps to rectify the error.

INCORPORATED RULE

C.R.C.P. 26(b)(5)(B):

If information produced in disclosures or discovery is subject to a claim of privilege or of protection as trial-preparation material the party making the claim may notify any party that received the information of the claim and the basis for it. After being notified, a party must not review, use or disclose the information until the claim is resolved; must take reasonable steps to retrieve the information if the party disclosed it before being notified; and shall give notice to the party making the claim within 14 days if it contests the claim. If the claim is not contested within the 14-day period, or is timely contested but resolved in favor of the party claiming privilege or protection of trial-preparation material, then the receiving party must also promptly return, sequester, or destroy the specified information and any copies that the receiving party has. If the claim is contested, the party making the claim shall present the information to the court under seal for a determination of the claim within 14 days after receiving such notice, or the claim is waived. The producing party must preserve the information until the claim is resolved, and bears the burden of proving the basis of the claim and that the claim was not waived. All notices under this Rule shall be in writing.

AUTHORITY

8 WIGMORE §§ 2290–2329

Ann M. Murphy, *Federal Rule of Evidence 502: The "Get Out of Jail Free" Provision—Or Is It?"* 41 N.M. L. Rev. 193 (2011)

COMPARISON TO FEDERAL RULE

Colorado Rule 502 is modeled after Federal Rule 502. The Colorado rule differs from the federal rule in terms of the binding effect of court rulings. The federal rule states that it applies to state proceedings and to certain federal arbitration proceedings. The Colorado rule limits the effect of a waiver ruling to "other proceedings" (which is intended to preclude applying a Colorado court's ruling to federal courts, courts in other states, or Colorado state and local agencies).

SIGNIFICANT CASES

[This rule became effective on March 22, 2016. There are not yet any reported cases applying or interpreting it.]

VI
WITNESSES

WITNESSES

Chapter 601

Rule 601. General Rule of Competency

Rule 601 reads as follows:

Every person is competent to be a witness except as otherwise provided in these rules, or in any statute of the State of Colorado.

ANALYSIS

In essence, the object of Rule 601 is to declare all persons competent to testify in all cases, criminal or civil, except where other Rules explicitly render a party incompetent or where an applicable state law disqualifies a witness. The reference to "any statute of the state of Colorado" preserves the statutory classifications of persons presently not competent as witnesses under Colorado law. *See* C.R.S. §§ 13-90-101 to 13-90-108. The purpose of Rule 601 is to create an assumption of competency except in expressly specified situations. Trial courts must make an individualized inquiry in each case to determine whether the trial testimony of a witness who has been hypnotized will be sufficiently reliable to qualify for admission.

INCORPORATED STATUTES
(selected statutory summaries)

§ 13-90-101.   Competent witnesses

All persons, whether parties to or interested in the suit, shall be competent witnesses in a civil action or proceeding, except as herein otherwise provided.

§ 13-90-102.   Colorado dead man's statute

A party or interested person may not testify on his own behalf when the adverse party represents a mentally incompetent person or the estate of a deceased person. The underlying policy is to prevent perjury and to protect the mentally incompetent and the estate of decedents from unjust claims, by preventing interested witnesses from testifying where the deceased cannot refute the claim.

§ 13-90-104.   Partners and joint contractors

In any action by or against a surviving partner or joint contractor no adverse party is competent to testify to any admission or conversation by any deceased partner or joint contractor unless some one or more of the surviving partners or joint contractors were also present at the time of the admission or conversation.

§ 13-90-105.   Assignment or release of claim

If a person is incompetent to testify under the provisions of C.R.S. § 13-90-102, he shall

123

not become competent by an assignment or release of his claim made for the purpose of allowing such person to testify.

§ 13-90-106(1)(a).   Persons of unsound mind

Persons who are of unsound mind at the time of their production for examination are prevented from testifying as witnesses.

§ 13-90-106(1)(b)(I).   Limitations on child witnesses

Children under ten years of age are prevented from being a witness unless they appear capable of "receiving" accurate impressions of the facts, "remembering" those facts, and "relating" them truly. This language clearly implies that the competency of a child under ten years of age as a witness is within the discretion of the trial court to determine and the Colorado courts have in various cases found children under ten years of age competent to testify.

§ 13-90-106(1)(b)(II).   Child witnesses in cases of sexual abuse, sexual assault, or incest

The proscription in C.R.S. § 13-90-106(1)(b)(I) does not apply to "children under ten years of age who appear incapable of receiving just impressions of the facts respecting which they are examined or of relating them truly."

§ 13-90-107.   Privileged communications

Seven categories of individuals are not permitted to give testimony about certain topics if the privilege is properly asserted. C.R.S. § 13-90-108, permits a person to waive the privilege provided by the previous section. For further discussion of privileges, see Chapter 501. *See also* CRE 602–608 as they relate to limitations on competency.

Highlights

Whether a member of a decision-making body can be questioned about his or her thinking during deliberations is an aspect of the general issue of witness competency. The Colorado Court of Appeals has ruled that a member of a county administrative board may not be questioned about the mental processes involved in contributing to a decision of that board, in *Gilpen County Board of Equalization v. Russell*, 941 P.2d 257 (Colo. 1997). This result is parallel to the Rule 606 provision concerning the competency of jurors.

AUTHORITY

WEISSENBERGER'S FEDERAL EVIDENCE §§ 601.1–.6

MCCORMICK §§ 61–67

3 WEINSTEIN 2d §§ 601.01–.05

3 MUELLER & KIRKPATRICK §§ 232–235

WIGMORE §§ 483–721

Ringland, *Child Sex Abuse Evidence Problems—Update 1988*, 14 U. DAYTON L. REV. 147 (1988)

Melton, *Children's Competency to Testify*, 5 LAW & HUMAN BEHAVIOR 73 (1981)

Comment, *The Uniformity-Conformity Dilemma Facing Draftsmen of Federal Rules of Evidence*, 69 COLUM. L. REV. 353 (1969)

COMPARISON TO FEDERAL RULE

Colorado Rule 601 and Federal Rule 601 both provide that all witnesses are competent to testify unless otherwise provided by the Rules. Colorado Rule 601 preserves statutory law pertaining to competency. Federal Rule 601 further provides that in civil actions as to which state law supplies the rule of decision, the competency of the witness is determined in accordance with state law. Please note that on Dec. 1, 2011 Federal Rule 601 was restyled. Please see Federal Rule 601 in the appendix for comparison.

SIGNIFICANT CASES

Just in Case Bus. Lighthouse, LLC v. Murray, 2013 Colo. App. LEXIS 1140 (2013) (whether an expert witness whose payment for testifying will be contingent on the outcome of the litigation should be precluded from testifying should be decided by the trial judge; preclusion of the testimony is possible, but the trial court should analyze whether the jury will be able to evaluate the credibility of the witness under the circumstances).

Breeden v. Stone (In re Estate of Breeden), 992 P.2d 1167 (Colo. 2000) (probate court did not abuse its discretion by denying petitioner's motion to dismiss two individuals as parties, thus barring their testimony as parties under the dead man's statute).

Gilpin County Bd. of Equalization v. Russell, 941 P.2d 257 (Colo. 1997) (in a civil non-jury case, the "mental process rule" excluded testimony of a member of a quasi-judicial body regarding the mental process or procedure employed by which the administrative decision was reached, absent a clear showing of illegal or unlawful action, misconduct, bias, or bad faith).

People v. Dist. Court for Summit County, 791 P.2d 682 (Colo. 1990) (where subsection 13-90-106(1)(b)(II) applies, the sole requirement imposed on the prospective child witness is that he or she be able to describe or relate in language appropriate for a child of that age the events or facts respecting which the child is examined).

People v. Dist. Court of El Paso County, 776 P.2d 1083 (Colo. 1989) (trial judge should consider eight factors to determine whether child's hearsay statement is sufficiently reliable to be admitted: spontaneity of statement; time gap between statement and child's upset or pain from alleged abuse; language of statement; use of leading questions; bias or motive for lying; intervening events; number of people who heard the statement; and general character of the child).

People v. Romero, 745 P.2d 1003 (Colo. 1987) (if, after considering the totality of circumstances, the court finds that hypnosis does not render witness's recollection and testimony unreliable, it may admit the testimony and allow cross-examination of the pretrial hypnosis as affecting credibility and weight of testimony. If hypnosis has rendered testimony unreliable, the testimony should be excluded).

In re Estate of Lopata, 641 P.2d 952 (Colo. 1982) (constitutionality of C.R.S. § 13-90-102 upheld).

Berger v. Coon, 606 P.2d 68 (Colo. 1980) (the dead man's statute does not bar plaintiffs from testifying if decedent's testimony is first admitted into evidence).

People v. Alley, 232 P.3d 272 (Colo. App. 2010) (drunk witness may be competent to stand trial if the jury is informed of the blood alcohol content of the prospective witness).

Crenshaw v. Bussey, 100 P.3d 568 (Colo. App. 2004) (when the purpose of a witness, as the purported common law wife and decedent's widow, is to gain a share of the estate, that witness cannot testify regarding her marriage with the decedent when its validity would diminish the interest of some heirs under Colorado's Dead Man statute, C.R.S. § 13-90-102).

People v. Flysaway, 807 P.2d 1179 (Colo. App. 1990) (cautionary instruction is necessary when child's hearsay statement is admitted).

People v. McKeehan, 732 P.2d 1238 (Colo. App. 1986) (witness who has been hypnotically relaxed without questioning or suggestion has not thereby been rendered incompetent to testify).

People v. Galloway, 677 P.2d 1380 (Colo. App. 1983) (witnesses who were never adjudicated insane were presumed to be competent and defendant had the burden to produce evidence to show otherwise).

WITNESSES

People v. McGhee, 677 P.2d 419 (Colo. App. 1983) (defendant convicted of selling heroin, appealed on the grounds that an involuntary psychiatric examination of a witness against him was not ordered. Appellate court affirmed, holding that the witness's heroin addiction and history of lying pertain to his credibility, not competency to testify).

David v. Powder Mtn. Ranch, 656 P.2d 716 (Colo. App. 1982) (the test for interest of a witness under the dead man's statute is whether he will gain or lose by direct legal operation of the judgment).

Chapter 602

Rule 602. Lack of Personal Knowledge

Rule 602 reads as follows:

> A witness may not testify to a matter unless evidence is introduced sufficient to support a finding that he has personal knowledge of the matter. Evidence to prove personal knowledge may, but need not, consist of the testimony of the witness himself. This rule is subject to the provisions of Rule 703, relating to opinion testimony by expert witnesses.

ANALYSIS

The preliminary interrogation of every witness must establish that the witness has first-hand knowledge or personal knowledge of the facts as to which he or she will testify. First-hand knowledge is knowledge acquired through one or more of the senses. Foundational testimony, as provided by Rule 602, may be developed from the witness whose competency is being established, and no extrinsic foundational evidence is required. Consequently, in a preliminary examination of a witness, it is only necessary to establish that he or she was in a physical position to see, hear or otherwise perceive the matters as to which he or she is to provide testimony.

Frequently, it will be established during cross-examination that the witness lacks first-hand knowledge to testify to certain facts presented in the direct examination testimony. Where this occurs, the cross-examining attorney should move to strike the direct examination testimony because of its failure to satisfy Rule 602. This rule does not govern the situation of a witness who testifies to a hearsay statement as such, if he has personal knowledge of the making of the statement. Rules 801 and 805 would be applicable.

AUTHORITY

WEISSENBERGER'S FEDERAL EVIDENCE §§ 602.1–.4

McCORMICK § 69

3 WEINSTEIN 2d §§ 602.01–.04

3 MUELLER & KIRKPATRICK §§ 236–237

2 WIGMORE §§ 650–70

COMPARISON TO FEDERAL RULE

Colorado Rule 602 is substantially identical to Federal Rule 602. However, on Dec. 1, 2011 Federal Rule 602 was restyled. Please see Federal Rule 602 in the appendix for comparison.

SIGNIFICANT CASES

Rock v. Arkansas, 483 U.S. 44 (1987) (criminal defendant's right to testify on her own behalf was violated by the Arkansas per se rule excluding all hypnotically refreshed testimony).

Howard-Walker v. People, 443 P.3d 1007 (Colo. 2019) (in a criminal case, admission of a detective's testimony as to why the defendant's girlfriend was upset was in error under CRE 602 because the detective did not have personal knowledge of why she was crying).

Pomeranz v. McDonald's Corp., 843 P.2d 1378 (Colo. 1993) (trial court's adherence to expense estimates was erroneous, given that petitioner's estimates of maintenance expenses on property were not supported by any other evidence that he possessed personal knowledge or that his opinion was rationally based on his own perception).

People v. Collins, 2021 Colo. App. LEXIS 266 (Colo. App. 2021) (in a case of sexual assault on a child, trial judge did not abuse discretion in finding that a child of six was a competent witness). Not selected for final or official publication as of June 1, 2021.

People v. Sparks, 914 P.2d 544 (Colo. App. 2018) (in a sexual assault on a minor case, Defendants' testimony that he knew the age of 14 year-old victim did not require that he possess personal knowledge under CRE 602, because admissions excluded from hearsay under CRE 801(d)(2) do not require that the declarant have personal knowledge).

Chapter 603

Rule 603. Oath or Affirmation

Rule 603 reads as follows:

> Before testifying, every witness shall be required to declare that he will testify truthfully, by oath or affirmation administered in a form calculated to awaken his conscience and impress his mind with his duty to do so.

ANALYSIS

Rule 603 requires that every witness must be sworn to testify truthfully. Although there is no rigid formula, the oath or affirmation must be such as may be "calculated to awaken his conscience and impress his mind with his duty to [testify truthfully]."

AUTHORITY

WEISSENBERGER'S FEDERAL EVIDENCE §§ 603.1–.3

McCORMICK § 63

3 WEINSTEIN 2d §§ 603.01–.05

3 MUELLER & KIRKPATRICK §§ 238–239

6 WIGMORE §§ 1818–29

Note, *A Reconsideration of the Sworn Testimony Requirement: Securing Trust in the Twentieth Century*, 75 MICH. L. REV. 1681 (1977)

COMPARISON TO FEDERAL RULE

Federal Rule 603 is similar to Colorado Rule 603 in that it requires a witness to declare his intention to testify truthfully. Please note that on Dec. 1, 2011 Federal Rule 603 was restyled. Please see Federal Rule 603 in the appendix for comparison.

SIGNIFICANT CASES

People v. Dist. Court, 791 P.2d 682 (Colo. 1990) (pursuant to C.R.S. § 13-90-106(1)(b)(II) a child under the age of ten may be competent to testify even if the child is not able to understand the difference between truth and lying. Rule 603, the Court notes, does not require a different result).

People v. Estorga, 612 P.2d 520 (Colo. 1980) (generally, if the Court determines that a witness can observe and relate facts accurately and understands his moral obligation to tell the truth, he is competent to testify).

Garrison v. People, 408 P.2d 60 (Colo. 1965) (it is within the discretion of the trial Court to determine whether a person has sufficient mental capacity to appreciate the nature and obligation of an oath and thereby determine whether or not a person should be permitted to testify).

Murray v. Just In Case Bus. Lighthouse, LLC, 374 P.3d 443 (Colo. 2016) (where a non-expert witness

WITNESSES

testifies by summarizing business documents, the trial court did not abuse its discretion because the evidence was so "complex and voluminous" that the testimony helped the jurors understand it).

Chapter 604

Rule 604. Interpreters

Rule 604 reads as follows:

> An interpreter is subject to the provisions of these rules relating to qualification as an expert and the administration of an oath or affirmation that he will make a true translation.

ANALYSIS

Rule 604 subjects an interpreter to the qualification requirements of other expert witnesses pursuant to Rule 702. Consistent with Rule 702, the determination of an interpreter's qualifications is an issue within the discretion of the trial court. Close relatives or friends of the witness are not precluded from serving as interpreters where such individuals qualify as experts.

Interpreters, like all experts, are subject to an attack on credibility. Nevertheless, where the trial judge finds that the interpreter satisfies the requirements of Rule 702 and allows the interpreter to testify, the accuracy of the translation becomes an issue for the trier of fact. In such cases, the credibility of the interpreter and his or her competence to translate, become issues for the jury.

AUTHORITY

WEISSENBERGER'S FEDERAL EVIDENCE §§ 604.1–.3

3 WEINSTEIN 2d §§ 604.01–.04

3 MUELLER & KIRKPATRICK §§ 240–241

6 WIGMORE § 1824

Chang & Araujo, *Interpreters for the Defense: Due Process for the Non-English-Speaking Defendant*, 63 CAL. L. REV. 801 (1975)

Note, *The Right to an Interpreter*, 25 RUTGERS L. REV. 145 (1970)

COMPARISON TO FEDERAL RULE

Colorado Rule 604 and Federal Rule 604 are substantially identical. However, on Dec. 1, 2011 Federal Rule 604 was restyled. Please see Federal Rule 604 in the appendix for comparison.

SIGNIFICANT CASES

United States ex rel. Negron v. New York, 434 F.2d 386 (2d Cir. 1970) (failure to provide a criminal defendant with an interpreter held to violate Due Process Clause).

People v. Mejia-Mendoza, 965 P.2d 777 (Colo. 1998) (interpreters are required to accurately communicate the substance of an individual's rights both in the courtroom and during informal settings, such as police interrogations).

People v. Munoz-Casteneda, 300 P.3d 944 (Colo. App. 2012) (the requirements of CRE 604 have no application where a fact witness gives testimony that includes an English translation of an out-of-court conversation with a non-English speaker).

People v. Avila, 797 P.2d 804 (Colo. App. 1990) (it was not a reversible error for the trial court to fail to administer an oath or affirmation of true translation to the interpreter, since no objection was made at trial, no prejudice to defendant has been shown, and the sworn testimony of the interpreter and a bilingual officer attending the trial show that the interpretation was true and accurate).

Chapter 605

Rule 605. Competency of Judge as Witness

Rule 605 reads as follows:

> The judge presiding at the trial may not testify in that trial as a witness. No objection need be made to preserve the point.

ANALYSIS

Rule 605 provides that the trial judge presiding at the trial may not testify in that trial as a witness, and further, that no objection need be interposed at trial to preserve error for appeal. The Rule, however, does not prevent a judge from testifying at a later trial about matters occurring in the original trial, such as where a trial judge is called as a witness in a hearing on a petition for postconviction relief from a previous judgment.

AUTHORITY

WEISSENBERGER'S FEDERAL EVIDENCE §§ 605.1–.4

MCCORMICK § 68

3 WEINSTEIN 2d §§ 605.01–.07

3 MUELLER & KIRKPATRICK §§ 242–244

6 WIGMORE § 1909

Saltzburg, *The Unnecessarily Expanding Role of the American Trial Judge*, 64 VA. L. REV. 39 (1978)

Hart, *Testimony by a Judge or Juror*, 44 MARQ. L. REV. 183 (1960)

COMPARISON TO FEDERAL RULE

In substance, Colorado Rule 605 and Federal Rule 605 are identical. However, on Dec. 1, 2011 Federal Rule 605 was restyled. Please see Federal Rule 605 in the appendix for comparison.

SIGNIFICANT CASES

Lillie v. United States, 953 F.2d 1188 (10th Cir. 1992) (error for trial judge to view the scene of the accident outside the record).

People v. Roehrs, 440 P.3d 1231 (Colo. App. 2019) (in a criminal case alleging harassment and retaliation against a witness, the trial court erred in denying the motion to recuse on the grounds that the judge presided over defendant's prior dependency neglect case and was a material witness to the defendant's conduct in question).

People v. Rogers, 800 P.2d 1327 (Colo. App. 1990) (a trial court's action in personally escorting the child victim to and from the witness stand could be perceived by the jury as an endorsement of the child's credibility and is reversible error).

WITNESSES

Chapter 606

Rule 606. Competency of Juror as Witness

Rule 606 reads as follows:

> **(a) At the trial.** A member of the jury may not testify as a witness before that jury in the trial of the case in which he is sitting as a juror. No objection need be made in order to preserve the point.
>
> **(b) Inquiry into validity of verdict or indictment.** Upon an inquiry into the validity of a verdict or indictment, a juror may not testify as to any matter or statement occurring during the course of the jury's deliberations or to the effect of anything upon his or any other juror's mind or emotions as influencing him to assent to or dissent from the verdict or indictment or concerning his mental processes in connection therewith. But a juror may testify about (1) whether extraneous prejudicial information was improperly brought to the jurors' attention, (2) whether any outside influence was improperly brought to bear upon any juror, or (3) whether there was a mistake in entering the verdict onto the verdict form. A juror's affidavit or evidence of any statement by the juror may not be received on a matter about which the juror would be precluded from testifying.

ANALYSIS

Rule 606(a) declares incompetent any witness who is a member of the jury impaneled to hear the case in question. No objection need be made in order to preserve the point.

Rule 606(b) governs the competency of a juror to testify at a subsequent proceeding concerning the original verdict or indictment. The first half of the first sentence of Rule 606(b) represents the embodiment of the common law tradition of protecting and preserving the integrity of jury deliberations by declaring jurors generally incompetent to testify as to any matter directly pertinent to, and purely internal to, the emotional or mental processes of the jury's deliberations. The Rule is designed to protect the finality of verdicts and to insure that jurors are insulated from being unceasingly harassed by defeated parties.

The remainder of the first sentence of Rule 606(b) recognizes situations in which a juror is competent to impeach a verdict or indictment after it has been returned. A juror may offer testimony concerning whether prejudicial information was improperly brought to the attention of the jury during deliberations. Finally, a juror may testify whether an outside influence was improperly brought to bear upon any member of the jury.

AUTHORITY

WEISSENBERGER'S FEDERAL EVIDENCE §§ 606.1–.5

WITNESSES

McCormick § 605

3 Weinstein 2d §§ 606.01–.07

3 Mueller & Kirkpatrick §§ 245–255

6 Wigmore § 1910

Christman, *Federal Rule of Evidence 606(b) and the Problem of "Differential" Jury Error*, 67 N.Y.U. L. Rev. 802 (1992)

Rank, *Federal Rule of Evidence 606(b) and the Post-trial Reformation of Civil Jury Verdicts*, 76 Minn. L. Rev. 1421 (1992)

Carlson & Sunberg, *Attacking Jury Verdicts: Paradigms for Rule Revision*, 1977 Ariz. St. L.J. 247 (1977)

COMPARISON TO FEDERAL RULE

Colorado Rule 606(a) and Federal Rule 606(a) are similar but according to Colorado Rule 606(a), no objection need be made in order to preserve the point. Please note that on Dec. 1, 2011 Federal Rule 606 was restyled. Please see Federal Rule 606 in the appendix for comparison.

Highlights

Amendments to the Federal Rules of Evidence approved by the judicial conference took effect December 1, 2006.

An amendment to Federal Rule of Evidence 606 clarifies that juror testimony may be received only for very limited purposes, including to report that the verdict reported was the result of a clerical mistake.

Those litigating criminal cases in Colorado should be aware of the recent consideration given by the Colorado Evidence Rules Committee to adding a fourth 606(b) exception for cases where there is evidence of racial stereotyping, bias, and animus expressed by any juror during jury deliberations. The reason for giving such consideration was the holding of the US Supreme Court in *Pena-Rodriguez v. Colorado*, 137 S. Ct. 855, 197 L. Ed. 2d 107 (2017), which held that the Sixth Amendment was controlling over evidentiary rules such as 606(b) which currently holds that jurors are incompetent to give testimony concerning racial bias expressed in jury deliberations. However, the Committee decided not to amend 606(b) for the time being, because racial stereotypes and animus in jury deliberations would in any case be a violation of the 6th amendment, and the committee felt that it needed more time to consider the ramifications of any such amendment to application of 606(b) in other contexts.

SIGNIFICANT CASES

People v. Richardson, 481 P.3d 1 (Colo. 2020) (in the absence of evidence demonstrating actual bias or prejudice, the trial judge was not obliged to recuse himself or his wife, who was a juror on the case).

People v. Richardson, 184 P.3d 755 (Colo. 2008) (jurors' affidavits stating that a jury had unanimously agreed on acquittal for particular offenses, in a case where the jury did not sign a verdict form regarding that offense, were not admissible).

People v. Harlan, 109 P.3d 616 (Colo. 2005) (in a first degree murder case the jury consulted the Bible to demonstrate a requirement of the death penalty for the crime; this could influence a typical juror to reject a life sentence; this jury misconduct under CRE 606(b) required the trial court to disregard the jury death sentence and impose a life sentence. In determining whether the jury has been exposed to extraneous information as contemplated under 606(b), non-exclusive factors to be considered by a court include: 1) how the information relates to critical issues in the case; 2) the authoritativeness of the source; 3) whether a juror initiated the search for the information; 4) whether the information obtained by one juror was presented to another juror; 5) whether the information was presented prior to reaching a unanimous verdict; and 6) whether the information would be likely to influence a "typical juror" to the defendant's detriment).

Hall v. Levine, 104 P.3d 222 (Colo. 2005) (in a malpractice case the jury returned a unanimous verdict and after the Court found that it was not unanimous and ordered a new trial; this was error, as CRE 606(b) precludes use of post-judgment jury statements to impeach a verdict that was represented to be unanimous).

People v. Wadle, 97 P.3d 932 (Colo. 2004) (jurors improperly consulted Internet information during deliberation; Court must apply objective test to misconduct: what effect misconduct would have on a "typical jury," not effect on present jury).

Stewart v. Rice, 47 P.3d 316 (Colo. 2002) (juror affidavits offered by defense counsel to show that jury's intent differed from the damages verdict they rendered were inadmissible because they did not meet the following two requirements for the admission of such evidence pursuant to CRE 606(b): (1) They were not offered to show that extraneous prejudicial information was brought to the jurors' attention, or (2) they were not offered to show that improper outside influence was exerted upon a juror).

Ravin v. Gambrell, 788 P.2d 817 (Colo. 1990) (in this civil case, reasonable probability that extraneous information or influence affected a verdict required reversal of conviction).

Neil v. Espinoza, 747 P.2d 1257 (Colo. 1987) (CRE 606(b) prohibits the use of any testimony by jurors for the purposes of resurrecting or impeaching a verdict, except in the limited instance of inquiry into validity of the verdict or indictment).

Wiser v. People, 732 P.2d 1139 (Colo. 1987) (while two incidents of juror misconduct during the deliberation phase were improper, reversal of the conviction was not required because there was no reasonable probability that extraneous information or influence affected the verdict).

Aldrich v. Dist. Court of Eighteenth Jud. Dist., 714 P.2d 1321 (Colo. 1986) (jury impeachment of verdict rule was extended to apply to eminent domain commissioners).

People v. Newman, 481 P.3d 1243 (Colo. App. 2020) (lawyer/juror's introduction into the jury room of a written legal definition based on the lawyer/juror's research outside the jury room constituted extraneous information sufficient to permit another junior's affidavit describing said incident to be received by the court in support of a motion for mistrial under CRE 606(b)).

People v. Harmon, 2011 Colo. App. LEXIS 1635 (Colo. App. 2011) (in appeal for conviction of knowing or reckless child abuse, appellate court reversed because trial court failed to respond to note by juror during trial that jury had decided guilt prior to deliberations. It was proper to inquire into the validity of the verdict because of the violation of due process under the 14th Amendment to the U.S. Constitution).

People v. Holt, 266 P.3d 442 (Colo. App. 2011) (in attempted alluding criminal case, when juror told other jurors based his own experience that penalty for this charge would only be "a slap on the wrist" it did not prejudice defendant because juror is entitled to bring own experience to attention of rest of jury during deliberation and looking up definition of alluding was not error because no evidence was presented indicating dictionary definition was different from legal definition).

People v. Rivers, 70 P.3d 531 (Colo. App. 2002) (where a judge in a criminal case declares mistrial based on jury deadlock, retrial does not violate defendant's double jeopardy rights if, pursuant to CRE 606 the court in a second trial refuses to consider affidavits of jurors in the first trial in which the jurors claimed that they believed that their deliberations were not final).

People v. Harrison, 58 P.3d 1103 (Colo. App. 2002) (court properly applied *Harper* and *Wiser* tests, *infra*, in denying motion for a mistrial in manslaughter case where jury was exposed to information during deliberations, and one of the jurors had a conversation with defendant's alibi witness during which juror made an evaluation of witness's credibility).

Reifschneider v. City and County of Denver, 917 P.2d 315 (Colo. App. 1995) (despite earlier juror confusion in a slip and fall case, which, after proper court assistance in providing the opportunity to amend verdict, a final, consistent verdict was rendered, it is inappropriate to set aside the verdict on court's belief that confusion still existed).

People v. Fox, 862 P.2d 1000 (Colo. App. 1993) (a jury foreman's act of discussing a case at a bar, about the qualities of a pistol during deliberations violated defendant's right to a fair trial by an impartial jury).

Montrose Valley Funeral Home v. Crippin, 835 P.2d 596 (Colo. App. 1992) (a party alleging juror misconduct may introduce evidence under CRE 606(b) to establish that external matters improperly influenced the jury).

Gambrell v. Ravin, 764 P.2d 362 (Colo. App. 1988) (under CRE 606(b) a juror is precluded from testifying as to matters occurring during course of deliberation, or effect of events in jury room upon his or other's mind or emotion, but may testify on question of whether extraneous prejudicial information was improperly brought to any juror's attention).

People v. Harrison, 746 P.2d 66 (Colo. App. 1987) (defendant may not claim prejudice resulting from his own conduct as grounds for setting aside the verdict or reversal).

People v. Black, 725 P.2d 8 (Colo. App. 1986); *People v. Collins*, 730 P.2d 293 (Colo. 1986) (defendant is not entitled to a new trial as a result of influence exerted upon jurors during deliberations absent evidence of threats, abuse or coercion, beyond mere argumentation).

Rome v. Gaffrey, 654 P.2d 333 (Colo. App. 1982) (since the jurors' confusion about the effect of their verdict was considered part of their mental processes, affidavits concerning this confusion were inadmissible because impeachment of a verdict which delves into the mental processes of jury deliberations is not permitted in Colorado).

People v. Borrelli, 624 P.2d 900 (Colo. App. 1980) (defendant was entitled to a new trial where, after the trial, it became known that the juror had given false answers to material questions on voir dire).

Malpica-Cue v. Fangmeier, 395 P.3d 1234 (Colo. App. 2017) (applying the 606(b)(3) exception prohibiting testimony by jurors, thus allowing jurors to testify that the jury had made a mistake by awarding damages in the incorrect amount).

Pena-Rodriguez v. Colorado, 137 S. Ct. 855, 197 L. Ed. 2d 107 (2017) (Where a juror makes a clear statement that references were made during jury deliberations to racial stereotypes or animus to convict a criminal defendant, the Sixth Amendment requires that the 606(b) rule prohibiting jurors from testifying as to what was discussed in jury deliberations give way in order to permit the trial court to consider the evidence of the juror's statement and any resulting denial of the jury trial guarantee").

People v. Bohl, 446 P.3d 907, 2018 Colo. App. LEXIS 1517 (Colo. App. 2018) (in a first-degree murder case, a defendant is not entitled to the contact information of a juror in order to allow further investigation of a juror's alleged misconduct of outside research of "scientific terms" if the trial court properly held a hearing to determine the extent of potential misconduct and determined there was no evidence of jury misconduct and no extraneous prejudicial information had been presented to the other jurors).

People v. Burke, 452 P.3d 124, 2018 Colo. App. LEXIS 1653 (Colo. App. 2018) (a trial court erred in granting a new trial based on a jurors statement that he considered the failure of the defendant to testify in reaching a verdict after a judges instruction not to do so; the rule 606(b) exception to the rule of juror incompetency in cases where extraneous prejudicial information was improperly brought to the judges attention is not applicable and thus cannot form the basis for granting a new trial).

Chapter 607

Rule 607. Who May Impeach

Rule 607 reads as follows:

> The credibility of a witness may be attacked by any party, including the party calling him. Leading questions may be used for the purpose of attacking such credibility.

ANALYSIS

Colorado Rule 607 provides that the credibility of a witness may be attacked by any party, including the party who called the witness. Rule 607 represents a change in preexisting Colorado law which prohibited the impeachment of a party's own witness.

Potential abuse in the literal application of Rule 607 is subject to control by the trial judge where, for example, a witness is called for the purpose of introducing otherwise inadmissible evidence for the purpose of impeachment. Rule 403 may be applied in such situations to prevent admissibility.

The law of evidence has recognized several specific techniques that might be used to diminish the credibility of witnesses. These techniques include prior inconsistent statement impeachment (self-contradiction); contradiction; prior acts and convictions; character impeachment (propensity for lack of veracity); exposure of perceptual incapacity; the exposure of mental incapacity; and the introduction of evidence to expose bias, prejudice, interest or motive to misrepresent.

AUTHORITY

WEISSENBERGER'S FEDERAL EVIDENCE §§ 607.1–.6

McCORMICK §§ 45–47

4 WEINSTEIN 2d §§ 607.01–.10

3 MUELLER & KIRKPATRICK §§ 256–259

WIGMORE §§ 896–918

COMPARISON TO FEDERAL RULE

Colorado Rule 607 is similar to Federal Rule 607. However, Colorado Rule 607 further provides that leading questions may be used for purposes of attacking credibility. Please note that on Dec. 1, 2011 Federal Rule 607 was restyled. Please see Federal Rule 607 in the appendix for comparison.

SIGNIFICANT CASES

Olden v. Kentucky, 488 U.S. 227 (1988) (defendant's rights under the confrontation clause were violated when trial court refused to allow him to impeach the alleged rape victim's testimony on cross-examination with evidence revealing a motive to fabricate the alleged crime).

United States v. Gossett, 877 F.2d 901 (11th Cir. 1989) (impeachment by a prior inconsistent statement may not be permitted when used as a strategy to put before the jury otherwise inadmissible evidence).

United States v. Webster, 734 F.2d 1191 (7th Cir. 1984) (abuse of the Rules of Evidence to permit a party to impeach his party with a prior statement simply to get hearsay evidence admitted).

Davis v. People, 310 P.3d 58 (Colo. 2013) (trial court properly allowed testimony from investigating detectives that they "didn't believe" one witness, felt another "obviously hadn't been entirely truthful," and that another's information was "true," on the theory that the testimony was offered for the limited purpose of providing "context for the detective's interrogation tactics and investigative decisions").

People v. Trujillo, 49 P.3d 316 (Colo. 2002) (defendant's unwarned custodial statements may only be used to impeach the defendant if he testifies, and may not be used to impeach other defense witnesses).

People v. Romero, 197 P.3d 302 (Colo. App. 2008) (proof that defendant had been incarcerated in the past could properly be introduced to impeach his testimony regarding his beliefs about procedures for work release; impeachment use may be allowable without regard to the requirements associated with Rule 404(b), although in this case, the requirements of that rule were satisfied).

People v. Gwinn, 428 P.3d 727 (Colo. App. 2018) (the prosecutor is permitted to impeach its own police officer witness if the testimony of the witness is contradicted by a previous statement regarding a sobriety examination report as long as the questions are direct references to the sobriety record and were asked in response to the conflicting statement).

Chapter 608

Rule 608. Evidence of Character and Conduct of Witness

Rule 608 reads as follows:

> **(a) Opinion and reputation evidence of character.** The credibility of a witness may be attacked or supported by evidence in the form of opinion or reputation, but subject to these limitations: (1) the evidence may refer only to character for truthfulness or untruthfulness, and (2) evidence of truthful character is admissible only after the character of the witness for truthfulness has been attacked by opinion or reputation evidence or otherwise.
>
> **(b) Specific instances of conduct.** Specific instances of the conduct of a witness, for the purpose of attacking or supporting the witness' character for truthfulness other than conviction of crime as provided in § 13-90-101, may not be proved by extrinsic evidence. They may, however, in the discretion of the court, if probative of truthfulness or untruthfulness, be inquired into on cross-examination of the witness (1) concerning the witness' character for truthfulness or untruthfulness, or (2) concerning the character for truthfulness or untruthfulness of another witness as to which character the witness being cross-examined has testified.
>
> The giving of testimony, whether by an accused or by any other witness, does not operate as a waiver of the accused's or the witness' privilege against self-incrimination when examined with respect to matters that relate only to character for truthfulness.

ANALYSIS

Rule 608 governs the technique of impeaching and bolstering a witness through a distinct witness who testifies to the primary witness's character trait of veracity. Colorado Rule 608 is unlike Federal Rule 608, in that it does not authorize the impeachment of a witness by raising an inference of untruthful character arising from cross-examination of that witness concerning unconvicted prior acts of misconduct.

The credibility or veracity of a witness who has taken the stand may be attacked by calling a character witness who is competent to testify to the reputation of the primary witness for untruthfulness. The format is as follows. The primary witness steps down from testifying. The proponent of the primary witness completes his case and rests. Then, the opponent of the primary witness, at a point later in the trial when he has an opportunity to call his own witnesses, calls a character witness. This character witness then testifies in regard to the reputation of the primary witness sought to be impeached.

The qualifications of an impeachment character witness are essentially the same as those qualifications applicable to a character witness under Rule 405. He must be a member of an appropriate community where the reputation of the person characterized is known. The character witness testifies to the reputation of the primary witness in regard to the character trait of veracity or truth-telling. The character witness may also be asked to state his personal opinion as to the veracity of the primary witness sought to be impeached. The character witness is not, however, permitted to testify to specific instances of untruthful conduct of the primary witness on direct examination. Specific acts of conduct of the primary witness may be elicited on cross-examination of the character witness in order to test the basis for his reputation or opinion testimony. It is unlikely that the cross-examiner is the proponent of the primary witness. He, consequently, is not interested in the exposure of prior specific acts of untruthfulness of the witness which he has offered and which the character witness is seeking to impeach.

Under Rule 608(b), a character witness may be impeached by cross-examination as to specific instances of conduct of the primary witness sought to be impeached. Such acts must be probative of truthfulness or untruthfulness and they may not be proven by "extrinsic evidence," i.e., evidence introduced after the character witness steps down from testifying. Further, giving testimony does not operate as a waiver of the privilege against self-incrimination when examined with respect to matters which relate only to credibility.

AUTHORITY

WEISSENBERGER'S FEDERAL EVIDENCE §§ 608.1–.10

McCORMICK § 41

4 WEINSTEIN 2d §§ 608.01–.30

3 MUELLER & KIRKPATRICK §§ 260–272

3 WIGMORE §§ 977–88

4 WIGMORE §§ 1100–44

8 WIGMORE § 2276

Okun, *Character and Credibility: A Proposal to Realign Federal Rules of Evidence 608 and 609*, 37 VILL. L. REV. 533 (1992)

Friedland, *On Common Sense and the Evaluation of Witness Credibility*, 40 CASE W. RES. L. REV. 165 (1989)

Kerper & MacDonald, *Federal Rule of Evidence 608(B): A Proposed Revision*, 22 AKRON L. REV. 283 (1989)

Ordover, *Balancing the Presumptions of Guilt and Innocence: Rules 404(B), 608(B) and 609(A)*, 38 EMORY L.J. 135 (1989)

Hale, *Specific Acts and Related Matters as Affecting Credibility*, 1 HASTINGS L.J. 89 (1950)

Note, *Witnesses Under Rule VI of the Proposed Federal Rules of Evidence*, 15 WAYNE L. REV. 1236 (1969)

Comment, *Use of Bad Character and Prior Convictions to Impeach a Defendant Witness*, 34 FORDHAM L. REV. 107 (1965)

COMPARISON TO FEDERAL RULE

Colorado Rule 608 is substantively identical to Federal Rule 608. However, on Dec. 1, 2011 Federal Rule 608 was restyled. Please see Federal Rule 608 in the appendix for comparison.

SIGNIFICANT CASES

People v. Penn, 2016 CO 32 (Colo. 2016) (police officer's testimony that he had reason to arrest the defendant was not equivalent to a prohibited opinion on the credibility of the person whose information had led to the arrest; that claimed equivalence was too attenuated to run afoul of the rule against direct comment on a witness's credibility).

People v. Vidauri, 2019 Colo. App. LEXIS 1333 (Colo. App. 2019) (in a criminal case alleging theft of public benefits, the court found that expert testimony on questionable aspects of defendant's benefit applications did not violate CRE 608 because the expert's testimony did not involve the defendant's truthfulness on a specific occasion).

Settle v. Basinger, 2013 Colo. App. LEXIS 261 (2013) (trial judge properly refused to permit cross-examination of an expert witness about her past drug and alcohol addiction problems; such conduct might reflect character for sobriety and obedience to law, but whether such conduct reflects on truthfulness was properly left to the sound discretion of the trial court).

People v. Wittrein, 221 P.3d 1076 (Colo. 2009) (experts may not offer their direct opinion on a child victim's truthfulness or their opinion on whether children tend to fabricate sexual abuse allegations).

People v. Segovia, 196 P.3d 1126 (Colo. 2008) (theft is probative of dishonesty, so inquiry into a witness's act of shoplifting is permissible under Rule 608(b)).

Liggett v. People, 135 P.3d 725 (Colo. 2006) (it was error, though not harmful, for prosecutor to ask defendant to comment on the veracity of another witness's testimony by repeatedly asking the defendant: ". . . was he lying?").

People v. Eppens, 979 P.2d 14 (Colo. 1999) (testimony by social worker that statements by child who was allegedly the victim of abuse were sincere was wrongly admitted, since Rule 608(a) allows only narrowly specified types of extrinsic evidence on this subject).

People v. Fasy, 829 P.2d 1314 (Colo. 1992) (where an expert had not provided a "detailed history" of assault, had not made any commentary which referred to the victim's "truthfulness or untruthfulness," and did not focus on the "truthfulness" of the statements, the testimony provided did not fit CRE 608(a), an exception to CRE 404(a)).

People v. Gaffney, 769 P.2d 1081 (Colo. 1989) (pediatrician's statement that medical history given by child sex abuse victim was "very believable" constituted impermissible opinion testimony on victim's character for truthfulness).

People v. Distel, 759 P.2d 654 (Colo. 1988) (in a disciplinary proceeding against attorney Dristel, the court held that the attorney's prior disciplinary record may be used during evidentiary phase of the proceedings to judge the attorney's credibility as a witness under CRE 608(b)).

Tevlin v. People, 715 P.2d 338 (Colo. 1986); *People v. Jensen*, 747 P.2d 1247 (Colo. 1987); *People v. Oliver*, 745 P.2d 222 (Colo. 1987) (to prove reversible error when an expert testifies as to the truthfulness of child's testimony, defendant must meet a two-part test: (1) was opinion testimony erroneously admitted into evidence, and (2) if so, did it substantially influence the verdict or affect the trial proceedings fairness).

Honey v. People, 713 P.2d 1300 (Colo. 1986) (even though opinion evidence as to lack of truthfulness of the complaining witness was improperly rejected, the court held such to be harmless error).

People v. Bowman, 669 P.2d 1369 (Colo. 1983) (defendant's Sixth Amendment right to confront witnesses was improperly denied by the trial court when it prohibited him from cross-examining a juvenile witness who provided the only evidence regarding many links in the prosecution's case).

People v. Cole, 654 P.2d 830 (Colo. 1982) (testimony as to the use of force by an arresting officer in unrelated events was not admissible, because it directed the jury's attention away from the case under consideration and permitted a direct attack on the general character of the witnessing officer. The attack must go to the credibility of the officer and not his general character).

People v. Sasson, 628 P.2d 120 (Colo. 1981) (the court held that the credibility of a defendant who testifies in his own behalf may be attacked by introduction of evidence of prior felony convictions, but not of prior misdemeanor convictions).

People v. Meyers, 617 P.2d 808 (Colo. 1980); *People v. Layton*, 612 P.2d 83 (Colo. 1980); *People v.*

Hampton, 619 P.2d 48 (Colo. 1980) (Colorado Supreme Court rejected arguments that use of a prior felony conviction for impeachment purposes during trial was unconstitutional).

People v. Serra, 361 P.3d 1122 (Colo. App. 2015) (character evidence to show a witness's truthful character was not permissible in response to cross-examination of that witness that she "took an oath to tell the truth" and her testimony was given "under oath," and that the case was "[n]ot about a personal agenda," because those questions did not attack the witness's overall character for truthfulness).

Leaf v Beihoffer, 338 P.3d 1136 (Colo. App. 2014) (in a civil tort case, court found that failure to file tax returns for several years, as opposed to a single year, is admissible under 608(b). Court adopted federal rule, and found such evidence is probative of truthfulness because it reflects a pattern of behavior rather than an isolated mistake).

People v. Thomas, 345 P.3d 959 (Colo. App. 2014) (in a vehicular homicide case, court ruled admission of extrinsic evidence that contradicts witness testimony does not violate CRE 608(b). In this case, defendant lied about employment status to obtain a bond reduction, and evidence of a phone recording admitting as much was found admissible during cross-examination. Court adopted federal precedent that testimony by defendant can open door to admission of extrinsic evidence to attack or support witness's truthfulness).

People v. Cook, 197 P.3d 269 (Colo. App. 2008) (admission of testimony by investigating officer that she thought alleged victims were credible was plain error, because Rule 608(a)(1) does not permit a witness to express an opinion that a person was telling the truth on a specific occasion).

People v. Gilbert, 12 P.3d 331 (Colo. App. 2000) (evidence of a witness's prior misdemeanor conviction for providing false information to police should have been admitted for impeachment purposes under Rule 608(b), but error was harmless in overall context of case).

People v. Lee, 989 P.2d 777 (Colo. App. 1999) (asking witnesses if they took seriously their oath to testify truthfully, and asking a witness if his own testimony was truthful, is permissible, and is not improper bolstering).

People v. Lesslie, 939 P.2d 443 (Colo. App. 1996) (cross-examination of a witness on the question of bigamy for impeachment was properly denied absent a conviction, arrest, charge, or evidence of a prior plea agreement not to prosecute).

People v. Saiz, 923 P.2d 197 (Colo. App. 1996) (testimony of two criminal defense lawyers in the form of opinion or reputation testimony about the truthfulness of an expert witness based on past experience is admissible as character evidence of truthfulness; Rule 608(a) makes no exceptions for expert testimony).

People v. Gillis, 883 P.2d 554 (Colo. App. 1994) (trial court did not err in allowing prosecutor to ask defendant about prior misdemeanor convictions for providing false information to the police for the limited purpose of evaluating defendant's credibility).

Wilkerson v. State, 830 P.2d 1121 (Colo. App. 1992) (where proffered evidence deals with the witness's general character, exclusion is proper; impeachment may not be accomplished by attacking the general character of a witness).

People v. Wheatley, 805 P.2d 1148 (Colo. App. 1990) (something more than the contradiction of a witness's testimony by other witness's testimony must occur before there is an "attack on the truthfulness character trait." Hence, opinion or reputation evidence of truthful character would be error).

People v. Snook, 729 P.2d 1026 (Colo. App. 1986) (expert's testimony that child was telling the truth when child testified was held to be prejudicial error).

People v. Myers, 714 P.2d 513 (Colo. App. 1985) (the Colorado Court of Appeals allowed a mother to testify that the child victim of alleged sexual assault had received counseling at the suggestion of the Department of Social Services. The court held this was not opinion evidence and therefore not subject to CRE 608(a)).

People v. Manners, 713 P.2d 1348 (Colo. App. 1985) (because it was not opinion nor reputation evidence, the statement concerning participation in prior robberies was inadmissible to impeach the credibility of a co-participant in a murder case).

People v. Koon, 713 P.2d 410 (Colo. App. 1985); *People v. Ross*, 745 P.2d 277 (Colo. App. 1987); *People v. Higa*, 735 P.2d 203 (Colo. App. 1987) (in sexual assault situations concerning very young child-victims, expert opinions may be given relating to general characteristics in regard to truthfulness; however, such opinions may not always be allowed in situations involving older children).

People v. Armstrong, 704 P.2d 877 (Colo. App. 1985) (court allowed inquiry into a misdemeanor conviction for impeachment purposes (contrary to C.R.S. § 13-90-101) because the conviction was for making a false police report concerning the same defendant which under 608(b) was a "specific instance of conduct" probative of untruthfulness).

People v. Saldana, 670 P.2d 14 (Colo. App. 1983) (defense improperly tried to cross-examine a police witness on his past use of marijuana. The trial court was correct in denying the proffered evidence, absent a showing that it would be probative of truthfulness or untruthfulness).

People v. Heredia-Cobos, 415 P.3d 860 (Colo. App. 2017) (adopting the rule in other jurisdictions that a defendant in a child sex assault case opens the door to otherwise inadmissible testimony under 608 when the defense challenged the child witness's credibility by suggesting the child had been coached).

Gay v. Foster, 2018 U.S. Dist. LEXIS 159032(D. Colo. 2018) (the trial court did not abuse its discretion when admitting the testimony of a detective, who having been called as a lay witness, testified concerning typical reactions of testifying witnesses based on his general experience and did not offer testimony that a particular witness testified truthfully).

People v. Koper, 488 P.3d 409, 2018 Colo. App. LEXIS 1325 (Colo. App. 2018) (the trial court erred in allowing the prosecutor to repeatedly ask the defendant if other witness's testimony were incorrect, wrong, or untrue, or whether the other witnesses had lied, because such questions fall within the general category of prohibited "are you lying" questions).

Herrera v. Lerma, 440 P.3d 1194 (Colo. App. 2018) (the trial court erred in finding that the medical expert's opinion on the American Medical Association Guides had probative value substantially outweighed by the danger of unfair prejudice because the jury is not likely to be confused by such testimony).

WITNESSES

Chapter 609

Rule 609. *(No Colorado Rule Codified)*
COLO. REV. STAT. § 13-90-101. Who May Testify—Interest

The statute reads as follows:

All persons, without exception, other than those specified in sections 13-90-102 to 13-90-108 may be witnesses. Neither parties nor other persons who have an interest in the event of an action or proceeding shall be excluded; nor those who have been convicted of crime; nor persons on account of their opinions on matters of religious belief. In every case the credibility of the witness may be drawn in question, as now provided by law, but the conviction of any person for any felony may be shown for the purpose of affecting the credibility of such witness. The fact of such conviction may be proved like any other fact, not of record, either by the witness himself, who shall be compelled to testify thereto, or by any other person cognizant of such conviction as impeaching testimony or by any other competent testimony. Evidence of a previous conviction of a felony where the witness testifying was convicted five years prior to the time when the witness testifies shall not be admissible in evidence in any civil action.

Highlights

Amendments to the Federal Rules of Evidence approved by the judicial conference took effect December 1, 2006.

An amendment to Federal Rule of Evidence 609 clarifies that automatic impeachment is allowed only when an element of the crime requires proof of deceit or if the underlying act of deceit readily can be determined from information such as the charging instrument.

ANALYSIS

The Colorado statute concerning impeachment by evidence of conviction of crime provides that for purposes of attacking the credibility of a witness, evidence that the witness has been convicted of a felony is admissible. For civil trials there is a limitation that the felony conviction must have occurred within five years of the time of testifying. There is no time limitation in criminal trials.

A defendant in a criminal case becomes a "witness" for purposes of this statute when the defendant testifies at the trial.

"Felony" in the statute means the classification of the crime at the time of the conviction. Foreign felonies may be shown. Juvenile adjudications are not convictions under the statute nor are expunged convictions.

AUTHORITY

MCCORMICK § 43

WIGMORE §§ 980–88

4 WIGMORE §§ 1106, 1116

Williams, *Witness Impeachment by Evidence of Prior Felony Convictions: The Time Has Come to Put on the New Man and Forgive the Felon,* 65 TEMP. L. REV. 893 (1992)

A Recommendation for Reform, 57 FORDHAM L. REV. 1 (1988)

Stiegelmeier, *Decriminalization of Municipal Offenses in Colorado,* 19 COLO. LAW. 1327 (1990)

Snider, *Effect of Criminal Guilty Pleas in Administrative Hearings,* 22 COLO. LAW. 1889 (1993)

Multz, *Cross-Examination in Criminal Cases,* 7 COLO. LAW. 1727 (Oct. 1978)

SIGNIFICANT CASES

Apodaca v. People, 712 P.2d 467 (Colo. 1985) (defendant's military conviction for rape constituted a felony conviction for purposes of Colorado's impeachment statute).

People v. Layton, 612 P.2d 83 (Colo. 1980) (statute which permits admission of evidence of prior felony convictions when a defendant chooses to testify does not deny equal protection, even though such evidence is inadmissible when defendant does not testify, since the classes of defendants who choose to testify and those who do not are not similarly situated and when defendant takes witness stand his credibility is in issue and evidence of prior felony convictions then becomes relevant).

People v. McNeely, 68 P.3d 540 (Colo. App. 2002) (where a trial court has entered a judgment of conviction and also sentenced defendant, that conviction may be used for purposes of impeachment at a later proceeding even if the appeal of that conviction is pending).

People v. Bradley, 25 P.3d 1271 (Colo. App. 2001) (absent special circumstances, under C.R.S. § 13-90-101 a defendant may be impeached with felony convictions that occurred after the offense for which he or she is being tried).

People v. Diaz, 985 P.2d 83 (Colo. App. 1999) (prior felony convictions were properly admitted to impeach defendant's testimony; § 13-90-101 does not violate the separation of powers doctrine by invading the Supreme Court's rulemaking power).

People v. Hardy, 677 P.2d 429 (Colo. App. 1983) (when defendant testifies, trial court may not foreclose use of name, nature, and date of his prior felony convictions for impeachment purposes; further examination into details of prior convictions is within trial court's discretion, provided that such details are relevant).

People v. Sasson, 628 P.2d 120 (Colo. App. 1980) (evidence of prior felony convictions is admissible to attack credibility of defendant who testifies on his own behalf, but his credibility may not be impeached by evidence of prior misdemeanor convictions).

People v. Medina, 583 P.2d 293 (Colo. App. 1978) (trial court has discretion to limit cross-examination by use of prior felony conviction to exclude detailed cross-questioning concerning facts involved in defendant's prior conviction, however, when defendant exercises his statutory privilege of testifying, all prior felony convictions and their nature may be shown to impeach his testimony).

Chapter 610

Rule 610. Religious Beliefs or Opinions

Rule 610 reads as follows:

> Evidence of the beliefs or opinions of a witness on matters of religion is not admissible for the purposes of showing that by reason of their nature his credibility is impaired or enhanced.

ANALYSIS

Rule 610 generally prohibits the introduction of evidence or interrogation of witnesses as to religious beliefs or opinions for the purpose of impeaching or bolstering a witness's credibility. The principles of inadmissibility contained in Rule 610 rest primarily upon grounds of unfair prejudice and minimal probative value.

Rule 610 does not preclude the admission of evidence of religious beliefs where the evidence is relevant in a manner other than to show that the witness's trustworthiness is enhanced or diminished by virtue of the belief. Consequently, the Rule does not prevent evidence tending to demonstrate bias or interest on the part of a witness, such as where the witness is affiliated with a church that is a party to the action.

AUTHORITY

Weissenberger's Federal Evidence §§ 610.1–.2

McCormick § 48

4 Weinstein 2d §§ 610.01–.03

3 Mueller & Kirkpatrick §§ 289–290

3 Wigmore § 936

Swancara, *Impeachment of Non-Religious Witness*, 13 Rocky Mtn. L. Rev. 336 (1941)

Note, *Evidence—Impeaching Witness by Showing Religious Belief*, 9 N.C. L. Rev. 77 (1930)

COMPARISON TO FEDERAL RULE

Colorado Rule 610 is substantially identical to Federal Rule 610. However, on Dec. 1, 2011 Federal Rule 610 was restyled. Please see Federal Rule 610 in the appendix for comparison.

SIGNIFICANT CASES

Conrad v. City and County of Denver, 656 P.2d 662 (Colo. 1982), *as mod.* (1983) (questioning witnesses about their religious beliefs was not objectionable under Rule 610, because the questioning was not used solely to enhance or impeach credibility but was relevant in determining standing, personal

149

knowledge, and basis for opinions that the effect of the nativity scene was to prefer the Christian religion).

People v. Mandez, 997 P.2d 1254 (Colo. App. 1999) (testimony by prosecution witness that Jesus Christ had saved his life and that he therefore understood the importance of telling the truth violated Rule 610).

Chapter 611

Rule 611. Mode and Order of Interrogation and Presentation

Rule 611 reads as follows:

> **(a) Control by court.** The court shall exercise reasonable control over the mode and order of interrogating witnesses and presenting evidence so as to (1) make the interrogation and presentation effective for the ascertainment of the truth, (2) avoid needless consumption of time, and (3) protect witnesses from harassment or undue embarrassment.
>
> **(b) Scope of cross-examination.** Cross-examination should be limited to the subject matter of the direct examination and matters affecting the credibility of the witness. The court may, in the exercise of discretion, permit inquiry into additional matters as if on direct examination.
>
> **(c) Leading questions.** Leading questions should not be used on the direct examination of a witness except as may be necessary to develop his testimony. Leading questions should be permitted on cross-examination. When a party calls a hostile witness, an adverse party, or a witness identified with an adverse party, interrogation may be by leading questions.

ANALYSIS

Rule 611 governs the trial court's control over the mode and order of interrogating witnesses and presenting evidence, the scope of cross-examination, and the use of leading questions.

Rule 611(a) accords the trial judge authority to control the examination of witnesses and the presentation of non-testimonial evidence. In the exercise of the trial court's discretion three guiding principles are indicated: (1) efficiency in ascertainment of the truth; (2) avoidance of needless consumption of time; and (3) protection of witnesses from harassment or undue embarrassment. Rule 611(a) seeks to advance goals similar to those underlying Rules 102 and 403, and consistent with the three objectives identified in Rule 611(a), the trial court has discretionary power over decisions such as whether and to what extent to allow re-direct and re-cross-examinations, whether a witness can be re-called, and whether a party may reopen its case.

Under Colorado Rule 611(b), cross-examination is permitted on the subject matter covered in the direct examination and on matters affecting the credibility of the witness. Examination of a witness beyond the scope of direct inquiry is permissible only if authorized by the trial judge in the exercise of his or her discretion.

WITNESSES

Rule 611(c) provides the court with discretion to control the use of leading questions. Leading questions suggest a particular answer by the form or substance of the interrogation. On direct examination, where the witness usually favors the calling party's case, leading questions are disapproved because the witness may readily accede to the version of the events stated in the examiner's question rather than describing the occurrence as he or she actually remembers it. On cross-examination, where the witness is likely aligned with the opposing party, leading questions are generally permissible because it is assumed that the witness is less susceptible to the question's suggestiveness.

Illustration

The following questions are likely to be held leading, depending upon the factual context in which they are asked:

Q: Isn't it a fact that you were at home on January 19, 1994?

Q: The light was green when you entered the intersection, isn't that true?

Q: Was it 6 o'clock or was it some other time?

Q: After the meeting with Mr. Johnson, did you go home?

Q: Am I correct in stating that you are a close friend of the accused?

Leading questions may be allowed on direct examination but only when necessary to develop testimony or when used to elicit preliminary matters which are usually undisputed. Accordingly, leading questions are frequently permitted when interrogating a young child, or where the witness has temporarily forgotten relatively undisputed facts. Leading questions are expressly authorized by the Rule when a party calls a hostile witness, an adverse party or a witness identified with an adverse party. A hostile witness is one who is so evasive or uncooperative on examination that his testimony is impeded. Usually, counsel asks the trial judge to have the witness declared hostile, thereby permitting counsel to proceed with a leading question form. The term "witness identified with an adverse party" is intended to apply broadly to an identification based upon employment by the party or by virtue of a demonstrated connection to an opposing party.

Often constitutional questions arise under this rule (see recent significant cases at end of chapter). The Colorado Court of Appeals recently looked at the scope of the Sixth Amendment right of confrontation. In this dependency and neglect action, *People ex rel. S.X.M.*, the court reviewed a case terminating the parental rights of a father. The trial court had allowed the child to testify by closed circuit television outside the father's presence. The child testified in the courtroom before the judge and jury and was cross-examined by father's counsel. The father was able to see the child by closed circuit television and talk to his lawyer during the examination, but the child was unable to see the father. The trial court had ordered this procedure after an evidentiary hearing where the trial court determined that the child would suffer serious emotional harm if forced to testify in front of her father. The Court of Appeals affirmed, the trial court since: (1) the child testified in the courtroom in from of the judge and jury; (2) the father observed the examination and could participate in cross-examination; and (3) the trial judge based his determination on evidence that seeing the father would harm the child. The Sixth Amendment did not require "face-to-face" confrontation. The procedure adopted by the trial judge was within the judge's discretion and not error.

AUTHORITY

WEISSENBERGER'S FEDERAL EVIDENCE §§ 611.1–.6

McCORMICK §§ 5, 6, 19–31

4 WEINSTEIN 2d §§ 611.01–.06

3 MUELLER & KIRKPATRICK §§ 291–322

3 WIGMORE §§ 768–80

5 WIGMORE §§ 1390–94

6 WIGMORE §§ 1884–94

8 WIGMORE § 2276

Ringland, *Child Sexual Abuse Evidence Problems—Update (1988)*, 14 U. DAYTON L. REV. 147 (1988)

Bergman, *A Practical Approach to Cross-Examination: Safety First*, 25 UCLA L. REV. 547 (1978)

Carlson, *Scope of Cross-Examination and the Proposed Federal Rules*, 32 FED. B.J. 244 (1973)

Carlson, *Cross-Examination of the Accused*, 52 CORNELL L.Q. 705 (1967)

Degnan, *Non-Rules Evidence Law: Cross-Examination*, 6 UTAH L. REV. 323 (1959)

Denbeaux & Risinger, *Questioning Questions: Objections to Form in the Interrogation of Witnesses*, 33 ARK. L. REV. 439 (1980)

Denroche, *Leading Questions*, 6 CRIM. L.Q. 21 (1963)

Friendly, *The Fifth Amendment Tomorrow: The Case for Constitutional Change*, 37 U. CIN. L. REV. 671 (1968)

Lawson, *Order of Presentation as a Factor in Jury Persuasion*, 56 KY. L.J. 523 (1968)

Marshall, *Marquis and Oskamp, Effects of Kind of Questions and Atmosphere of Interrogation on Accuracy and Completeness of Testimony*, 84 HARV. L. REV. 1620 (1971)

Westen, *Order of Proof: An Accused's Right to Control the Timing and Sequence of Evidence in His Defense*, 66 CAL. L. REV. 935 (1978)

COMPARISON TO FEDERAL RULE

Colorado Rule 611 and Federal Rule 611 are functionally identical. However, on Dec. 1, 2011 Federal Rule 611 was restyled. Please see Federal Rule 611 in the appendix for comparison.

SIGNIFICANT CASES

Maryland v. Craig, 497 U.S. 836 (1990) (Sixth Amendment confrontation clause does not require face-to-face confrontation of child witness by defendant when all other courtroom safeguards of defendant's rights are present and trial court determines that child witness would be traumatized at hearing by seeing the defendant).

United States v. Havens, 446 U.S. 620 (1980) ("a defendant's statements made in response to proper cross-examination reasonably suggested by the defendant's direct examination are subject to otherwise proper impeachment by the government, albeit by evidence that has been illegally obtained and that is inadmissible on the government's direct case, or otherwise, as substantive evidence of guilt").

Garner v. People, 436 P.3d 1107 (Colo. 2019) (in a manslaughter case, the trial court's admission of victim-witness' in-court identifications of the defendant was not plain error, even though each witness failed to identify the defendant in a photographic array before trial and three years had elapsed between the crime and the confrontations).

Warden v. Exempla, Inc., 291 P.3d 30 (Colo. 2012) (evidentiary rules afford a party presenting rebuttal evidence significant leeway so long as the evidence rebuts some portion of an opposing party's claim; if evidence that is proper rebuttal also supports a party's case in an additional way, that additional relevance does not bar its admission as rebuttal).

WITNESSES

People v. Skufca, 176 P.3d 83 (Colo. 2008) (trial court's ruling that, if a defendant chose to testify, the People could cross-examine him about prior drug transactions to the extent that the defendant opened the door to that topic was proper; when a criminal defendant testifies in his or her own defense, the breadth of waiver of Fifth Amendment rights is determined by the scope of relevant cross examination).

People v. Harris, 762 P.2d 651 (Colo. 1988) (Supreme Court affirmed the Court of Appeals holding that defendant was entitled to cross-examination of prosecution's witness).

Banek v. Thomas, 733 P.2d 1171 (Colo. 1986) (in an action against deputy sheriff for assault and battery, the Colorado Supreme Court held that evidence of a prior criminal charge may be admitted for impeachment purposes when plaintiff denied he had resisted arrest in incident).

Le Masters v. People, 678 P.2d 538 (Colo. 1984) (where there is no nexus between the defendant's direct examination and the suppressed evidence, the latter's admission would destroy the defendant's right to take the stand. However, since other evidence was overwhelming here, the Court of Appeal's error was held harmless).

People v. Bowman, 669 P.2d 1369 (Colo. 1983) (defendant's Sixth Amendment right to confront witnesses was improperly denied by the trial court when it prohibited him from cross-examining a juvenile witness who provided the only evidence regarding many links in the prosecution's case).

People v. Raffaelli, 647 P.2d 230 (Colo. 1982); *People v. Loscutoff*, 661 P.2d 274 (Colo. 1983) (Rule 611(b) limits the scope of cross-examination to the subject matter of the direct examination and matters which affect the credibility of the witness. Unless the restriction of cross-examination is so severe as to constitute a denial of that right, the extent to which cross-examination should be allowed rests within the trial court's discretion).

People v. Rios, 462 P.3d 322 (Colo. App. 2020) (in a criminal menacing case, the trial court's denial of mistrial on that grounds that the prosecutor improperly commented on the defendant's silence was not in error because the defendant's objection to the prosecutor's comment was sustained, and the defense declined the offer to further instruct the jury).

People ex rel. S.X.M., 271 P.3d 1124 (Colo. App. 2011) (citing *Maryland v. Craig*, court allowed testimony of child witness to be used in trial adjudicating the child as dependent and neglected where trial court denied "face-to-face" confrontation).

People v. Liggett, 2005 Colo. App. LEXIS 45 (Jan 13, 2005) (improper to ask witness if other witnesses were lying and prosecutor repeatedly referring to defendant as "con man" but harmless error).

People v. James, 40 P.3d 36 (Colo. App. 2001) (where a prosecution witness had admitted in cross-examination the details of a plea agreement in exchange for his testimony, the trial court acted within its discretion in prohibiting further questioning trying to show that the witness could have been prosecuted as a habitual offender when defense counsel knew the witness's record was insufficient to be subject to habitual criminal prosecution).

People v. Johnson, 30 P.3d 718 (Colo. App. 2000) (where the prosecution learned after cross-examining a witness that the witness had been convicted earlier of a felony, the trial court acted properly in allowing the prosecution to recall that witness for impeachment and in permitting the defense to reopen its direct examination to elicit the conviction from the witness prior to the prosecution's second cross-examination).

People v. Scarlett, 985 P.2d 36 (Colo. App. 1998) (cross-examination of defendant concerning the amount of alcohol he consumed before he was involved in a traffic accident was not beyond the scope of his direct examination, since the defendant's direct testimony sought to minimize the recklessness of his driving; a defendant's testimony can be rebutted, contradicted, and impeached as with any other witness).

People v. Raehal, 971 P.2d 256 (Colo. App. 1998) (plain error was not committed when prosecution used leading questions in the direct examination of a young sexual assault victim, because the testimony was difficult and confusing).

People v. Gillis, 883 P.2d 554 (Colo. App. 1994) (there was no clear abuse of discretion by the trial court in allowing the prosecutor, upon redirect, to ask leading questions of a witness in order to clarify confusing testimony given during cross-examination).

People v. Sallis, 857 P.2d 572 (Colo. App. 1993) (trial court erred in not allowing the prosecutor an opportunity to fully develop surrounding facts and inconsistencies in the defense of a case involving the threatening and sexual assault of a young boy).

Knowles v. Board of Ed. Sch. Dist. No. RE-1, 857 P.2d 553 (Colo. App. 1993) (where petitioner in an administrative proceeding did not object or take exception to the questions on cross-examination asking whether "[I]s it your testimony that [the student] lied . . .," and where the record does not reflect that the result of the hearing was "specifically affected" as a result of these questions, allowing such questions on cross-examination did not constitute "plain error").

People v. Nunez, 684 P.2d 945 (Colo. App. 1984) (a defendant may impeach a witness's credibility on cross-examination by inquiring into the nature of a prosecutorial promise or deal motivating the witness to testify against the defendant. However, the prosecution may then question the witness about promises or deals to dispel any unfavorable innuendo cast on the witness by defendant's cross-examination).

Bruce Hughes, Inc. v. Ingels & Associates, Inc., 653 P.2d 88 (Colo. App. 1982) (the purpose of Rule 611(c) is to enlarge the class of witnesses identified as adverse by permitting (1) leading questions on cross-examination and (2) interrogation by leading questions when a party calls a hostile witness, adverse party, or a witness identified with an adverse party).

People v. Gwinn, 428 P.3d 727 (Colo. App. 2018) (the prosecutor is permitted to impeach its own police officer witness if the testimony of the witness is contradicted by a previous statement regarding a sobriety examination report as long as the questions are direct references to the sobriety record and were asked in response to the conflicting statement).

People v. Gutierrez, 432 P.3d 579 (Colo. 2018) (trial court did not abuse its discretion in denying a request to have a witness testify remotely by Skype after attempts to accommodate the People's difficulty in procuring the witness's presence due to witness's surgery and injury).

Chapter 612

Rule 612. Writing Used to Refresh Memory

Rule 612 reads as follows:

> If a witness uses a writing to refresh his memory for the purpose of testifying, either—
> (1) while testifying, or
> (2) before testifying, if
> the court in its discretion determines it is necessary in the interests of justice, an adverse party is entitled to have the writing produced at the hearing, to inspect it, to cross-examine the witness thereon, and to introduce in evidence those portions which relate to the testimony of the witness. If it is claimed that the writing contains matters not related to the subject matter of the testimony the court shall examine the writing in camera, excise any portions not so related, and order delivery of the remainder to the party entitled thereto. Any portion withheld over objections shall be preserved and made available to the appellate court in the event of an appeal. If a writing is not produced or delivered pursuant to order under this rule, the court shall make any order justice requires, except that in criminal cases when the prosecution elects not to comply, the order shall be one striking the testimony or, if the court in its discretion determines that the interests of justice so require, declaring a mistrial.

ANALYSIS

According to Rule 612, the recollection of a witness may be refreshed through the use of a document. The writing is used to revive the memory of the witness, and it must provide sufficient stimulus that the witness has a present, independent recollection of the matter. In order to apply the Rule properly, it is imperative to recognize that the writing is not the evidence. It is the refreshed recollection in the form of testimony that is the evidence. As a consequence, it is important to appreciate that the writing need not be admissible under the Rules. There is no necessity of compliance with the best evidence rule, the authentication rule or the hearsay rule. Frequently, a document used to refresh recollection is marked for the purposes of the record, however, even though it is not being offered as evidence.

Utilizing the technique of present recollection refreshed, the witness at trial must be incapable of recalling all of the pertinent facts as to which he or she has first-hand knowledge and as to which he or she has been called to testify. The witness is then handed the writing by trial counsel. The proponent of the witness then asks the witness to read the writing silently in order to refresh his or her recollection. The witness is then asked if his or her recollection is refreshed, and if he or she then has a present recollection, the witness provides testimony from revived memory.

WITNESSES

When a writing is used as a memory jogging device, the writing must be shown to opposing counsel on request. Rule 612 also expands the traditional rule by permitting production of a writing within the judge's discretion even if the writing was only used prior to trial to stimulate the witness's memory. The existence of such a document used prior to trial would normally be exposed during the course of cross-examination of the witness by the witness's opponent. A recess may be requested where the pretrial memory jogging document is not readily available for production.

Practical Application of Rule 612

It should be noted that when a document is used at trial in an effort to refresh the recollection of a witness, the document must be produced for adverse counsel. Where, however, the document is used prior to testifying in order to refresh the witness's recollection, the document is subject to production in the discretion of the trial judge subject to the interests of justice. Accordingly, documents used at trial to refresh recollection must be delivered to adverse counsel on request. In this context Rule 612 does not provide for discretion. The discretion provided by Rule 612 applies only to those documents used prior to trial to refresh recollection.

Where a claim is made that the writing used to refresh recollection contains matters which are unrelated to the litigation and which have not affected the witness's testimony, the court has the duty to inspect the writing *in camera* to excise any unrelated or irrelevant portions. The remainder is delivered to the adverse party. Where a party fails to produce documents in compliance with the trial court's order, the court may make any further order necessitated by the ends of justice, including in criminal cases, ordering a mistrial where the prosecution fails to comply.

Practical Considerations

The technique of refreshing a witness's recollection must be distinguished from the hearsay exception, "past recollection recorded," the subject of Rule 803(5). Under the technique of refreshing recollection, the witness reviews the writing to revive his memory of the material event and then proceeds to testify on the basis of present, personal knowledge. The writing itself is not offered as evidence. It merely serves as a memory jogging device, and compliance with the hearsay rule, the authentication rule or the so-called best evidence rule is not required. In contrast, under the "past recollection recorded" exception to the general proscription against hearsay, the document itself is offered as the evidence. Rule 803(5) may operate to admit written hearsay in certain instances where the witness's present recollection remains absent or incomplete and cannot be refreshed by the writing. Under Rule 803(5) the witness's trial testimony establishes the foundational fact that recollection was complete at the time of writing and that the facts were accurately recorded in the document. Obviously, where a writing is offered into evidence, it must comply with all the rules regarding the admissibility of documentary evidence, one of which is the hearsay rule. Where a writing is offered, one of the hearsay exceptions available to admit the out-of-court statement is Rule 803(5). Of course, other exceptions might be available as well.

Where a document fails to revive the recollection of a witness, the document may be admissible as "past recollection recorded" under Rule 803(5). *See* Analysis for Rule 803(5). In this regard, it should be appreciated that the Rules of Evidence essentially provide for a three-tiered preference. First, the unaided testimony of a witness is preferred. Second, if the unaided testimony is not available, the law then prefers refreshed recollection. Third, if the witness's recollection cannot be revived, the recorded recollection exception to the hearsay rule may be available to admit the document which contains the witness's prior knowledge of the facts in question.

AUTHORITY

WEISSENBERGER'S FEDERAL EVIDENCE §§ 612.1–.7

4 WEINSTEIN 2d §§ 612.01–.09

3 MUELLER & KIRKPATRICK §§ 323–328

McCORMICK § 9

3 WIGMORE §§ 758–65

A Deposition Primer, Part II: At the Deposition, 11 COLO. LAW. 1215 (1982)

Rule 612 Revisited, 11 COLO. LAW. 1553 (1982)

Kalo, *Refreshing Recollection: Problems with Laying a Foundation,* 10 RUTGERS-CAM. L.J. 233 (1979)

Maguire & Wuick, *Testimony: Memory and Memoranda,* 3 HOS. L.J. 1 (1957)

COMPARISON TO FEDERAL RULE

Colorado Rule 612 is similar in substance to Federal Rule 612. However, on Dec. 1, 2011 Federal Rule 612 was restyled. Please see Federal Rule 612 in the appendix for comparison.

SIGNIFICANT CASES

People v. Clary, 950 P.2d 654 (Colo. App. 1997) (there was no error where a handwritten notation on the back of a payroll record that was not written contemporaneously with the document was admitted as a basis for refreshing the recollection of the testimony of a prosecution witness).

WITNESSES

Chapter 613

Rule 613. Prior Statements of Witnesses

Rule 613 reads as follows:

> **(a) Examining witness concerning prior inconsistent statements for impeachment purposes.** Before a witness may be examined for impeachment by prior inconsistent statement the examiner must call the attention of the witness to the particular time and occasion when, the place where, and the person to whom he made the statement. As a part of that foundation, the examiner may refer to the witness statement to bring to the attention of the witness any purported prior inconsistent statement. The exact language of the prior statement may be given.
>
> Where the witness denies or does not remember making the prior statement, extrinsic evidence, such as deposition, proving the utterance of the prior evidence is admissible. However, if a witness admits making the prior statement, additional extrinsic evidence that the prior statement was made is inadmissible.
>
> Denial or failure to remember the prior statement is a prerequisite for the introduction of extrinsic evidence to prove that the prior inconsistent statement was made.

ANALYSIS

Under Rule 613 a witness may be impeached through the introduction of evidence of a statement made by that witness prior to trial that is inconsistent with the testimony he has provided at trial. Before a witness may be examined for impeachment by prior inconsistent statement, the examiner must call his attention to the particular time, place, and person to whom he made the statement.

As a part of that foundation, the examiner may refer to the specific witness's statement and may give the exact language of the prior statement.

Under Federal Rule 613(b), a witness may be impeached by "extrinsic evidence." Where such evidence is introduced, the witness must be given an opportunity to explain or deny the inconsistent statement and the opposing party must have the opportunity to interrogate the witness concerning the statement.

A Colorado statute, § 16-10-201, requires the admission of a witness's prior inconsistent statement for substantive purposes in a criminal trial, when certain foundation requirements are met. A statement that qualifies for admission under the statute may be used for impeachment purposes even if it would not otherwise satisfy the foundation requirements of Rule 613. Rule 613 requires that a witness must have denied or failed to remember the prior statement before it can be proved by extrinsic evidence. The statute has no such requirement.

Practical Application of Rule 613

Extrinsic evidence is testimony or documentary evidence that is submitted to the trier of fact after the conclusion of the testimony of the witness sought to be impeached. Usually, it involves the calling of a distinct witness to provide the testimony as to the prior inconsistent statement or to authenticate the document containing the prior contradictory statement.

Constitutional Considerations

When a defendant exercises his right to testify at trial, statements ordinarily subject to the exclusionary rule and constitutionally inadmissible in the prosecution's case-in-chief are often admissible to impeach the defendant's inconsistent testimony. The United States Supreme Court has held that the exclusionary rule is not "a license to use perjury by way of defense." *See Harris v. New York*, 401 U.S. 222 (1971). The possibility that this impeachment exception will encourage police misconduct is merely "speculative" and therefore outweighed by the furtherance of the truth-seeking function of the court. The impeachment exception, however, may not be extended beyond the defendant's own testimony to include other defense witnesses. *See James v. Illinois*, 493 U.S. 307 (1990).

In *Michigan v. Harvey*, 494 U.S. 344 (1990), statements obtained in violation of the accused's Sixth Amendment right to counsel were admitted at trial for impeachment purposes. The United States Supreme Court held that, although these statements may not be used as substantive evidence, they may be used to impeach the defendant's inconsistent trial testimony.

STATUTES

§ 16-10-201.   Inconsistent statement of witness—competency of evidence

(1) Where a witness in a criminal trial has made a previous statement inconsistent with his testimony at the trial, the previous inconsistent statement may be shown by any otherwise competent evidence and is admissible not only for the purpose of impeaching the testimony of the witness, but also for the purpose of establishing a fact to which his testimony and the inconsistent statement relate, if:

(a)   The witness, while testifying, was given an opportunity to explain or deny the statement or the witness is still available to give further testimony in the trial; and

(b)   The previous inconsistent statement purports to relate to a matter within the witness's own knowledge.

AUTHORITY

WEISSENBERGER'S FEDERAL EVIDENCE §§ 613.1–.8

4 WEINSTEIN 2d §§ 613.01–.05

3 MUELLER & KIRKPATRICK §§ 329–333

MCCORMICK §§ 34–39

3A WIGMORE §§ 1017–46

Hale, *Impeachment of Witnesses by Prior Inconsistent Statements*, 10 S. CAL. L. REV. 135 (1937)

Ladd, *Some Observations on Credibility: Impeachment of Witnesses*, 52 CORNELL L.Q. 239 (1967)

Slough, *Impeachment of Witnesses, Common Law Principles and Modern Trends*, 34 IND. L.J. 1 (1958)

Comment, *Hearsay Under the Proposed Federal Rules: A Discretionary Approach*, 15 WAYNE L. REV. 1077 (1969)

Hearsay in Criminal Cases Under the Colorado Rules of Evidence: An Overview, 50 U. COLO. L. REV. 277 (1979)

COMPARISON TO FEDERAL RULE

Colorado Rule 613 differs from Federal Rule 613 in that it requires the examiner to disclose the particular time and occasion when, the place where, and the person to whom the statement was made. The Federal Rule does not require this disclosure before examining a witness for impeachment by prior inconsistent statements. Additionally, only the Federal Rule requires that the witness be afforded an opportunity to explain or deny the prior inconsistent statement and the opposite party is afforded an opportunity to interrogate the witness thereon, or the interests of justice otherwise require. On Dec. 1, 2011 Federal Rule 613 was restyled. Please see Federal Rule 613 in the appendix for comparison.

SIGNIFICANT CASES

Michigan v. Harvey, 494 U.S. 344 (1990) (statements taken in violation of defendant's Sixth Amendment right to counsel were admissible to impeach the defendant's testimony).

James v. Illinois, 493 U.S. 307 (1990) (the impeachment exception to the exclusionary rule may not be extended beyond the defendant's own testimony to include other defense witnesses).

People v. Welsh, 80 P.3d 296 (Colo. 2003) (in a case for first degree murder where the defendant raised the defense of not guilty by reason of insanity, the defendant's silence when asked by officers what happened at the time of the murder "was inadmissible for impeachment purposes because it did not sufficiently contradict the defendant's later statements to mental health experts that she did not recall the shooting").

People v. Saiz, 32 P.3d 441 (Colo. 2001) (trial court did not abuse its discretion by excluding videotaped inconsistent statements of defendant's minor son as cumulative, since a detective had already conceded that the child had made the conflicting statements, and defense counsel merely offered to impeach the child by showing his prior inconsistent statements on videotape as opposed to offering them for substantive purposes pursuant to C.R.S. § 16-10-201; requiring evidence to be "otherwise competent" under C.R.S. § 16-10-201 allows trial court to exclude probative evidence as being prejudicial or cumulative, and excluding the videotape was not a deprivation of a constitutional right to cross-examine or to present a defense).

Montoya v. People, 740 P.2d 992 (Colo. 1987) (as long as statutory foundation requirements for substantive admissibility are satisfied, the hearsay impediment of using prior inconsistent statements for proving the truth of the matter asserted may be eliminated; satisfying the statute's foundation requirements also permits use of a statement for impeachment purposes).

Appel v. Sentry Life Ins. Co., 739 P.2d 1380 (Colo. 1987) (the court held that the examiner could not impeach a witness with a deposition taken in an unrelated case because the opposing party was neither "present or represented at the taking of the deposition" nor given "reasonable notice thereof").

People v. Aguirre, 839 P.2d 483 (Colo. App. 1992) (witness's statements made following arrest were not made in furtherance of conspiracy but rather were admissible as prior inconsistent statements).

People v. Ball, 821 P.2d 905 (Colo. App. 1991) (prosecutor's threat to set aside witness's previously bargained plea did not render the witness's testimony from that trial involuntary or untrustworthy for impeachment of coconspirator at second trial).

WITNESSES

Gunnison v. McCabe Hereford Ranch, Inc., 702 P.2d 768 (Colo. App. 1985) (court stipulated value of land was not allowed to be used as a prior inconsistent statement, because there was a two-year time difference and the stipulation was a negotiated settlement compromise).

Transamerica Ins. Co. v. Pueblo Gas & Fuel Co., 519 P.2d 1201 (Colo. App. 1973) (the court set forth Rule 613, "First, a proper foundation must be laid for impeachment by prior inconsistent statement by specifically calling attention of the witness to the particular time and occasion when, the place where, and the person to whom he made the statements . . . . Before a party can offer proof the witness must be afforded an opportunity to deny, admit, or explain circumstances under which the purported statement was made").

Chapter 614

Rule 614. Calling and Interrogation of Witnesses by Court

Rule 614 reads as follows:

(a) **Calling by court.** The court may, on its own motion or at the suggestion of a party, call witnesses and all parties are entitled to cross-examine witnesses thus called.

(b) **Interrogation by court.** The court may interrogate witnesses, whether called by itself or by a party.

(c) **Objections.** Objections to the calling of witnesses by the court or to interrogation by it may be made at the time or at the next available opportunity when the jury is not present.

ANALYSIS

Rule 614 applies in civil and criminal cases and permits the trial judge to call and interrogate witnesses. Where the trial judge elects to call a witness, all parties are allowed to examine that witness. The power of the trial court to interrogate witnesses is, of course, subject to the restriction that the trial judge must maintain his or her status as an impartial arbiter.

Rule 614(c) permits trial counsel to make objections to either the court's calling of its own witness or the court's questioning of any witness. In addition, Rule 614(c) provides that such objection is timely if it is made at the earliest opportunity outside of the hearing of the jury.

AUTHORITY

WEISSENBERGER'S FEDERAL EVIDENCE §§ 614.1–.4

4 WEINSTEIN 2d §§ 614.01–.05

3 MUELLER & KIRKPATRICK §§ 334–337

MCCORMICK § 8

3 WIGMORE § 784

9 WIGMORE § 2484

Close, *The Right and Duty of a Trial Court to Call Witnesses in Civil Actions*, 25 INS. COUNS. J. 278 (1958)

Newark & Samuels, *Let the Judge Call the Witness*, 1969 CRIM. L. REV. 399

Comment, *Evidence—Impeachment of Witness Called by Court*, 20 WAYNE L. REV. 1385 (1974)

Note, *The Power of a Trial Judge to Call a Witness—A Tool to Mend Defects*, 21 S.C. L. REV. 224 (1969)

Note, *The Trial Judge's Use of His Power to Call Witnesses—An Aid to Adversary Presentation*, 51 NW. U. L. REV. 761 (1957)

COMPARISON TO FEDERAL RULE

Colorado Rule 614 is substantively identical to Federal Rule 614. Please note that on Dec. 1, 2011 Federal Rule 614 was restyled. Please see Federal Rule 614 in the appendix for comparison.

SIGNIFICANT CASES

People in Interest of Archuleta, 653 P.2d 93 (Colo. App. 1982) (on appeal of an order extending her commitment to a mental hospital, defendant claimed she was prevented from having a fair trial because the judge questioned her after the parties had concluded their examination of her. This alleged error was precluded because no contemporaneous objection was made. Additionally, Rule 614(b) specifically allowed for court interrogation of witnesses and there was no showing that the patient was prejudged by the questioning).

Chapter 615

Rule 615. Exclusion of Witnesses

Rule 615 reads as follows:

> At the request of a party the court shall order witnesses excluded so that they cannot hear the testimony of other witnesses, and it may make the order of its own motion. This rule does not authorize exclusion of (1) a party who is a natural person, or (2) an officer or employee of a party which is not a natural person designated as its representative by its attorney, or (3) a person whose presence is shown by a party to be essential to the presentation of his cause.

ANALYSIS

Under Rule 615 a party has the right to the separation of witnesses upon timely request. Where the request is made, the trial court lacks the discretion to deny the request except in regard to certain necessary witnesses expressly identified in the Rule. A party may not be subject to the exclusion order.

A party includes:

- A natural person
- An employee or agent of a party who is not a natural person as designated by its attorney
- Another person whose presence is shown to be necessary to the presentation of the cause (e.g., an expert witness)

The Rule is intended to:

- Insure that a party has adequate opportunity to prepare and present his case and, in a criminal case, to confront his accusers
- Permit a legal entity to participate in a trial to the same extent as a natural person
- Permit counsel to present his or her client's case effectively. For example: A prosecutor may need a police officer or the complaining witness at counsel table to present the state's case. In such cases it should be rare that both the police officer and the complaining witness would be present. Other persons who may be necessary for adequate presentation might include the parent of a child-party, an interpreter for a party who does not speak English, or an expert who observes testimony for purposes of his own testimony.

It should be noted that this Rule relates to persons at counsel table who may also be witnesses, and it does not apply to persons who will not be witnesses, e.g., co-counsel, investigators, clerks, or secretaries.

AUTHORITY

WEISSENBERGER'S FEDERAL EVIDENCE §§ 615.1–.3

4 WEINSTEIN 2d §§ 615.01–.07

3 MUELLER & KIRKPATRICK §§ 338–341

6 WIGMORE §§ 1837–41

Hood, *Witness Immunity Under Colorado Law*, 27 COLO. LAW. 37 (1998)

Comment, *Witnesses Under Article VI of the Proposed Federal Rules of Evidence*, 15 WAYNE L. REV. 1236, 1247–49

Note, *Witnesses—Enforcing a Sequestration Order to Exclude Witnesses—Barring the Witness from Testifying*, 11 U. KAN. L. REV. 410 (1963)

A Deposition Primer, Part I: Setting Up the Deposition, 11 COLO. LAW. 938 (1982)

COMPARISON TO FEDERAL RULE

Colorado Rule 615 is substantively identical to Federal Rule 615. Please note that on Dec. 1, 2011 Federal Rule 615 was restyled. Please see Federal Rule 615 in the appendix for comparison.

SIGNIFICANT CASES

State v. Melendez, 102 P.3d 315 (Colo. 2004) (trial court precluded the testimony of a defense witness who allegedly violated a sequestration order; the Supreme Court reversed because the trial court did not have any proof that the violation occurred and preclusion of a witness's testimony is not harmless ever).

People v. Cheeks, 682 P.2d 484 (Colo. 1984) (the Colorado Supreme Court held that an investigator who was designated by the prosecution as its representative under CRE 615(2) should not have been sequestered since "CRE 615 places natural and non-natural parties on an equal plane; both are entitled to have one potential witness who is not subject to sequestration." The trial court does not retain discretion to tip this balance against a non-natural party).

People v. Bobian, 461 P.3d 643 (Colo. App. 2019) (in a murder and assault case, the prosecutor's question asking a detective to address the consistency of the other witnesses' testimony was not plain error even though the detective was the only witness permitted to remain in the courtroom while all other witnesses were sequestered).

People v. Villalobos, 159 P.3d 624 (Colo. App. 2006) (CRE 615 applies to witnesses, not attorneys; therefore, a sequestration order is not violated when an attorney discusses one witness's testimony with another witness who is bound by a sequestration order).

Hamon Contractors, Inc. v. Dist. Court, 877 P.2d 884 (Colo. App. 1994) (trial court abused its discretion in excluding corporate plaintiffs representative from attending pretrial deposition of plaintiffs employee, absent evidence that plaintiff's employee would be intimidated by or would alter his testimony because of representative's presence).

Williamson v. School Dist. No. 2, 695 P.2d 1173 (Colo. App. 1984) (trial court's refusal to sequester defendant's witnesses at plaintiffs' request was not reversed on appeal, because plaintiffs failed to show abuse of discretion, especially considering they failed to make the sequestration motion until after plaintiffs had completed their case-in-chief on the third day of trial).

VII
OPINIONS AND EXPERT TESTIMONY

Chapter 701

Rule 701. Opinion Testimony by Lay Witnesses

Rule 701 reads as follows:

> If the witness is not testifying as an expert, the witness' testimony in the form of opinions or inferences is limited to those opinions or inferences which are (a) rationally based on the perception of the witness and (b) helpful to a clear understanding of the witness' testimony or the determination of a fact in issue, and (c) not based on scientific, technical, or other specialized knowledge within the scope of Rule 702.

ANALYSIS

Rule 701 governs the admissibility of opinion testimony from a lay witness. Before an opinion from a lay witness is permitted, two circumstances must exist. First, consistent with Rule 602, the opinion must be rationally based upon first-hand perceptions by the witness, and second, the opinion must facilitate an understanding of the witness's testimony.

Some things simply cannot be expressed in terms other than an opinion. Obvious examples would be testimony about color, speed of a vehicle, and the like. Opinion testimony is permitted in more complex circumstances where the opinion will facilitate a more complete understanding of the witness's testimony. Such circumstances might include the identity of a person, elements of a person's health, age, or appearance. Another area in which a lay witness is permitted to give opinion testimony under controlled circumstances relates to sanity or intoxication. In either case, a foundation is necessary to establish that the witness has had sufficient perceptions to form an opinion based upon those perceptions of the witness. The degree to which a witness may give an opinion, of course, is predicated in part upon whether and the extent to which the witness has sufficient life experiences that would permit making a judgment as to the matter involved.

Highlights

Robinson v. People, 927 P.2d 381 (Colo. 1996), exemplifies treatment of the requirement in Subsection (b) of Rule 701 that lay witness testimony must be "helpful" to the determination of a fact in issue. Testimony of a police officer was offered as lay witness testimony to identify the accused as a robber depicted in a surveillance video taken during a robbery, where the robber had attempted to disguise his identity. The issue is: Does CRE 701 permit a police officer to give lay opinion testimony regarding the identity of a person depicted in a video or photograph? This was a case of first impression in Colorado, and the Colorado Supreme Court looked to federal jurisdictions for interpretation because FRE 701 is identical to CRE 701. Federal jurisdictions have ruled in favor, as did the Colorado Supreme Court, of allowing lay witness testimony regarding the identity of a person depicted in a surveillance video or photograph so long as there is some basis for concluding that the lay witness is more likely to identify the accused than the jury. As a prerequisite, the Court did not require "intimate familiarity" with the accused, nor did it require that the accused have altered his appearance at the time of the crime, to allow the police officer to testify to the robber's identity.

It is important to note that lay opinions may be determined to be not "helpful" under the Rule whenever the jury can readily draw the necessary inferences and conclusions without the aid of the opinion. Likewise, such opinions are not helpful when they are confusing or excessively time consuming.

Accordingly, the Rule vests considerable discretion in the trial court and mandates care in determining whether the jury will be aided by lay opinion testimony in reaching a just result. Furthermore, in a proper case, lay opinion testimony otherwise admissible may be excluded by the trial court if the probative value of the testimony is sufficiently outweighed by the considerations set forth in Rule 403.

Practical Application of Rule 701

Any question that asks a lay witness to speculate as to certain facts will likely be "not helpful" under Rule 701. Consequently, a question such as "What would have happened if your son had survived the accident?" is likely to be subject to objection based upon its speculative nature.

AUTHORITY

WEISSENBERGER'S FEDERAL EVIDENCE §§ 701.1–.4

McCORMICK § 11

4 WEINSTEIN 2d §§ 701.01–.08

3 MUELLER & KIRKPATRICK §§ 342–347

7 WIGMORE §§ 1917–29

Ladd, *Expert Testimony*, 5 VAND. L. REV. 414 (1952)

Spies, *Opinion Evidence*, 15 ARK. L. REV. 105 (1960)

Tyree, *The Opinion Rule*, 10 RUTGERS L. REV. 601 (1956)

Williams, *Law and Practice in the Identification of Controlled Drugs by Lay Testimony*, 11 CRIM. L. BULL. 814 (1975)

STATUTES

§ 16-8-109.   Testimony of lay witness

In any trial or hearing in which the mental condition of the defendant is an issue, witnesses not specifically trained in psychiatry or psychology may testify as to their observation of the defendant's actions and conduct, and as to conversations which they have had with him bearing upon his mental condition, and they shall be permitted to give their opinions or conclusions concerning the mental conditions of the defendant.

COMPARISON TO FEDERAL RULE

In substance, Colorado Rule 701 is now identical to Federal Rule 701. In 2000, Federal Rule 701 was amended by the addition of a clause clarifying that a lay witness's testimony is not admissible if it is based on "scientific, technical or other specialized knowledge within the scope of 701." The purpose of this clause was to foreclose the possibility of an expert opinion masquerading as a lay witness opinion. In 2002, the Colorado Supreme Court in *People v. Stewart*, 55 P.3d 107, relied upon this federal amendment to Rule 701 in interpreting CRE 701, even though the Colorado Rule had not yet been amended to conform to the Federal Rule. However, on February 15, 2003, the federal amendment was adopted in CRE 701. Then on Dec. 1, 2011 Federal Rule 701 was restyled. Please see Federal Rule 701 in the appendix for comparison.

SIGNIFICANT CASES

United States v. Scheffer, 523 U.S. 303 (1998) (Military Rule of Evidence 707, which requires a per se exclusion of the opinion of a polygraph examiner, does not violate a criminal defendant's right to prevent relevant evidence, nor does the application of this rule forbidding a defendant from entering exculpatory lie-detector evidence violate that defendant's Fifth or Sixth Amendment right to counsel).

People v. Murphy, 484 P.3d 678 (Colo. 2021) (in a prosecution for distribution of meth, a police officer's conclusion regarding inferences he drew from a witness's body language was admissible as lay witness testimony).

Vigil v. People, 455 P.3d 332 (Colo. 2019) (a police officer's testimony that the defendant's shoes visually matched shoeprints he photographed at the crime scene was admissible as a lay opinion because an ordinary person can visually compare a shoe to an imprint of a shoe).

People v. Kubuugu, 433 P.3d 1214 (Colo. 2019) (a police officer's testimony, based on training and experience, that he detected the smell of metabolized alcohol and inferred when the defendant drank based on that odor exceeded the scope of lay testimony and thus required qualification of the witness as an expert).

Howard-Walker v. People, 443 P.3d 1007 (Colo. 2019) (a detective's testimony, based on training and experience, on whether a gun in a video was real based on the size of the barrel of the gun exceeded the scope of lay testimony and thus required qualification of the witness as an expert).

Campbell v. People, 443 P.3d 72 (Colo. 2019) (a police officer's testimony, based on training and experience, concerning roadside sobriety tests and interpretation of their results exceeded the scope of lay testimony and thus required qualification of the witness as an expert).

People v. Acosta, 338 P.3d 472 (Colo. 2014) (in a child sexual assault case, the court found testimony from a witness describing defendant as "very guilty looking" when leaving the scene of crime admissible under CRE 701. The court reasoned that the witness had observed defendant personally before and after the crime, in addition to being friends. The court further concluded that the testimony also complied with CRE 704, as it was phrased as a response, not asserting a particular legal standard, and that the witness had a rational basis for forming an opinion as to how defendant appeared).

Dunlap v. People, 173 P.3d 1054 (Colo. 2007) (testimony by a registered nurse that the defendant's conduct seemed psychotic was expert testimony, not the kind of opinion permitted to be given by a lay witness under C.R.S. § 16-8-109).

People v. Stewart, 55 P.3d 107 (Colo. 2002) (where a police officer testified as to accident reconstruction without being qualified as an expert, testimony was inadmissible in as much as it contained specialized knowledge which was only admissible if witness was qualified pursuant to CRE 701).

People v. Dunlap, 975 P.2d 723 (Colo. 1999) (polygraph evidence is per se inadmissible in criminal trials, and this exclusionary rule does not violate any Constitutional rights).

Robinson v. People, 927 P.2d 381 (Colo. 1996) (a police officer may give lay opinion testimony that the accused is the robber depicted in a videotape taken by an automatic surveillance camera if he is personally familiar with the accused; such level of familiarity only goes to the weight to be given to the testimony and not to its admissibility).

Pomeranz v. McDonald's Corp., 843 P.2d 1378 (Colo. 1993) (where there was no indication that the owner had ever personally paid a maintenance bill, he was not permitted to testify as to the prospective damages incurred in this area).

Witcher v. Canon City, 716 P.2d 445 (Colo. 1986) (corporation's president was permitted to testify as to the life expectancy of a bridge built by his corporation, either as an expert, or in the alternative, based on his own perception, having worked in the field for 30 years).

People v. Nhan Dao Van, 681 P.2d 932 (Colo. 1984) (both a paramedic and an investigator for the coroner's office were allowed to give lay testimony that the victim was dead, and describe the victim's physical condition as they observed it. They did not have to be qualified as experts prior to giving this testimony).

Sherry v. Jones, 292 P.2d 746 (Colo. 1956) (a person of reasonable intelligence and ordinary experience in life may express an opinion as to how fast an automobile or other moving object that he saw, was going at a particular time, without further proof of qualification) *See also Colorado & S. R. Co. v. Webb*, 85 P. 683 (Colo. 1906).

People v. Oliver, 474 P.3d 207 (Colo. App. 2020) (in a case against defendant for introduction of contraband, the admission of a correctional officer's law witness testimony that he had seen similar types of contraband used to cause bodily injury or death did not violate CRE 701 because it was based on personal experience and knowledge and did not require specialized experience, knowledge, or training).

People v. Rodriguez, 2021 Colo. App. LEXIS 548 (Colo. App. 2021) (in a domestic violence assault case, officer's testimony as to wife's 911 voice recording was admissible as lay witness testimony despite the fact that officer relied on noise canceling headphones to identify wife's voice). Not selected for final or official publication as of June 1, 2021.

People v. Bobian, 461 P.3d 643 (Colo. App. 2019) (a detective's testimony, based on training and experience, regarding blood patterns and tool markings was beyond the scope of lay witness testimony and thus required qualification of the witness as an expert, however the admission of this testimony was held to be harmless error).

People v. Shanks, 467 P.3d 1228 (Colo. App. 2019) (in a case of first impression, the Colorado Court of Appeals held that expert testimony regarding historical cell site data designed to determine the general geographic location of a cell phone is inherently reliable and does not require a Shreck hearing, and it is distinguishable from the controversial theory of granulization, which is the allegedly faulty premise that a cell phone will always connect to closest tower and thus show the specific location of the phone's user).

People v. Dominguez, 454 P.3d 364 (Colo. App. 2019) (a police agent's testimony, based on training and experience, regarding the use of an electronic scale to weigh drugs, the price range for methamphetamine, the amount of methamphetamine for personal use, and code word usage exceeded the scope of lay testimony and thus required qualification of the witness as an expert).

People v. Glover, 363 P.3d 736 (Colo. App. 2015) (a detective could properly testify about the features of a social networking website without being qualified as an expert on that topic, since the information in the testimony has based on an investigation).

Melssen v. Auto-Owners Ins. Co., 285 P.3d 328 (Colo. App. 2012) (where a witness was permitted to testify both as an expert and a lay witness, his testimony about cracks he saw in a foundation was properly treated as lay witness testimony).

People v. Graybeal, 155 P.3d 614 (Colo. App. 2007) (trial court was within its discretion to permit lay witnesses to testify that a substance they had observed was marijuana; evidence supported a conclusion that these witnesses possessed prior experiences with marijuana and based their identification on its appearance, taste, and distinctive smell).

People v. Walters, 821 P.2d 887 (Colo. App. 1991) (when victim's coworker personally heard verbally abusive phone conversation from the defendant to the victim, her characterization of those statements was permissible lay witness testimony).

Pyles-Knutzen v. Board of County Comm'rs, 781 P.2d 164 (Colo. App. 1989) (in a personal injury action, the injured motorist was allowed to testify as to what impact his injuries would have on his income, where his testimony was based on his own perception).

Sandoval v. Birx, 767 P.2d 759 (Colo. App. 1988) (an animal control officer was permitted to give lay testimony as to whether a dog had vicious tendencies, after observing the dog daily for a month after the dog bit someone).

People v. Brown, 731 P.2d 763 (Colo. App. 1986) (a witness's testimony regarding his method of identifying duct tape and paper tears was not admitted to establish his expertise, but to show his perception of the evidence. Upon such showing, it was proper to allow him to give lay testimony).

People v. Brewer, 720 P.2d 583 (Colo. App. 1985) (police officer was permitted to give an opinion on whether the defendant left the hospital voluntarily, when the officer did not personally see the defendant leave, and was making inferences from talking with the defendant).

Murray v. Just In Case Bus. Lighthouse, LLC, 374 P.3d 443 (Colo. 2016) (where a non-expert witness testifies by summarizing business documents, the trial court did not abuse its discretion by allowing such testimony because the evidence was so "complex and voluminous" that the testimony helped the jurors understand it).

People v. Ramos, 417 P.3d 902 (Colo. App. 2017) A secretary's testimony about the amount of missing money based on her own calculation of the "difference between what defendant said the fundraiser made and the amount of money that defendant deposited in the PTSA bank account" was properly admitted as lay opinion under CRE 701 because it was a "basic mathematical calculation" not requiring specialized knowledge.

People v. Bryant, 428 P.3d 669 (Colo. App. 2018) (a police officer is deemed an expert rather than a lay person when he offers testimony on the street name for the drug PCP when he acquired such knowledge from his specialized training and experience as a police officer).

People v. Murphy, ___ P.3d ___, 2019 Colo. App. LEXIS 423 (Colo. App. 2019) (a police officer is deemed an expert rather than a lay witness when he interprets a suspect's body language based on specialized knowledge from his training and experience as a police officer, and therefore must be qualified as an expert).

Chapter 702

Rule 702. Testimony by Experts

Rule 702 reads as follows:

> If scientific, technical, or other specialized knowledge will assist the trier of fact to understand the evidence or to determine a fact in issue, a witness qualified as an expert by knowledge, skill, experience, training, or education, may testify thereto in the form of an opinion or otherwise.

ANALYSIS

Rule 702 governs the admissibility of testimony by experts and it performs four distinct functions. First, it expressly authorizes the use of expert testimony. Second, the Rule establishes standards to be applied in determining whether expert testimony should be admitted in a particular case. Third, the Rule provides criteria to be applied in determining whether an individual qualifies as an expert. Fourth, the Rule governs the form of expert testimony.

In understanding expert testimony, it should be appreciated that there are essentially two types of witnesses at the trial of a lawsuit. First, a lay witness testifies because he or she has firsthand knowledge of relevant facts. Second, an expert may testify, not because he or she has firsthand knowledge of relevant facts, but rather because of special expertise which will assist the trier of fact in interpreting the facts of the case.

While the test for the use of expert testimony requires that the trier of fact be aided by the testimony, the standard is a relative one which will depend upon the particular subject, the particular witness, and the facts of the litigation. By necessity, the trial court has a substantial degree of discretion in determining whether to permit expert testimony in a particular case. This discretion should also extend to the trial court's determination of whether the state of the art in the particular discipline permits a rational and reliable opinion to be asserted by an expert.

Rule 702 addresses the qualifications necessary to accord a witness expert status. Under the Rule, a witness may qualify as an expert by reason of his or her knowledge, skill, experience, training or education. It is important to note that any one of these characteristics may qualify an individual as an expert, although in the usual case, more than one of these factors will be present.

Federal law in this field is controlled by *Daubert v. Merrell Dow Pharmaceuticals, Inc.*, 509 U.S. 579 (1993), the opinion in which the United States Supreme Court held that under the Federal Rules of Evidence, the so-called *Frye* test (*Frye v. United States*, 293 F. 1013, 54 App. D.C. 46 (1923)) does not apply to determine whether expert testimony may be offered on a particular subject. The *Frye* test, or the "general acceptance test," provides that an expert opinion based on a scientific technique is admissible only where the technique is generally accepted as reliable in the relevant scientific community. The Court held that the express language of the pertinent Federal Rules of Evidence places appropriate limits on the admissibility of purportedly scientific evidence by requiring the trial judge to ensure that an expert's testimony rests on a reliable foundation.

In Colorado state courts, this issue is controlled by *People v. Shreck*, 22 P.3d 68 (Colo. 2001), in which the Colorado Supreme Court declined to require use of either the *Frye* or *Daubert* tests for admission of scientific evidence. It held that Rules 702 and 403 should govern admissibility of all novel and non-novel scientific evidence. The court stated that in ruling on admissibility of scientific evidence, a trial court must issue specific findings in the context of these Rules, and must focus on the reliability of the scientific principles involved, the qualifications of the proposed witness, the usefulness of the testimony to the jury, and on the totality of the circumstances of the particular case.

In *Shreck*, the Court, recognizing the fact-specific nature of admitting scientific evidence, refused to establish set factors for a CRE 702 reliability analysis. However, the Court used the reasoning in *Kumho Tire Co. v. Carmichael*, 526 U.S. 137 (1998), to identify that the four factors outlined in *Daubert v. Merrell Dow Pharmaceuticals, Inc.*, 509 U.S. 579 (1993): "(1) whether the technique can and has been tested; (2) whether the theory or technique has been subjected to peer review and publication; (3) the scientific technique's known or potential rate of error, and the existence and maintenance of standards controlling the technique's operation; and (4) whether the technique has been generally accepted," may be used in a reliability analysis. The Court, however, emphasized that other factors may also be relevant in a CRE 702 reliability analysis.

Traditionally, the primary purpose for qualifying a witness as an expert has been to enable that individual to express his or her opinion on a central matter in issue. Rule 702 authorizes expert testimony in the form of opinion "or otherwise." The "or otherwise" language of Rule 702 is designed to permit an expert to provide relevant scientific, professional, technical or other principles as a basis for an application of those principles to the relevant issues by the trier of fact.

Caution should be exercised in assuring that the subject matter of the expert witness's testimony relates to the expertise the witness brings to the courtroom.

Illustration

In a criminal prosecution, X is prosecuted for possession of marijuana and a police chemist is qualified as an expert in identifying the marijuana. The chemist testifies that he thought the substance was marijuana because the container the substance was in looked like ones he saw used in Mexico. Such opinion is suspect because the basis of the opinion is not directly related to his qualification as a police chemist.

AUTHORITY

WEISSENBERGER'S FEDERAL EVIDENCE §§ 702.1–.5

MCCORMICK § 13

4 WEINSTEIN 2d §§ 702.01–.08

3 MUELLER & KIRKPATRICK §§ 348–353

Rackham, *Challenging the Unreliable Damages Expert—Part I*, COLO. LAW. 119 (Oct. 2003)

Rackham, *Challenging the Unreliable Damages Expert—Part II*, COLO. LAW. 103 (Nov. 2003)

Golanski, *Judicial Scrutiny of Expert Testimony in Environmental Tort Litigation*, 9 PACE ENVTL. L. REV. 399 (1992)

Strong, *Language and Logic in Expert Testimony: Limiting Expert Testimony by Restrictions of Function, Reliability and Form*, 71 OR. L. REV. 349 (1992)

Weinstein, *Rule 702 of the Federal Rules of Evidence Is Sound: It Should Not Be Amended*, 138 F.R.D. 631 (1991)

Fassett, *The Third Circuit's Unique Response to Expert Testimony on Eyewitness Perception: Is What You See What You Get?*, 19 SETON HALL 697 (1989)

McLaughlin, *Discovery and Admissibility of Expert Testimony*, 63 NOTRE DAME L. REV. 760 (1988)

Myers, Bays, Becker, Berliner, Corwin & Saywitz, *Expert Testimony in Child Sexual Abuse Litigation*, 68 NEB. L. REV. 1 (1989)

Ringland, *Child Sex Abuse Evidence Problems—Update 1988*, 14 U. DAYTON L. REV. 147 (1988)

Selecting an Expert Witness, COLO. LAW. 1464 (1983)

Addison, *Expert Testimony on Eyewitness Perception*, 82 DICKINSON L. REV. 465 (1978)

Decker & Handler, *Voiceprint Identification—Out of the Frye Pan and into Admissibility*, 26 AM. U. L. REV. 314 (1977)

Diamond & Louisell, *The Psychiatrist as an Expert Witness: Some Ruminations and Speculations*, 63 MICH. L. REV. 1335 (1965)

Donaher, Piehler, Twerski, & Weinstein, *The Technological Expert in Products Liability Litigation*, 52 TEX. L. REV. 1303 (1974)

Finkelstein, *A Statistical Analysis of Guilty Plea Practice in the Federal Court*, 89 HARV. L. REV. 293 (1975)

Giannelli, *The Admissibility of Novel Scientific Evidence: Frye v. United States, a Half Century Later*, 80 COLUM. L. REV. 1197 (1980)

O'Connor, *That's the Man: A Sobering Study of Eyewitness Identification and the Polygraph*, 49 ST. JOHN'S L. REV. 1 (1974)

STATUTES

§ 16-3-309 C.R.S. (2002).   Admissibility of laboratory test results

(1) When evidence is seized in so small a quantity or unstable condition that qualitative laboratory testing will not leave a sufficient quantity of the evidence for independent analysis by the defendant's expert and when a state agent, in the regular performance of his duties, can reasonably foresee that the evidence might be favorable to the defendant, the trial court shall not suppress the prosecution's evidence if the court determines that the testing was performed in good faith and in accordance with regular procedures designed to preserve the evidence which might have been favorable to the defendant.

(2) The trial court shall consider the following factors in determining, pursuant to subsection (1) of this section, whether the state has met its obligation to preserve the evidence:

(a) Whether or not a suspect has been identified and apprehended and whether or not the suspect has retained counsel or has had counsel appointed for him at the time of testing;

(b) Whether the state should have used an available test method more likely to preserve the results of seized evidence;

(c) Whether, when the test results are susceptible to subjective interpretation, the state should have photographed or otherwise documented the test results as evidence;

(d) Whether the state should have preserved the used test samples;

(e) Whether it was necessary for the state agency to conduct quantitative analysis of the evidence;

(f) Whether there is a sufficient sample for the defendant's expert to utilize for analysis and the suspect or defendant has made a specific request to preserve such sample;

(g) If paragraph (f) of this subsection (2) cannot be complied with, in view of the small amount of evidence, or when the state's duty to preserve the evidence would otherwise be enhanced, whether it was reasonable for the state to have contacted the defendant to determine if he wished his expert to be present during the testing.

(3) With regard to testing performed on blood, urine, and breath samples which form the basis for a conclusion upon which a statutory presumption arises, it is hereby declared to be the public policy of the state of Colorado that when the prosecution's evidence of test results is sought to be excluded from the trier of fact in a criminal proceeding because the testing destroyed evidence which might have been favorable to the defense, it shall be open to the proponent of the evidence to urge that the testing in question was performed in good faith and in accordance with regular procedures designed to preserve the evidence which might have been favorable to the defense, and, in such instances, the evidence so discovered should not be kept from the trier of fact if otherwise admissible.

(4) For all other types of blood analysis, breath analysis, and urine analysis and for laboratory testing, such as serial number restoration, firearms testing, and gunpowder pattern testing, it is hereby declared to be the public policy of the state of Colorado that, when the prosecution's evidence of test results is sought to be excluded from the trier of fact in a criminal proceeding because of the destruction of evidence upon which the test was performed, it shall be open to the proponent of the evidence to urge that the testing in question was performed in a reasonable, good faith belief that it was proper and, in such instances, the evidence so discovered should not be kept from the trier of fact if otherwise admissible.

(5) Any report or copy thereof or the findings of the criminalistics laboratory shall be received in evidence in any court, preliminary hearing, or grand jury proceeding in the same manner and with the same force and effect as if the employee or technician of the criminalistics laboratory who accomplished the requested analysis, comparison, or identification had testified in person. Any party may request that such employee or technician testify in person at a criminal trial on behalf of the state before a jury or to the court, by notifying the witness and other party at least fourteen days before the date of such criminal trial.

(6) In no event shall evidence be suppressed which results from laboratory testing performed before identification of a suspect for the sole reason that the later identified suspect or his attorney was not present at the time of the testing.

(7) This section is necessary to identify the characteristics of evidence which will be admissible in a court of law. This section does not address or attempt to prescribe court procedure.

COMPARISON TO FEDERAL RULE

In substance, Colorado Rule 702 is identical to Federal Rule 702(a), but does not include clauses intended to incorporate into the Federal Rule the holdings of *Daubert v. Merrell Dow Pharmaceuticals, Inc.*, 509 U.S. 579 (1993) and numerous decisions applying *Daubert*. Please note that on Dec. 1, 2011 Federal Rule 702 was restyled. Please see Federal Rule 702 in the appendix for comparison.

SIGNIFICANT CASES

Williams v. Illinois, 132 S. Ct. 2221 (2012) (DNA analysis prepared in the context of criminal investigation was not covered by the Confrontation Clause for a variety of rationales, no single one of which accrued majority support).

Bullcoming v. New Mexico, 131 S. Ct. 2705 (2011) (blood alcohol report prepared by a state crime lab was covered by the Confrontation Clause).

Melendez-Diaz v. Massachusetts, 557 U.S. 305 (2009) (admission of sworn certificate by laboratory analyst to show that seized material was cocaine violated defendant's Confrontation Clause rights because the out-of-court statement was testimonial).

United States v. Scheffer, 523 U.S. 303 (1998) (while the *Daubert* holding replaces the *Frye* doctrine and therefore removes the requirement of an absolute limitation on admissibility of "lie detector" evidence, a jurisdiction does not violate a defendant's constitutional right to present evidence by continuing to maintain such a per se prohibition, given the wide range of scientific points of view on the accuracy of such tests).

Daubert v. Merrell Dow Pharmaceuticals, Inc., 509 U.S. 579 (1993) ("general acceptance" is no longer the standard for admissibility of scientific evidence. A new, more liberal five-part test should be applied: (1) Is the theory testable, and has it been tested, (2) had it been subjected to peer review and publication, (3) does it have a known or potential error rate, (4) does it have standards controlling its operation, and (5) has it attracted widespread acceptance within its relevant scientific community).

Vigil v. People, 455 P.3d 332 (Colo. 2019) (a police officer's testimony that the defendant's shoes visually matched shoeprints he photographed at the crime scene was admissible as a lay opinion because an ordinary person can visually compare a shoe to an imprint of a shoe).

Kutzly v. People, 442 P.3d 838 (Colo. 2019) (a social worker's expert testimony regarding the behavior of abused children was reasonably reliable and thus admissible because it was based on his educational background and experience counseling purported abuse victims and offenders, notwithstanding the absence of confirmations of these cases of abuse or scientific studies).

People v. Kubuugu, 433 P.3d 1214 (Colo. 2019) (a police officer's testimony, based on training and experience, that he detected the smell of metabolized alcohol and inferred when the defendant drank based on that odor exceeded the scope of lay testimony and thus required qualification of the witness as an expert).

Howard-Walker v. People, 443 P.3d 1007 (Colo. 2019) (a detective's testimony, based on training and experience, on whether a gun in a video was real based on the size of the barrel of the gun exceeded the scope of lay testimony and thus required qualification of the witness as an expert).

Campbell v. People, 443 P.3d 72 (Colo. 2019) (a police officer's testimony, based on training and experience, concerning roadside sobriety tests and interpretation of their results exceeded the scope of lay testimony and thus required qualification of the witness as an expert).

Davis v. People, 310 P.3d 58 (Colo. 2013) (trial court properly allowed testimony from investigating detectives that they "didn't believe" one witness, felt another "obviously hadn't been entirely truthful," and that another's information was "true," on the theory that the testimony was offered for the limited purpose of providing "context for the detective's interrogation tactics and investigative decisions").

Core-Mark Midcontinent, Inc. v. Sonitrol Corp., 300 P.3d 963 (Colo. 2012) (trial court erroneously suggested that testimony about how alleged code violations might have affected the spread of a fire was required to be based on a scientific or technical analysis; specialized knowledge about building codes can be an adequate basis for such testimony).

Golob v. People, 180 P.3d 1006 (Colo. 2008) (where the prosecution questioned its own expert about a defense expert's conclusions regarding impressions made by boots, the trial court erred in prohibiting direct testimony by that defense expert; the prosecution had opened the door, and decisions regarding admissibility of defense expert testimony in criminal cases may be more susceptible of reversal because of sensitivity to the needs of criminal defendants).

People v. Wilkerson, 114 P.3d 874 (Colo. 2005) (where a defendant offers an expert's scientifically quantified testimony that the defendant more likely than not fired a weapon accidentally, a trial court may bar the expert from testifying if the expert's conclusions are based on unreliable information and the expert failed to test the weapon in question or to provide statistical or expert interpretation of the test results).

People v. Mojica-Simental, 73 P.3d 15 (Colo. 2003) (C.R.S. § 16-3-309(5) applies to DUI cases. The defendant's affirmative duty to request the presence of lab technician at trial, as required by the statute, does not, on its face, violate the defendant's right to confrontation because the defendant may preserve the right to confrontation with minimal effort).

People v. Shreck, 22 P.3d 68 (Colo. 2001) (reversing a trial court's exclusion of DNA evidence, the court held that Rules 702 and 403, rather than the *Frye* test or *Daubert* factors, govern admissibility of all novel and non-novel scientific evidence; in ruling on admissibility of scientific evidence, a trial court must issue specific findings in the context of these Rules, with a focus on the reliability of the scientific principles involved, the qualifications of the proposed witness, the usefulness of the testimony to the jury, and on the totality of the circumstances of the particular case).

Brooks v. People, 975 P.2d 1105 (Colo. 1999) (the *Frye* and *Daubert* tests are inapplicable to evidence of canine scent tracking; rather than using those tests a court must first consider admissibility under 702 and then determine if the evidence is unfairly prejudicial under CRE 403).

Huntoon v. TCI Cablevision, 969 P.2d 681 (Colo. 1998) (neuropsychologist is not automatically disqualified from giving expert testimony regarding the physical cause of brain injury, unless the testimony fails to satisfy the requirements set out in CRE 702).

Gerrity Oil & Gas Corp. v. Magness, 946 P.2d 913 (Colo. 1997) (where a negligence claim was based on administrative regulations establishing a duty of care, and such duty of care was within the common knowledge and experience of ordinary persons, the regulations constitute valid evidence of the duty owed and preclude the necessity of expert witness testimony on that issue).

People v. Campbell, 847 P.2d 228 (Colo. 1992) (expert testimony regarding studies which show a weak correlation between eyewitness confidence and reliability of identification is admissible to rebut the assumption of confidence in eyewitness identification).

Cardiel v. Brittian, 833 P.2d 748 (Colo. 1992) (it was within the trial court's discretion to disallow fellow inmate to testify as an expert in a habeas corpus proceeding: even though his job duties at the prison included working with habeas petitions and parole issues, he was not employed by the Department of Corrections or the parole board).

People v. Fasy, 829 P.2d 1314 (Colo. 1992) (psychologist's testimony that victim's delay in reporting the incident was consistent with posttraumatic stress disorder was found to be helpful to the jury, and as such, was admissible as opinion evidence).

Lanari v. People, 827 P.2d 495 (Colo. 1992) (when there is an objection with respect to proposed expert testimony, the court must be apprised of the substance of the proposed testimony in order to exercise its discretion).

Melville v. Southward, 791 P.2d 383 (Colo. 1990) (a doctor's testimony regarding a school of medicine other than his area of expertise is admissible only if by reason of knowledge, training, or education, he is so familiar with the other specialty that he is as informed as an expert in that field would be); *Greene v. Thomas*, 662 P.2d 491 (Colo. App. 1982); *Sanchez v. Lauffenburger*, 784 P.2d 855 (Colo. App. 1989).

People v. Hampton, 746 P.2d 947 (Colo. 1987) (any flaws in expert testimony go to the weight of the testimony, not to the admissibility, so long as it is subject to cross-examination).

People v. Marston, 2021 Colo. App. LEXIS 177 (Colo. App. 2021) (in a DWI case, testimony of the prosecution's expert interpreting the subject's responses to the horizontal gaze nystagmus test was properly admitted). Not selected for final or official publication as of June 1, 2021.

People v. Ambrose, 2021 Colo. App. LEXIS 643 (Colo. App 2021) (a police officer's testimony explaining the procedures he used in operating the I-9000 breathalyzer machine was improperly admitted as lay witness testimony despite the fact that it was based on specialized knowledge; however the error was harmless). *Cert granted. Ambrose v. People*, 2021 Colo. LEXIS 237 (Colo. 2021).

People v. Grosko, 2021 Colo. App. LEXIS 338 (Colo. App. 2021) (in a pimping case, court properly qualified prosecution witness as an expert in commercial sex trafficking, pimping, and prostitution). Not selected for final or official publication as of June 1, 2021.

Trujillo v. Vail Clinic, Inc., 480 P.3d 721 (Colo. App. 2020) (the exposition of the theory of cranial compression ischemic encephalopathy was sufficiently based on scientific principles to support the admissibility of such testimony by an expert witness).

People v. Ornelas-Licano, 2020 Colo. App. LEXIS 732 (Colo. App. 2020) (in an attempted murder case, a police officer's expert testimony, based on his own experiment, regarding the angle from which the defendant fired a shot in the direction of another officer was held to be inadmissible because of insufficient foundation that this experiment was scientifically reliable). *Cert granted. People v. Ornelas-Licano*, 2021 Colo. LEXIS 203 (Colo. 2021).

People v. Yachik, 469 P.3d 582 (Colo. App. 2020) (the prosecution's witness who testified on the defendant's "grooming" of victims in a child sexual assault case was improperly admitted because the court failed to make specific findings of the reliability, relevance, and usefulness of the testimony).

People v. Bobian, 461 P.3d 643 (Colo. App. 2019) (a detective's testimony, based on training and experience, regarding blood patterns and tool markings was beyond the scope of lay witness testimony and thus required qualification of the witness as an expert, however the admission of this testimony was held to be harmless error).

People v. Vidauri, 2019 Colo. App. LEXIS 1333 (Colo. App. 2019) (although an expert possessed no academic or experience-based credentials, her ten years of experience working for the Colorado Department of Human Services as a case manager, benefits technician, and fraud investigator was found to be sufficient to find her qualified as an expert in medical assistance benefits eligibility determinations).

Lorenzen v. Pinnacol Assur., 457 P.3d 100 (Colo. App. 2019) (in a bad faith breach of insurance case, the court properly excluded an expert's theory of causation of the plaintiff's injury as not scientifically reliable).

People v. Murphy, 2019 Lexis 423 (Colo. App, March 21, 2019) (a police officer's testimony, based on training and experience, interpreting a witness's body language exceeds the scope of lay testimony and thus requires qualification of the witness as an expert).

People v. Cooper, 2019 Lexis 231 (Colo. App. February 21, 2019) (in an assault case, it was improper to admit expert testimony on abusive intimate relationships without evidence of an existing abusive relationship in the case at bar).

People v. Dominguez, 454 P.3d 364 (Colo. App. 2019) (a police agent's testimony, based on training and experience, regarding the use of an electronic scale to weigh drugs, the price range for methamphetamine, the amount of methamphetamine for personal use, and code word usage exceeded the scope of lay testimony and thus required qualification of the witness as an expert).

People v. Wilson, 318 P.3d 538 (Colo. App. 2013) (trial court was within its discretion in refusing to hold a *Shreck* hearing regarding testimony by a fingerprint expert; this is an example of a circumstance in which the reliability of an expert's methods is properly taken for granted).

People v. Tunis, 318 P.3d 524 (Colo. App. 2013) (DNA analysis with the Y-STR method was properly admitted, along with results of a counting method analysis based on a group of 3,500 samples).

Melssen v. Auto-Owners Ins. Co., 285 P.3d 328 (Colo. App. 2012) (where a witness was permitted to testify both as an expert and a lay witness, his testimony about cracks he saw in a foundation was properly treated as lay witness testimony).

People v. Tucker, 232 P.3d 194 (Colo. App. 2009) (trial court did not abuse its discretion when it refused to admit testimony of expert witness whose testimony was not useful to the jury because it was not relevant and did not "fit" with defendant's assertion of lack of intent).

Estate of Ford v. Eicher, 220 P.3d 939 (Colo. App. 2008) (where theory of an expert witness regarding the cause of injuries to an infant child was untestable, testimony was held to be reliable and thus admissible under CRE 702 because it was based on a process of elimination and supported by several peer reviewed medical journal articles).

Luster v. Brinkman, 205 P.3d 410 (Colo. App. 2008) (testimony by a board-certified obstetrician was properly admitted; the testimony was helpful to the jury because it was not clear how the litigated injury came about, the testimony assisted the jury because it offered contrary medical opinions from which the jury could choose the theory it found more convincing, there is support in reliable medical literature, although it is contested, that the injury could occur without the negligence of the attending physician, and the expert's medical theories were based on reliable scientific principles, including his personal experience).

People v. Laurent, 194 P.3d 1053 (Colo. App. 2008) (although an expert had not followed a "written analytical method" in testing material found in the defendant's trash, the trial court properly admitted the expert's testimony because the laboratory which conducted the testing was certified by a third-party accreditation society that audits lab procedures to ensure that the standard operating procedures meet minimum standards, both the Infrared Spectroscopy and the Gas Chromatography/Mass Spectrometry methods used by the expert to conduct the chemical tests followed Colorado Bureau of Investigation standard operating procedures, standard procedures were used to maintain the instruments and to detect any error during the tests, and the expert had used the same techniques "hundreds or thousands of times" during her career, both in Colorado and when she worked for the Georgia Bureau of Investigations).

People v. Rojas, 181 P.3d 1216 (Colo. App. 2008) (DNA mixture evidence can properly be admitted; issues of reliability of interpretation of mixed samples go to weight, and not to admissibility, of evidence).

Farmland Mut. Ins. Cos. v. Chief Indus., 170 P.3d 832 (Colo. App. 2007) (in determining the likely cause of a fire, proper scientific method can involve reasoning by the process of elimination).

People v. Wallin, 167 P.3d 183 (Colo. App. 2007) (trial court was within its discretion in admitting expert testimony on reasons why victims of domestic violence may recant their allegations).

People v. Mintz, 165 P.3d 829 (Colo. App. 2007) (expert testimony was properly admitted showing the typical behavioral traits of an abused child; testimony based on hypothetical questions related to the facts of the current case was also proper).

People v. Johnson, 74 P.3d 349 (Colo. App. 2002) (where defendant was charged with attempting to murder his wife by slashing her with knife in front of their two children, expert testimony regarding "battered woman's syndrome" and "cycle of violence" was relevant and helpful to the jury even though there was no evidence of prior domestic violence between the defendant and the victim).

People v. Masters, 33 P.3d 1191 (Colo. App. 2001) (in a sexual assault and murder case, the trial court properly admitted the defendant's narratives and drawings depicting sexually violent scenes, and properly permitted an expert witness to explain the relevance of the drawings and narratives).

People v. Ramirez, 1 P.3d 223 (Colo. App. 1999) (narcotics detective was properly permitted to testify as to typical mode or operation of narcotics couriers).

People v. Miller, 981 P.2d 654 (Colo. App. 1998) (testimony of defendant's expert witness was inadmissible because it was inconsistent with the defendant's story, drew conclusions that should have been left for the jury, and was not helpful to the jury; it would have been based on a survey about people's feelings related to possible sexual attacks by strangers, whereas the victim and defendant in this case were not strangers.

Colwell v. Mentzer Invs., Inc., 973 P.2d 631 (Colo. App. 1998) (plaintiff's expert could testify about the effect stress, caused from an accident with the defendant, had on plaintiff's multiple sclerosis; because the expert testimony was based on the expert's specialized knowledge of MS, and was helpful to the jury's understanding of the disputed issues, it was properly admitted under CRE 702).

People v. Bornman, 953 P.2d 952 (Colo. App. 1997) (where a licensed used car dealer of 12 years testified as an expert witness about the value of a make of vehicle which he previously appraised but never actually sold, the trial court did not abuse its discretionary powers determining the sufficiency of the qualifications of the witness as an expert).

Tran v. Hilburn, 948 P.2d 52 (Colo. App. 1997) (the test in Colorado for admission of novel scientific evidence is set forth in *Frye v. United States*, 293 F. 1013 (D.C. Cir. 1923); therefore such evidence must be generally accepted within the scientific community before such evidence may be used to bolster the testimony of an expert in a field of science).

Klein v. State Farm Mut. Auto. Ins. Co., 948 P.2d 43 (Colo. App. 1997) (an osteopath was certified as an expert in occupational medicine and provided testimony in areas of medicine where he was not a certified expert; the trial court did not abuse its discretion in allowing the doctor's testimony about the reasonableness and necessity of such services irrespective of the fact that he was not certified as an expert in those areas of medicine).

Department of Higher Educ. v. Singh, 939 P.2d 491 (Colo. App. 1997) (the admission of testimony in an administrative hearing was within the ALJ's discretion to determine whether the witness was one who possessed the requisite knowledge, skill, experience, training, or education to qualify as an expert in the field of data entry performance in the data processing industry).

People v. Lesslie, 939 P.2d 443 (Colo. App. 1996) (in a criminal eavesdropping case, where an expert witness was trained in law and was a member of the Colorado Bar, his testimony was properly excluded because it was based on a legal conclusion which the court determined was unnecessary and might confuse the jury).

People v. Lanari, 926 P.2d 116 (Colo. App. 1996) (in a first-degree murder case, the trial court properly excluded expert testimony of a psychiatrist which supported the defendant's "heat of passion" defense, because the defendant's testimony did not clearly establish that he acted in the "heat of passion" and because the psychiatrist's offer of proof described few, if any, facts upon which he relied in forming his opinion and did not provide examples or criteria that might have assisted the jury in evaluating the evidence).

People v. Price, 903 P.2d 1190 (Colo. App. 1995) (trial court's admission of expert testimony concerning why anyone would fabricate a military background was not an abuse of discretion during the sanity portion of a trial when the testimony helped the trier of fact understand the mental conditions related to post-traumatic stress disorder).

People v. Kemp, 885 P.2d 260 (Colo. App. 1994) (the broad discretion of a trial court to deny expert testimony concerning the reliability of eyewitness identification will not be reversed by the appellate court unless the ruling is manifestly erroneous).

People v. Perryman, 859 P.2d 263 (Colo. App. 1993) (even though shoe print identification involves no highly technical or scientific theories, the trial court did not abuse its discretion in allowing an expert to testify regarding shoe print identification after he was properly qualified as an expert in the field).

People v. Martinez, 841 P.2d 383 (Colo. App. 1992) (resident in psychiatry was properly qualified as an expert in the field 6 months prior to the licensing exam, when he was responsible for performing diagnosis and providing treatment independently).

Brewer v. American & Foreign Ins. Co., 837 P.2d 236 (Colo. App. 1992) (qualification of expert witnesses is a matter for the discretion of the court, and absent abuse, should not be disturbed on review).

Koehn v. R.D. Werner Co., 809 P.2d 1045 (Colo. App. 1990) (prior to admitting expert testimony, there must first be a showing that the proposed testimony would be helpful to the jury in understanding a complex technical or scientific theory, or help them to understand a fact at issue).

Coffee v. Inman, 728 P.2d 376 (Colo. App. 1986) (the court correctly determined CPAs to be experts on the issue of accounts receivable).

Durkee v. Oliver, 714 P.2d 1330 (Colo. App. 1986) (failure to consider knowledge, training, and education in determining the qualifications of an expert witness is potential error, regardless of the witness's experience in the area).

Venalonzo v. People, 388 P.3d 868 (Colo. 2017) (in a sexual assault case involving children, the court found that testimony by a forensic interviewer that "children are not very good at understanding physical measurements, that they often use generalities when speaking, and that they often reveal secrets to other children before they tell adults" was lay testimony because "an ordinary person who interacts with children can recognize these behaviors"; however, testimony about the significance of the children gesturing on their bodies to demonstrate where they had been touched, and the distinction between "core versus peripheral" details, required specialized experience, and was expert testimony requiring expert witness qualification).

People v. Garrison, 411 P.3d 270 (Colo. App. 2017) (testimony about the traceability of an IP address is not within the knowledge or experience of ordinary people and therefore was not admissible as lay testimony).

Romero v. People, 393 P.3d 973 (Colo. 2017) (the concept of grooming as it relates to a sexual predator's methods of acquiring victims is not within the knowledge or experience of ordinary people and therefore was not admissible as lay witness testimony).

People v. Campbell, 425 P.3d 1163, 2018 Colo. App. LEXIS 70 (Colo. App. 2018) (witness with experience as a worker for the manufacturer of the ankle monitor worn by defendant was properly qualified to testify as an expert on GPS technology).

People v. Ramos, 388 P.3d 888 (Colo. 2018) (a detective's technical testimony about blood spatter evidence was not within the knowledge or experience of ordinary people since he relied upon nineteen years of experience as a police officer, nine years as a detective, and his work on thousands of cases involving blood evidence, and was therefore not admissible as lay witness testimony).

Black v. Black, 422 P.3d 592 (Colo. App. 2018) (the testimony of an expert witness on cycles of violence in a domestic abuse case is inadmissible because it is irrelevant and unfairly prejudicial when he is not personally acquainted with the parties and the prosecution fails to proffer any evidence of prior abuse).

People v. Kubuugu, 433 P.3d 1214 (Colo. 2019) (a deputy testifying in a DUI case on the intoxication level of the defendant is considered an expert witness, and not a lay witness when he can opine the volume of alcohol ingested based off of the metabolized smell of alcohol on the defendant).

Chapter 703

Rule 703. Bases of Opinion Testimony by Experts

Rule 703 reads as follows:

> The facts or data in the particular case upon which an expert bases an opinion or inference may be those perceived by or made known to the expert at or before the hearing. If of a type reasonably relied upon by experts in the particular field in forming opinions or inferences upon the subject, the facts or data need not be admissible in evidence in order for the opinion or inference to be admitted. Facts or data that are otherwise inadmissible shall not be disclosed to the jury by the proponent of the opinion or inference unless the court determines that their probative value in assisting the jury to evaluate the expert's opinion substantially outweighs their prejudicial effect.

ANALYSIS

Rule 703 identifies permissible sources of facts or data upon which the expert may base his or her opinion or inference. The expert may predicate his or her opinion on first-hand knowledge, or in the alternative, the expert may draw upon facts or data made known to the expert at or before the hearing. Additionally, the Rule provides that if the facts or data are of the type reasonably relied upon by experts in the field, they are a permissible source of information even if they would not be admissible in evidence.

Where an expert has personal knowledge of the facts or data underlying his or her opinion, this basis is a permissible predicate for his or her testimony. For example, an attending physician who treated an injured plaintiff would have first-hand knowledge of the facts which could permissibly support expert opinion testimony as to the permanence of plaintiff's disability. In this case, the expert is aware of the supporting data by reason of his or her first-hand experience.

Alternative bases for expert testimony are sources in regard to which the expert does not have personal knowledge. For example, the expert may base his or her opinion on reports prepared by others. If such material is inadmissible, it nevertheless is an appropriate basis for expert testimony provided it is the type of information reasonably relied upon by experts in the field.

AUTHORITY

WEISSENBERGER'S FEDERAL EVIDENCE §§ 703.1–.5

MCCORMICK § 15

4 WEINSTEIN 2d §§ 703.01–.06

3 MUELLER & KIRKPATRICK §§ 354–359

3 WIGMORE § 687

Becker & Orenstein, *The Federal Rules of Evidence After Sixteen Years—The Effect of "Plain Meaning" Jurisprudence, the Need for an Advisory Committee on the Rules of Evidence, and Suggestions for Selected Revision of the Rules*, 60 GEO. WASH. L. REV. 857 (1992)

Imwinkelried, *The "Bases" of Expert Testimony: The Syllogistic Structure of Scientific Testimony*, 67 N.C. L. REV. 1 (1988)

Larson, *The Admissibility of Expert Testimony on Child Sexual Abuse Accommodation Syndrome as Indicia of Abuse: Aiding the Prosecution in Meeting Its Burden of Proof*, 16 OHIO N.U. L. REV. 81 (1989)

Admissibility of Governmental Studies to Prove Causation, 11 COLO. LAW. 1822 (1982)

Diamond & Louisell, *The Psychiatrist as an Expert Witness: Some Ruminations and Speculations*, 63 MICH. L. REV. 1335 (1965)

Maguire & Hahesy, *Requisite Proof of Certainty: An Analysis and Proposal for a Federal Evidence Rule*, 20 WAYNE L. REV. 781 (1974)

Rheingold, *The Basis of Medical Testimony*, 15 VAND. L. REV. 473 (1962)

Note, *Hearsay Bases of Psychiatric Opinion Testimony: A Critique of Federal Rule of Evidence 703*, 51 S. CAL. L. REV. 129 (1977)

COMPARISON TO FEDERAL RULE

In substance, Colorado Rule 703 is identical to Federal Rule 703. However, on Dec. 1, 2011 Federal Rule 703 was restyled. Please see Federal Rule 703 in the appendix for comparison.

SIGNIFICANT CASES

Kumho Tire Co. v. Carmichael, 526 U.S. 137 (1999) (*Daubert* is a flexible test that applies to testimony from other experts who are not scientists, where the expert's testimony is reliable and based on the expert's knowledge and experience of his discipline).

Delaware v. Fensterer, 474 U.S. 15 (1985) (admission of an expert opinion did not violate criminal defendant's rights under the confrontation clause of the Sixth Amendment, even though the expert could not recall the method whereby he arrived at his opinion).

People v. Martinez, 74 P.3d 316 (Colo. 2003) (in a case against the defendant for murder in the first degree for knowingly killing a child under 12 years old, expert's testimony of an accident scenario was inadmissible under a 703 and 403 analysis as to the question of defendant's *mens rea* because the expert "did not show how the accident scenarios relate to shaken-impact syndrome." However, such testimony is "as the basis of [the expert's] opinion that a subdural hematoma results from massive, violent force").

Pueblo West Metropolitan Dist. v. Southeastern Colorado Water Conservancy Dist., 717 P.2d 955 (Colo. 1985) (there is no error in allowing one expert witness to testify as to the specifics in a case, and disallowing another, when the expert not permitted to testify as to specifics is not familiar with the conditions in the present case and the other is).

People v. Cauley, 32 P.3d 602 (Colo. App. 2001) (in trial for criminally negligent child abuse, testimony of coroner and pediatrician regarding rib fractures found during the autopsy was admissible, since the pediatrician used it as the basis of her opinion that the child had died as a result of shaken baby syndrome, the testimony was relevant to provide context to the coroner's observations, the evidence was not prior bad acts evidence, the experts' opinions were based upon facts reasonably relied on by experts in the medical field, and the trial court gave a limiting instruction; even though the coroner stated that he did not rely on the evidence in reaching his conclusion that the daughter had suffered from shaken baby syndrome, if the admission was erroneous it was harmless error).

People v. Martinez, 841 P.2d 383 (Colo. App. 1992) (expert testimony of licensed supervising physicians is customarily based on psychiatrist in residency reports and therefore was properly admitted).

People v. Pflugbeil, 834 P.2d 843 (Colo. App. 1992) (treating doctors opinion testimony, made in reliance on sources usually relied on by psychiatrist in making diagnosis, was properly admitted in an involuntary commitment proceeding).

In re Marriage of Keyser, 820 P.2d 1194 (Colo. App. 1991) (when two experts in assessment give different valuations for property, the weight to be given to each valuation technique is a matter for the trial court, depending on the court's determination of reliability of data used by each expert).

Walford v. Blinder, Robinson & Co., 793 P.2d 620 (Colo. App. 1990) (a professor of economics was properly qualified as an expert on economic damages, and allowed to rely on a prospectus including audited financial reports and other data which was given to him in preparation for trial upon which to base his opinion).

Whitney v. Anderson, 784 P.2d 830 (Colo. App. 1989) (data underlying an expert's opinion must come from one of three sources: (1) first-hand observation, (2) presentation at trial, including hypotheticals, and (3) presentation to the expert outside the courtroom. If his opinion is based on data from other than these sources, it is not admissible).

Harvey v. Dyer, 731 P.2d 777 (Colo. App. 1986) (even if data is of the type reasonably relied upon by experts in the field, it must still be helpful to the trier of fact in determining a fact at issue in order for the expert's opinion to be admissible).

People v. Beasley, 608 P.2d 835 (Colo. App. 1980) (while a doctor is not disqualified from expressing his opinion when he has received information from a source other than his own examination, he may not base his conclusions solely on that information).

Dorsey & Whitney LLP v. RegScan, Inc., 488 P.3d 324, 2018 Colo. App. LEXIS 214 (Colo. App. 2018) ("Otherwise inadmissible" as used in CRE 703 refers to evidence that cannot be admitted under the rules of evidence, not evidence that simply has not been admitted).

Chapter 704

Rule 704. Opinion on Ultimate Issue

Rule 704 reads as follows:

> Testimony in the form of an opinion or inference otherwise admissible is not objectionable because it embraces an ultimate issue to be decided by the trier of fact.

ANALYSIS

Rule 704 provides that testimony in the form of an opinion is not subject to exclusion solely because it addresses the ultimate issue in the case. The Rule applies both to expert and lay testimony.

Rule 704 provides that ultimate issue testimony "otherwise admissible" is not subject to exclusion, and consequently, the testimony at issue must minimally satisfy the requirements of all Rules of Evidence. For example, Rule 701 governs opinions offered by a lay witness. The ultimate issue testimony of a lay person must be rationally based on facts perceived by the witness in order to be admissible. Moreover, under Rule 701 the opinion or inference is not admissible if it does not assist the trier of fact in the determination of a factual issue. When the jury can easily draw the inference from a simple recitation of facts by the witness, the witness's opinion on the ultimate issue might be subject to exclusion under Rule 701 even though Rule 704 would not afford a basis for exclusion.

Under Rule 702 the expert's special body of knowledge must assist the trier of fact in determining a fact in issue or in understanding the evidence. It is the inability of the unaided jury to reach the ultimate opinion that renders the expert opinion vital. For this reason, an ultimate issue opinion from a properly qualified expert should not be excluded except in the extreme case where the expert opinion is inherently misleading or unfairly prejudicial.

A persuasive interpretation of the abolition of the ultimate issue rule in Rule 704 is found in the Federal Advisory Committee Notes:

> The abolition of the ultimate issue rule does not lower the bars so as to admit all opinions. Under Rules 701 and 702, opinions must be helpful to the trier of fact, and Rule 403 provides for exclusion of evidence which wastes time. These provisions afford ample assurances against the admission of opinions which would merely tell the jury what result to reach, somewhat in the manner of the oath-helpers of an earlier day. They also stand ready to exclude opinions phrased in terms of inadequately explored legal criteria. Thus the question, "Did T have capacity to make a will?" would be excluded, while the question, "Did T have sufficient mental capacity to know the nature and extent of his

property and the natural objects of his bounty and to formulate a rational scheme of distribution?" would be allowed.

AUTHORITY

WEISSENBERGER'S FEDERAL EVIDENCE §§ 703.1–.5

McCORMICK § 12

4 WEINSTEIN 2d §§ 704.01–.06

3 MUELLER & KIRKPATRICK §§ 360–362

7 WIGMORE §§ 1920–21

Nossel, *The Admissibility of Ultimate Issue Expert Testimony by Law Enforcement Officers in Criminal Trials*, 93 COLUM. L. REV. 231 (1993)

Ladd, *Expert Testimony*, 5 VAND. L. REV. 414 (1952)

Stoebuck, *Opinions on Ultimate Facts: Status, Trends, and a Note of Caution*, 41 DEN. L. C. J. 226 (1964)

Note, *Evidence-Expert Testimony—The Ultimate-Issue Rule*, 40 CHI.-KENT L. REV. 147 (1963)

Note, *Opinion Testimony "Invading the Province of the Jury,"* 20 U. CIN. L. REV. 484 (1951)

COMPARISON TO FEDERAL RULE

Colorado Rule 704 differs from the Federal Rule by the Colorado omission of the Federal exception to the general rule set forth by both FRE 104(a) and FRE 704(b). FRE 704(b) provides that no expert witness may testify as to whether a criminal defendant did or did not have the requisite mental state which is an element of the crime. CRE 704 does not provide for this exception. On Dec. 1, 2011 Federal Rule 704 was restyled. Please see Federal Rule 704 in the appendix for comparison.

SIGNIFICANT CASES

People v. Rowerdink, 756 P.2d 986 (Colo. 1988) (in a prosecution for possession of incendiary devices, testimony characterizing fabric strips as "wicks" attached to bottles was admissible, because the testimony was based on the physical observations of the witness).

People v. Collins, 730 P.2d 293 (Colo. 1986) (a lay witness may testify as to an ultimate issue of fact, but questioning lay witnesses must elicit factual, rather than legal, opinions).

People v. Jiron, 2020 Colo. App. LEXIS 542 (Colo. App. 2020) (a blood expert's testimony in a DWI case about the defendant's blood alcohol level was properly admitted because the scientist rendered his own conclusion by means of his independent review of the evidence) *cert. granted.* **Jiron v. People**, 2021 Colo. LEXIS 9 (Colo. 2021).

Silverberg v. Colantuno, 991 P.2d 280 (Colo. App. 1998) (expert testimony by a lawyer which embraced an ultimate issue was admissible where it was found helpful to the court and jury in terms of "sorting out" business transactions).

Peiffer v. State Farm Mut. Auto. Ins. Co., 940 P.2d 967 (Colo. App. 1996) (in an action for breach of contract and bad faith, expert testimony that the insurer violated the Unfair Claims Settlement Practices Act in denying further no-fault payments was properly allowed even though such testimony was a combination of law and fact, because the testimony was relevant to the bad faith claim, explained complex issues of insurance company claims management practices, related to a subject the jury was expressly permitted to consider, and any prejudice created by the testimony did not outweigh its probative value).

People v. Payne, 461 P.3d 630 (Colo. App. 2019) (where a defendant is charged with assaulting an officer while in custody, an officer's layperson testimony that he believed the defendant was not free to leave did not improperly usurp the jury's role, because the officer did not state that the defendant was guilty, but only that he was not free to leave.).

People v. Baker, 2019 Colo. App. LEXIS 1679 (Colo. App. 2019) (expert testimony was improper in a securities fraud case, because the expert witness assessed another witness's testimony, indicated a belief in a particular version of the facts, and made conclusions properly reserved to the jury).

People v. Lawrence, 2019 Colo. App. LEXIS 819 (Colo. App. 2019) (expert testimony was proper in a Colorado securities fraud case, where the expert did not give his opinion as to the defendant's guilt, but instead only testified as to what qualified as a security) *cert. granted sub nom. **Lawrence v. People***, 2020 Colo. App. LEXIS 44 (Colo. 2020)

Hines v. Denver & Rio Grande W.R. Co., 829 P.2d 419 (Colo. App. 1991) (in a wrongful death action, the trial court correctly admitted the opinion of the plaintiff's expert witness that the train was operated negligently, when her opinion was based upon numerous violations of safety policies, despite the fact that the testimony touched on an ultimate issue).

People v. Rivers, 727 P.2d 394 (Colo. App. 1986) (court found that a pathologist's testimony that a murder victim was attacked in two stages was a factual opinion, and did not go to the ultimate issue of whether the defendant acted after deliberation).

People v. Robles-Sierra, 488 P.3d 337, 2018 Colo App. LEXIS 305 (Colo. App. 2018) (where a defendant is charged with distribution of child pornography through a file-sharing software (ARES) and his defense is that he didn't know that the images he was downloading were accessible to others, testimony by the prosecution's expert witness that said software is accessible by others, does not usurp the function of the jury in as much as the expert did not testify on the defendant's intent).

Chapter 705

Rule 705. Disclosure of Facts or Data Underlying Expert Opinion

Rule 705 reads as follows:

The expert may testify in terms of opinion or inference and give reasons therefor without first testifying to the underlying facts or data, unless the court requires otherwise. The expert may in any event be required to disclose the underlying facts or data on cross-examination.

ANALYSIS

Rule 705 sets forth the procedure governing the disclosure of the facts or data used by an expert in formulating his or her opinion. Under the Rule, the expert need not first disclose the underlying basis for his or her opinion unless the court in its discretion requires such a sequence. Consequently, the Rule is designed to provide flexibility in the presentation of expert testimony. Moreover, the Rule implicitly rejects the necessity of a hypothetical question.

Rule 705 provides that the expert may give reasons for the opinion. It is normally during this stage of the interrogation that the expert witness provides a thorough explanation for the opinions and inferences that have been stated. The expert systematically explains his or her reasoning, or provides the jury with an elucidation of the application of his or her expertise to the identified operative facts supporting the opinion.

AUTHORITY

WEISSENBERGER'S FEDERAL EVIDENCE §§ 705.1–.5

McCORMICK § 14

4 WEINSTEIN 2d §§ 705.01–.08

3 MUELLER & KIRKPATRICK §§ 363–365

2 WIGMORE §§ 672–86

Ladd, *Expert Testimony*, 5 VAND. L. REV. 414, 426–27 (1952)

Moller, *Cross-Examining the Plaintiff's Medical Expert*, 42 INS. COUNSEL J. 198 (1975)

Note, *A Reconsideration of the Admissibility of Computerized Evidence*, 126 U. PA. L. REV. 425 (1977)

Note, *Expert Witness and Hypothetical Questions*, 13 W. RES. L. REV. 755 (1962)

COMPARISON TO FEDERAL RULE

In substance, Colorado Rule 705 is identical to Federal Rule 705. However, on Dec. 1, 2011 Federal Rule 705 was restyled. Please see Federal Rule 705 in the appendix for comparison.

SIGNIFICANT CASES

Roberts v. C & M Ready Mix Concrete Co., 767 P.2d 769 (Colo. App. 1988) (when the expert witness's opinion that the victim of a car accident suffered no permanent damage was based on a hypothetical rate of speed, it was proper for the trial court to allow the opposing counsel to question him as to whether his opinion would be the same if the rate of speed was greater).

Great W. Sugar Co. v. N. Natural Gas Co., 661 P.2d 684 (Colo. App. 1984) (expert testimony may not be based on facts which are contrary to evidence).

People v. Alward, 654 P.2d 327 (Colo. App. 1982) (when a psychiatrist testified concerning the defendant's mental state, and based his opinion on episodes of the defendant's conduct, it was not error for the trial court to allow the prosecution to ask the psychiatrist on cross-examination whether his opinion would change when shown other examples of the defendant's conduct which were unknown to the expert).

Stone v. Caroselli, 653 P.2d 754 (Colo. App. 1982) (so long as hypothetical questions are known to the court to be hypotheticals and not assertions of fact, it is not error to allow expert witnesses to give opinion based on those hypotheticals).

Chapter 706

Rule 706. Court Appointed Experts

Rule 706 reads as follows:

(a) **Appointment.** The court may on its own motion or on the motion of any party enter an order to show cause why expert witnesses should not be appointed, and may request the parties to submit nominations. The court may appoint any expert witnesses agreed upon by the parties, and may appoint expert witnesses of its own selection. An expert witness shall not be appointed by the court unless he consents to act. A witness so appointed shall be informed of his duties by the court in writing, a copy of which shall be filed with the clerk, or at a conference in which the parties shall have opportunity to participate. A witness so appointed shall advise the parties of his findings, if any; his deposition may be taken by any party; and he may be called to testify by the court or any party. He shall be subject to cross-examination by each party, including a party calling him as a witness.

(b) **Compensation.** Expert witnesses so appointed are entitled to reasonable compensation in whatever sum the court may allow. The compensation thus fixed is payable from funds which may be provided by law in criminal cases and civil actions and proceedings involving just compensation under the fifth amendment. In other civil actions and proceedings the compensation shall be paid by the parties in such proportion and at such time as the court directs, and thereafter charged in like manner as other costs.

(c) **Disclosure of appointment.** In the exercise of its discretion, the court may authorize disclosure to the jury of the fact that the court appointed the expert witness.

(d) **Parties' experts of own selection.** Nothing in this rule limits the parties in calling expert witnesses of their own selection.

ANALYSIS

There has been a trend toward allowing court appointed expert witnesses for many years. Colorado courts have been allowed to appoint experts for some time via C.R.C.P. 53.

Rule 706 sets out the procedure to be followed when the trial judge, pursuant to Rule 614, calls an expert as a court witness. This rule addresses traditional concerns in its requirements that: a court-appointed expert advise the parties of his findings, his deposition may be taken by any party, he may be called to testify by any party, and he is subject to cross-examination by each party.

Rule 706(b) provides for compensation for the court-appointed expert and under Rule 706(c) the court need not disclose to the jury the fact that a witness is a court-appointed expert. This helps minimize the potential danger that a court-appointed expert may acquire an aura of infallibility. A tendered instruction addressing this potential danger may be appropriate where it is made known to the jury that the expert is court-appointed. This rule has been seldom used in Colorado, probably because most trial judges recognize the extreme danger of a jury giving the court's expert an aura of infallibility. The danger of agreeing to a potentially adverse witness is apparent.

Rule 706(d) merely grants no monopoly to the judge in calling expert witnesses.

This rule may be an excellent source of experts in cases where one party or the other cannot afford but requires an expert to fairly present his case.

AUTHORITY

JAMISON'S COLORADO RULES OF EVIDENCE § 706 I.P.I. (1994)

MUELLER & KIRKPATRICK'S FEDERAL RULES OF EVIDENCE § 706

2 WIGMORE § 563

9 WIGMORE § 2484

95 A.L.R.2d 383

CALIFORNIA EVIDENCE CODE §§ 730–731

Impartial Medical Testimony—Revisited, 34 TEMP. L.Q. 416 (1961)

COMPARISON TO FEDERAL RULE

In substance, Colorado Rule 706 is identical to Federal Rule 706. However, on Dec. 1, 2011 Federal Rule 706 was restyled. Please see Federal Rule 706 in the appendix for comparison.

SIGNIFICANT CASES

Kelton v. Ramsey, 961 P.2d 569 (Colo. App. 1998) (trial courts lack authority to appoint experts to aid parties in litigation; courts only possess authority to appoint expert witnesses for the purpose of providing testimony).

Durbin v. Bonanza Corp., 716 P.2d 1124 (Colo. App. 1986) (the appointment of an expert pursuant to CRE 706 is not per se inconsistent with procedures for establishing a disputed boundary).

VIII
HEARSAY

HEARSAY

Chapter 801

Rule 801. Definitions

Rule 801 reads as follows:

The following definitions apply under this article:

(a) Statement. A "statement" is (1) an oral or written assertion or (2) nonverbal conduct of a person, if it is intended by him to be communicative.

(b) Declarant. A "declarant" is a person who makes a statement.

(c) Hearsay. "Hearsay" is a statement other than one made by the declarant while testifying at the trial or hearing, offered in evidence to prove the truth of the matter asserted.

(d) Statements which are not hearsay. A statement is not hearsay if—

(1) Prior statement by witness. The declarant testifies at the trial or hearing and is subject to cross-examination concerning the statement, and the statement is (A) inconsistent with his testimony, or (B) consistent with his testimony and is offered to rebut an express or implied charge against him of recent fabrication or improper influence or motive, or (C) one of identification of a person made after perceiving him, or

(2) Admission by party-opponent. The statement is offered against a party and is (A) the party's statement in either an individual or a representative capacity or (B) a statement of which the party has manifested his adoption or belief in its truth; or (C) a statement by a person authorized by the party to make a statement concerning the subject; or (D) a statement by the party's agent or servant concerning a matter within the scope of the agency or employment, made during the existence of the relationship, or (E) a statement by a co-conspirator of a party during the course and in furtherance of the conspiracy. The contents of the statement shall be considered but are not alone sufficient to establish the declarant's authority under subdivision (C), the agency or employment relationship and scope thereof under subdivision (D), or the existence of the conspiracy and the participation therein of the declarant and the party against whom the statement is offered under subdivision (E).

ANALYSIS

Definition of "statement," "declarant" and "hearsay"

The hearsay rules govern the admissibility of out-of-court statements, that is, statements that are made by a person other than while testifying at the trial at which the statement is offered into evidence. The law of evidence has developed a system of exclusion, which rejects the admission of certain out-of-court statements that fail to satisfy accepted standards of reliability. Usually, testimony received at trial is accompanied by the safeguards of cross-examination, oath, and the opportunity to observe the demeanor of the witness. Hearsay is inherently unreliable because it is lacking in these safeguards. The general hearsay exclusionary Rule is codified in Rule 802, and it will operate on statements defined as hearsay pursuant to the definitions contained in Rule 801.

"Statement" defined.   Rule 801(a) provides the definition of a "statement" and must be considered in conjunction with the definition of hearsay in Rule 801(c) which uses the term "statement." Evidence not meeting the definition of a "statement" will not be considered hearsay under the basic definition. Rule 801(a) provides that a "statement" may be either an oral or a written assertion, or conduct of a person which is intended by that person to be communicative. Accordingly, documentary evidence almost inevitably contains out-of-court statements. Likewise, any oral statement made outside of the courtroom, subsequently reported by a distinct individual or the same individual as a witness on the stand, is a statement under the definitional scheme of Rule 801. It should nevertheless be noted, that not all oral or written out-of-court statements are hearsay. Whether an out-of-court statement is hearsay is determined by the application of Rule 801(c), which requires a determination of whether the out-of-court statement is offered for its truth.

Nonverbal conduct.   According to Rule 801(a), certain nonverbal conduct may be a statement for the purposes of the hearsay system. Certain nonverbal signals are obviously the equivalent of words for the purposes of communication. Such signals would include nodding, pointing, and the sign language of the hearing impaired. Such conduct may be hearsay if the conduct is intended as communicative and if the intended communication is offered for its truth. Other types of cognitive nonverbal conduct are more difficult to analyze. In certain situations, the conduct of a person may reflect his or her belief, and in certain situations a person's belief which is established by his conduct might be relevant in a particular case. Under Rule 801 the question of whether conduct may be a statement is resolved exclusively by the determination of whether the actor subjectively intended to make a cognitive communication. Where evidence of conduct is offered on a theory that it is not intended by the actor as a communication, and consequently not subject to exclusion under the hearsay system, the burden of showing that a communication is intended should logically fall on the party objecting to the admission of the evidence on hearsay grounds.

"Declarant" defined.   Rule 801(b) defines "declarant" as a person who makes a statement. Consequently, in conjunction with Rule 801(a), a declarant is a person who makes an oral or written statement or who engages in intentionally assertive nonverbal conduct. It should be noted that the definition of declarant employs the term "person." Under the hearsay system, only a person may make a statement, and as a result, machine or animal statements cannot be hearsay.

"Hearsay" defined.   Rule 801(c) codifies the generally accepted definition of hearsay. Hearsay is defined as a statement, other than the one made by the declarant while testifying at the trial or hearing, offered in evidence to prove the truth of the matter asserted. Two key components should be identified in applying the definition of hearsay. The first component of the hearsay definition relates to statements which are made outside of the courtroom. Hearsay potentially involves any statement made outside the courtroom by any person, even a statement made by a person who becomes a witness. The second element of the hearsay definition provides that the out-of-court statement must be "offered in evidence to prove the truth of the matter asserted." This element requires an examination of whether the statement is offered to prove the substance of its contents. Where an out-of-court statement is offered for its truth and determined to be hearsay, the evidence

is presumptively inadmissible, and admissibility may only be achieved through the vehicle of the exception to the basic definition, an exception to the exclusionary rule, or some other basis identified in Rule 802.

Non-hearsay out-of-court. Not all out-of-court statements are relevant in a manner that relies upon their truthfulness, and when an out-of-court statement is relevant in a manner that does not depend upon the truth of the statement, the out-of-court statement is not hearsay under the definition. Such a statement will not be excluded by the hearsay system, because the exclusionary rule contained in Rule 802 only operates on statements defined as hearsay. Statements which are not offered for their truth, and consequently are non-hearsay out-of-court statements, generally fall into certain patterns. These patterns include: (1) statements offered for the effect on a listener; (2) verbal acts or operative facts; (3) state of mind; and (4) prior inconsistent statements used for impeachment. It should be recognized that there is no requirement to fit a particular out-of-court statement within one of these classes to qualify it as admissible non-hearsay. Nevertheless, these traditionally recognized categories are helpful in discerning whether a particular statement should be classified as non-hearsay.

Statements of the witness—inconsistent statements

Rule 801(d)(1) contains vehicles for the admission of prior out-of-court statements of a witness, i.e., a person who testifies at the trial at which the out-of-court statement is offered. Rule 801(d)(1)(A) relates exclusively to prior inconsistent statements used in conjunction with the impeachment technique of self-contradiction. *See* Rule 613. Where the out-of-court statement is inconsistent with the witness's trial testimony, the prior statement may be considered for its truth. It may be considered as substantive evidence, and the jury may base its verdict upon it. Where the prior inconsistent statement conforms to the exception, the opponent of the witness sought to be impeached is not entitled to a limiting instruction requiring the jury to consider the prior statement only for impeachment. The prior statement has a dual purpose; it may be considered for impeachment as well as substantive evidence.

Statements of the witness—prior consistent statements

Rule 801(d)(1)(B) applies to prior statements used to rehabilitate a witness. No oath or cross-examination attending the prior statement is necessary for the prior consistent statement to be considered as substantive evidence. This subdivision has very narrow application. The exception is only triggered where there has been an inference of fabrication, fraud or improper motive of such a nature that a prior consistent statement would be probative to negate such an inference.

Statements of the witness—prior identification

Rule 801(d)(1)(C) does not apply in the context of impeachment or rehabilitation. Rather, it applies to the situation where a witness is present at trial and a prior out-of-court identification made by that witness is offered into evidence. This exception is available where a witness testifies to earlier statements made as to the identity of a particular person. The identification may have been a line-up identification, a street identification or even a photographic array identification. It is imperative, however, that the person who made the out-of-court identification be a witness at trial and be subject to cross-examination.

Statement by party-opponent

Rule 801(d)(2)(A) provides for the admissibility of statements by a party opponent. Hearsay offered through this exception must involve an out-of-court statement by a party where the out-of-court statement is offered against the party at trial. Consequently, as foundational testimony, the witness who heard the party make a statement must be prepared to testify that he had first-hand knowledge of the statement and that the statement was made by the party against whom it is offered.

Under Rule 801(d)(2)(B) an out-of-court statement may be attributable to a party through express or implied adoption. In a number of jurisdictions, this very limited principle has been misapplied and enlarged to create the erroneous notion that if a statement is made in the presence of the parties it is not hearsay, or at least is admissible hearsay by virtue of the parties' presence alone.

Authorized statements and statements of agents or servants

Under Rule 801(d)(2)(C) a statement by a person which is authorized by a party will be attributed to that party. The statement is imputed to the party and considered to be his statement for the purposes of the hearsay rule. Foundational evidence is necessary to establish that the declarant was an agent of the party opponent, and that the declarant had "speaking authority" to make declarations on behalf of the party opponent. Rule 801(d)(2)(D) authorizes the admission of a statement by a party's agent or servant concerning a matter within the scope of the agency or employment. To utilize this hearsay exception, the proponent of evidence must establish a foundation that the declarant was an employee or agent of the party against whom the statement is offered. Second, the statement must merely "concern" a matter within the scope of the agency or employment. No express or implied speaking authority need be given to the agent or employee. Finally, the statement must have been made while the employment or the agency existed. Statements made after the employment or agency has terminated do not qualify under this exception.

Coconspirator statements

Rule 801(d)(2)(E) provides for the admission of coconspirator statements. The statement of a member of a conspiracy is attributed to the coconspirator party against whom the statement is offered at trial. To utilize this exception, the proponent must establish that there was a conspiracy, that both the declarant and the party against whom the statement is offered were members of the conspiracy, and that the statement, in fact, furthered or advanced the conspiracy. In regard to the last element, common sense dictates that a confession to the police does not advance a conspiracy.

Constitutional Developments

Crawford v. Washington, 541 U.S. 36 (2004), rejected the prior "reliability" test for determining whether admission of hearsay could violate the Confrontation Clause. The Court announced the only due process procedures that will satisfy the demands of the Confrontation Clause: (1) If hearsay is testimonial, the declarant must come to court, be a witness and testify in the presence of the defendant, and be available for cross-examination; or (2) if the declarant of testimonial hearsay is unavailable to be a witness, the defendant must have had a prior adequate opportunity to cross-examine the declarant.

In *Crawford*, the Court reversed an assault conviction of Michael D. Crawford because the trial court allowed into evidence a tape-recorded statement from his wife describing the incident to the police. The wife did not testify at the trial because of the Washington state marital privilege, which prohibits spouses from testifying against each other. The Court stated that under any definition of "testimonial" declaration the wife's hearsay statement could not be used as evidence because the defendant never had an opportunity to cross-examine her. The Court declined to give a specific definition of "testimony." Clearly, the narrow legal definition that "testimony" is the oral statement made by a witness in a trial and subject to cross-examination is not the definition of "testimony" the Court used in *Crawford*. Justice Scalia in the opinion hints at a broader, more common dictionary type of definition: "those who bear testimony"; "typically a solemn declaration or affirmation made for the purpose of establishing or proving some fact"; and "statements that were made under circumstances which would lead an objective witness reasonably to believe that the statement would be available for use at a later trial."

In the 2006 cases of *Davis v. Washington*, 547 U.S. 813 (2006) and *Hammon v. Indiana*, 546 U.S. 1088 (2006) the Supreme Court further developed the holding in *Crawford* by clarifying what qualifies as testimonial evidence. Specifically, the court held that,

"Statements are non-testimonial when made in the course of police interrogation under circumstances objectively indicating that the primary purpose of the interrogation is to enable police assistance to meet an ongoing emergency. They are testimonial when the circumstances objectively indicate that there is no such ongoing emergency, and that the primary purpose of the interrogation is to establish or prove past events potentially relevant to later criminal prosecution" *Id.* at 2273.

In *Davis*, the defendant was convicted of felony violation of a domestic no-contact order. The relevant evidence admitted was a tape recording of a 911 call in which the victim identified her assailant by name during and shortly after an assault. The court reasoned that since the purpose of the 911 operating in soliciting the victim's statements were not in contemplation of a prosecution but rather an attempt to assess an ongoing emergency the statements were not testimonial

In *Hammon*, the defendant was convicted of a domestic battery. After police responded to a domestic disturbance, they separated the victim and the defendant and interrogated both in an attempt to determine what had taken place. At trial the victim's statements and an affidavit were introduced by one of the police officers. The court reasoned that at the time the statement was made the emergency was not ongoing as the alleged battery has ceased, the police were on the scene, and the victim and defendant were separated. Rather, the court concluded that the police were attempting to establish or prove past events which would be relevant to a criminal prosecution, and that the statement was therefore testimonial.

The courts in Colorado have continued to grapple with the testimonial/non-testimonial distinction and the application of the confrontation clause principles as set forth in *Crawford* and *Davis*. *See* the case annotations herein: *Marshall v. People*, 309 P.3d 943 (Colo. 2013); *Hinojos-Mendoza v. People*, 169 P.3d 662 (Colo. 2007); *People v. Vigil*, 127 P.3d 916 (Colo. 2006); *People v. Cevallos-Acosta*, 140 P.3d 116 (Colo. App. 2005).

The new Confrontation Clause jurisprudence brings additional importance to the concept of *forfeiture by wrongdoing.* Cases related to confrontation and forfeiture are found at the conclusion of Chapter 804 of this Manual.

Significant Cases

People v. Sparks, 434 P.3d 713 (Colo. App. 2018) (where the record is insufficient for a proper review of an alleged constitutional violation, the court may decline to rule; here the defense's failure to object to the testimony of police detective testifying on the age of the victim in a sexual assault on a child case meant that the record was insufficient).

Nicholls v. People, 396 P.3d 675 (Colo. 2017) (statements by defendant's co-conspirator did not implicate the defendant's right to Confrontation under the Colorado Constitution because the statements were made to co-conspirator's cellmate rather than law enforcement and were therefor considered nontestimonial).

People v. Deleon, 454 P.3d 299, 2017 Colo. App. LEXIS 1467 (Colo. App. 2017) (Cert. Denied) (in a case of sexual assault on a minor, the defense council's objection was not directed to the witness's statements, which were properly admitted under 803(4) statements made for purpose of medical diagnosis: first, because the objection was based on a speculative inference that the victims statement would be interpreted as implying that the victim's mother believed she was lying; second, the defense failed to ask the court to recall the declarant victim to testify; and third, in any case was harmless error).

STATUTES

§ 13-25-135. Evidence of admissions—civil proceedings—unanticipated outcomes—medical care

(1) In any civil action brought by an alleged victim of an unanticipated outcome of medical care, or in any arbitration proceeding related to such civil action, any and all statements, affirmations, gestures, or conduct expressing apology, fault, sympathy, commiseration, condolence, compassion, or a general sense of benevolence which are made by a health care provider or an employee of a health care provider to the alleged victim, a relative of the alleged victim, or a representative of the alleged victim and which relate to the discomfort, pain, suffering, injury, or death of the alleged victim as the result of the unanticipated outcome of medical care shall be inadmissible as evidence of an admission of liability or as evidence of an admission against interest.

(2) For purposes of this section, unless the context otherwise requires:

(a) "Health care provider" means any person licensed or certified by the state of Colorado to deliver health care and any clinic, health dispensary, or health facility licensed by the state of Colorado. The term includes any professional corporation or other professional entity comprised of such health care providers as permitted by the laws of this state.

(b) "Relative" means a victim's spouse, parent, grandparent, stepfather, stepmother, child, grandchild, brother, sister, half brother, half sister, or spouse's parents. The term includes said relationships that are created as a result of adoption. In addition, "relative" includes any person who has a family-type relationship with a victim.

(c) "Representative" means a legal guardian, attorney, person designated to make decisions on behalf of a patient under a medical power of attorney, or any person recognized in law or custom as a patient's agent.

(d) "Unanticipated outcome" means the outcome of a medical treatment or procedure that differs from an expected result.

§ 16-10-201.   Inconsistent statement of witness—competency of evidence

(1) Where a witness in a criminal trial has made a previous statement inconsistent with his testimony at the trial, the previous inconsistent statement may be shown by any otherwise competent evidence and is admissible not only for the purpose of impeaching the testimony of the witness, but also for the purpose of establishing a fact to which his testimony and the inconsistent statement relate, if:

(a) The witness, while testifying, was given an opportunity to explain or deny the statement or the witness is still available to give further testimony in the trial; and

(b) The previous inconsistent statement purports to relate to a matter within the witness's own knowledge.

§ 6-1-111.   Information and evidence confidential and inadmissible-when

(1) Any testimony obtained by the attorney general or a district attorney [in a consumer protection act investigation] pursuant to compulsory process under this article or any information derived directly or indirectly from such testimony shall not be admissible in evidence in any criminal prosecution against the person so compelled to testify. The provisions of this subsection (1) shall not be construed to prevent any law enforcement officer from independently producing or obtaining the same or similar facts, information, or evidence for use in any criminal prosecution.

(2) Subject to the provisions of section 6-1-110 (2), the records of investigations or intelligence information of the attorney general or a district attorney obtained under this article [consumer protection act investigation] may be deemed public records available for inspection by the general public at the discretion of the attorney general or district attorney. This subsection (2) shall not be construed to prevent the attorney general or a district attorney from issuing public statements describing or warning of any course of conduct or any conspiracy which constitutes a deceptive trade practice, whether on a local, statewide, regional, or nationwide basis.

§ 19-2-511.   Statements

(1) No statements or admissions of a juvenile made as a result of the custodial interrogation of such juvenile by a law enforcement official concerning delinquent acts alleged to have been committed by the juvenile shall be admissible in evidence against such juvenile unless a parent, guardian, or legal or physical custodian of the juvenile was present at such interrogation and the juvenile and his or her parent, guardian, or legal or physical custodian were advised of the juvenile's right to remain silent and that any statements made may be used against him or her in a court of law, of his or her right to the presence of an attorney during such interrogation, and of his or her right to have counsel appointed if he or she so requests at the time of the interrogation; except that, if a public defender or counsel representing the juvenile is present at such interrogation, such statements or admissions may be admissible in evidence even though the juvenile's parent, guardian, or legal or physical custodian was not present.

(2) (a) Notwithstanding the provisions of subsection (1) of this section, statements or admissions of a juvenile may be admissible in evidence, notwithstanding the absence of

a parent, guardian, or legal or physical custodian, if the court finds that, under the totality of the circumstances, the juvenile made a knowing, intelligent, and voluntary waiver of rights and:

(I) The juvenile is eighteen years of age or older at the time of the interrogation or the juvenile misrepresents his or her age as being eighteen years of age or older and the law enforcement official acts in good faith reliance on such misrepresentation in conducting the interrogation;

(II) The juvenile is emancipated from the parent, guardian, or legal or physical custodian; or

(III) The juvenile is a runaway from a state other than Colorado and is of sufficient age and understanding.

(b) For the purposes of this subsection (2), "emancipated juvenile" is defined in section 19-1-103 (45).

(3) Notwithstanding the provisions of subsection (1) of this section, statements or admissions of a juvenile shall not be inadmissible in evidence by reason of the absence of a parent, guardian, or legal custodian if the juvenile was accompanied by a responsible adult who was a custodian of the juvenile or assuming the role of a parent at the time.

(4) For the purposes of this section, "physical custodian" is defined in section 19-1-103 (84).

(5) Notwithstanding the provisions of subsection (1) of this section, the juvenile and his or her parent, guardian, or legal or physical custodian may expressly waive the requirement that the parent, guardian, or legal or physical custodian be present during interrogation of the juvenile. This express waiver shall be in writing and shall be obtained only after full advisement of the juvenile and his or her parent, guardian, or legal or physical custodian of the juvenile's rights prior to the taking of the custodial statement by a law enforcement official. If said requirement is expressly waived, statements or admissions of the juvenile shall not be inadmissible in evidence by reason of the absence of the juvenile's parent, guardian, or legal or physical custodian during interrogation. Notwithstanding the provisions of this subsection (5), a county social services department and the department of human services, as legal or physical custodian, may not waive said requirement.

(6) Notwithstanding the provisions of subsection (1) of this section, statements or admissions of a juvenile shall not be inadmissible into evidence by reason of the absence of a parent, guardian, or legal or physical custodian, if the juvenile makes any deliberate misrepresentations affecting the applicability or requirements of this section and a law enforcement official, acting in good faith and in reasonable reliance on such deliberate misrepresentation, conducts a custodial interrogation of the juvenile that does not comply with the requirements of subsection (1) of this section.

Trends and Developments

The statute articulated above is a relatively knew statute, pertaining to statements admissibility of Juveniles, at a court proceeding. The Supreme Court noted an additional factor required when determining whether a juvenile is in custody. When considering the totality of the circumstances, the court must also consider the age of the juvenile. *People v. N.A.S.*, 329 P.3d 285, 2014 CO 65. In a recent opinion, the Court of Appeals noted an important aspect of when a statement covered by 19-2-511 is prohibited and when such statement may be permitted. In *People v. Richardson*, the Court of Appeals stated, that the trial court did not err in denying defendant's motion to suppress statements made during a phone conversation with a victim who was a minor. First, the standards for determining whether a party's consent is voluntary for the purpose of the eavesdropping and wiretapping statutes are less stringent than the standards applicable to questions of voluntariness arising in the context of alleged violations of constitutional rights. Second, the victim was not in custody when he agreed to the recording but rather was given in an effort to assist in the apprehension and prosecution of defendant. *People v. Richardson*, 2014 COA 50—[published April 24, 2014].

HEARSAY

AUTHORITY

WEISSENBERGER'S FEDERAL EVIDENCE §§ 801.1–.25

McCORMICK §§ 246, 248–50

5 WEINSTEIN 2d §§ 801.01–.34

4 MUELLER & KIRKPATRICK §§ 368–430

2 WIGMORE § 267

5 WIGMORE § 1361

6 WIGMORE § 1766

BEST, EVIDENCE: EXAMPLES AND EXPLANATIONS, Chapters 3–4

Lathi, *Sex Abuse, Accusations of Lies, and Videotaped Testimony: A Proposal for a Federal Hearsay Exception in Child Sexual Abuse Cases*, 68 U. COLO. L. REV. 507 (1997)

Humphreys, *In Search of the Reliable Conspirator: A Proposal Amendment to Federal Rule of Evidence 801(d)(2)(E)*, 30 AM. CRIM. L. REV. 337 (1993)

Rice, *Should Unintended Implications of Speech Be Considered Nonhearsay? The Assertive/Nonassertive Distinction Under Rule 801(a) of the Federal Rules of Evidence*, 65 TEMP. L. REV. 529 (1992)

Weissenberger, *Unintended Implications of Speech and the Definition of Hearsay*, 65 TEMP. L. REV. 857 (1992)

Milich, *Re-Examining Hearsay Under the Federal Rules: Some Method of the Madness*, 39 KAN. L. REV. 893 (1991)

Blakely, *You Can Say That If You Want - The Redefinition of Hearsay in Rule 801 of the Proposed Federal Rules of Evidence*, 35 OHIO ST. L.J. 601 (1974)

Falknor, *The "Hear-say" Rule as a "See-Do" Rule: Evidence of Conduct*, 33 ROCKY MTN. L. REV. 133 (1961)

Falknor, *"Indirect" Hearsay*, 31 TUL. L. REV. 3 (1956)

Falknor, *Silence as Hearsay*, 89 U. PA. L. REV. 192 (1940)

Finman, *Implied Assertions as Hearsay: Some Criticism of the Uniform Rules of Evidence*, 14 STAN. L. REV. 682 (1962)

Graham, *"Stickperson Hearsay": A Simplified Approach to Understanding the Rule Against Hearsay*, 4 U. ILL. L. REV. 877 (1982)

McCormick, *The Borderland of Hearsay*, 39 YALE L.J. 489 (1983)

Maguire, *The Hearsay System: Around and Through the Thicket*, 14 VAND. L. REV. 741 (1961)

Morgan, *Hearsay*, 25 MISS. L.J. 1 (1953)

Morgan, *Hearsay Dangers and the Application of the Hearsay Concept*, 62 HARV. L. REV. 177 (1948)

Rucker, *The Twilight Zone of Hearsay*, 9 VAND. L. REV. 453 (1956)

Tribe, *Triangulating Hearsay*, 87 HARV. L. REV. 957 (1974)

Wellborn, *The Definition of Hearsay in the Federal Rules of Evidence*, 61 TEX. L. REV. 49 (1982)

COMPARISON TO FEDERAL RULE

Federal Rule 801(a) differs from Colorado Rule 801(a) in its description of the type of nonverbal conduct that is defined as a statement. The Federal Rule treats a person's nonverbal conduct as a statement if the person intends the conduct to be an "assertion." The Colorado Rule treats a person's nonverbal conduct as a statement if the person intends the conduct to be "communicative."

Federal Rule 801(d)(1)(A) requires that prior inconsistent statements must have been made under oath subject to the penalty of perjury to be eligible for exclusion from the definition of hearsay. Colorado Rule 801(d)(1)(A) does not impose such a requirement in order for prior inconsistent statements to be eligible for exclusion from the definition of hearsay. This treatment of prior inconsistent statements is consistent with a separate Colorado statute governing treatment of prior inconsistent statements in criminal cases. *See* C.R.S. § 16-10-201. Federal Rule 801(d)(1)(B) defines two kinds of prior consistent statements as *not* hearsay. One of these kinds of prior statements is a prior statement offered to rebut a charge of recent fabrication or motivation, and the other is a prior statement offered to rehabilitate the credibility of a witness that has been attacked on another ground. The Colorado rule includes only the first of these two kinds of prior consistent statements.

Please note that on Dec. 1, 2011 Federal Rule 801 was restyled. Please see Federal Rule 801 in the appendix for comparison.

SIGNIFICANT CASES

Beech Aircraft Corp. v. Rainey, 488 U.S. 153 (1988) (a judge advocate report regarding the crash of a military aircraft was admissible under Federal Rule 803(8) where portions of the report contained opinions and the author's statement as to probable cause of crash).

Coy v. Iowa, 487 U.S. 1012 (1988) (defendant's right to face-to-face confrontation was violated where a screen was placed between child sexual assault victims and defendant during their testimony).

United States v. Owens, 484 U.S. 554 (1988) (admission of prior out-of-court identification statement did not violate the Confrontation Clause of the Sixth Amendment or Federal Rule 801, where the witness testified he was unable to explain the basis for the identification because of memory loss).

Bourjaily v. United States, 483 U.S. 171 (1987) (under Federal Rule 801(d)(2)(E) the trial court may examine hearsay statements sought to be admitted in making a preliminary factual determination of whether a conspiracy existed).

Tennessee v. Street, 471 U.S. 409 (1985) (under Federal Rule 801(c), an accomplice's confession was not considered a hearsay statement where offered to rebut defendant's testimony that his own confession was a coerced "copy" of the accomplice's confession).

People v. Garcia, 479 P.3d 905 (Colo. 2021) (in order to determine whether a statement is testimonial, a trial court must analyze "whether, in light of all circumstances, viewed objectively, the primary purpose of [procuring the statement is] 'to creat[e] an out-of-court substitute for trial testimony.'"

Cain v. People, 327 P.3d 249 (Colo. 2014) (A defendant on trial for driving under the influence did not open-the-door for admission of the results of his preliminary breath test for blood alcohol content when he testified that he had not been drinking. Colo. Rev. Stat. § 42-4-1301(6)(i)(III) prohibits the use of preliminary breath test results at trial for all purposes, including impeachment).

Davis v. People, 310 P.3d 58 (Colo. 2013) (Under C.R.S. section 16-10-201, which permits the introduction at trial of a witness's previous inconsistent statement not only for the purpose of impeachment but also for the purpose of establishing a fact, a witness's actual or feigned memory loss is tantamount to denial and therefore can support the introduction of previous statements in which the witness recalled facts that the witness testifies she does not remember at trial).

People v. Greenlee, 200 P.3d 363 (Colo. 2009) (murder defendant's own statement two months prior to shooting the victim that he planned to shoot and kill a woman was not hearsay because it was the defendant's own out-of-court statement).

Golob v. People, 180 P.3d 1006 (Colo. 2008) (expert's testimony that another expert agreed with his conclusions was inadmissible hearsay; the second expert's conclusions were not used as a basis for the first expert's findings but rather were used to bolster them).

Hinojos-Mendoza v. People, 169 P.3d 662 (Colo. 2007) (report prepared in a Colorado Bureau of Investigation lab, finding that seized substance was cocaine, was hearsay that was testimonial for purposes of the Confrontation Clause).

People v. Moreno, 160 P.3d 242 (Colo. 2007) (admission of hearsay pursuant to the statute governing statements by child sexual assault victims violates a defendant's Confrontation Clause rights, unless the defendant has forfeited those rights in some way).

Arteaga-Lansaw v. People, 159 P.3d 107 (Colo. 2007) (statements made to police when they came to the declarant's house in response to her report of a robbery were testimonial and therefore subject to Confrontation Clause restrictions; they were made when there was no current threat and were retrospective in nature).

Raile v. People, 148 P.3d 126 (Colo. 2006) (where police questioned the defendant in the absence of an on-going emergency, statements made in response to interrogation were testimonial and thus inadmissible under Confrontation Clause).

Compan v. People, 121 P.3d 876 (Colo. 2005) (hearsay statements given by the victim to her friend regarding domestic abuse which were not made under circumstances which would lead an objective witness reasonably to believe that the statement would be available for use later at trial, were not testimonial).

People v. Eppens, 979 P.2d 14 (Colo. 1999) (Rule 801(D)(1)(b) is not the only provision under which evidence of a person's prior consistent statements may be admitted; even if a statement does not meet the requirements of that rule to avoid the hearsay prohibition, it may still be admitted, if relevant, for the non-hearsay purpose of rehabilitation).

Blecha v. People, 962 P.2d 931 (Colo. 1998) (a co-defendant's statement made after the crime was committed and not made in furtherance of the conspiracy is outside the scope of the coconspirator exclusion of hearsay).

People v. Meier, 954 P.2d 1068 (Colo. 1998) (a statement made by a defendant is an admission under CRE 801(d)(?), and is not hearsay; the rationale for this exclusion from the hearsay definition is that the defendant has the opportunity to explain his own words when they are offered against him).

Burlington Northern Railroad Co. v. Hood, 802 P.2d 458 (Colo. 1990) (personal injury plaintiff's out-of-court statement that he was not suffering from certain injuries should have been treated as admissible to show that he was not suffering from those injuries at the time he made the statement, under Rule 801(d)(2)(A) as an admission).

People v. Bowers, 801 P.2d 511 (Colo. 1990) (testimony about alleged sex abuse victim's use of anatomically correct dolls in response to out-of-court questions about her claimed abuse was hearsay, since the victim intended her positioning of the dolls to be communicative).

People v. Drake, 748 P.2d 1237 (Colo. 1988) (out-of-court statements to a psychiatrist are not hearsay when used to show the reason for the psychiatrist's opinion about the speaker rather than to show that the facts contained in the statements were true).

Montoya v. People, 740 P.2d 992 (Colo. 1987) (as long as the foundation requirements of C.R.S. § 16-10-201 are satisfied, a prior inconsistent statement may be proved with otherwise competent extrinsic evidence without meeting the foundational requirements of CRE 613; evidence admissible under

C.R.S. § 16-10-201 may be used for substantive or impeachment purposes since the statute eliminates hearsay considerations).

Williams v. People, 724 P.2d 1279 (Colo. 1986) (coconspirator admissions must be shown to have been made in furtherance of the conspiracy; a statement by an alleged coconspirator which detracts from another co-conspirator's alibi cannot be characterized as in furtherance of the conspiracy and is thus outside the definition of the coconspirator admission provision).

People v. Green, 629 P.2d 1098 (Colo. 1981) (silence as a lack of response to an incriminating statement can be an admission, but this doctrine will not apply if there were emotional or physical impediments to a response; in this case the silent party was involved in an argument with the speaker and knew that the speaker was armed).

People v. Collins, 2021 Colo. App. LEXIS 266 (Colo. App. 2021) (the decision of a trial judge to allow a six-year-old child to testify while a comfort dog was present did not violate defendant's confrontation right: ". . . a defendant's confrontation rights do not carry with it the right to impose discomfort on any witness.") Not selected for final or official publication as of June 1, 2021.

People v. Chirinos-Raudales, 2021 Colo. App. LEXIS 419 (Colo. App. 2021) (for purposes of applying the child hearsay rule (paragraph 13-25-129 C.R.S. 220) the relevant age of the child is that applicable to the general offence, not the age relevant to sentence enhancement). Not selected for final or official publication as of June 1, 2021.

People v. Knapp, 2020 Colo. App. LEXIS 1296 (Colo. App. 2020) (in an assault case, State's evidence of the defendant's brother-in-law calling the defendant a "wife beater" was properly admitted as part of the res gestae as it explained the defendant's motives for his actions). Not selected for final or official publication as of June 1, 2021.

People v. Dominguez, 454 P.3d 364 (Colo. App. 2019) (in a possession of a controlled substance with intent to distribute case, text messages sent to the defendant's phone were held to be non-hearsay verbal acts, not offered for the truth, and were thus admissible).

People v. Cohen, 440 P.3d 1256 (Colo. App. 2019) (the concept of "opening the door" to otherwise inadmissible hearsay evidence is applicable only to the extent necessary to remove any unfair prejudice which might otherwise have ensued from the introduction of the original hearsay evidence).

People v. Cohen, 440 P.3d 1256 (Colo. App. 2019) (in a theft trial where the defendant, a formerly licensed attorney, was accused of misappropriating clients' funds, Colorado Office of Attorney Regulation Counsel complaints were deemed to be out-of-court testimonial statements and inadmissible as violative of the Confrontation Clause).

People v. Smalley, 369 P.3d 737 (Colo. App. 2015) (hearsay rule did not bar introduction of a recording of a telephone conversation between the defendant and another person; the defendant's own words are exempted from the definition of hearsay, and the other person's words were relevant not for their truth but to provide context for the defendant's expression of relief made after hearing those words).

People v. Glover, 363 P.3d 736 (Colo. App. 2015) (statements in a defendant's social network web page were properly admitted as statements of a party opponent).

People v. Stroud, 2014 COA 58 (Colo. App. 2014) (§ 19-3-207(3) which bars admissions made during a dependency and neglect case from use in a criminal prosecution only applies to a formal admission or denial of the allegations. It does not apply to other statements made during the hearing. Such statements are admissible at a subsequent criminal trial as party admissions under 801(d)(2)).

McLaughlin v. BNSF Railway Co., 300 P.3d 925 (Colo. App. 2012) (the entire transcript of the plaintiff's interview with a claims investigator employed by the defendant was properly admitted as a response to a general charge of fabrication, and also to provide context for the plaintiff's testimony during cross-examination).

People v. Hagos, 250 P.3d 596, 623 (Colo. App. 2009) (where the victim recorded several telephone conversations between himself and the defendant, the defendant's own statements in the recorded conversations were admissions under CRE 801(d)(2)(A) and the utterances of the victim were not hearsay because they were offered for the limited purpose of putting the defendant's responses in context).

People v. Buckner, 228 P.3d 245 (Colo. App. 2009) (holding that electronically stored information in a cell phone, including the list of incoming and received calls, is not hearsay because it is neither a "person" nor a "declarant" making a communicative "statement" within the meaning of CRE 801).

People v. Espinoza, 195 P.3d 1122 (Colo. App. 2008) (state department of revenue records including statement that defendant had been served with proof that his driver's license had been suspended were not testimonial; they existed before the defendant committed any actions for which he was prosecuted and reflected normal administrative work of the government agency).

People v. Kendall, 174 P.3d 791 (Colo. App. 2007) (testimony that the defendant stated in a telephone call that he was not the defendant was not hearsay, when offered to show that the caller was, in fact, the defendant).

People v. Gash, 165 P.3d 779 (Colo. App. 2006) (statements made by victim to witness at a family gathering before the victim disappeared were not testimonial, as their primary purpose was not to establish past events potentially relevant to a later criminal prosecution).

Vista Resorts, Inc. v. Goodyear Tire & Rubber Co., 117 P.3d 60 (Colo. App. 2004) (in an action claiming defective hot water hose it was not hearsay to allow evidence of 950 complaints received by Goodyear to prove notice and market "stigma").

People v. Robson, 80 P.3d 912 (Colo. App. 2003) (in a trial for sexual assault where the prosecution only presents defendant's confession and his opportunity to commit the crime without independent corroborating evidence of the crime, CRE 801(d) does not supersede the *corpus delicti* doctrine requiring independent corroboration and the charges were properly dismissed).

People v. Sweeney, 78 P.3d 1133 (Colo. App. 2003) (in a case where defendant was found guilty of two counts of aggravated robbery and one count of conspiracy to commit aggravated robbery, testimony by a witness that a participant not the defendant said to witness " 'if you say anything, you know what's going to happen,' and points at [defendant], and at that time [defendant] lifted up his shirt, and tapped on his gun," that although the defendant said nothing, his conduct was more than mere silence and indicated an adoption of the other participant's statements relegating his conduct to an adopted admission).

People v. Richardson, 58 P.3d 1039 (Colo. App. 2002) (in murder case against defendant charged with causing death by ligature strangulation, use of a mannequin by prosecutor during the trial to demonstrate the manner in which victim was tied was not a communicative hearsay statement but an illustration of trial testimony).

People v. James, 40 P.3d 36 (Colo. App. 2001) (statements made by the defendant to a prosecution witness and offered against the defendant were admissible as admissions under CRE 801(d)(2)(A), and statements of coconspirators were admissible under CRE 801(d)(2)(E) where the declarants were members of the conspiracy, the statements were made in furtherance of the conspiracy, at least two other persons corroborated each alleged hearsay statement, and all but one of the declarants themselves testified at trial and confirmed their roles in the conspiracy).

People v. Fisher, 9 P.3d 1189 (Colo. App. 2000) (trial court did not commit error by allowing the prosecutor to impeach a prosecution witness with prior inconsistent statements made in a police interview where the witness's in-court testimony deviated from her prior statements).

Klein v. State Farm Mut. Auto. Ins. Co., 948 P.2d 43 (Colo. App. 1997) (the court properly allowed into evidence a report and addenda issued from an independent medical examiner which was provided to prove the defendant's reliance upon the opinion of the examiner for the non-payment of medical services provided on behalf of the plaintiff; the report and addenda were not hearsay because they were not admitted to prove the truthfulness of the facts and opinions of the medical condition of the plaintiff).

People v. McCoy, 939 P.2d 537 (Colo. App. 1997) (where the Youthful Offender System (YOS), in a quasi-judicial proceeding, revoked a convicted juvenile felon's YOS sentence, remanding the defendant to the adult correctional system, the defendant's due process rights do not include the imposition of the rules of evidence and the YOS may therefore introduce hearsay evidence which may be used against the defendant without exception).

People v. Newton, 940 P.2d 1065 (Colo. App. 1996) (in an aggravated robbery, theft, and menacing case, where a witness refused to answer questions based on a privilege against self-incrimination, the court improperly allowed testimony of a detective about the witness's statement during out-of-court questioning as a prior inconsistent statement, because asserting one's privilege against self-incrimination is not testimony for the purposes of 801(d)(1)(A)).

People v. Segura, 923 P.2d 266 (Colo. App. 1995) (victims' prior consistent statements were properly admitted since their statements rebutted a charge of fabrication and were made before the alleged fabrication).

Stevens v. Humana of Delaware, Inc., 832 P.2d 1076 (Colo. App. 1992) (hospital employee's statement that other medical personnel were absent during crucial time of childbirth was hearsay, when introduced to support finding of personnel's absence; exceptions applied to permit its admission).

People v. Walters, 821 P.2d 887 (Colo. App. 1991) (testimony about volume and intensity of victim's screams during alleged assault was admissible, since screams were not intended to be communicative).

People v. Franklin, 782 P.2d 1202 (Colo. App. 1989) (out-of-court statement "Now is not a good time to go out" should have been treated as hearsay when sought to be introduced to support finding that speaker believed that a crime of violence was about to occur outside).

People v. Sparks, 434 P.3d 713, 2018 Colo. App. LEXIS 30 (Colo. App. 2018) (in a sexual assault on a minor case, Defendants' testimony that he knew the age of 14 year-old victim did not require that he possess personal knowledge under CRE 602, because admissions excluded from hearsay under CRE 801(d)(2) do not require that the declarant have personal knowledge).

People v. Lujan, 484 P.3d 718, 2018 Colo. App. LEXIS 986 (Colo. App. 2018) (testimony by a police officer rebutting the testimony of another officer that the defendant was not upset about the victim's death should not be excluded as self-serving hearsay because the statements are about the defendant's demeanor and thus do not involve hearsay).

People v. Godinez, 457 P.3d 77, 2018 Colo. App. LEXIS 1908 (Colo. App. 2018) (contradictory out of court statements about the defendant's whereabouts on the day of the crime are admissible as non hearsay because they were not offered for their truth, but rather for their falsity and their effect on the police investigation; thus, admission of the statements did not violate the defendant's confrontation rights. Further, the co-conspirator exception does not apply to a co-conspirator's out of court statements alleging an alibi, since the statements were not made in furtherance of the conspiracy but rather to cover-up the conspiracy).

Chapter 802

Rule 802. Hearsay Rule

Rule 802 reads as follows:

> Hearsay is not admissible except as provided by these rules or by the civil and criminal procedural rules applicable to the courts of Colorado or by any statutes of the State of Colorado.

ANALYSIS

The hearsay rule is a general rule of exclusion of statements falling within the definition of hearsay under Rule 801. Once having established that the evidence is hearsay, it is inadmissible unless the proponent of the declaration can bring it within an exception to the basic definition under Rule 801(d), within an exception under either Rule 803 or Rule 804, or within some other basis identified in Rule 802.

Analysis of hearsay. Hearsay issues are subject to systematic analysis. The analysis may be made in the following manner:

1. Is the witness testifying to an out-of-court "statement" for purposes of the hearsay rule? (*See* Rule 801(a).)

2. If so, is the out-of-court statement being offered to prove the truth of the matter asserted in the statement? (*See* Rule 801(c).) It may be offered to prove only that the statement was made, not that the statement is true. In such cases the statement is not hearsay, and if otherwise admissible, may be subject to a limiting instruction under Rule 105.

3. If the statement is offered to prove the truth of the statement, is it exempted under Rule 801(d)(1), "Prior statements by a witness," or Rule 801(d)(2), "Statements of a party-opponent"?

4. If the statement is not exempted by Rule 801(d), is it subject to an exception under Rule 803? The availability of the declarant is not a material requisite to the Rule 803 exceptions.

5. Is the declarant unavailable as defined by Rule 804(a)? If so, does the statement fit within one of the exceptions under Rule 804(b)? Each of these exceptions has as a prerequisite the unavailability of the declarant.

6. Is the statement admissible pursuant to a statute or rule of procedure?

7. If it is a criminal case, does the prosecution's use of a hearsay exception pass constitutional muster relative to rights of confrontation and due process? Hearsay

otherwise admissible may be inadmissible under the Constitution in criminal cases if offered against the accused.

8.   Again, in a criminal case even if a statement is hearsay and not subject to a specific exception, is it offered by the defendant and would the defendant be denied due process by its exclusion? *See Chambers v. Mississippi* 410 U.S. 284 (1973).

AUTHORITY

WEISSENBERGER'S FEDERAL EVIDENCE § 802.1

5 WEINSTEIN 2d §§ 802.01–.06

4 MUELLER & KIRKPATRICK §§ 431–432

Martin, *Admissibility of Hearsay Evidence in Administrative Hearings*, 27 COLO. LAW. 65 (1998)

Epps, *Passing the Confrontation Clause Stop Sign: Is All Hearsay Constitutionally Admissible?*, 77 KY. L.J. 7 (1989)

COMPARISON TO FEDERAL RULE

Colorado Rule 802 is parallel to Federal Rule 802. However, on Dec. 1, 2011 Federal Rule 802 was restyled. Please see Federal Rule 802 in the appendix for comparison.

SIGNIFICANT CASES

People v. Loveall, 231 P.3d 408, 414–415 (Colo. 2010) (the minimum due process required at a parole revocation hearing was violated when the prosecution failed to reveal the identity of the hearsay declarants until shortly before the hearing).

Baldwin v. Huber, 223 P.3d 150 (Colo. App. 2009) (statement was sufficiently reliable to be admitted in the driver's license revocation case where the hearsay assertions made by the arresting officer were sworn and made by him in the course of his police officer duties and the licensee had a right to subpoena the involved officers but failed to do so).

People v. Moses, 64 P.3d 904 (Colo. App. 2002) (probation violation may be established by hearsay testimony that the defendant failed a drug test if the probation officer is subject to cross-examination).

People v. Franklin, 782 P.2d 1202 (Colo. App. 1989) (out-of-court statement "Now is not a good time to go out" should have been treated as hearsay when sought to be introduced to support finding that speaker believed that a crime of violence was about to occur outside).

Chapter 803

Rule 803. Hearsay Exceptions; Availability
of Declarant Immaterial

Rule 803 reads as follows:

The following are not excluded by the hearsay rule, even though the declarant is available as a witness:

(1) Spontaneous present sense impression. A spontaneous statement describing or explaining an event or condition made while the declarant was perceiving the event or condition.

(2) Excited utterance. A statement relating to a startling event or condition made while the declarant was under the stress of excitement caused by the event or condition.

(3) Then existing mental, emotional, or physical condition. A statement of the declarant's then existing state of mind, emotion, sensation, or physical condition (such as intent, plan, motive, design, mental feeling, pain, and bodily health), but not including a statement of memory or belief to prove the fact remembered or believed unless it relates to the execution, revocation, identification, or terms of declarant's will.

(4) Statements for purposes of medical diagnosis or treatment. Statements made for purposes of medical diagnosis or treatment and describing medical history, or past or present symptoms, pain, or sensations, or the inception or general character of the cause or external source thereof insofar as reasonably pertinent to diagnosis or treatment.

(5) Recorded recollection. A past recollection recorded when it appears that the witness once had knowledge concerning the matter and; (A) can identify the memorandum or record, (B) adequately recalls the making of it at or near the time of the event, either as recorded by the witness or by another, and (C) can testify to its accuracy. The memorandum or record may be read into evidence but may not itself be received unless offered by an adverse party.

(6) Records of regularly conducted activity. A memorandum report, record, or data compilation, in any form, of acts, events, conditions, opinions, or diagnosis, made at or near the time by, or from information transmitted by, a person with knowledge, if kept in the course of a regularly conducted business activity, and if it was the regular practice of that business activity to make the memorandum, report, record, or data compilation, all as shown by the testimony of the custodian or other qualified witness, or by certification that complies with Rule 902(11), Rule 902(12), or a statute permitting certification, unless the source of information or the method or circumstances of preparation indicate a lack of trustworthiness. The term "business" as used in this

paragraph includes business, institution, association, profession, occupation, and calling of every kind, whether or not conducted for profit.

(7) Absence of entry in records kept in accordance with the provisions of paragraph (6). Evidence that a matter is not included in the memoranda reports, records, or data compilations, in any form, kept in accordance with the provisions of paragraph (6), to prove the nonoccurrence or nonexistence of the matter, if the matter was of a kind of which a memorandum, report, record, or data compilation was regularly made and preserved, unless the sources of information or other circumstances indicate lack of trustworthiness.

(8) Public records and reports. Unless the sources of information or other circumstances indicate lack of trustworthiness, records, reports, statements, or data compilations in any form, of public offices or agencies, setting forth (A) the activities of the office or agency, or (B) matters observed pursuant to duty imposed by law as to which matters there was a duty to report excluding, however, in criminal cases matters observed by police officers and other law enforcement personnel, or (C) in civil actions and proceedings and against the Government in criminal cases, factual findings resulting from an investigation made pursuant to authority granted by law.

(9) Records of vital statistics. Records or data compilations, in any form, of births, fetal deaths, deaths, or marriages, if the report thereof was made to a public office pursuant to requirements of law.

(10) Absence of a Public Record. Testimony—or a certification under Rule 902—that a diligent search failed to disclose a public record or statement if:

(A) the testimony or certification is admitted to prove that

(i) the record or statement does not exist; or

(ii) a matter did not occur or exist, if a public office regularly kept a record or statement for a matter of that kind; and

(B) in a criminal case, a prosecutor who intends to offer a certification provides written notice of that intent at least 14 days before trial, and the defendant does not object in writing within 7 days of receiving the notice—unless the court sets a different time for the notice or the objection.

(11) Records of religious organizations. Statements of births, marriages, divorces, deaths, legitimacy, ancestry, relationship by blood or marriage, or other similar facts of personal or family history, contained in a regularly kept record of a religious organization.

(12) Marriage, baptismal, and similar certificates. Statements of fact contained in a certificate that the maker performed a marriage or other ceremony or administered a sacrament, made by a clergyman, public official, or other person authorized by the rules or practices of a religious organization or by law to perform the act certified, and purporting to have been issued at the time of the act or within a reasonable time thereafter.

(13) Family records. Statements of fact concerning personal or family history contained in family Bibles, genealogies, charts, engravings on rings, inscriptions on family portraits, engravings on urns, crypts, or tombstones, or the like.

(14) Records of documents affecting an interest in property. The record of a

document purporting to establish or affect an interest in property, as proof of the content of the original recorded or filed document and its execution and delivery by each person by whom it purports to have been executed, if the record is a record of a public office and an applicable statute authorizes the recording of documents of that kind in that office.

(15)   Statements in documents affecting an interest in property.   A statement contained in a document purporting to establish or affect an interest in property if the matter stated was relevant to the purpose of the document, unless dealings with the property since the document was made have been inconsistent with the truth of the statement or the purport of the document.

(16) Statements in ancient documents.   A statement in a document that was prepared before January 1, 1998, and whose authenticity is established.

(17) Market reports, commercial publications.   Market quotations, tabulations, lists, directories, or other published compilations, generally used and relied upon by the public or by persons in particular occupations.

(18) Learned treatises.   To the extent called to the attention of an expert witness upon cross-examination or relied upon by him in direct examination, statements contained in published treatises, periodicals, or pamphlets on a subject of history, medicine, or other science or art, established as a reliable authority by the testimony or admission of the witness or by other expert testimony or by judicial notice. If admitted, the statements may be read into evidence and may be received as exhibits, as the court permits.

(19) Reputation concerning personal or family history.   Reputation among members of his family by blood, adoption, or marriage, or among his associates, or in the community, concerning a person's birth, adoption, marriage, divorce, death, legitimacy, relationship by blood, adoption, or marriage, ancestry, or other similar fact of his personal or family history.

(20)   Reputation concerning boundaries or general history.   Reputation in a community, arising before the controversy, as to boundaries of or customs affecting lands in the community, and reputation as to events of general history important to the community or state or nation in which located.

(21)   Reputation as to character.   Reputation of a person's character among his associates or in the community.

(22) Judgment of previous conviction.   Evidence of a final judgment, entered after a trial or upon a plea of guilty or *nolo contendere*, adjudging a person guilty of a crime punishable by death or imprisonment in excess of one year, to prove any fact essential to sustain the judgment, but not including, when offered by the Government in a criminal prosecution for purposes other than impeachment, judgments against persons other than the accused. The pendency of an appeal may be shown but does not affect admissibility.

(23) Judgment as to personal, family, or general history, or boundaries.   Judgments as proof of matters of personal, family or general history, or boundaries, essential to the judgment, if the same would be provable by evidence of reputation.

(24)   [Transferred to Rule 807]

ANALYSIS

Hearsay exceptions; availability of declarant immaterial

(1) Spontaneous present sense impression

In order for an out-of-court statement of a declarant to be admissible as a present sense impression, the statement must be spontaneous, and it must be made while the declarant is perceiving the facts in question. There is no necessity of a startling event. Consequently, the foundational requirement for application of this exception requires establishing that the declarant had first-hand knowledge of the event perceived, and that the statement made by the declarant described the event or condition. It must be established that the statement was made contemporaneously with the event or immediately after the event. The out-of-court statement must describe the event, and any expansion beyond what is perceived would not be admissible as a statement of present sense impression.

Illustration

If Norb testifies that Ralph said, "There goes that Acme Service truck through the red light. I saw that truck getting its brakes repaired yesterday," the second sentence is not admissible under Rule 803(1). The sentence involves a recollection of past events and is not a report of the immediate sense impression.

---

(2) Excited utterance

An excited utterance is an admissible out-of-court statement which is made in response to a startling event during the trauma or stress of the event. In order for the exception to apply, there must be an extremely startling or shocking event. Foundational evidence as to the existence of the event may be established through the out-of-court statement of the declarant himself. It must further be established as a foundation that the declarant had personal knowledge of the event, and that, as a subjective matter, the declarant was under extreme stress when he made the statement. Because stress can continue for a period of time after a startling event, the statement need not be made immediately after the startling event has occurred. *Compare* Rule 803(1). The statement must also "relate" to the startling event in question and the term "relate" is broader than the term "describe" which is operative in the context of Rule 803(1).

The excited utterance may expand upon a description of the event as long as the statement in some way relates to the startling event.

Illustration

Bystander observing an accident states to a companion, "Look at that blue car crash that red light!" Immediately after the accident, before the dust has yet settled, a passenger in the car says of the driver, "Oh my God, why did he drink those three beers before we left work?"

In the first statement, the present sense impression exception limits the scope of statement to a description of the event. Under the excited utterance exception, Rule 803(2), if the reflective processes remain stilled, the declaration is admissible as to a matter pertinent to the event even if it relates to an occurrence at another time. Therefore, what the passenger said with regard to events affecting his ability to drive would be admissible even though it pertained to events occurring at another time.

The Doctrine of Res Gestae

This exception and the "excited utterance" exception in Rule 803(2) treat statements sometimes referred to as *res gestae* statements. The doctrine of *res gestae* has long been disdained by judges and legal scholars. Judge Learned Hand, in *United States v. Matot*, 146 F.2d 197, 198 (2d Cir. 1944), expressed his dissatisfaction with the doctrine and said, "[I]t is a phrase which has been accountable for so much confusion that it had best be denied any place whatever in legal terminology; if it means anything but an unwillingness to think at all, what it covers cannot be put in less intelligible terms." Dean Wigmore disliked the use of the term, saying "There are words enough to describe the Rules of Evidence. Even if there were no accepted name for the doctrine, any name would be preferable to an empty phrase so encouraging to looseness of thinking and uncertainty of decision." 6 WIGMORE, EVIDENCE § 1767 at 180, 182–183 (3d ed. 1940).

Courts have long used the doctrine of *res gestae* (things done) as a "catch-all" device and a vehicle to expand the scope of the exceptions to the hearsay rule. *Res gestae* is generally defined by courts as circumstances, facts, and declarations which arise from a main fact or event, and are explanatory of that main fact or event, and are so closely connected to be considered part of the main fact or event, and illustrative of its character. While the doctrine was thought of as obsolete in recent years, Colorado appellate courts have resurrected the doctrine in their decisions, allowing the admissibility of evidence that would otherwise be excluded, so long as the evidence is relevant and its probative value substantially outweighs the probability of unfair prejudice.

The doctrine is most often referred to in connection with evidence of past crimes committed by a person who is charged with another crime. Cases of this type are discussed in Chapter 404. It may also be used as a means for admitting statements that would otherwise be barred by the hearsay exclusionary rule. On some occasions, courts have admitted statements under the *res gestae* rationale even though the statements lacked the specific requirements for admission under specific exceptions covering, for example, excited utterances, contemporaneous statements, declarations of bodily condition, and declarations of state of mind.

In *People v. Blecha*, 940 P.2d 1070 (Colo. App. 1996), the court referred to the possibility that a statement that failed to satisfy the requirements of the coconspirator exception to the hearsay rule might nonetheless be admissible as a *res gestae* statement, if circumstances showed that although it had been made after the end of a conspiracy there was a showing that a specific plan of further concealment had been made. In that case, no such showing was made and the *res gestae* rationale for admission was not proper.

In *People v. Agado*, 964 P.2d 565 (Colo. App. 1998), evidence of a domestic fight before the defendant murdered a man at his girlfriend's house was admissible as *res gestae* evidence; the fight was "part and parcel of the crime charged" and provided the jury with necessary background information.

(3) Then existing mental, emotional, or physical condition

Rule 803(3) provides for the admissibility of statements made by the declarant concerning his state of mind, emotions, sensations, or physical condition. The out-of-court statement must refer to then existing subjective qualities of the declarant. The out-of-court statement may not refer to qualities that existed at a prior point in time. For example, the statement, "I felt ill yesterday," would not qualify under the exception. An out-of-court statement which looks forward to some act and expresses an intent or plan to do some act in the future is admissible under Rule 803(3). Intent is considered to be a mental condition under the exception, and consequently, the statement "I intend to go to Boston" would be comprehended by the exception. The Rule specifically provides that out-of-court statements relating to the execution, revocation, identification, or terms of the declarant's will are admissible. Such statements of belief must be made by the testator in regard to his own will. The rule otherwise, however, does not comprehend statements of belief when such statements are used to prove the fact believed.

Illustration

The following statements, if relevant, would generally satisfy Rule 803(3) depending upon the context in which the out-of-court statement is made:

I am ill.

I am tired.

I have a pain in my chest.

I feel dizzy.

I am afraid.

I like Norb.

I am depressed.

I am happy.

I plan to sell my house.

I don't plan to go on any trips this year.

---

(4) Statements for purposes of medical diagnosis or treatment

Rule 803(4) provides for the admissibility of certain statements made in subjective contemplation of medical treatment or diagnosis. The out-of-court declarant must subjectively believe that the statement is being made in anticipation of treatment or diagnosis. The statement usually will be made to a physician, but the out-of-court statement may be made to someone other than a physician where the out-of-court declarant subjectively believes that he is making the statement in contemplation of receiving treatment or diagnosis. For example, the statement could be made to a nurse, an ambulance attendant, or even to a member of the declarant's family. The subjective contemplation of treatment or diagnosis is the significant foundational requirement which must be established to utilize the exception.

Rule 803(4) conditions admissibility of statements made for the purpose of obtaining medical treatment or diagnosis upon the objective standard that such hearsay declarations must be "reasonably pertinent" to the treatment or diagnosis sought. The exception consequently operates as a vehicle for the admission of statements of medical history, past and present symptoms and conditions, past and present pain or sensations, the inception or cause of the medical condition or illness and the external source, if any, of the medical condition, injury or illness. The fact that a doctor solicited or took the information should be sufficient evidence that the statement is reasonably pertinent to diagnosis or treatment. Nevertheless, the requirement of pertinency to diagnosis and treatment does, of course, impose a real limitation in certain cases.

Statements concerning fault or guilt are not reasonably pertinent to diagnosis or treatment. A declarant's out-of-court statements that his injury resulted, for example, from the defendant's negligent driving, refusing to provide a safe work environment or failing to maintain a reasonably safe condition or diagnosis and treatment of an injury, will fall outside the scope of the exception.

The distinction between declarations by the patient for purposes of treatment or for purposes of diagnosis has been abandoned. This exception may be invoked even as to statements made for purposes of medical evaluation in preparation for trial. See Rule 703 with regard to the requisites of disclosure of the basis for an expert opinion.

Trends and Developments

Recently, the Colorado Supreme Court reversed a 2011 Court of Appeals ruling in *Kelly v. Haralampopoulos*, 327 P.3d 255 (Colo. 2014). The case was a medical malpractice action that arouse out of a failed biopsy procedure, which left the victim in a vegetative state. A statement by the victim's former girlfriend asking if the victim's cocaine use could have contributed to his injuries was admitted, at trial, as a statement made for medical diagnosis or treatment under 803(4).

The Court of Appeals found that the trial court had abused its discretion in admitting the evidence. It held that an 803(4) exception did not apply to the statement because the victim was already in a vegetative state when the statement was made, and treatment was no longer possible.

Reinvigorating the 803(4) distinction between "treatment" and "diagnosis," the Colorado Supreme Court reversed. The court held that a statement made for the purpose of medical "treatment" suggests that it is made in conjunction with developing a course of action to treat a patient's medical condition. The court then distinguished the present case as one involving a statement made for "diagnosis," finding that diagnosis is the process of determining the nature, source, or cause of a patient's medical condition. Therefore, a statement made for the purpose of diagnosis does not carry with it the same prospective focus that treatment has. Because of this, the court held that the former girlfriend's statement was properly admitted at trial as a statement made for medical diagnosis under 803(4).

---

(5) Recorded recollection

In contrast to the device of refreshing a witness's recollection under Rule 612, Rule 803(5) provides for the admission of a written document which contains a recorded recollection. The Federal Rules and rules of many states condition use of the recorded recollection exception on a showing that the witness's current memory of the information in the record is insufficient for full and accurate testimony, but the Colorado rule omits that requirement. Thus, a document can be eligible for treatment under this provision whether or not its proponent has used it to refresh or to attempt to refresh a witness's recollection.

It must be established that the memorandum or record containing the witness's past recollection concerns a matter of which the witness once had personal knowledge. Second, the document must have been prepared when the matter was fresh in the memory of the witness.

If a writing qualifies as a past recollection recorded, it is read into evidence and is not received as an exhibit. The purpose of this limitation is to avoid elevating this type of declaration above testimonial evidence. It ought to be afforded no greater opportunity for scrutiny than is afforded testimonial evidence unless the party against whom the writing is offered desires that it be subjected to closer scrutiny.

(6) Records of regularly conducted activity

Rule 803(6) is commonly referred to as the "business record exception" but its application goes far beyond business entities, and records of associations, clubs, or other organizations may qualify under this exception.

In order for an out-of-court statement to be admitted under this exception, there must be a business record or writing. As a general proposition, an oral business record does not qualify under this exception. In order to establish the proper foundation for the admission of a business record, testimony from an appropriate foundation witness must be used. The witness must have first-hand knowledge of the method by which the business in question prepares, stores and maintains its records. Generally, the foundation witness is a custodian or records librarian, but any witness with the requisite first-hand knowledge of the business's record keeping procedures may qualify. The foundation witness testifies that the record in question was prepared by an employee of the business in question who had a duty to report the information. The foundation witness further testifies that the person preparing the record or contributing information to the record had personal knowledge of the facts or events reported, and that the report was prepared at or near the time of the event that is recorded. The witness must also testify that it is the regular practice or custom of the business in question to make and retain the type of record involved.

It is important to recognize that the preparer of the document must have had a business duty to report the information, and likewise he must have relied upon reports made to him by persons who also have a business duty to report the information. A business document which records information that is not within the personal knowledge of individuals with a business duty to report the information is not admissible under this exception as to the information provided by third persons.

Practical Application

Quite frequently, business records contain statements of persons who are not employees of the business which keeps the record and who do not have a business duty to report accurately to that business. Such third party statements recorded in business records are not comprehended by this particular exception, whereas all statements of persons who have a business duty to report to the business which keeps the records are encompassed by the exception. Statements of third persons are only admissible when contained in a business record where they satisfy the multiple hearsay requirements of Rule 805. Under Rule 805, the third party statement must have an independent basis of admissibility pursuant to an exception to the basic definition, a hearsay exception, a non-hearsay basis, or some other basis identified in Rule 802.

An opponent of a business record may seek to exclude the record because it was a document prepared in subjective contemplation of litigation. The operative language in Rule 803(6) is: ". . . unless the source of information or the method or circumstances of preparation indicate a lack of trustworthiness." Even though complying with all the parameters of the business records exception, documents prepared for use in litigation are excludable within the discretion of the trial judge. The case of *Palmer v. Hoffman*, 318 U.S. 109 (1943), held that such litigation-oriented documents are not prepared in the "regular course of business."

(7) Absence of entry

Rule 803(7) serves the purpose of permitting a fact to be proven by the absence of an entry in the same manner and under the same conditions as Rule 803(6) permits facts to be proven by the existence of an entry. Of course, where an entry is absent, evidence to that effect may not represent hearsay at all, since the preparer of the record (the declarant) may intend to make no assertion about matters not mentioned. Where no assertion is subjectively intended, there can be no out-of-court statement and, consequently, no hearsay.

The foundational requirements for evidence offered pursuant to Rule 803(7) are, with obvious adjustments, substantially similar to those for evidence offered under Rule 803(6). Instead of demonstrating that a record is of the type routinely kept by a business, the proponent of evidence under Rule 803(7) must demonstrate that such a business routinely kept records of matters like the entry not made. In similar fashion, instead of showing a contemporaneous recording, the proponent must be prepared to demonstrate that the matter not mentioned was of such a nature that had it occurred, it would have alerted the record-keeper and been promptly recorded.

Proof that payments have not been made as indicated by the absence of notations on account ledger, or proof that the patient has not reported a claimed injury to his doctor by reference to absence of notation on the medical chart, could be established by use of this exception. In such cases, special attention should be given in qualifying the record to establish that it would be customary for those responsible to make such notations had information been provided to them.

(8) Public records and reports

Rule 803(8) permits proof of the activities of a public office or agency by means of its records. Foundational requirements for this exception are easily satisfied, and where the record is properly authenticated pursuant to Article 9, it will be presumed that responsible persons, acting in the course of their official duties, prepared and maintained accurate entries based upon reliable information.

Examples of evidence admissible as proof of the activities of official agencies include:

1. Accounting records of governmental agencies;

2. Documents and journal entries of courts, legislative bodies and administrative tribunals;

3. Certificates of title, registry, death and birth;

4. Records of licensing agencies; and

5. Records of deeds and conveyances.

Rule 803(8) also provides for the admission of matters which are observed and reported under a legal duty and which are external to the agency or public office. The admissibility of reports of matters observed is conditioned on three requirements. First, the governmental employer's agent who is the source of the information must have personal knowledge of the event or condition described in the report, as the qualifying phrase "matters observed" clearly imports. Second, the source must be under a legal duty to report the information. Third, the official agency must be legally required to prepare and maintain the record, as the term "duty" implies.

Finally, Rule 803(8) provides for the admissibility of factual findings resulting from an investigation made pursuant to authority granted by law. The admissibility of investigative reports is parallel to federal practice. *See Beech Aircraft Corporation v. Rainey*, 488 U.S. 153 (1988). Such reports may contain opinions or evaluations resulting from an investigation.

The Rule explicitly prohibits the introduction of public reports in the following situations: (1) records of matters observed by police and other law enforcement personnel, by the prosecution in criminal cases; (2) records of factual findings of investigations, by either the prosecution or the defense in criminal cases. These restrictions should apply to any record qualifying under Rule 803(8) but offered pursuant to Rule 803(6).

In similar fashion to the exception provided for business records in Rule 803(6), Rule 803(8) contains a clause authorizing exclusion where trustworthiness is demonstrably compromised. Accordingly, an official record otherwise satisfying the requirements of the Rule, may be excluded on the basis that the circumstances surrounding the source of the information or the manner of its recording indicate an unusual degree of unreliability.

Current Trends and New Developments

The Supreme Court of Colorado has interpreted C.R.S. 42-4-1301 (2013), relating to inadmissible evidence pertaining to Preliminary Breath Tests (PBT). That statue prohibits the results of a preliminary screening test, to be admitted into any court action, outside a hearing held to determine if a law enforcement officer had probably cause to believe that the driver committed a violation of driving under the influence. The Supreme Court in *Cain v. People*, considered whether the results of a preliminary breath test ("PBT") for blood alcohol content are admissible for impeachment purposes. The Supreme court held, that under this section, the PBT results may not be used as a evidence in ANY court action except as specifically provided in the statute itself. Since the statute does not explicitly allow for using the results for impeachment purposes, PBT results may shall not be admitted. *Cain v. People*, 2014 CO 49M, ¶ 1.

The court further distinguished this case from those in other jurisdiction where evidence of this kind was permissible, as a case involving a statute that expressly prohibits the admission of PBT results in a criminal trial to determine if the defendant is guilty. The statue specifically limits the use of PBT results to hearings conducted to determine if a police officer had probable cause to arrest the defendant on suspicion of DUI or DWAI. 42-4-1301(6)(i)(III). The court notes the importance of this restriction because in a probable cause hearing, the issue is whether, at the tine of the arrest, "the facts and circumstances within the arresting officer's knowledge are sufficient to warrant a person of reasonable caution to believe an offense has been or is being committed." *Cain v. People*, 2014 CO 49M, ¶ 16.

(9) Records of vital statistics

Rule 803(9) creates a hearsay exception for public records relating to births, fetal deaths, deaths, and marriages. It allows the contents of such records to be introduced as substantive evidence, thereby facilitating the proof of a wide variety of information contained in such records.

(10) Absence of a Public Record

Rule 803(10) admits evidence of the absence of a public record or entry in order to prove either the absence of certain documents or the nonexistence or nonoccurrence of a matter regarding which there would normally be a public record. The Rule is similar in effect to the provisions of Rule 803(7), which governs proof of the absence of an entry in the records of a regularly conducted business activity. *See* Analysis to Rule 803(7).

(11), (12), (13) Records of religious organizations; marriage, baptismal, and similar certificates; family records

These three exceptions relate to proof of births, marriages, divorces, deaths, legitimacy, relationships, and ancestry. The circumstantial guarantee of trustworthiness of such records and certificates lies in the lack of motivation to fabricate inherent in the information recording process and in the opportunity for scrutiny of the information by others who may be in a position to verify or protest the data recorded. Requirements of authentication of Article IX must be met.

An interesting problem of the best evidence rule, Article X, arises where an inscription on an urn, crypt or tombstone is being introduced under this exception. Since the tombstone is being offered to prove its written contents, a photograph of the tombstone or testimony of the inscription would be secondary evidence. Nevertheless, the requisite showing of the unavailability of the original would be easily met in such a case. Since the best evidence rule requires only a showing that the original is not available, any evidence of the tombstone inscription would be admissible. This might be a tombstone rubbing, photograph, or even one testifying as to what he saw on the stone. Any concerns of reliability of such evidence go to the credibility and probative value and not to its admissibility.

(14), (15) Records of documents affecting an interest in property; statements in documents affecting an interest in property

Rule 803(14) recognizes a hearsay exception for all statements contained in a properly recorded deed establishing the interest in the property. Rule 803(15) creates a similar exception for statements relevant to the property interest so long as the dealings with respect to the property since execution of the document are consonant with the statement.

Illustration 1

X offers recorded deed to Blackacre to prove that at the time of execution grantor was an unmarried person.

Objection: Hearsay.

Court: Overruled.

The ruling is correct so long as the instrument is recordable and it was properly recorded.

HEARSAY

Illustration 2

A offers an unrecorded lease to Blackacre to prove the existence of a described monument used as part of the property description.

Objection: Hearsay.

Court: Overruled.

The ruling is correct as long as it was established by way of foundation that dealings with respect to the property since execution of the lease were consonant with the declaration.

It should be noted that Rule 803(15) does not require the document to have been recorded or to be subject to recordation. Also, documents affecting personal property as well as real property are within the scope of Rule 803(15), for example, contracts, bills of sale, security agreements, wills, estate inventories, and other documents that establish or affect an interest in property.

Documents embraced by the exception may be self-authenticating under Rule 902(1), concerning domestic public documents, or Rule 902(9), concerning certified domestic records of regularly conducted activity, or they may qualify as ancient documents under Rule 901(b)(8).

(16) Statements in ancient documents

The "ancient document" hearsay exception applies to documents that were prepared prior to January 1, 1998 and whose authenticity can be established. The ancient document hearsay exception, Rule 803(16), directly complements Rule 901(b)(8), which provides for the authentication of a document that is in excess the same date of January 1, 1998, which is found in its proper repository, and which manifests no indications of suspicion as to the document's authenticity. Consequently, utilizing the ancient document authentication technique will simultaneously satisfy the hearsay exception.

The ancient document hearsay exception applies only to writings, but it contains no restriction as to the type of writing that will qualify. Consequently, Rule 803(16) may be applied to documents of formal nature, such as wills and deeds as well as other types of writings, such as letters, leases, powers of attorney, receipts, maps and public surveys.

(17) Market reports, commercial publications

Rule 803(17) authorizes the admission of certain books and reports as substantive proof of the information contained in such sources. The exception applies to market quotations, tabulations, lists, directories, or other published compilations. These reports and publications are admissible where the proponent by way of foundation shows that the publication is one that is both generally used and generally relied upon either by the public or by persons in particular occupations.

Data that is admissible under this exception should include:

1.   Weather data, either in the meteorological reports or even in the almanac.

2.   Stock market reports as evidence of value of securities on a given day.

3.   Telephone directories to prove telephone numbers (e.g., as part of evidence of authentication of a telephone conversation under Rule 901(b)(6)).

4.   Mail order catalogues to establish value.

5. City directories to establish addresses.

6. Blue or red books to prove automobile values.

7. Membership lists to prove enrollment or membership in institutions or organizations.

Many of the writings falling within this exception would be self-authenticating under Rule 902(3), "Official publications"; Rule 902(4), "Newspapers and periodicals"; or Rule 902(5), "Trade inscriptions and the like." Others would be easily authenticated under Rule 901(b)(7), "Public records or reports"; or Rule 901(b)(8), "Ancient documents or data compilations."

(18) Learned treatises

Rule 803(18) creates a hearsay exception for statements contained in published treatises, periodicals or pamphlets on a subject of history, medicine or other science or art established as a reliable authority to the extent that such statements are called to the attention of an expert witness upon cross-examination or relied upon by him in direct examination. The reliability of the authority may be established by the testimony or admission of the witness, by other expert testimony, or by judicial notice. Once the authority is established as reliable, statements contained in treatises and the like which are addressed on direct or cross-examination may be considered as substantive evidence and may, in the court's discretion, be received as exhibits. To prevent the possibility of misuse of the evidence by the jury, however, statements contained in books and articles may not be offered as substantive evidence independent of expert testimony.

(19), (20), (21) Reputation exceptions

These exceptions reflect the essential hearsay nature of reputation evidence. Reputation is simply the composite of a large number of out-of-court declarations evincing belief in a particular fact or set of facts. These exceptions permit proof of matters relating to personal or family history, boundaries or general history, or a person's character by reputation evidence. The reputation concerning boundaries or general history must have arisen prior to the matter in controversy.

Rule 803(21) serves to re-enforce other Rules which allow the introduction of reputation testimony in specific situations. For example, under Rule 404(a)(1), an accused in a criminal trial may authorize evidence of his character and if he or she does so, the prosecution may offer character evidence in rebuttal. In addition, under Rule 404(a)(2), the accused and the prosecution may, under certain circumstances, offer evidence relating to the character of the victim. In these instances, and also in situations where character itself is "in issue," Rule 405 permits proof of character to be established by testimony as to reputation. The function of Rule 803(21) is to insure that where reputation evidence is admissible, it may be received for the truth of the matter asserted. Moreover, the reference to "associates" and "community" in Rule 803(21) refers to a variety of settings such as business, church or social groups, and the only prerequisite to use of the exception is a showing that the person characterized is sufficiently known in the group in question to have permitted others to have become acquainted with him or her such that a reputation has developed.

(22) Judgment of previous conviction

Subject to express restrictions, Rule 803(22) authorizes the admission of felony convictions in subsequent civil and criminal actions in order to prove any fact essential to the previous criminal judgment. The evidence offered must be that of a final judgment, entered after a trial or guilty plea, but not upon a plea of *nolo contendere*. Additional limitations provide that the previous conviction must relate to a crime punishable by death or imprisonment in excess of one year and that in criminal prosecution, the government may not utilize the prior conviction of persons other than the accused for a purpose other than impeachment. It should be noted that the evidence offered pursuant to Rule 803(22) is merely probative, rather than conclusive, of the fact sought to be proved. In other words, it merely serves as evidence as to the consequential fact sought to be proven.

Subject to the limitations of the Rule, this hearsay exception admits evidence of previous convictions in criminal and civil actions as proof of any fact essential to sustain the conviction. Consequently, the proponent must establish not only the conviction itself through, for example, introduction of a certified record, but he or she must also establish that the fact sought to be proved was essential to sustain the prior judgment. Accordingly, the trial judge must determine that issue as a preliminary matter, based upon an examination of the entire record of the prior case, if necessary. Admissibility of a prior conviction to prove a fact essential to that determination also depends upon its relevancy in the litigation in which it is offered. In this respect the proponent may not run afoul of the forbidden inference of Rule 404(b). *See* Analysis to Rule 404.

Finally, it should be noted that this exception does not impinge upon res judicata or collateral estoppel, but it merely makes a felony conviction evidence of the facts underlying the conviction. Moreover, the exception does not give rise either to a shifting of the burden of persuasion or the shifting of the burden of production by establishing a rebuttable presumption.

(23) Judgment as to personal, family, general history, or boundaries

Rule 803(23) authorizes the admissibility of a judgment as substantive proof of certain matters in a subsequent action. The matters which may be proved by this method are limited to those of personal, family or general history, or boundaries. The exception is further circumscribed by the requirements that the facts sought to be proved must have been essential to the prior judgment and that the matter must be one which would be provable by reputation evidence. The exception is consequently limited in application.

The doctrines of res judicata and collateral estoppel must be distinguished from the principles reflected in Rule 803(23). The hearsay exception permits the use of judgments as evidence. Nevertheless, such evidence is not conclusive and may be rebutted in the same fashion as any other evidence. This use of a judgment is distinct from the concept of res judicata, in which a judgment operates as a bar to further litigation between the same parties concerning the same subject matter. It is also distinguishable from collateral estoppel, which operates as a bar to re-litigation of facts previously litigated between the same parties. A judgment offered under Rule 803(23), then, is merely probative of the fact to which it is relevant.

The elements of this exception are:

1. The judgment pertains to matters of personal, family, general history or boundaries;

2. The matter was essential to the judgment;

3. Res judicata or collateral estoppel do not take the matter out of the realm of proof; and

4. The matter is one which could also be proved by the reputation exceptions Rules 803(19) or 803(20).

See Analysis to Rule 803(22), "Judgment of previous conviction."

STATUTES

§ 13-25-129.   Statements of child victim of unlawful sexual offense against a child or of child abuse—hearsay exception

(1) An out-of-court statement made by a child, as child is defined under the statutes which are the subject of the action, describing any act of sexual contact, intrusion, or penetration, as defined in section 18-3-401, C.R.S., performed with, by, on, or in the presence of the child declarant, not otherwise admissible by a statute or court rule which provides an exception to the objection of hearsay, is admissible in evidence in any criminal, delinquency, or civil proceedings in which a child is a victim of an unlawful sexual offense, as defined in section 18-3-411(1), C.R.S., or in which a child is the subject of a proceeding alleging that a child is neglected or dependent under section 19-1-104(1)(b), C.R.S., and an out-of-court statement by a child, as child is defined under the statutes which are the subject of the action, describing any act of child abuse, as defined in section 18-6-401, C.R.S., to which the child declarant was subjected or which the child declarant witnessed, not otherwise admissible by a statute or court rule which provides an exception to the objection of hearsay, is admissible in evidence in any criminal, delinquency, or civil proceedings in which a child is a victim of child abuse or the subject of a proceeding alleging that a child is neglected or dependent under section 19-1-104(1)(b), C.R.S., and an out-of-court statement made by a person under thirteen years of age describing all or part of an offense contained in part 1 of article 3 of title 18, C.R.S., or describing an act of domestic violence as defined in section 18-6-800.3(1), C.R.S., not otherwise admissible by statute or court rule which provides an exception to the objection of hearsay is admissible in evidence in any criminal, delinquency, or civil proceeding, if:

(a)   The court finds in a hearing conducted outside the presence of the jury that the time, content, and circumstances of the statement provide sufficient safeguards of reliability; and

(b)   The child either:

(I)   Testifies at the proceedings; or

(II)   Is unavailable as a witness and there is corroborative evidence of the act which is the subject of the statement.

(2) If a statement is admitted pursuant to this section, the court shall instruct the jury in the final written instructions that during the proceeding the jury heard evidence repeating a child's out-of-court statement and that it is for the jury to determine the weight and credit to be given the statement and that, in making the determination, the jury shall consider the age and maturity of the child, the nature of the statement, the circumstances under which the statement was made, and any other relevant factor.

(3) The proponent of the statement shall give the adverse party reasonable notice of his intention to offer the statement and the particulars of the statement.

§ 13-25-129.5.   Statements of persons with developmental disabilities—hearsay exception

(1) An out-of-court statement made by a person with an intellectual and developmental disability, as defined in *section 25.5-10-202 (26)(a), C.R.S.*, not otherwise admissible by a statute or court rule that provides an exception to the objection of hearsay is admissible in any criminal or delinquency proceeding in which the person is alleged to have been a victim if the conditions of subsection (5) of this section are satisfied.

(2)   (a) An out-of-court statement made by a person with and intellectual and developmental disability, as defined by *25.5-10-202 (26)(a), C.R.S.*, that describes all or part of an offense described in paragraph (b) of this subsection (2) performed with, by, on, or in the presence of the declarant, and that is not otherwise admissible by a statute or

court rule that provides an exception to the objection of hearsay, is admissible in any criminal, delinquency or, civil proceeding if the conditions of subsection (5) of this section are satisfied.

(b) The exceptions described in paragraph (a) of this subsection (2) applies to an out-of-court statement made by a person with a developmental disability, which statement describes all or part of any of the following offenses:

(i) Sexual assault, as described in *section 18-3-402, C.R.S.;*

(ii) Unlawful sexual conduct, as described in section 18-3-404, C.R.S.;

(iii) Sexual assault on a child, as described in section 18-3-405, C.R.S.;

(iv) Sexual assault on a child by one in a position of trust, as described in section 18-3-405.3, C.R.S.;

(v) Internet sexual exploitation of a child, described in section 18-3-405.4, C.R.S.;

(vi) Sexual assault on a client by a psychotherapist, as described in described in section 18-3-405.5, C.R.S.;

(vii) Incest, as described in section 18-6-301, C.R.S.;

(viii) Aggravated incest, as described in section 18-6-302, C.R.S.;

(ix) Human trafficking of a minor for involuntary servitude, as described in section 18-3-503, C.R.S., or human trafficking of a minor for sexual servitude, as described in section 18-3-504 (2), C.R.S.;

(x) Sexual exploitation of a child, as described in section 18-6-403, C.R.S.;

(xi) Indecent exposure, as described in section 18-7-302, C.R.S.; or

(xii) Criminal attempt to commit any of the acts as specified in this paragraph (b).

(3) An out-of-court statement by a person with an intellectual and developmental disability, as defined in section 25.5-10-202 (26)(a), C.R.S., that describes any act of child abuse, as defines in section 18-6-401, C.R.S., to which the declarant was subjected or which the declarant witnessed, and that is not otherwise admissible by a statute or court rule that provides and exception to the objection of hearsay, is admissible in evidence in any criminal, delinquency, or civil proceeding in which a child is alleged to be a victim of child abuse or the subject of a proceeding alleging that a child is neglected or dependent under *section 19-1-104 (1)(b), C.R.S.*, if the conditions of subsection (5) of this section are satisfied

(4) An out-of-court statement by a person with an intellectual and developmental disability, as defined in *section 25.5-10-202 (26)(a), C.R.S.*, that describes all or part of an offense contained in part 1 of article 3 of title 18, C.R.S., of that describes an act of domestic violence as defined in section 18-6-800.3 (1) C.R.S., not otherwise admissible by a statute or court rule that provides and exception to the objection of hearsay, is admissible in evidence in any criminal, delinquency, or civil proceeding if the conditions of subsection (5) of this section are satisfied.

(5) The exceptions to the objection of hearsay described in subsections (1), (2), (3), and (4) of this section shall apply only if the court finds in a hearing conducted outside the presence of the jury that the time, content, and circumstances of the statement provide sufficient safeguards of reliability; and either:

(a) The statement is a nontestimonial statement; or

(b) (i) The declarant testifies at the proceedings; or

(ii) If the declarant is unavailable to testify, the defendant has had an opportunity to cross-examine the declarant in a previous proceeding and there is corroborative evidence of the act which is the subject of the statement.

(6) If a statement is admitted pursuant to this section, the court shall instruct the jury in the final written instructions that during the proceeding the jury heard evidence repeating a person's out-of-court statement, that it is for the jury to determine the weight and credit to be given the statement, and that, in making the determination, the jury shall consider the nature of the statement, the circumstances under which the statement was made, and any other relevant factor.

(7) The proponent of the statement shall give the adverse party reasonable notice of his or her intention to offer the statement and the particulars of the statement.

§ 42-4-1301.   Driving Under the influence, Driving while impaired-driving with excessing alcohol content

Statutes states in relevant part the following: The below stated statute reflects changes current through all laws passed at the Second Regular Session of the Sixty-Ninth General Assembly of the State of Colorado (2014) and changes approved by the electorate at the November 2014 election.

. . . (6)(i)

(I) following the lawful contact with a person who has been driving a motor vehicle or vehicle and when a law enforcement officer reasonably suspects that person was driving a motor vehicle or vehicle while under the influence of or while impaired by alcohol, the law enforcement may conduct a preliminary screening test using a device approved by the executive directors of the department of public health and environment after first advising the driver that the driver may either refuse or agree to provide a sample of the driver's breath for such preliminary test; except that, if the driver is under twenty-one years of age, the law enforcement officers may, after providing such advisement to the person, conduct such preliminary screening test if the officer reasonably suspects that the person has consumed any alcohol.

(II) The results of this preliminary screening test may be used by a law enforcement officer in determining whether probably cause exists to believe such person was driving a motor vehicle or vehicle in violation of this section and whether to administer a test pursuant to section *42-4-1301.1(2)*.

(III) Neither the results of such preliminary screening test nor the fact that the person refused such test shall be used in any court action except in a hearing outside of the presence of a jury, when such hearing is held to determine if a law enforcement officer has probable cause to believe that the driver committed a violation of this section. The results of such preliminary screening test shall be made available to the driver or the driver's attorney on request.

(j) In any trial for a violation of this section, if, at the time of the alleged offense, the person possessed a valid medical marijuana registry identification card, as defined in section 25-1.5-106(2)(e), C.R.S., issues to himself or herself, the prosecution shall not use such fact as part of the prosecution shall not use such fact as part of the prosecution's case in chief.

(k) In any traffic stop, the driver's possession of a valid medical marijuana registry identification card, as defined in section 25-1.5-106(2)(e), C.R.S., issued to himself or herself shall not, in the absence of other contributing factors, constitute probable cause for a peace officer to require the driver to submit to an analysis of his or her blood.

§ 18-4-414   Evidence of Value

(1) For purposes of this part 4, when theft occurs from a store, evidence of the retail value of the thing involved shall be prima facie evidence of the value of the thing involved. Evidence offered to prove retail value may include, but shall not be limited to, affixed labels and tags, signs, shelf tags, and notices.

(2) For the purposes of this part 4, in all cases where theft occurs, evidence of the value of the thing involved may be established through the sale price of other similar property and may include, but shall not be limited to, testimony regarding affixed labels and tags, signs, shelf tags, and notices tending to indicate the price of the thing involved. Hearsay evidence shall not be excluded in determining the value of the thing involved.

AUTHORITY

WEISSENBERGER'S FEDERAL EVIDENCE §§ 803.1–.88

5 WEINSTEIN 2d § § 803.01–.30

4 MUELLER & KIRKPATRICK §§ 433–478

McCORMICK §§ 254–420

5 WIGMORE §§ 1420–1684

6 WIGMORE §§ 1690–1764

Eaton & Perruso, *E-Mail as Evidence*, 27 COLO. LAW. 43 (1998)

Turner, *Admissibility of Accident Reports into Evidence Under Federal Rule of Evidence 803(8)(C)*, 35 TRIAL LAW. GUIDE 137 (1991)

Weissenberger, *Hearsay Puzzles: An Essay on Federal Evidence Rule 803(3)*, 64 TEMP. L. REV. 145 (1991)

Goldman, *Distorted Vision: Spontaneous Exclamations as a "Firmly Rooted" Exception to the Hearsay Rule*, 23 LOY. L.A. L. REV. 453 (1990)

Imwinkelried, *The Importance of the Memory Factor in Analyzing the Reliability of Hearsay Testimony: A Lesson Slowly Learnt—and Quickly Forgotten*, 41 FLA. L. REV. 215 (1989)

Mosteller, *Child Sexual Abuse and Statements for the Purpose of Medical Diagnosis or Treatment*, 67 N.C. L. REV. 257 (1989)

Ringland, *Child Sex Abuse Evidence Problems—Update 1988*, 14 U. DAYTON L. REV. 146 (1988)

Tuerkheimer, *Convictions Through Hearsay in Child Sexual Abuse Cases: A Logical Progression Back to Square One*, 72 MARQ. L. REV. 47 (1988)

McFarland, *Dead Men Tell Tales: Thirty Times Three Years of the Judicial Process After Hillmon*, 30 VILL. L. REV. 1 (1985)

Arnold, *Presenting Business Records as Evidence in Federal Court*, 32 PRAC. LAW. 19 (1986)

Comment, *Reason and the Rules: Personal Knowledge and The Co-conspirator Hearsay*, 135 U. PA. L. REV. 1265 (1987)

Falknor, *The Hearsay Rule and Its Exceptions*, 2 UCLA L. REV. 43, 60–62 (1954)

Foster, *Present Sense Impressions: An Analysis and a Proposal*, 10 LOY. U. L.J. 299 (1979)

Hutchins & Slesinger, *Some Observations on the Law of Evidence: Spontaneous Exclamations*, 46 COLUM. L. REV. 432 (1946)

Morgan, *Res Gestae*, 12 WASH. L. REV. 91 (1937)

Slough, *Res Gestae*, 2 U. KAN. L. REV. 246 (1954)

Slough, *Spontaneous Statements and the State of Mind*, 46 IOWA L. REV. 224 (1961)

Waltz, *The Present Sense Impression Exception to the Rule Against Hearsay: Origins and Attitudes*, 66 IOWA L. REV. 869 (1981)

Hinton, *States of Mind and the Hearsay Rule*, 1 U. CHI. L. REV. 394 (1934)

Morgan, *Hearsay Dangers and the Application of the Hearsay Concept*, 62 HARV. L. REV. 177 (1948)

Payne, *The Hillmon Case—An Old Problem Revisited*, 41 VA. L. REV. 1011 (1955)

Rice, *The State of Mind Exception to the Hearsay Rule: A Response to "Secondary" Relevance*, 14 DUQ. L. REV. 219 (1975–76)

Seidelson, *State of Mind Exception to the Hearsay Rule*, 13 DUQ. L. REV. 251 (1974)

Note, *Medical Testimony and the Hearsay Rule*, WASH. U. L.Q. 192 (1964)

Note, *Evidence—Admissibility of Expressions of Pain and Suffering*, 51 MICH. L. REV. 902 (1953)

Morgan, *The Relation Between Hearsay and Preserved Memory*, 40 HARV. L. REV. 712 (1927)

Note, *Past Recollection Recorded: The "Forward Looking" Federal Rules of Evidence Lean Backwards*, 50 NOTRE DAME L. REV. 737 (1975)

Hale, *Hospital Records as Evidence*, 14 S. CAL. L. REV. 99 (1941)

Laughlin, *Business Entries and the Like*, 46 IOWA L. REV. 276 (1961)

Powell, *Admissibility of Hospital Records into Evidence*, 21 MD. L. REV. 22 (1961)

Comment, *A Reconsideration of the Admissibility of Computer-Generated Evidence*, 126 U. PA. L. REV. 425 (1977)

Note, *Admissibility of Computer-Kept Records*, 55 CORNELL L.Q. 1033 (1970)

Comment, *Computer Print-Outs of Business Records and Their Admissibility in New York*, 31 ALB. L. REV. 61 (1967)

Alexander, *Hearsay Exception for Public Records in Federal Criminal Trials*, 47 ALB. L. REV. 699 (1983)

McCormick, *Can the Courts Make Wider Use of Reports of Official Investigations?*, 42 IOWA L. REV. 256 (1961)

Comment, *The Admissibility of Police Reports Under the Federal Rules of Evidence*, 71 NW. U. L. REV. 691 (1976)

Comment, *Evaluative Reports By Public Officials—Admissible as Official Statements?*, 30 TEX. L. REV. 112 (1951)

Hale, *Proof of Facts of Family History*, 2 HASTINGS L.J. (1950)

Comment, *Admissibility of Hearsay Evidence on Matters of Family History*, 5 ARK. L. REV. 58 (1951)

Wickes, *Ancient Documents and Hearsay*, 8 TEX. L. REV. 451 (1930)

Note, *Recitals in Ancient Documents*, 46 IOWA L. REV. 448 (1961)

McElroy, *Public Surveys—The Latest Exception to the Hearsay Rule*, 28 BAYLOR L. REV. 59 (1976)

Sorenson & Sorenson, *The Admissibility and Use of Opinion Research Evidence*, 28 N.Y.U. L. REV. 1213 (1953)

Note, *Mercantile Credit Reports as Evidence*, 44 MINN. L. REV. 719 (1960)

Note, *Public Opinion Surveys as Evidence: The Pollsters Go to Court*, 66 HARV. L. REV. 498 (1953)

Bush, *Criminal Convictions as Evidence in Civil Proceedings*, 29 MISS. L.J. 276 (1959)

Cowen, *The Admissibility of Criminal Convictions in Subsequent Civil Proceedings*, 40 CAL. L. REV. 225 (1952)

Note, *Use of Record of Criminal Conviction in Subsequent Civil Action Arising from the Same Facts as the Prosecution*, 64 MICH. L. REV. 702 (1966)

Note, *Judgments as Evidence*, 46 IOWA L. REV. 400 (1961)

Note, *Effect of a Criminal Conviction in Subsequent Civil Suits*, 50 YALE L.J. 499 (1941)

COMPARISON TO FEDERAL RULE

Colorado Rule 803(1) requires that a present sense impression statement be "spontaneous." Federal Rule 803(1) applies to statements made immediately after the declarant perceived the event or condition. Colorado Rule 803(1) requires that the statement be made while the declarant was perceiving the event or condition. There is no similar requirement in Federal Rule 803(1). In Colorado Rule 803(5), there is no requirement that the maker of a recorded recollection have currently insufficient memory to testify about the subject of the record; Federal Rule 803(5) imposes such a requirement. While Colorado Rule 803(18) exempts certain statements in learned treatises from the hearsay exclusion, as does Federal Rule 803(18), the Colorado Rule differs from the corresponding Federal Rule by allowing the judge discretion to treat such statements as exhibits, a possibility explicitly rejected in the Federal Rule. Please note that on Dec. 1, 2011 Federal Rule 803 was restyled. Please see Federal Rule 803 in the appendix for comparison. Also, in considering differences between the federal and state rule 803, account should be taken of Colorado Statute 13 CRS 25-129.5 (setting forth a hearsay exception for statements of developmentally disabled persons) which has no counterpart in the Federal Rules of Evidence.

Similar to the new Colorado rule on ancient documents, Federal Rule 803(16) excludes statements in ancient documents prepared before January 1, 1998, and whose authenticity is established, from hearsay.

SIGNIFICANT CASES

Ohio v. Clark, 135 S. Ct. 2173 (2015) (statements by a very young child to a teacher were not testimonial, despite a statute imposing a duty on the teacher to report statements like the child's to law enforcement, because the child declarant could not have had any idea that his words would be used by the state, because the primary purpose of the conversation in which he made his statements was to protect him, and because the statements had attributes that made them likely to be reliable).

Williams v. Illinois, 132 S. Ct. 2221 (2012) (DNA analysis prepared in the context of criminal investigation was not covered by the Confrontation Clause for a variety of rationales, no single one of which accrued majority support).

Melendez-Diaz v. Massachusetts, 557 U.S. 305 (2009) (sworn certificates prepared by laboratory analyst showing seized material was cocaine do not qualify as business or public records under Rule 803(6) & (8) because they were prepared specifically for use at trial, therefore testimonial and subject to confrontation under the Sixth Amendment).

Beech Aircraft Corp. v. Rainey, 488 U.S. 153 (1988) (a judge advocate report regarding the crash of a military aircraft was admissible under Federal Rule 803(8) where portions of the report contained opinions and the author's statement as to probable cause of crash).

Kelly v. Haralampopoulos, 327 P.3d 255 (Colo. 2014) (in a medical malpractice case, a statement made to the plaintiff's physician asking if the plaintiff's cocaine use could have contributed to his injuries qualified as a statement made for medical diagnosis or treatment under 803(4) because it was offered for the purpose of determining the nature, source, or cause of a patient's medical condition).

Kinney v. People, 187 P.3d 548 (Colo. 2008) (the hearsay exception for public records and reports applies to a judgment of acquittal).

People v. Moreno, 160 P.3d 242 (Colo. 2007) (statutory provision that would permit testimonial out-of-court statements by a child to be introduced even if a defendant has no opportunity to cross-examine the declarant violates the Confrontation Clause rights under the United States Constitution).

Pena v. People, 173 P.3d 1107 (Colo. 2007) (out-of-court statement by alleged victim that her wrists were sore from having been held down was properly admitted under the hearsay exception for statements describing a declarant's then-existing physical condition; additionally, the requirements of C.R.S. § 13-25-129 that an unavailable declarant's statement have sufficient safeguards of reliability and sufficient corroboration were satisfied; the victim related the assault incident to her aunt spontaneously, with no evidence of leading questions; her language was appropriate for a thirteen-year-old; the statements were made within hours after the incident, the victim had no motive to fabricate, and corroboration was provided by evidence of a phone call by the defendant, medical evidence consistent with sexual assault, and DNA evidence).

People v. Vigil, 127 P.3d 916 (Colo. 2006) (statements made to a physician by young child who was allegedly the victim of a sexual assault were not testimonial for Confrontation Clause purposes; the child could not have anticipated that they would be used in a trial).

People v. Mojica-Simental, 73 P.3d 15 (Colo. 2003) (C.R.S. § 16-3-309(5) applies to DUI cases. The defendant's affirmative duty to request the presence of lab technician at trial, as required by the statute, does not, on its face, violate the defendant's right to confrontation because the defendant may preserve the right to confrontation with minimal effort).

People v. Harris, 43 P.3d 221 (Colo. 2002) (declarant's reply to a police officer's question about whether he agreed with another person's statement was hearsay).

People v. Garcia, 826 P.2d 1259 (Colo. 1992) (for admission of a hearsay statement as an excited utterance, there must be direct or circumstantial evidence adequate to support a jury finding that the declarant had an opportunity to observe the event that is the subject of the statement).

People v. Czemerynski, 786 P.2d 1100 (Colo. 1990) (statement by declarant identifying a person who was calling on the telephone qualified as a spontaneous utterance, and could be treated as admissible hearsay).

Morrison v. Bradley, 655 P.2d 385 (Colo. 1982) (statements by father that he planned to pay for son's education after high school and planned to buy a truck for him were admissible under the exception in Rule 803(3) for statements showing "state of mind").

People v. Tran, 469 P.3d 568 (Colo. App. 2020) (in a trial for burglary and possession of burglary tools, a retail store's sign that, "Tran (defendant) no longer allowed (entry) . . ." was within the business records exception to hearsay rule).

People v. Knapp, 2020 Colo. App. LEXIS 1296 (Colo. App. 2020) (in an assault case, State's evidence of the defendant's brother-in-law calling the defendant a "wife beater" was properly admitted as part of the res gestae as it explained the defendant's motives for his actions). Not selected for final or official publication as of June 1, 2021.

People v. N.T.B., 457 P.3d 126 (Colo. App. 2019) (in order for evidence stored in an account on a remote cloud server to be admitted as a business record exception to the hearsay rule, a foundation must be laid by means of a custodian's testimony that the records were made in the regular course of business, input accurately within a reasonable amount of time, and transmitted by a reliable person with knowledge).

People v. Hard, 342 P.3d 572 (Colo. App. 2014) (in a drug possession case where a police officer testified that he identified a defendant's pills as schedule II and III controlled substances by referencing a website which contained descriptions and photographs of various pharmaceutical drugs (Drugs.com), the trial court erred by admitting the testimony about the website as market report under 803(17). The court found that the website was not necessary for identification of the drugs, and that it was not a reliable source despite its mission statement).

People v. Marciano, 2014 COA 92M (Colo. App. 2014) (in a theft case where the defendant's bank statements were admitted at trial as business records under 803(6), the appellate court held that the trial court did not abuse its discretion by admitting the statements, despite a lack of foundation. The court found that the nature of bank records and their trustworthiness, due the to the fastidious nature of record keeping in financial institutions, which is often required by governmental regulation, along with the records as a whole, can establish a sufficient foundation for the bank records' admission.

Therefore, the records were judicially noticeable as business records).

People v. Miranda, 2014 COA 102 (Colo. App. 2014) (in a case where two years lapsed between an assault on a juvenile victim and the creation of a list of the sexual assaults introduced at trial under 803(5), the court held that the time span was not so long that the victim could not accurately recall the events recorded. 803(5) imposes no specific time constraint on the timing of the preparation and adoption of memoranda).

People v. Tyme, 315 P.3d 1270 (Colo. App. 2013) (alleged victim's statements to a sexual assault nurse examiner (SANE) were properly admitted under the hearsay exception for statements for medical diagnosis or treatment, since the SANE testified that she relied on the medical history to guide her examination and used it "to diagnose and treat," and also testified that SANEs normally rely on similar historics to guide their diagnosis and treatment).

People v. Blackwell, 251 P.3d 468 (Colo. App. 2010) (the declarant's report to a security guard that a black taurus sped off from the parking lot where the shooting occurred was not admissible as an excited utterance because the declarant's voice was "calm and just kind of casual" and there was no evidence that the declarant witnessed the shooting).

Saint John's Church in the Wilderness v. Scott, 194 P.3d 475 (Colo. App. 2008) (out-of-court statements by one declarant that protest demonstrations at a church made her feel scared and another declarant that because of the demonstrations, she planned to forbid her son from participating at a service at the church were properly admitted under the state of mind exception because the first statement was about the declarant's feelings and the second statement was about the declarant's plans).

People v. Welsh, 176 P.3d 781 (Colo. App. 2007) (statements of victim that he wished to end his relationship with the defendant who killed him were properly admitted under Rule 803(3) because his state of mind was relevant to the defendant's motive for her actions).

People v. Cevallos-Acosta, 140 P.3d 116 (Colo. App. 2005) (statement to 911 operator seeking help was not testimonial for Confrontation Clause purposes).

A-1 Auto Repair & Detail, Inc. v. Bilunas-Hardy, 93 P.3d 598 (Colo. App. 2004) (in a civil action for conversion and civil theft after defendant already found guilty of two counts of theft in a separate criminal trial on same facts, previous criminal judgment may be admitted under 803(22) hearsay exception and "issue preclusion will bar litigation in a civil trial of an issue previously litigated in a criminal trial, provided the requisites for the application of issue preclusion are satisfied).

People v. Joyce, 68 P.3d 521 (Colo. App. 2002) (in kidnapping trial, testimony by attending emergency room physician that victim stated that he was handcuffed by defendant was admissible under the medical diagnosis and treatment exception to the hearsay rule).

People v. Welsh, 58 P.3d 1065 (Colo. App. 2002) (in murder case in which defendant pled not guilty by reason of insanity and defense offered expert testimony of a psychiatrist concerning defendant's sanity, and prosecution rebutted said testimony with a written transcript of another judge's finding regarding the expert's credibility in a different case, said written transcript violated the defendant's right to confront the witnesses against her in that it failed to meet the requirements of unavailability of the declarant and a showing that the statement possessed particularized guarantees of trustworthiness).

Leiting v. Mutha, 58 P.3d 1049 (Colo. App. 2002) (an administrative law judge's decision offered into evidence at a civil trial is not automatically admitted under CRE 803(8)(C) since portions of the decision are not factual findings but are an accumulation of inadmissible information).

People v. Rogers, 68 P.3d 486 (Colo. App. 2002) (in murder case, prosecution witness's testimony that prior to the murder victim stated that she was afraid of defendant falls within the state of mind exception to the hearsay rule).

People v. Pineda, 40 P.3d 60 (Colo. App. 2001) (in a trial for child abuse, the trial court properly balanced the probative value versus the prejudicial effect in admitting a child victim's hearsay statements under C.R.S. § 13-25-129).

People v. Cardenas, 25 P.3d 1258 (Colo. App. 2000) (evidence that the victim, prior to his death, told his sister that he was "getting afraid" of the defendant because of the defendant's increased drug use was properly admitted under the Rule 803(3) state of mind exception to the hearsay rule).

People v. Martinez, 18 P.3d 831 (Colo. App. 2000) (hearsay statements made by the victim of assault were properly admitted as excited utterances under CRE 803(2) despite the fact that they were made in response to questions; the victim's injuries were severe, the victim made the statements while in an agitated emotional state, and the time between the startling event and the statements was brief).

People v. Mossmann, 17 P.3d 165 (Colo. App. 2000) (in a violation of custody case, it was error to exclude hearsay evidence offered only to show the defendant's state of mind; the evidence would have established the defendant's affirmative defense that he reasonably believed that his conduct was necessary to preserve the child from danger to his welfare).

Hauser v. Rose Health Care Systems, 857 P.2d 524 (Colo. App. 1993) (business records exception properly applies to price quotation documents from a computer supplier, in an action by plaintiff alleging breach of a contract which authorized plaintiff to renegotiate existing agreements defendant had with suppliers, since the plaintiff and defendant both relied upon such documents in their businesses, and the documents were prepared as part of regular business activity of the supplier).

People v. Fincham, 799 P.2d 419 (Colo. App. 1990) (children's statements describing a parent's abduction were admissible as excited utterances; they were made less than two hours after the crime, they were prompted by only general questions, and one child cried during the conversation).

People v. King, 765 P.2d 608 (Colo. App. 1988), *aff'd*, 785 P.2d 596 (statements to a nontreating physician are admissible under Rule 803(4), but the declarant's purpose in making the statements must have been consistent with the rationale behind the rule making it reasonable for the physician to rely on the information).

People v. Galloway, 726 P.2d 249 (Colo. App. 1986) (hearsay statements by a seven-year-old alleged victim of sexual assault were properly admitted under the excited utterance, child victim of a sexual assault, and medical treatment exceptions to the hearsay exclusion rule; confrontation concerns were satisfied by the victim's actual availability for cross-examination).

Kelln v. Colorado Dep't of Revenue, Motor Vehicle Div., 719 P.2d 358 (Colo. App. 1986) (in civil driver's license revocation hearing, Rule 803(8) allowed admissibility of a chemical laboratory report showing a driver's blood alcohol level; the arresting officer had a duty to report the results stated in the laboratory report).

Downing v. Overhead Door Corp., 707 P.2d 1027 (Colo. App. 1985) (a business record's reliability for purposes of Rule 803(6) can be established with evidence that it was made pursuant to routine procedures for systematic conduct of the record maker's business).

Ed Hackstaff Concrete, Inc. v. Powder Ridge Ridge Conndominium "A" Owners' Asso., 679 P.2d 1112 (Colo. App. 1984) ("batch tickets" offered to show that concrete used in repairs contained added water, which were prepared by persons with personal knowledge of the facts set forth in the tickets under established business procedures, were covered by the business records exception to the hearsay exclusion rule).

People v. Manyik, 383 P.3d 77 (2016) (in a murder case, statements made in a phone call by defendant that his former girlfriend " 'was throwing him under the bus', that she had invited the victim over so that (the defendant) would shoot him, and that she and the victim had been planning to move to Arizona together, not only spoke to a past mental state but also addressed the mental state of someone else" and therefore did not fall under the CRE 803(3) exception to the hearsay rule).

Pernell v. People, 411 P.3d 669 (Colo. 2018) (the trial court erred when it admitted victim's statement detailing her rape and false imprisonment as an excited utterance under 803(2), because the victim had several interludes of "reflective thought," before making her statement; however the error was harmless due to overwhelming evidence against the defendant and the defense's extensive cross examination of the victim).

Fritzler v. Mitchell (In re Estate of Fritzler), 413 P.3d 163 (Colo. App. 2017) (in a case dealing with the "testamentary capacity" of testator who amended his will days before his death, medical records should have been admitted under 803(6) Business Records exception because, although the testifying custodian's lacked personal knowledge of each document's authenticity, lack of knowledge should have only affected "the weight of {the} evidence, not its admissibility" and additionally many or the documents contained in the record bore the signature of the person preparing the report making them independently verifiable).

State ex. Rel. v. Robert J. Hopp & Assocs., LLC, 422 P.3d 617 (Colo. App. 2018) (in this case regarding fraudulent billing practices, a spreadsheet containing invoicing data and prepared by data aggregation software provider is admissible under the business record hearsay exception because the data entered was within the knowledge of the defendants and was part of their regularly conducted business).

People ex rel. E.R., ___ P.3d ___. 2018 Colo. App. LEXIS 610 (Colo. App. 2018) (in a child custody case, test results showing that the mother of a child born premature had tested positive for methamphetamine at the child's birth are admissible hearsay to prove the unfitness of the mother under C.R.E. 803(4) because they are reasonably pertinent to the child's diagnosis or treatment).

People v. Jaeb, 434 P.3d 785 (Colo. App. 2018) (As an assertion of the value of a stolen U-Haul trailer, a "total loss notice" supplied by the theft victim to the prosecution is inadmissible hearsay under C.R.S. § 18-4-414 because it is not reliable proof of retail value as is the kind specified in the statute as "affixed labels and tags, signs, shelf tags, and notices"; nor is it admissible under the business record exception because it was created at the request of a testifying witness long after the theft occurred and just two months before trial, and therefore was not created during the ordinary course of business).

Chapter 804

Rule 804. Hearsay Exceptions; Declarant Unavailable

Rule 804 reads as follows:

(a) Definition of unavailability. "Unavailability as a witness" includes situations in which the declarant—

(1) is exempted by ruling of the court on the ground of privilege from testifying concerning the subject matter of his statement; or

(2) persists in refusing to testify concerning the subject matter of his statement despite an order of the court to do so; or

(3) testifies to a lack of memory of the subject matter of his statement; or

(4) is unable to be present or to testify at the hearing because of death or then existing physical or mental illness or infirmity; or

(5) is absent from the hearing and the proponent of a statement has been unable to procure his attendance (or in the case of a hearsay exception under subdivision (b)(3) or (4) his attendance or testimony) by process or other reasonable means.

A declarant is not unavailable as a witness if his exemption, refusal, claim of lack of memory, inability, or absence is due to the procurement or wrongdoing of the proponent of his statement for the purpose of preventing the witness from attending or testifying.

(b) Hearsay exceptions. The following are not excluded by the hearsay rule if the declarant is unavailable as a witness:

(1) Former testimony. Testimony given as a witness at another hearing of the same or a different proceeding, or in a deposition taken in compliance with law in the course of the same or another proceeding, if the party against whom the testimony is now offered, or, in a civil action or proceeding, a predecessor in interest, had an opportunity and similar motive to develop the testimony by direct, cross, or redirect examination.

(2) (No Colorado Rule Codified)

(3) Statement against interest. A statement that:

(A) a reasonable person in the declarant's position would have made only if the person believed it to be true because, when made, it was so contrary to the declarant's proprietary or pecuniary interest or had so great a tendency to invalidate the declarant's claim against someone else or to expose the declarant to civil or criminal liability; and

(B) is supported by corroborating circumstances that clearly indicate its trustworthiness, if it is offered in a criminal case as one that tends to expose the

---

declarant to criminal liability.

(4)   Statement of personal or family history.   (A) A statement concerning the declarant's own birth, adoption, marriage, divorce, legitimacy, relationship by blood, adoption, or marriage, ancestry, or other similar fact of personal or family history, even though declarant had no means of acquiring personal knowledge of the matter stated; or (B) a statement concerning the foregoing matters, and death also, of another person, if the declarant was related to the other by blood, adoption, or marriage or was so intimately associated with the other's family as to be likely to have accurate information concerning the matter declared.

(5)   [Transferred to Rule 807]

(6)   (No Colorado Rule codified). See this section for Colorado cases treating forfeiture by wrongdoing.

ANALYSIS

(a) Definition of unavailability

Rule 804 establishes a principle of preference for the admissibility of certain types of hearsay. The preference is for in-court testimony over hearsay, and, further, for certain forms of hearsay over a total loss of the evidence. In contrast to the Rule 803 exceptions, the admissibility of the Rule 804 exceptions is dependent upon laying a foundation satisfactory to the court that the declarant is unavailable as a witness. As to the standard of proof for the foundation, see Analysis to Rule 104.

Rule 804(a) identifies five types of situations in which a declarant is determined to be unavailable as a witness and in which the condition to the use of the Rule 804(b) exceptions is satisfied. Although the language of Rule 804(a) emphasizes the unavailability of the declarant, the significant issue is whether the declarant's testimony is unavailable. In each of the first three types of situations identified in Rule 804(a), the declarant may be physically present in the courtroom, but hearsay is admissible because his or her testimony is not available. Also, it should be noted that Rule 804(a) provides that if the proponent of the hearsay statement procured the unavailability of the declarant, the declarant is not considered to be unavailable.

Burden of proving unavailability.   Rule 804 places the burden of establishing the unavailability of a declarant on the proponent of the hearsay and the court must determine whether the declarant is unavailable as a witness. While Rule 804 treats all types of unavailability uniformly, consistent with the Sixth Amendment, there may be a more stringent application of the unavailability standard in criminal cases where the evidence is offered against the accused. *See* Analysis to Rule 801.

Privilege.   Rule 804(a)(1) provides that a witness's valid assertion of privilege, exempting him from testifying, satisfies the unavailability requirement of Rule 804. The witness's mere assertion of the privilege, however, is not sufficient to make the witness unavailable. Rather, the court must rule that the assertion of the privilege is justified.

Refusal to testify.   Rule 804(a)(2) extends the definition of unavailability to include situations in which a witness refuses to testify. The Rule requires that the proponent of the hearsay show more than an indication by the potential witness of an unwillingness to testify. Specifically, the witness must disobey a court order to testify, and this disobedience by the witness in the face of a court order distinguishes a refusal to testify from an assertion of privilege. Without the requirement of disobedience of a court order, the mistaken assertion of a privilege would satisfy the requirement of unavailability.

Lack of memory. Rule 804(a)(3) extends prior law by providing that a hearsay declarant is unavailable if he or she testifies to a lack of memory as to the content of the out-of-court declaration. The Rule adopts the modern position that the value of the hearsay outweighs the danger arising from the potential for perjury.

Death or infirmity. Rule 804(a)(4) follows the long established tradition in treating as unavailable a declarant who is determined to be dead. As in other instances of unavailability, the burden for demonstrating the death of the declarant is upon the proponent of the hearsay. Rule 804(a) also provides that a witness is unavailable where he or she is subject to a mental or physical infirmity. An obvious difference between infirmity and death is that an infirmity may not be permanent. If an infirmity is temporary, the trial can be continued in the court's discretion until the witness is available.

Absence. Rule 804(a)(5) provides that if a person is absent and his testimony cannot be procured by process or other reasonable means, the witness is not available. The Rule imposes on the proponent of the hearsay an obligation to employ "reasonable means" in attempting to procure the witness.

(b) Hearsay exceptions

(1) Former testimony

Rule 804(b)(1) creates a hearsay exception for former testimonial statements by an unavailable declarant where two conditions are satisfied: (1) the statement must have been made while the declarant was testifying as a witness in a proceeding and (2) the party against whom the statement is offered, or in civil cases a predecessor in interest, must have had an opportunity and similar motive to develop the declarant's testimony by direct, re-direct, or cross-examination at the time the statement was made.

Exception qualified. Several qualifications of this exception should be noted. First, the Rule addresses the hearsay issue only, and it does not affect an objection to the prior testimony evidence based upon some other ground where the live testimony of like content or effect would be objectionable. Second, Rule 804(b)(1) is not the only basis for the admission of a transcript or a deposition. A transcript or a deposition could conceivably satisfy numerous other hearsay exceptions. Third, Rule 804(b)(1) does not dictate the manner in which the former testimony must be proved at trial. Customarily, however, when evidence is admitted pursuant to this hearsay exception, the transcript is merely read into the record in the presence of the trier of fact. Finally, where only a portion of the former testimony or deposition is introduced, the adverse party is entitled to introduce other portions that should in fairness be construed by the trier of fact. *See* Rule 106.

Circumstances. In applying Rule 804(b)(1), it should be noted that the declarant's statements must have been made at a deposition, hearing, or a proceeding. The term "proceeding" should, absent any statutory definition, be broadly interpreted so as to encompass any form of official inquiry conducted in accordance with law, including judicial, administrative and legislative forms. The term "testimony" should be restricted to only those statements which are sworn, subject to perjury, and on the record.

Tests. Two key tests must be satisfied in order to admit hearsay pursuant to this exception. These tests are "the opportunity test" and "the similar motive test." It should be noted that these tests focus on the party against whom the hearsay, i.e., the transcript, is offered. Focusing on the party against whom the hearsay is offered facilitates the fairness rationale which underpins this exception. "The opportunity test" provides that the party against whom the hearsay is offered must have had an opportunity to examine the declarant at the former hearing. The party against whom the hearsay is offered, must have effectively been present at the former hearing and had an opportunity to conduct some type of examination of that declarant when he or she provided testimony at the former hearing. Only an opportunity is necessary. No actual examination need have taken place. The examination in question could be a cross-examination, a direct examination, or a re-direct examination. It should be noted that in a civil case, the party's "predecessor in interest" will qualify if that predecessor had an opportunity to examine the declarant.

Highlights

The exact purport of the "predecessor in interest" language in the Rule is less than clear. While an expansive reading of this language would appear to reduce the opportunity requirement to a nullity, some federal courts interpreting the identical language in the cognate Federal Rule have read the language broadly to include virtually anyone who would satisfy the similar motive requirement. *See Lloyd v. American Export Lines, Inc.*, 580 F.2d 1179 (3d Cir. 1978). In contrast, the same language in the Federal Rule has been subjected to strict application, and it has been held that only a predecessor in privity in the property sense will qualify under the Rule. *See In re IBM Peripheral EDP Devices Antitrust Litigation*, 444 F. Supp. 110 (N.D. Cal. 1978). While reliability and fairness may not be sacrificed by the broader interpretation of the predecessor in interest requirement, the stricter reading more logically comports with the customary meaning of the term "predecessor in interest," and moreover, it preserves the obvious intent of the Rule to require more than simply a similarity in motive as between the party developing the testimony at the prior proceeding and the party against whom it is offered at the instant proceeding.

Similar motive test.   Under the "similar motive test," the party against whom the hearsay is offered must have had a motive at the former proceeding in examining the declarant that is similar to the motive this party would have in examining the declarant if the declarant were now available at the instant trial. The motive in question pertains to the motive to develop or refute facts. It should be noted that an identical motive is not required.

Illustration

Assume that D is charged with two distinct crimes of murder and robbery involving one occurrence, and further that the crimes are the subject of two distinct trials. The murder case is tried first and at this trial an occurrence witness, X, who was present at the scene testifies to all the pertinent facts on behalf of the prosecution. The occurrence witness, X, dies before the trial of the second case, the robbery case, and is, consequently, unavailable. At the robbery trial, the prosecution may seek to introduce the transcript of X's testimony given at the murder trial. The transcript may be admissible under the prior testimony exception to the hearsay rule because D, the defendant, had the opportunity at the earlier trial to cross-examine the occurrence witness, and also, the defendant presumably had a motive at the earlier trial in cross-examining the occurrence witness that is similar to the motive he would have if the witness were available for testimony at the instant robbery trial.

(2) Statement under belief of impending death

The Colorado Rules omit paragraph 804(b)(2), so that after paragraph 804(b)(1), the next substantive paragraph is 804(b)(3). The subject matter of Federal Rule 804(b)(2), statements given under belief of impending death, is treated in a separate Colorado statute, shown below. The general rationale for a hearsay exception for "dying declarations" is that no person would intentionally meet his maker with a lie on his lips. In modern terms, some believe that psychological forces at the moment of death lead to an impulse to speak truthfully. The Colorado statute has broader application than the Federal Rule. It allows a dying declaration on any subject to be admitted in any type of trial or hearing, if the following foundation is established: (1) the declarant was conscious of impending death and had no hope of recovery; (2) the statement was voluntary and not the result of persuasion; (3) the statement was not a reply to interrogatories intended to lead to a particular statement; (4) the declarant was of sound mind at the time; and (5) the declarant is dead at the time the statement is sought to be introduced.

HEARSAY

Illustration

In a homicide case against Jackson, the witness is a physician.

Q: Did you see the declarant (victim) prior to his death?

A: Yes.

Q: How long before he died did you arrive on the scene?

A: Five minutes.

Q: Was there anyone else present?

A: The ambulance attendant.

Q: Did the victim say anything to you?

Objection: Hearsay. The foundation has not been laid for a dying declaration.

Court: Sustained.

Q: *(On voir dire of witness)* Did the ambulance attendant say anything to you?

A: Yes. He said the victim told him that he knew he had only a few minutes to live and hoped that a priest would come before he died.

Q: How soon after you arrived did the victim die?

A: About five minutes.

Q: What did the victim say to you prior to his death?

A: He said, "Jackson shot me. And now I have got to die."

Objection: Move to strike the answer; hearsay.

Court: Overruled.

The rulings by the court are correct. The point of the first objection is that there had been no foundation established that the declarant was aware of his

> impending death. The statement by the ambulance driver established on voir dire, while probably not admissible under any exceptions to the hearsay rule, would be sufficient under Rule 102 to establish the foundation for a dying declaration. *See* Analysis to Rule 102. There is evidence from which the court could conclude that the victim was under a belief of impending death, and his declaration was made concerning the cause of that death. Therefore, the requirements of the dying declaration have been met.

(3) Statement against interest

Rule 804(b)(3) codifies the historical exception to the hearsay rule for statements against interest. The Rule encompasses the traditional exception for statements against the financial or proprietary interests of the declarant and statements which tend to subject the declarant to civil liability. It significantly expands the traditional exception, however, to include statements which tend to subject the declarant to criminal punishment, i.e., statements against penal interest.

Foundations. The foundational requirements for statements against interest under Rule 804(b)(3) are as follows:

1. The declarant must be unavailable as defined in Rule 804(a);

2. The declarant must have first-hand knowledge as contemplated by Rule 602;

3. The nature of the statement must be such that a reasonable person would not have uttered it unless he or she believed it to be true;

4. The statement must be contrary to a pecuniary, proprietary, or penal interest at the time of its utterance; and

5. The rule expressly provides that corroborating circumstances are required when a statement is offered to exculpate a defendant.

Statement of party-opponent distinguished. It is critical to appreciate the distinction between declarations constituting statements against interest, identified in Rule 804(b)(3), and those which are statements of a party-opponent as defined in Rule 801(d)(2). Statements of a party opponent are excluded from the hearsay definition under the Rule's evidentiary scheme without regard to: (1) whether the declarant is unavailable; (2) whether the statement was against any particular interest when made; (3) whether the party had any first-hand knowledge of the underlying events; or (4) whether any sort of reasonable person test is satisfied.

(4) Statements of personal or family history

Rule 804(b)(4)(A) admits statements concerning an unavailable declarant's own personal or family history, embracing such topics as "birth, adoption, marriage, divorce, legitimacy, relationship by blood." Rule 804(b)(4)(B) admits declarations concerning these subjects pertaining to another person if the declarant was related by blood, adoption, or marriage, or "was so intimately associated with the other's family as to be likely to have accurate information concerning the matter declared."

The conditions to the admission of statements of personal or family history are threefold:

1. Unavailability of the declarant as defined in Rule 804(a) must be established;

2. The statement must be restricted to the subject matters described in the Rule; and

3. An appropriate relation to or association with the family in question must be shown.

(5) Transferred to Rule 807.

(6) Forfeiture by Wrongdoing. (No Colorado Rule codified.)

Colorado's treatment of the consequences of rendering a witness unavailable is developed under the state's common law and is not the subject of a rule, in contrast to treatment of this subject under the Federal Rules of Evidence.

STATUTES

§ 13-25-119.   Dying declarations

(1) The dying declarations of a deceased person are admissible in evidence in all civil and criminal trials and other proceedings before courts, commissions, and other tribunals to the same extent and for the same purposes that they might have been admissible had the deceased survived and been sworn as a witness in the proceedings, under the following restrictions. To render the declarations of the deceased competent evidence, it must be satisfactorily proved:

(a) That at the time of the making of such declaration he was conscious of approaching death and believed there was no hope or recovery;

(b) That such declaration was voluntarily made, and not through the persuasion of any person;

(c) That such declaration was not made in answer to interrogatories calculated to lead the deceased to make any particular statement;

(d) That he was of sound mind at the time of making the declaration.

AUTHORITY

WEISSENBERGER'S FEDERAL EVIDENCE §§ 804.1–.34

McCORMICK §§ 253–61, 276–87, 322

5 WEINSTEIN 2d §§ 804.01 .08

4 MUELLER & KIRKPATRICK §§ 479–507.2

5 WIGMORE §§ 1370, 1371, 1386–89, 1402–15, 1430–52, 1455–77, 1480–1503, 1660–69

7 WIGMORE §§ 2098–99

Litt, *Dying Declarations*, 27 COLO. LAW. 49 (1998)

Weissenberger, *The Former Testimony Hearsay Exception: A Study in Rulemaking, Judicial Revisionism, and the Separation of Powers*, 67 N.C. L. REV. 295 (1989)

Kirkpatrick, *Confrontation and Hearsay: Exemptions From the Constitutional Unavailability Requirement*, 70 MINN. L. REV. 665 (1986)

Comment, *Evidence—Hearsay Exception—Requirements for Unavailability of Witness in Criminal Case Under the Federal Law of Evidence*, 29 RUTGERS L. REV. 133 (1975)

Comment, *Evidence: The Unavailability Requirement of Declaration Against Interest Hearsay*, 55 IOWA L. REV. 477 (1969)

Hale, *Proof of Facts of Family History*, 2 HASTINGS L.J. 1 (1950)

Note, *Pedigree*, 46 IOWA L. REV. 414 (1962)

Comment, *Admissibility of Hearsay Evidence on Matters of Family History*, 5 ARK. L. REV. 58 (1951)

Jefferson, *Declarations Against Interest: An Exception to the Hearsay Rule*, 58 HARV. L. REV. 1 (1944)

Morgan, *Declarations Against Interest*, 5 VAND. L. REV. 451 (1952)

Note, *Declaration Against Penal Interest: What Must Be Corroborated Under the Newly Enacted Federal*

Rules of Evidence, Rule 804(b)(3)?, 9 VAL. U. L. REV. 421 (1975)

Note, *Declarations Against Interest: A Critical Review of the Unavailability Requirement*, 52 CORNELL L.Q. 301 (1967)

Quick, *Some Reflections on Dying Declarations*, 6 HOW. L.J. 109 (1960)

Note, *Dying Declarations*, 46 IOWA L. REV. 375 (1961)

COMPARISON TO FEDERAL RULE

Colorado Rule 804 is substantially the same as Federal Rule 804. It omits treatment of dying declarations, which is provided in Federal Rule 804(b)(2), due to the existence of C.R.S. § 13-25-119, a specific statute on that subject. The Colorado dying declarations statute allows the admissibility of more statements than would be admitted under the federal provision. The Federal Rule is limited to civil cases and homicide prosecutions; the Colorado statute applies to all proceedings. The Federal Rule is limited to statements on the subject of the cause of the declarant's impending death; the Colorado statute has no subject matter limitation. In one minor aspect, the Federal Rule takes a position that is more pro-admissibility than the Colorado statute's position: under the Colorado statute, the declarant must be dead for the statute to apply; in contrast, the Federal Rule requires that the declarant must have believed that death was imminent when the declarant made the statement, but the rule can still apply if the declarant makes an unexpected recovery and survives. Please note that on Dec. 1, 2011 Federal Rule 804 was restyled. Please see Federal Rule 804 in the appendix for comparison.

SIGNIFICANT CASES

Ohio v. Clark, 135 S. Ct. 2173 (2015) (statements by a very young child to a teacher were not testimonial, despite a statute imposing a duty on the teacher to report statements like the child's to law enforcement, because the child declarant could not have had any idea that his words would be used by the state, because the primary purpose of the conversation in which he made his statements was to protect him, and because the statements had attributes that made them likely to be reliable).

Michigan v. Bryant, 562 U.S. 344 (2011) (dying declaration of murder victim to police admissible against defendant, because it was not testimonial, but given to assist police in ongoing emergency).

Giles v. California, 554 U.S. 353 (2008) (a defendant whose wrongful conduct causes the unavailability at trial of a hearsay declarant retains his or her Confrontation Clause right to prohibit introduction of that declarant's testimonial hearsay, unless the defendant's wrongful conduct was specifically intended to prevent the declarant from testifying).

Crawford v. Washington, 541 U.S. 36 (2004) (Court rejects the *Roberts* balancing test for reliability of testimonial statements at trial requiring that unavailability of witness and a prior opportunity to cross-examine both be met before testimonial statements can be offered as a hearsay exception. The Court stated that confrontation is the "only indicium of reliability sufficient to satisfy constitutional demands" of reliability of testimonial statements).

Williamson v. United States, 512 U.S. 594 (1994) (the statement against interest exception applies only to portions of a declarant's statement that are individually self-inculpatory).

Marshall v. People, 309 P.3d 943 (Colo. 2013) (results of a urine test performed by laboratory personnel could properly be introduced through testimony of the lab supervisor who reviewed the test results, determined that the data accurately made a determination concerning the presence of drugs in the urine, and certified the results; for these reasons she was not a surrogate for the technician and her testimony therefore did not violate the Confrontation Clause; additionally, the requirement of C. R. S. section 16-3-309(5) that the lab employee who accomplished the analysis must be made available to testify was satisfied, since the supervisor performed the final analysis and therefore accomplished the analysis under the plain meaning of the statute).

Vasquez v. People, 173 P.3d 1099 (Colo. 2007) (defendant forfeits the right to confront a witness when a preponderance of evidence supports a finding by the judge that (1) the witness is unavailable; (2) the defendant was involved in, or responsible for, procuring the unavailability of the witness; and (3) the defendant acted with the intent to deprive the criminal justice system of evidence; however, the evidence must be within the coverage of an exception to the hearsay exclusionary rule to be admissible).

People v. Moreno, 160 P.3d 242 (Colo. 2007) (use of videotaped interview with an alleged child victim of sexual wrongdoing violated the defendant's Confrontation Clause rights; forfeiture of those rights was not established because there was no showing that the defendant had any intention of subverting the criminal justice system by preventing or dissuading the child from witnessing against him).

People v. Fry, 92 P.3d 970 (Colo. 2004) (in an assault case where the defendant set his girlfriend on fire prosecution's evidence of preliminary hearing testimony violated defendant's confrontation rights because of the limited scope of cross-examination allowed at a preliminary hearing).

Bernal v. People, 44 P.3d 184 (Colo. 2002) (in kidnapping and robbery case, statement of prosecution witness that he "admitted to taking the car, but adamantly denied being in the robbery" may have met the requirements of the statement against interest; nevertheless, because the Confrontation Clause requires that an admission of an out-of-court statement fall within a deeply rooted exception to the hearsay rule, and statements against interest do not qualify as a firmly rooted exception, the statement was inadmissible under the Confrontation Clause due to a failure of the prosecution to show indicia of reliability or a particularized guarantee of trustworthiness).

People ex rel. Faulk v. Dist. Court of the Eleventh Judicial Dist., 667 P.2d 1384 (Colo. 1983) (unavailability, for purposes of applying rule of criminal procedure that allows a deposition to be used at trial if witness is unable to attend because of sickness or infirmity, is to be determined at time of trial in light of then-current circumstances).

People v. Mackey, 185 Colo. 24, 521 P.2d 910 (Colo. 1974) (murder victim's statement in response to question by a police officer about who had shot victim was an admissible dying declaration; the victim was conscious of approaching death, there was no persuasion or leading questions, the declaration was voluntary, and facts could support a conclusion that the victim was of sound mind when he spoke).

People v. Hagos, 250 P.3d 596 (Colo. App. 2009) (where declarant was unavailable, his "statement against interest" needed to bear indicia of reliability because statements against interest are *not* firmly rooted under the Confrontation Clause).

Margenau v. Bowlin, 12 P.3d 1214 (Colo. App. 2000) (deposition testimony can be admissible in a civil trial if it meets the requirements of CRCP 32; inapplicability of Rule 804(b)(1) because of an inadequate showing of the deponent's unavailability does not bar admission of the deposition).

People v. Hernandez, 899 P.2d 297 (Colo. App. 1995) (for determining unavailability, "good faith effort" does not require the exhaustive utilization of every possible means of securing the witness, especially where no evidence supports the presumption that the witness would even obey the court in appearing for trial).

People v. Atkins, 844 P.2d 1196 (Colo. App. 1992) (statements which allegedly demonstrated that the speaker was sorry that he had shot victim and that he had not meant the victim to die were not against the speaker's penal interest, since they were intended to mitigate a first-degree murder charge; Rule 803(3) would not therefore permit their admission).

People v. Bowman, 738 P.2d 387 (Colo. App. 1987) (transcript of witness's testimony in prior trial could properly be introduced in current murder and arson trial, notwithstanding that the prior testimony was vague and had been subject only to limited cross-examination by the defendant; witness had died prior to current trial).

People v. Raffaelli, 701 P.2d 881 (Colo. App. 1985) (statements related to facts that baby died, the dates of her birth and death, and her parentage were admissible under Rule 840(b)(4), since they are statements concerning matters of personal or family history).

People v. Raffaelli, 701 P.2d 881 (Colo. App. 1985) (declarant's statements that she had shaken a baby, that the baby had rolled off a table while under her care, and that she sometimes spanked the baby, tended to subject the declarant to possible criminal liability; therefore they were admissible under the Rule 804(b)(3) exception).

People v. Thompson, 413 P.3d 306 (Colo. App. 2017) (statements that are "related collaterally neutral" to a statement against interest under 804(4) are admissible to provide the jury context to the self-inculpatory remark).

Nicholls v. People, 396 P.3d 675 (Colo. App. 2017) (co-conspirators nontestimonial statements outlining premeditated plan to murder defendants three children were admissible as a statement against interest under 804(b)(3) because the third party was unavailable, the statements tended to subject the declarant to criminal liability, and the statements were of "neutral character" rather than a "self-serving character").

Chapter 805

Rule 805. Hearsay Within Hearsay

Rule 805 reads as follows:

Hearsay included within hearsay is not excluded under the hearsay rule if each part of the combined statements conforms with an exception to the hearsay rule provided in these rules.

ANALYSIS

Rule 805 expressly authorizes the admission of multiple hearsay where each element or level of hearsay conforms to an exception to the hearsay rule. While this is not explicitly set forth in the language of the Rule, Rule 805 implicitly authorizes the admission of multiple levels of out-of-court statements offered for their truth where each level conforms to either a hearsay exception or to an exception to the definition of hearsay. These latter exceptions are set forth in Rules 801(d)(1) and 801(d)(2).

Illustration 1

Where an admission of a party admissible under Rule 801(d)(2) is contained within a business record admissible under Rule 803(6), the entire document is admissible.

Illustration 2

Where a party's prior inconsistent statement not under oath offered only for its impeachment value is contained within a public record admissible under Rule 803(8), both levels of out-of-court statement may be received.

Illustration 3

Negligence action, *P v. D.*   P is injured and is taken to the emergency room. Statement in the hospital record by emergency room nurse:

"P brought in by his brother B. Observed severe laceration of head, P appears unconscious.

B states P was struck by D in the crosswalk."

Objection: Self-serving.

Court: Sustained.

The ruling is correct for the wrong reason.

The record could come in under Rule 803(6) upon adequate authentication and qualification. The statement by B is not part of the business record, and it is admissible as an observation of the emergency room nurse only if B's statement qualifies under some other hearsay exception since he is under no duty to the hospital to report incidents accurately. If B's statement as to P's condition qualified under Rule 803(4), it might be admissible. Otherwise, B's statement should be excised. The fact that B's statement serves P's interests is not the reason for exclusion. The reason is that it is multiple hearsay and no exception applies to the second level declaration.

Rule 805 does not limit admissibility to double, i.e., two level, hearsay. Rather, multiple hearsay exceeding two levels of out-of-court statements is admissible as long as each level of out-of-court statement satisfies an exception to the hearsay rule.

One difficulty with multiple hearsay is that the reliability of the evidence is diminished by each additional layer of hearsay. In this context Rule 403 may operate to authorize the court to exclude multiple hearsay where the court determines the reliability of the evidence has been diminished to an unacceptable extent.

AUTHORITY

WEISSENBERGER'S FEDERAL EVIDENCE § 805.1–.2

MCCORMICK § 313

5 WEINSTEIN 2d §§ 805.01–.06

4 MUELLER & KIRKPATRICK §§ 508–509

5 WIGMORE §§ 1361–63

COMPARISON TO FEDERAL RULE

In substance, Colorado Rule 805 is identical to Federal Rule 805. However, on Dec. 1, 2011 Federal Rule 805 was restyled. Please see Federal Rule 805 in the appendix for comparison.

SIGNIFICANT CASES

People v. Guilbeaux, 761 P.2d 255 (Colo. 1988) (admissibility of a copy of a child's drawing which was annotated by a police officer allegedly to reflect statements made by the child's mother about the drawing, required analysis of multiple levels of hearsay).

People v. Raffaelli, 701 P.2d 881 (Colo. App. 1985) (a doctor's report containing quotations of another person's statements could not be used as the basis for a witness's testimony at trial even though the person's statements might be covered by an exception to the hearsay exclusion, since there was no showing that the doctor's report itself was covered by any exceptions to the hearsay exclusion).

People v. Sparks, 434 P.3d 713, 2018 Colo. App. LEXIS 30 (Colo. App. 2018) (in a sexual assault on a minor case, defendants' testimony that he knew the age of 14 year-old victim did not require that he possess personal knowledge under CRE 602, because admissions excluded from hearsay under CRE 801(d)(2) do not require that the declarant have personal knowledge).

Chapter 806

Rule 806. Attacking and Supporting Credibility of Declarant

Rule 806 reads as follows:

When a hearsay statement, or a statement defined in Rule 801(d)(2), (C), (D), or (E), has been admitted in evidence, the credibility of the declarant may be attacked, and if attacked may be supported, by any evidence which would be admissible for those purposes if declarant had testified as a witness. Evidence of a statement or conduct by the declarant at any time, inconsistent with his hearsay statement, is not subject to any requirement that he may have been afforded an opportunity to deny or explain. If the party against whom a hearsay statement has been admitted calls the declarant as a witness, the party is entitled to examine him on the statement as if under cross-examination.

ANALYSIS

Rule 806 delineates the procedure for attacking and supporting the credibility of declarant's hearsay statements. Recognizing that admissions by authorized persons, agents, or coconspirators are technically not hearsay under an exception to the basic definition, Rule 806 treats such admissions as hearsay for the purposes of impeaching or rehabilitating the declarant. *See* Rule 801(d). Rule 806 authorizes the admissibility of any evidence that would be used to impeach or rehabilitate a declarant of hearsay if that declarant had testified as a witness. The Rule reflects the position that justice is best served by the presentation of all evidence relevant to the reliability of statements made out of court. Where a party calls as a witness the declarant whose hearsay has been admitted against him, Rule 806 provides that the party may examine the declarant on the hearsay as if on cross-examination. Rule 806 complements Rule 611(c), which provides for cross-examination of hostile and adverse witnesses by the proponent of the witness, Rule 607, which allows a party to impeach his or her own witness.

Illustration

Impeachment evidence would be permitted, for example, in attacking the credibility of a declarant whose statement qualified under the dying declaration exception even though the court had found that the requisites of the dying declaration had been met. Such requisites are predicated upon the assumption that the person will not meet his maker with a lie on his lips. Impeachment might take the form of establishing that the declarant had a bad reputation for veracity through a character witness. Also, a witness might be called who would testify that the declarant had an extreme bias against the defendant. None of this evidence would affect the admissibility of the evidence in the first instance, but it would affect the credibility to be attached to the declarant's hearsay statement.

AUTHORITY

WEISSENBERGER'S FEDERAL EVIDENCE §§ 806.1–.4

MCCORMICK § 37

5 WEINSTEIN 2d §§ 806.01–.07

4 MUELLER & KIRKPATRICK §§ 510–511

3A WIGMORE § § 1025–39

COMPARISON TO FEDERAL RULE

In substance, Colorado Rule 806 is identical to Federal Rule 806. However, on Dec. 1, 2011 Federal Rule 806 was restyled. Please see Federal Rule 806 in the appendix for comparison.

SIGNIFICANT CASES

Burlington Northern Railroad Co. v. Hood, 802 P.2d 458 (Colo. 1990) (a prior inconsistent statement of hearsay declarant may be admitted for impeachment purposes; it may also be admissible for substantive purposes if the declarant testifies at the trial and is subject to cross-examination).

King v. People, 785 P.2d 596 (Colo. 1990) (hearsay statements, such as those made by criminal defendant to defense-retained psychiatrist, could be subject to impeachment under Rule 806).

People v. Krueger, 296 P.3d 294 (Colo. App. 2012) (where defendant cross-examined a prosecution witness and used that cross-examination to bring the defendant's own exculpatory out-of-court statements into evidence, impeachment of the defendant-declarant by means of his past felony convictions was proper).

People v. Dore, 997 P.2d 1214 (Colo. App. 1999) (where defendant introduced his own hearsay statement, evidence that he had been convicted of a felony was properly admitted, to impeach the credibility of his hearsay statement).

People v. Ball, 821 P.2d 905 (Colo. App. 1991) (prosecutor was properly allowed to introduce transcript of unavailable witness's testimony from an earlier trial of defendant, and was also properly allowed to introduce testimony seeking to impeach that former testimony with quotations of inconsistent statements allegedly made by the unavailable witness).

People v. Short, 425 P.3d 1208 (Colo. App. 2018) (a defendant's exculpatory self-serving hearsay, admitted under the rule of completeness, is not subject to impeachment under CRE 806. The prosecution can choose to admit the complete statement—and forfeit any objection to the part of the statement favoring defendant—or admit no part of the statement at all). ***But See People v. Davis***, 218 P.3d 718 (Colo. App. 2008).

Chapter 807

Rule 807. Residual Exception

Rule 807 reads as follows:

A statement not specifically covered by Rule 803 or 804 but having equivalent circumstantial guarantees of trustworthiness, is not excluded by the hearsay rule, if the court determines that (A) the statement is offered as evidence of a material fact; (B) the statement is more probative on the point for which it is offered than any other evidence which the proponent can procure through reasonable efforts; and (C) the general purposes of these rules and the interests of justice will best be served by admission of the statement into evidence. However, a statement may not be admitted under this exception unless the proponent of it makes known to the adverse party sufficiently in advance of the trial or hearing to provide the adverse party with a fair opportunity to prepare to meet it, the proponent's intention to offer the statement and the particulars of it, including the name and address of the declarant.

ANALYSIS

Rule 807 provides for the admission of hearsay statements which do not fall within a specific exception under Rules 803 and 804, but which have "equivalent circumstantial guarantees of trustworthiness," provided the statements satisfy certain additional requirements. This residual exception provides a vehicle for admitting hearsay "in situations unanticipated by the other exceptions, but involving equal guarantees of trustworthiness."

Hearsay offered under this exception must satisfy five requirements to be admissible. First, the statements must possess "circumstantial guarantees of trustworthiness" which are "equivalent" to those supporting the specific hearsay exceptions. In assessing reliability, courts should consider a variety of factors, for example, whether circumstances present psychological motivations to be truthful. Second, the evidence "must be offered as evidence of a material fact." Third, the hearsay statement must be "more probative on the point for which it is offered than any other evidence which the proponent can procure through reasonable efforts." This requirement imposes a duty of diligence on the proponent in seeking better evidence than the proffered hearsay. Fourth, the proponent must show that its admission would serve "the general purposes of these rules and the interests of justice." Finally, the statement is not admissible unless the proponent notifies the opponent of his intention to offer it "sufficiently in advance of trial or hearing to provide the adverse party with a fair opportunity to prepare to meet it."

Rule 807 was adopted in November 1998 and effective as of January 1, 1999. It is comprised of components from preexisting rules, specifically Rule 803(24) and Rule 804(b)(5). The purpose behind this reconfiguration of the rules was to facilitate amendments to Rules 803 and 804. No change in meaning was intended.

Practical Considerations

The proponent of evidence offered under the residual exception bears the burden of proving that the five requirements have been satisfied. Admissibility of the statement is determined by the trial court pursuant to Rule 104(a). Where all the requirements are met, the court nevertheless retains discretion to exclude the statement pursuant to Rule 403 to prevent unfair prejudice, confusion of the issues, or undue delay. Further, constitutional considerations may bar admission.

AUTHORITY

WEISSENBERGER'S FEDERAL EVIDENCE § 807

5 WEINSTEIN 2d §§ 803.01–.04

COMPARISON TO FEDERAL RULE

Federal Rule 807

On Dec. 1, 2019 Federal Rule 807 was amended. See Federal Rule 807 in the appendix. The amendment removed the requirement of an equivalence analysis, and instead requires "sufficient guarantees of trustworthiness" based on the totality of the circumstances and an analysis of any corroborating evidence. The amendment removes the requirement that a statement be offered as evidence of a material fact. Additionally, the amendment requires notice to be in writing and to include the substance of the statements. It provides a notice exception for good cause and eliminates the requirement for notice to include the declarant's address.

SIGNIFICANT CASES

United States v. Ismoila, 100 F.3d 380 (5th Cir. 1996) (at trial for credit card fraud, the trial court admitted records from over 40 banks which contained letters, affidavits, and reports of calls from customers reporting unauthorized charges or missing/stolen credit cards as "business records" under Rule 803(6); on appeal, the court held that these documents did not satisfy the "business records" exception as documents from card holders were not prepared in the regular course of the credit holders' business; therefore, the court found these documents admissible under the residual exception to the hearsay rule, Rule 803(24) and 804(b)(5) (now Rule 807)).

United States v. Coney, 51 F.3d 164 (8th Cir. 1995) (trial court did not abuse its discretion in refusing to admit a report under the residual hearsay exception where the defendant offered the report only 45 minutes before she wanted to introduce it at trial).

United States v. Blackburn, 992 F.2d 666 (7th Cir. 1993) (construing former Rule 803(24); computer printouts of eyeglass analysis requested by the FBI from a private company were not admissible as business records because they were not kept in the regular course of business; court found that the records were admissible under the residual hearsay exception).

People v. Preciado-Flores, 66 P.3d 155 (Colo. App. 2002) (in trial in which defendant is charged with accessory to homicide, testimony of victim's sister, offered by defendant as a residual exception under Rule 807 and which concerned defendant's involvement in the Mexican drug trade which resulted in threats to the defendant, were properly excluded on grounds that witness had no independent knowledge of these facts and could not provide guarantees of trustworthiness).

People v. Thompson, 413 P.3d 306 (Colo. App. 2017) (a child that is developmentally delayed is not "ipso facto unreliable" for purposes of complying with the trustworthiness provision of the 807 residual exception. The court looked at the content and circumstances of the out of court statements and found sufficient degrees of reliability).

People v. Lujan, 484 P.3d 718, 2018 Colo. App. LEXIS 986 (Colo. App. 2018) (the victim's statements that she was being abused by the defendant and that the defendant had tried strangling her prior to her death are sufficiently trustworthy under the residual hearsay exception because they were testified to by friends who had personally witnessed the abuse and thereby found to be "nontestimonial, not motivated by a police investigation, and prompted by questions based on personal observations of the victim's bodily injuries").

People v. Jackson, 474 P.3d 60, 2018 Colo. App. LEXIS 796 (Colo. App. 2018) (witness testimony of inculpatory statements by the defendant were sufficiently trustworthy under the residual hearsay exception regardless of the witness' efforts to downplay his own role in the crime because his testimony was consistent and nonetheless placed him at the scene).

Former Rules 803(24) and 804(b)(5)

The Supreme Court of Colorado merged Rules 803(24) and 804(b)(5), both "catch-all" exceptions, into a new Rule 807, mirroring Federal Rule 807. The cases decided under the old Colorado rules are listed below. The same standards of circumstantial guarantees of trustworthiness are applied under the new Colorado Rule 807 as under old Rules 803(24) and 804(b)(5).

Hock v. New York Life Ins. Co., 876 P.2d 1242 (Colo. 1994) (Rule 803(24) could properly be basis for admitting out-of-court written statements by business operator prepared outside the course of routine business, where the trial court found that there were indicia of accuracy and that substitute methods of establishing the facts contained in the statements were not practical).

People v. Fuller, 788 P.2d 741 (Colo. 1990) (under the "residual exception" to the hearsay rule, when the declarant is unavailable as a witness, a hearsay statement may be admitted when there are circumstantial guarantees of trustworthiness, when the statement is offered as evidence of material facts, when the statement is more probative on the points for which it is offered than any other evidence which could be reasonably procured, when the general purposes of the rules of evidence and the interests of justice are best served by the admission of the statement, and when the adverse party had adequate notice in advance of trial of the intention of the proponent of the statement, specific findings must be made on the record to support use of this exception).

Haralampopoulos v. Kelly, 2011 Colo. App. LEXIS 1890 (Colo. App. 2011) (In a medical malpractice case, evidence of cocaine use two years prior to injury was not admissible because it did not fit qualifications required for 807).

People v. Blackwell, 251 P.3d 468 (Colo. App. 2010) (no reversible error when court excluded audio recorded statement for lack of reliability under CRE 807 based on conflicting evidence).

People v. Webster, 987 P.2d 836 (Colo. App. 1998) (a written statement made by a defense witness confined to her bed was inadmissible; the defense did not seek to justify its admission under CRE 804(b)(5) until the case was on appeal, and had not provided the required advance notice to the plaintiff).

People v. Melanson, 937 P.2d 826 (Colo. App. 1996) (in the defendant's trial for a murder which occurred some 18 years prior to the time of trial, the court properly allowed statements by three deceased witnesses to be read into the record under the "catch-all" exception rule of 804(b)(5), because the court in its discretion determined that the statements were trustworthy and material, that they would aid in establishing the defendant's travel shortly after the victim's disappearance, and that the interests of justice would best be served by admission).

IX
AUTHENTICATION AND IDENTIFICATION

AUTHENTICATION

Chapter 901

Rule 901. Requirement of Authentication or Identification

Rule 901 reads as follows:

(a) General provision. The requirement of authentication or identification as a condition precedent to admissibility is satisfied by evidence sufficient to support a finding that the matter in question is what its proponent claims.

(b) Illustrations. By way of illustration only, and not by way of limitation, the following are examples of authentication or identification conforming with the requirements of this rule:

(1) Testimony of witness with knowledge. Testimony that a matter is what it is claimed to be.

(2) Non-expert opinion on handwriting. Non-expert opinion as to the genuineness of handwriting, based upon familiarity not acquired for purposes of the litigation.

(3) Comparison by trier or expert witness. Comparison by the trier of fact or by expert witnesses with specimens which have been authenticated.

(4) Distinctive characteristics and the like. Appearance, contents, substance, internal patterns, or other distinctive characteristics, taken in conjunction with circumstances.

(5) Voice identification. Identification of a voice, whether heard firsthand or through mechanical or electronic transmission or recording, by opinion based upon hearing the voice at any time under circumstances connecting it with the alleged speaker.

(6) Telephone conversations. Telephone conversations, by evidence that a call was made to the number assigned at the time by the telephone company to a particular person or business, if (A) in the case of a person, circumstances, including self-identification, show the person answering to be the one called, or (B) in the case of business, the call was made to a place of business and the conversation related to business reasonably transacted over the telephone.

(7) Public records or reports. Evidence that a writing authorized by law to be recorded or filed and in fact recorded or filed in a public office, or a purported public record, report, statement, or data compilation, in any form, is from the public office where items of this nature are kept.

(8) Ancient documents or data compilation. Evidence that a document or data compilation, in any form, (A) is in such condition as to create no suspicion concerning its authenticity, (B) was in a place where it, if authentic, would likely be, and (C) that

was prepared before January 1, 1998.

(9) Process or system. Evidence describing a process or system used to produce a result and showing that the process or system produces an accurate result.

(10) Methods provided by statute or rule. Any method of authentication or identification provided by Colorado Rules of Procedure, or by statute of the State of Colorado.

ANALYSIS

(a) General provision

Authentication and identification are terms which apply to the process of laying a foundation for the admission of such nontestimonial evidence as documents and objects. Authentication and identification may also refer to foundational evidence which identifies a person's voice on a tape recording or in a telephone conversation. Conceptually, the function of authentication or identification is to establish, by way of preliminary evidence, a connection between the evidence offered and the relevant facts of the case. Authentication and identification involve laying a foundation which establishes the "connective relevancy" of the evidence.

The standard of authentication as provided in Rule 901(a) operates to screen out certain evidence which cannot meet a threshold test of connective relevancy. Rule 901(a) provides that "the requirement of authentication or identification as a condition precedent to admissibility is satisfied by evidence sufficient to support a finding that the matter in question is what its proponent claims." The "sufficient to support a finding" standard merely means that foundational evidence must be sufficient to constitute a rational basis for a jury decision that the primary evidence is what its proponent claims it to be. If the proponent claims the object to be a murder weapon taken from the scene of a crime, the proponent must submit sufficient preliminary evidence to support such a finding. Likewise, if a proponent offers a letter which he claims to have been executed by the plaintiff, he must submit sufficient foundational evidence to support such a finding.

Two key points should be recognized in conjunction with the threshold standard for authentication. First, the foundational evidence need not be absolutely conclusive as to whether the evidence in question connects to the facts of the case. Only evidence sufficient to support a finding need be submitted as a foundation. Second, once the judge determines the threshold test of authentication or identification has been met, and has submitted the evidence to the jury, the jury need not accept the foundational evidence as truthful. The jury need not believe that the primary evidence is in any way connected to the facts of the case. The jury may reject the authenticity of the evidence and decline to believe the foundational witness's testimony.

(b) Illustrations

Rule 901(b) provides illustrations of authentication and identification which may be used to meet the threshold standard of authentication or identification provided in Rule 901(a). The illustrations set forth in Rule 901(b) should not be considered as directives to use particular types of foundations. Rather, the illustrations are suggestive of the means by which the threshold standard of Rule 901(a) may be satisfied.

(1) Testimony of a witness with knowledge

Most frequently, the illustration contained in Rule 901(b)(1) will be used. Rule 901(b)(1) provides that any person who has first-hand knowledge that a matter is what its proponent claims may testify to such facts and establish the foundation for connective relevancy. For example, custody authentication falls within the category of authentication through testimony. Under this technique the authenticating witness or witnesses account for the precise whereabouts of an object from the time it was found in connection with the relevant facts of the case until the moment it is offered into evidence. Where more than one person has had custody of an item, a chain of custody may be accounted for. The use of chain of custody authentication is usually required in the discretion of the trial judge where identification of an object would be difficult because of a lack of distinctive characteristics such as a serial number or signature.

Another illustration of Rule 901(b)(1) would be the testimony provided by an authenticating witness regarding the execution of a document. Where connective relevancy involves attributing authorship or execution to a particular individual, a person who has had first-hand knowledge of the execution may testify that the document offered at trial is the same one executed by a particular individual. Such foundational testimony connects the document offered at trial with the actual execution by a particular person.

Illustration

Counsel: Did you have occasion on February 12, 1990 to meet with the defendant and Mr. Johnstone?

Witness: Yes I did.

Counsel: Please describe the nature of that occasion.

Witness: I happened to attend a meeting at Mr. Johnstone's office which involved the review and execution of certain documents.

Counsel: I hand you now what has been marked as Plaintiff's Exhibit No. 3 and ask you if you recognize that document.

Witness: Yes, it was one of the documents that was reviewed on that date.

Counsel: I direct your attention to the signature at the bottom of the page. Were you present at the time that signature was executed?

Witness: Yes, I actually saw the defendant execute that document at the meeting. That is the signature I saw the defendant put at the bottom of the page.

Counsel: Your Honor, we now would like to offer this exhibit into evidence based on the authentication provided by this witness.

Judge: Is there an objection?

Opposing counsel: No, your Honor.

Judge: Then it will be received into evidence and it may be published to the jury.

The authentication of a photograph may also be established through the testimony of a witness. The foundational witness testifies that the photograph being offered at trial is a faithful and accurate representation of the object or scene depicted. The authenticating witness, through his testimony, connects the photograph offered at trial with the relevant facts of the case where the relevant facts are related to the scene, event or object depicted.

(2) Non-expert opinion on handwriting

The authenticity of a document may also be established through non-expert opinion on handwriting. Rule 901(b)(2) codifies the principle that non-expert foundational opinion may be used to attribute the handwriting on an offered exhibit to a particular individual. Under this technique a person familiar with the handwriting of an individual provides foundational testimony that, based on his knowledge of the individual's handwriting, the document was written by the individual in question. The document is being connected to a particular individual who authored it where such execution or authorship is a relevant fact of the case.

Obviously, the authenticating witness must have sufficient familiarity with the handwriting of the document's author to render a valuable opinion as to authorship. The burden is on the proponent of the document to establish, as part of the foundation, that the authenticating witness has the requisite familiarity.

Illustration

Q: Mr. Johnson, how do you know the plaintiff, Mr. Murphy?

A: I have been his business partner for five years. We operate a car rental agency.

Q: During those five years, have you had an opportunity to observe Mr. Murphy sign his name?

A: Yes, I see him sign his name several times a day.

Q: Would you know his signature if you were to see it?

A: I am certain I would.

Q: I hand you now what has been marked as Plaintiff's Exhibit Number 16. Please look at the signature at the bottom of page 3. Do you recognize that signature?

A: Yes.

Q: Whose signature is it?

A: Mr. Murphy's.

---

(3) Comparison by trier or expert witness

Authentication or identification of a document may be established through the device of comparison of an offered document with specimens or exemplars which have been authenticated. Rule 901(b)(3) provides for the authentication device of comparison to be used to attribute authorship to a particular individual. Where an expert makes the comparison between the offered exhibits and the authenticated specimen, the expert must be qualified as provided in Article VII of the Rules. *See* Analysis to Rule 702.

Regardless of whether an expert is utilized, the specimen used for the basis of comparison must be authenticated through the normal authentication process. In order to avoid confusion, it is helpful to use a specimen or exemplar which is unquestionably authentic. A signature card from a bank is often used. Alternatively, in order to avoid confusion, a stipulation may be sought to establish the conclusive authenticity of the specimen or exemplar. It should be noted that a lay witness is not qualified to render an opinion as to the similarity between the specimen and the handwriting on the offered exhibit. Only opinion testimony from an expert is appropriate. When no expert is utilized for the purpose of rendering an opinion as to authenticity, the exemplar and the offered exhibit are both tendered to the jury for their consideration in determining whether or not the offered exhibit is authentic.

Statutory procedure. C.R.S. § 13-25-104 provides:

Comparison of a disputed writing, with any writing proved to the satisfaction of the court to be genuine, shall be permitted to be made by witnesses in all trials and proceedings, and the evidence of witnesses respecting the same may be submitted to the court and jury as evidence of the genuineness or otherwise of the writing in dispute.

Constitutional Considerations

A handwriting or voice specimen of a defendant in a criminal case may be obtained by compulsion without violating the defendant's Fifth or Sixth Amendment rights. *Gilbert v. California*, 388 U.S. 263 (1967).

---

(4) Distinctive characteristics and the like

Distinctive contents of a document may be the basis for authentication under Rule 901(b)(4). For example, a letter might be authenticated and attributed to a particular author where the letter reveals knowledge that only one individual would possess. This technique is occasionally referred to as the reply doctrine technique where the unique information revealed in the letter indicates that the author is replying to prior correspondence.

Many documents may be authenticated by virtue of their custody. Custody, considered in conjunction with appearance, contents, and substance may be used to authenticate a business record under Rule 901(b)(4). In addition to requiring the foundation to satisfy the hearsay rule, business records must also be authenticated. Custodial authentication is established by a foundation witness who testifies that he has personal knowledge of the business's system of maintaining records. *See* Rule 901(b)(1). The foundational witness further provides testimony that the record or writing being offered at trial was removed from the business's files prior to trial and brought to the courtroom by the witness. Alternatively, the witness may testify that he recognizes the document offered at trial as one which was removed from the business's files by virtue of its distinctive characteristics or contents. Usually, a witness qualified to establish the foundation for Rule 803(6) will also be qualified to establish the foundation for authentication of the business record under Article IX. A similar technique is used for public records and reports pursuant to Rule 901(b)(7).

(5) Voice identification

Just as the authentication of a document involves attributing authorship to a particular individual, the authentication of an oral statement involves identifying the individual who made the statement. Rules 901(b)(5) and (6) illustrate methods by which oral statements may be attributed to a particular speaker where the identification of the speaker is relevant in a case.

Voice identification is established by opinion evidence, that is, by testimony of a witness that, based upon his or her familiarity with a speaker's voice, it is the witness's belief that the voice sought to be identified or authenticated is that of the specific speaker. It is clear from the provisions of Rule 901(b)(5) that anyone who has heard the voice of the alleged speaker, at any time, may offer opinion testimony sufficient to identify the voice. Such a witness need not offer conclusive proof on the issue of identity, but must merely offer testimony sufficient to establish a finding of identity.

The proponent of voice identification testimony must establish by way of foundation that the witness has some familiarity with the alleged speaker's voice. Pursuant to the Rule, this foundation may be established by showing that the witness has heard the voice sought to be identified under circumstances connecting it with the alleged speaker. Accordingly, the requisite familiarity may arise from exposure to the alleged speaker's voice prior to or subsequent to the conversation or communication sought to be authenticated. In the typical situation, however, a witness offering an opinion on voice identification will do so based upon his prior familiarity with the voice in question.

(6) Telephone conversations

Rule 901(b)(6) provides for authentication of telephone conversations. The Rule is designed to apply specifically to calls initiated by the person who offers the foundational evidence. In other words, it pertains to outgoing calls. The Rule applies to telephone calls to both individuals and business establishments, and a slightly different foundational requirement is indicated for each. The Rule provides a method for attributing oral statements to a particular speaker or to a person who speaks for a particular business establishment where the identity of the speaker is relevant to an issue in the case.

In order to utilize this provision, there must be evidence that a call was placed to a number assigned at the time by the telephone company to a particular person or business. This evidence may consist of testimony or other proof such as, for example, telephone company records. In regard to an individual, there must be circumstantial evidence that identifies the person who answered the call as the one who was intended to be called. This requirement may be satisfied by the testimony that the recipient identified himself or herself, or by other circumstances that are probative of identity. In regard to a call to a business, the foundation must include evidence that the call was made to a place of business and that the conversation related to business reasonably transacted over the phone. If the answering person has purported to speak for the business, it is not necessary that his or her individual identity be established, as long as the conversation is circumstantially probative of the identity of the place of business.

(7) Public records or reports

Rule 901(b)(7) provides for the authentication of public records based upon a preliminary showing that the records are from a public office where records of that type are kept. Accordingly, a party may authenticate public records by foundational evidence that, prior to the trial, such records were in the custody of an appropriate public office. It should be noted that the Rule includes within its scope writings that are authorized by law to be recorded or filed in a public office and that are in fact so recorded or filed.

Authentication of public records pursuant to Rule 901(b)(7) contemplates that the original record itself will be offered into evidence. Due to the inconvenience or impossibility of producing the original record in court, the proponent may seek to introduce a copy. If the copy is certified, it may be authenticated pursuant to Rule 902. If the copy is not certified, it may also be offered into evidence and authenticated pursuant to Rule 901(b)(7). In this case, however, the proponent must also satisfy the best evidence requirements identified in Rule 1005. *See* Analysis to Rule 1005.

The Rule will apply to such writings as judicial records, legislative records, records of administrative agencies, records of correctional institutions and law enforcement agencies, coroner's records and reports, tax returns, selective service files, weather reports, patent office reports, military records, and any other official records from an office of any level of government, domestic as well as foreign.

(8) Ancient documents or data compilation

Rule 901(b)(8) provides a method for authenticating any document or data compilation on the combined bases of age and corroborating circumstances as to genuineness. The threshold standard of admissibility may be satisfied by showing that a document or data was prepared before January 1, 1998, that its condition creates no suspicion as to its genuineness, and that it was kept or found in a place where, if authentic, it would likely be retained.

Authentication of an ancient document or data compilation under Rule 901(b)(8) simultaneously satisfies the hearsay requirements of Rule 803(16). Nevertheless, the proponent may need to address best evidence considerations and must address general relevancy principles in order to insure the admissibility of the document or data compilation.

(9) Process or system

Rule 901(b)(9) provides a method for authenticating the resulting product of a process or system. Authentication under this Rule is established by foundational evidence which describes the process or system and which shows that the process or system produces an accurate result.

While the method of establishing authenticity provided by the Rule may be utilized in connection with any process or system, Rule 901(b)(9) will frequently be used to authenticate computer results. It should be noted that there is no requirement under Rule 901(b)(9) that printouts have been produced in the regular course of business, although this factor may be significant if Rule 803(6) is used as a basis for satisfying the hearsay system. The Rule will, of course, be utilized for authenticating results from processes or systems other than computer systems, such as x-ray films, motion pictures, audio recordings, police radar systems, medical tests such as electrocardiograms, and certain out-of-court experiments, polls and surveys.

(10) Methods provided by statute or rule

Rule 901(b)(10) is in effect a clarifying provision, and the Rule preserves methods of authentication or identification provided by certain legislative provisions and by Rules promulgated by the Supreme Court of Colorado.

AUTHORITY

WEISSENBERGER'S FEDERAL EVIDENCE §§ 901.1–.43

McCORMICK §§ 218, 220–21, 223–26, 228

5 WEINSTEIN 2d §§ 901.01–.12

5 MUELLER & KIRKPATRICK §§ 512–537

2 WIGMORE §§ 570, 658, 660, 666, 694–97

5 WIGMORE §§ 1638(a), 1651, 1672–84

7 WIGMORE §§ 1997–2015, 2128–35, 2138–46, 2148–54, 2158–60, 2162, 2164, 2167

Hearsay in Criminal Cases Under the Colorado Rules of Evidence: An Overview, 50 U. COLO. L. REV. 277 (1979)

Alexander & Bickel, *The Authentication of Documents Requirements: Barrier to Falsehood or to Truth*, 10 SAN DIEGO L. REV. 266 (1973)

Broun, *Authentication and Contents of Writings*, 1969 LAW AND THE SOCIAL ORDER 611 (1969)

Strong, *Liberalizing the Authentication of Private Writings*, 10 CORNELL L. REV. 284 (1967)

Levin, *Authentication and the Content of Writings*, 10 RUTGERS L. REV. 632 (1956)

Decker & Handler, *Voiceprint Identification Evidence—Out of the Frye Pan and into Admissibility*, 26 AM. U. L. REV. 314 (1977)

Kamine, *The Voiceprint Technique: Its Structure and Reliability*, 6 SAN DIEGO L. REV. 213 (1969)

Weintraub, *Voice Identification, Writing Exemplars and the Privilege Against Self-Incrimination*, 10 VAND. L. REV. 485 (1976)

Comment, *Authentication and the Best Evidence Rule Under the Federal Rules of Evidence*, 16 WAYNE L. REV. 195 (1969)

COMPARISON TO FEDERAL RULE

Effective March 2021, 901 (b)(8) changed from the 20-year timeframe was replaced with documents prepared before January 1, 1998, whereas the federal rule maintains the previous 20-year timeframe. However, on Dec. 1, 2011 Federal Rule 901 was restyled. Please see Federal Rule 901 in the appendix for comparison.

SIGNIFICANT CASES

People v. Fry, 92 P.3d 970 (Colo. 2004) (in an assault case where the defendant set his girlfriend on fire prosecution's evidence of preliminary hearing testimony violated defendant's confrontation rights because of the limited scope of cross-examination allowed at a preliminary hearing).

People v. Mascarenas, 666 P.2d 101 (Colo. 1983) (where bottles of drugs stolen from a pharmacist were in the pharmacist's possession a day before trial, the fact that the police had initialed, catalogued, and photographed the bottles when they were seized from the defendant, and where the pharmacist testified that they were the drugs stolen from his pharmacy, satisfied the chain of custody rule for authenticity of evidence because there was no indication that the drugs had been altered).

People v. Abad, 2021 Colo. App LEXIS 89 (Colo. App. 2021) (police officer's testimony that he requested and received a thumb drive from Drop Box containing sexually explicit images, downloaded them to a disk, and testified that the contents were accurate, sufficiently authenticated the images). Not selected for final or official publication as of June 1, 2021.

People v. Gonzales, 2019 Colo. App. LEXIS 345 (Colo. App. 2019) (in a first-degree murder trial, voice recordings were properly authenticated by a witness's testimony identifying defendant's voice on the tape and circumstances of the tape's discovery).

People v. Dominguez-Castor, 2020 Colo. App. LEXIS 12 (Colo. App. 2020) (Facebook communications were properly authenticated by evidence showing that the defendant was the owner of the account and author of the messages).

People. v. N.T.B., 457 P.3d 126 (Colo. App. 2019) (in a case charging defendant with sexual exploitation of a child, video evidence stored with an internet-based file storage company was properly authenticated by the investigator's testimony that defendant had previously admitted ownership of the account associated with the illicit material).

People v. Glover, 363 P.3d 736 (Colo. App. 2015) (in a first degree murder case, the court found that Facebook messages are analogous to phone records or emails, and can be authenticated through CRE 901(b)(1) or 901(b)(4). In this case, messages linking defendant to an accomplice were found on Facebook and allowed into evidence. At trial, a records custodian of Facebook verified the information, and no evidence was presented that anyone other than defendant ever used account, therefore the court concluded the Facebook messages satisfied CRE 901(b) and were properly admitted).

People v. Vasquez, 155 P.3d 588 (Colo. App. 2006) (where evidence of a defendant's forged check resulted from a police search of the defendant's driver's license number, evidence of any form of a public record, report, or statement being retrieved from a public office where such items are kept is sufficient to satisfy the authenticity and identification requirement).

Rojhani v. Meagher, 22 P.3d 554 (Colo. App. 2000) (it was error to exclude a document on lack of authentication grounds when the defendant stipulated that all medical records documents meet the foundation requirements of Rule 803).

People v. Bielecki, 964 P.2d 598 (Colo. App. 1998) (certified public records of previous convictions were self-authenticating and sufficient to establish the defendant's habitual offender status).

People v. Lesslie, 939 P.2d 443 (Colo. App. 1996) (in a criminal eavesdropping case where a listening device, installed in a bar restroom, was recovered by the CBI one year after the alleged incidents occurred, the trial court properly admitted testimony of two witnesses as authenticating the listening device pursuant to 901(b)(1); they identified it as having been removed from the bar restroom).

People v. Slusher, 844 P.2d 1222 (Colo. App. 1992) (testimony by a witness regarding a document purporting to be a lease agreement created on a certain date, which the witness had retrieved from the defendant's computer files, did not satisfy CRE 901(a)'s authentication requirement that the document be a "true record and not doctored," because the witness also testified that is was possible for someone with sufficient knowledge of computers to tamper with the computer's internal clock).

McClellan v. State, Dep't of Revenue, Motor Vehicle Div., 731 P.2d 769 (Colo. App. 1986) (documents including a driver's license revocation notice, copies of a breath test record and procedure sheet, computer printouts of the plaintiff's arrest and case reports, and copies of the plaintiff's vehicle impound report and summons were properly verified by the arresting officer because an attestation to the accuracy of the reports was signed by the officer and notarized, and the officer identified the documents under oath and testified that they were correct).

People v. Gable, 647 P.2d 246 (Colo. App. 1982) (a voice heard over the telephone could be identified by a witness who heard the voice at any time including after the phone call, and by circumstantial evidence where the witness had held previous face-to-face conversations with the speaker, and had heard the speaker identifying himself over the telephone).

People v. Holder, 632 P.2d 607 (Colo. App. 1981) (records of long-distance telephone calls made from a motel which were sent to the motel bookkeeper by a telephone company were admissible as business records, because the bookkeeper's lack of personal knowledge concerning the accuracy of the numbers affected only the weight of the evidence, not its admissibility).

People v. Heisler, ___P.3d___, 2017 Colo. App. LEXIS 536 (Colo. App. 2017) (proper authentication of text messages requires that a witness with personal knowledge of the messages testifies that the text accurately reflects the content of the messages and identifies the purported sender by showing that the phone number from which the messages were sent was assigned to, associated with, or controlled by the purported sender).

People ex rel. A.C.E-D, 433 P.3d 153 (Colo. App. 2018) (Facebook messages require two showings to be admissible; the party seeking admission must show that the records were those of Facebook, and that the communications recorded were made by the purported party; A Facebook message authenticated through the defendant's name, image, and witness testimony regarding the defendant's writing characteristics, meets the heightened authentication requirements to be admissible).

People v. Gonzales, 474 P.3d 124, 2019 Colo. App. LEXIS 345 (Colo. App. 2019) (a voicemail is properly authenticated under rule 901 where a police officer who had previously interrogated the suspect testifies that he recognizes the voice. The court declines to apply the common law rule that if "no witness with independent knowledge of the [voicemail's] content can verify the accuracy of the recorded conversation, the proponent must present a witness who can verify the reliability of the recording process, by establishing the factors laid out in Alonzi: the competency of the recorder, the reliability of the recording system, the absence of any tampering with the recording, and the identification of the speakers").

Chapter 902

Rule 902. Self-Authentication

Rule 902 reads as follows:

Extrinsic evidence of authenticity as a condition precedent to admissibility is not required with respect to the following:

(1) Domestic public documents under seal. A document bearing a seal purporting to be that of the United States, or of any State, district, Commonwealth, territory, or insular possession thereof, or the Panama Canal Zone, or the Trust Territory of the Pacific Islands, or of a political subdivision, department, officer or agency thereof, and a signature purporting to be an attestation or execution.

(2) Domestic public documents not under seal. A document purporting to bear the signature in his official capacity of an officer or employee of any entity included in paragraph (1) hereof, having no seal, if a public officer having a seal and having official duties in the district or political subdivision of the officer or employee certifies under seal that the signer had the official capacity and that the signature is genuine.

(3) Foreign public documents. A document purporting to be executed or attested in his official capacity by a person authorized by the laws of a foreign country to make the execution or attestation, and accompanied by a final certification as to the genuineness of signature and official position (A) of the executing or attesting person, or (B) of any foreign official whose certificate of genuineness of signature and official position relates to the execution or attestation or is in a chain of certificates of genuineness of signature and official position relating to the execution or attestation. A final certification may be made by a secretary of embassy or legation, consul general, consul, vice consul, or consular agent of the United States, or a diplomatic or consular official of the foreign country assigned or accredited to the United States. If reasonable opportunity has been given to all parties to investigate the authenticity and accuracy of official documents, the court may, for good cause shown, order that they be treated as presumptively authentic without final certification or permit them to be evidenced by an attested summary with or without final certification.

(4) Certified copies of public records. A copy of an official record or report or entry therein, or of a document authorized by law to be recorded or filed and actually recorded or filed in a public office, including data compilations in any form, certified as correct by the custodian or other person authorized to make the certification, by certificate complying with paragraph (1), (2), or (3) of this rule or complying with any Federal or Colorado Rule of Procedure, or with any Act of the United States Congress, or any

statute of the State of Colorado.

(5) Official publications. Books, pamphlets, or other publications purporting to be issued by public authority.

(6) Newspapers and periodicals. Printed materials purporting to be newspapers or periodicals.

(7) Trade inscriptions and the like. Inscriptions, signs, tags, or labels purporting to have been affixed in the course of business and indicating ownership, control, or origin.

(8) Acknowledged documents. Documents accompanied by a certificate of acknowledgment executed in the manner provided by law by a notary public or other officer authorized by law to take acknowledgments.

(9) Commercial paper and related documents. Commercial paper, signatures thereon, and documents relating thereto to the extent provided by general commercial law.

(10) Presumptions under legislative Act. Any signature, document, or other matter declared by Act of the Congress of the United States, or by any statute of the State of Colorado to be presumptively or prima facie genuine or authentic.

(11) Certified domestic records of regularly conducted activity. The original or a duplicate of a domestic record of regularly conducted activity that would be admissible under Rule 803(6) if accompanied by an affidavit of its custodian or other qualified person, in a manner complying with any Colorado statute or rule prescribed by the Colorado Supreme Court, certifying that the record—

    (a) was made at or near the time of the occurrence of the matters set forth by, or from information transmitted by, a person with knowledge of those matters;

    (b) was kept in the course of the regularly conducted activity; and

    (c) was made by the regularly conducted activity as a regular practice.

A party intending to offer a record into evidence under this paragraph must provide written notice of that intention to all adverse parties, and must make the record and affidavit available for inspection sufficiently in advance of their offer into evidence to provide an adverse party with a fair opportunity to challenge them.

(12) Certified foreign records of regularly conducted activity. In a civil case, the original or a duplicate of a foreign record of regularly conducted activity that would be admissible under Rule 803(6) if accompanied by a written declaration by its custodian or other qualified person certifying that the record—

    (a) was made at or near the time of the occurrence of the matters set forth by, or from information transmitted by, a person with knowledge of those matters;

    (b) was kept in the course of the regularly conducted activity; and

    (c) was made by the regularly conducted activity as a regular practice.

The declaration must be signed in a manner that, if falsely made, would subject the maker to criminal penalty under the laws of the country where the declaration is signed. A party intending to offer a record into evidence under this paragraph must provide written notice of that intention to all adverse parties, and must make the record and declaration available for inspection sufficiently in advance of their offer into evidence to provide an adverse party with a fair opportunity to challenge them.

ANALYSIS

The theory of self-authentication is that certain documents are self-evidently genuine on their face, and consequently, the proponent of the document is relieved of the obligation of meeting the threshold test of proving that the document is what he claims it to be. Self-authentication relieves the proponent from submitting foundational testimony regarding connective relevancy. In considering self-authenticating documents, two factors should not be overlooked. First, while self-authentication does relieve the proponent of the document from submitting foundational testimony as to authenticity, it does not guarantee admissibility of the document. Other issues, such as best evidence and hearsay, must be addressed in considering the admissibility of the document. Second, it is important to recognize that a self-authenticating document is not conclusively genuine. While self-authentication does relieve the proponent of submitting authentication evidence, the jury may still determine in rendering its final decision that the document is not genuine, i.e., it is not what its proponent claims it to be.

(1) Domestic public documents under seal

Rule 902(1) extends the doctrine of self-authentication to domestic public documents bearing a seal of an appropriate entity or officer and an appropriate signature purporting to be an attestation or execution of the document. To qualify as a public document under the Rule it need only be the type of document susceptible to the legitimate use of the official seal. The Rule retains the traditional reliance on the official seal as a means of authenticating a document.

(2) Domestic public documents not under seal

Rule 902(2) applies to domestic public documents not under seal. If the document is not under seal but is signed by an officer or public employee, it can be authenticated by a certification under seal by an officer having a seal and official duties in the district or political subdivision. The certification must state that the signer has the official capacity to sign the document and that the signature is genuine.

(3) Foreign public documents

Rule 902(3) provides for the self-authentication of foreign public documents. For the foreign public document to be self-authenticating, it must be executed or attested by an authorized official and there must be a certificate by an appropriate United States officer that the signature of the attesting or executing foreign official is genuine and lawful. If the appropriate United States officer is unable to ascertain the lawfulness or the legitimacy of the attesting or executing foreign official, he need only attest to the authenticity and legitimacy of the signature and official position of the last officer in the chain of such certificates. According to the Rule, the final certification by the United States official can be dispensed with for good cause.

(4) Certified copies of public records

Rule 902(4) states that certified copies of public or official records need no additional authentication. The Rule requires that the copy be of a public or official record, that the custodian or other authorized person certify the copy, and that the certificate comply with Rules 902(1)–(3), a specific statute, or other court rule. The copy should be certified as a correct copy by the custodian or other authorized person.

(5) Official publications

Rule 902(5) applies the doctrine of self-authentication to books, pamphlets and other publications purporting to be issued by a public authority. The Rule relieves the proponent from establishing an extrinsic foundation that the publication was actually printed or issued by public authority. Although not explicitly stated in the Rule, it would seem that the Rule would apply to the official publications of any of the entities described in Rule 902(1).

(6) Newspapers and periodicals

Rule 902(6) makes the doctrine of self-authentication applicable to non-official printed materials purporting to be newspapers or periodicals. The Rule also by its express terms includes notices and advertisements contained in the identified publications. This provision may be used to prove the contents of newspapers or periodicals, for example, in a libel action, or in an action involving deceptive advertising. Periodicals and newspapers may also be used as proof of collateral matters such as the date and place of publication. Finally, it must be remembered that Rule 902 only provides for authentication, and other issues such as best evidence and hearsay must be addressed before admissibility is attained.

(7) Trade inscriptions and the like

Rule 902(7) accords self-authenticating status to trade inscriptions, signs, tags or labels, as long as they purport to have been affixed in the course of business and are indicative of ownership, control or origin. Generally, this type of evidence will be introduced to prove ownership or control, for example, in a products liability action.

The Rule is justified because there is only a slight risk of forgery of items within the purview of the Rule due to the difficulty of reproduction and because trademark infringement involves serious penalties. Substantial efforts are devoted to inducing the public to buy and otherwise acquire items in reliance on brand names, and substantial protection is given by the law. The Rule requires that the inscription, label, or the like purport to have been affixed in the course of "business."

The term "business" should be interpreted liberally to include any ongoing enterprise or institution regardless of its commercial or non-commercial nature, including, for example, a private university or social organization that uses an identifying inscription or symbol.

(8) Acknowledged documents

Rule 902(8) provides that documents accompanied by a certificate of acknowledgment are self-authenticating and, consequently, do not require an extrinsic foundation. The certificate of acknowledgment serves as *prima facie* evidence that the document is what it purports to be. Rule 902(8) is not limited to title documents, and it applies to any type of document that is properly acknowledged.

The acknowledgment required is a certificate executed by a notary public or other officer authorized to take acknowledgments in the jurisdiction where the certificate is executed. In addition, the certificate must be executed in the manner provided by law.

(9) Commercial paper and related documents

Rule 902(7) expressly adopts the principles of general commercial law in applying the doctrine of self-authentication to commercial paper, signatures on commercial paper and documents relating to commercial paper.

(10) Presumption under legislative act

Rule 902(8) confers self-authenticating status to any signature, document or other matter that is declared to be authentic by an Act of the Congress of the United States or by a statute of the State of Colorado. By its express terms, the Rule incorporates any federal or Colorado law that declares a matter to be presumptively or *prima facie* genuine or authentic. It should be noted that statutes that grant "presumptive" authenticity to a matter go beyond the doctrine of self-authentication in the sense that the trier of fact is bound by the presumption in the absence of evidence sufficient to support a finding to the contrary. *See* Analysis to Rule 301.

(11) Certified domestic records of regularly conducted activity

Rule 902(11) extends the doctrine of self-authentication to domestic records of regularly conducted activity. Any documentation that would be admissible under 803(6) plus an affidavit of its custodian which complies with Colorado law attesting to § 102(11)(a), (b) and (c) is admissible as evidence. Notice to all adverse parties in advance of offering such "business records" is required.

(12) Certified foreign records of regularly conducted activity

In civil cases foreign "business records" are admissible if they comply with Rules 803(6) and 902(11) and the declaration is signed in a manner that if false made would subject the maker to a criminal penalty in the foreign country where signed.

AUTHORITY

WEISSENBERGER'S FEDERAL EVIDENCE §§ 902.1–.19

McCORMICK §§ 218, 283, 308

5 WEINSTEIN 2d §§ 902.01–.12

5 MUELLER & KIRKPATRICK §§ 538–548

4 WIGMORE § 1234

5 WIGMORE §§ 1677, 1680, 1684

7 WIGMORE §§ 2129–30, 2150, 2152, 2161 65

Note, *Evidence—Authentication of Documents—Proof of Publication*, 15 S. CAL. L. REV. 115, 117 (1941)

Strong, *Liberalizing the Authentication of Private Writings*, 52 CORNELL L.Q. 284 (1976)

Note, *Evidence—Authentication—Necessity of Proof of Genuineness of Documents*, 39 TEMP. L.Q. 109, 111 (1955)

Bigham, *Presumptions, Burden of Proof and the Uniform Commercial Code*, 21 VAND. L. REV. 177, 195 (1968)

COMPARISON TO FEDERAL RULE

Colorado Rules 902(4) and (10) differ from Federal Rule 902 in that while Federal Rule 902(4) refers only to Acts of Congress and rules of the United States Supreme Court, Colorado Rule 902(4) additionally refers to Colorado statutes and the Federal and Colorado Rules of Procedure. Federal Rule 902(10) also refers only to Acts of Congress, whereas Colorado Rule 902(10) additionally refers to Colorado statutes. The intent of these sections of the Colorado Rules, however, is identical to that of the Federal Rules. Please note that on Dec. 1, 2011 Federal Rule 902 was restyled. Please see Federal Rule 902 in the appendix for comparison.

On September 13, 2016, the Judicial Conference approved and transmitted Federal Rule 902(13) to the Supreme Court. Federal Rule 902(13) includes certified data copied from an electronic device, storage medium, or file, and is on track to become effective December 1, 2017.

SIGNIFICANT CASES

People v. Harris, 914 P.2d 434 (Colo. App. 1995) (in a trial including five habitual offender counts, the trial court properly admitted judgments of convictions into evidence; all the documents were accompanied by a certificate attesting that they were true and accurate copies taken from public records over which a custodian had authority, and there was no additional requirement pursuant to Rule 902).

People v. Morise, 859 P.2d 247 (Colo. App. 1993) (the fact that newspaper articles containing statements allegedly made by the defendant were self-authenticating under CRE 902(6) did not affect the fact that the articles were nevertheless inadmissible as hearsay).

Smith v. Weindrop, 833 P.2d 856 (Colo. App. 1992) (promissory notes are self-authenticating under CRE 902(9), and their production without endorsement of payment constitutes prima facie evidence of non-payment of some amount; when produced in addition to foreclosure documents they constituted sufficient evidence to establish the amount of the defendant's liability).

People v. More, 668 P.2d 968 (Colo. App. 1983) (although regularly promulgated administrative rules are presumed valid under CRE 902(5), once a foundation objection is raised as to whether compliance with a statute requiring public notice of the rules has occurred, the proponent of the evidence has the burden of establishing their authenticity).

Chapter 903

Rule 903. Subscribing Witness' Testimony Unnecessary

Rule 903 reads as follows:

The testimony of a subscribing witness is not necessary to authenticate a writing unless required by the laws of the jurisdiction whose laws govern the validity of the writing.

ANALYSIS

Rule 903 provides that authentication of a writing need not involve the testimony of a subscribing witness unless such testimony is required by the laws of the jurisdiction whose laws govern the validity of the writing. Consequently, where there is no applicable statutory or common law provision requiring testimony of a subscribing witness, authentication of a document may be established in accordance with the provisions of Rules 901 or 902.

AUTHORITY

WEISSENBERGER'S FEDERAL EVIDENCE §§ 903.1–.3

McCORMICK § 220

5 WEINSTEIN 2d §§ 903.01–.02

5 MUELLER & KIRKPATRICK §§ 549–550

4 WIGMORE §§ 1287–1321

COMPARISON TO FEDERAL RULE

In substance, Colorado Rule 903 is identical to Federal Rule 903. However, on Dec. 1, 2011 Federal Rule 903 was restyled. Please see Federal Rule 903 in the appendix for comparison.

AUTHENTICATION

X
CONTENTS OF WRITINGS, RECORDINGS AND PHOTOGRAPHS

WRITINGS

Chapter 1001

Rule 1001. Definitions

Rule 1001 reads as follows:

For purposes of this article the following definitions are applicable:

(1) Writings and recordings. "Writings" and "recordings" consist of letters, words, or numbers, or their equivalent, set down by handwriting, typewriting, printing, photostating, photographing, magnetic impulse, mechanical or electronic recording, or other form of data compilation.

(2) Photographs. "Photographs" include still photographs, X-ray films, video tapes, and motion pictures.

(3) Original. An "original" of a writing or recording is the writing or recording itself or any counterpart intended to have the same effect by a person executing or issuing it. An "original" of a photograph includes the negative or any print therefrom. If data are stored in a computer or similar device, any printout or other output readable by sight, shown to reflect the data accurately, is an "original."

(4) Duplicate. A "duplicate" is a counterpart produced by the same impression as the original, or from the same matrix, or by means of photography, including enlargements and miniatures, or by mechanical or electronic re-recording, or by chemical reproduction, or by other equivalent techniques which accurately reproduce the original.

ANALYSIS

The collection of Rules contained in Article X were historically known as the "best evidence rule." The best evidence rule has frequently been criticized as a misnomer, because the rule does not require the best evidence as a general proposition of law. Rather, the rule in certain instances requires original evidence. The essence of the best evidence rule, as it is applied in Article X, provides that in proving the contents of a writing, recording or photograph, the original is preferentially required. The rule further provides that if the original is unavailable through no fault of the proponent of the evidence, secondary evidence may be admitted. It should be noted that the best evidence rule does not apply to proving the contents of physical objects or things other than writings, recordings or photographs, and there is no general requirement that the most probative evidence be used to prove a fact in every instance. Evidence need only be relevant under Rule 401 to satisfy the threshold qualification of admissibility under Rule 402.

"Secondary evidence." Article X contains no express definition of "secondary evidence." Nevertheless, it is clear that secondary evidence may be defined as any evidence which is

probative of the contents other than the original itself. Consequently, secondary evidence of the contents of a document could be testimony of a person with first-hand knowledge of the contents or it could be a hand-transcribed copy. It should be noted that, except in regard to Rule 105 governing public records, Article X does not erect a hierarchy of secondary evidence such that, for example, a hand-transcribed copy is preferred to oral testimony. Once an exception to the requirement for the original is established, any secondary evidence may be used to prove contents.

Writings and recordings. Rule 1001(1) defines "writings and recordings" in their broadest sense, to include any setting down of "letters, words, or numbers or their equivalent" by virtually any means constituting a writing or recording. Moreover, a writing or recording is not only a setting down or inscription of letters and numbers, but also any compilation or recording of data such as might be produced by a computer, modern electronic device or other newly developed machine or technique.

Practical Application of the "Best Evidence Rule"

Article X of the Rules of Evidence, the so-called best evidence rule, applies only where the contents of a writing, recording or photograph are sought to be proven. Generally, if a party is seeking to establish the terms of a dispositive document such as a contract, lease, will or trust, the so-called best evidence rule will apply and will require the original if it is available. If, however, some other fact concerning a document is sought to be proven, for example, its delivery, the best evidence rule does not apply. Moreover, the best evidence rule is a rule of mandatory preference. It prefers the original if it is available. Secondary evidence may be used, however, to establish the contents of a writing, recording or photograph where it is authorized under Rule 1002.

Photographs. Rule 1001(2) defines photographs to include, "still photographs, x-ray films, videotapes, and motion pictures." It should be noted that offering a photograph at trial will only involve the best evidence rule where the contents of the photograph itself are at issue. In the case of an allegedly obscene film, for example, the film's contents must be proved in order to establish the purported obscenity. Nevertheless, where a photograph of an item (itself not a writing, recording or photograph) is available to prove the appearance of the item, the best evidence rule does not operate to prefer the photograph over other evidence. Proof of the appearance of the object of the photograph is not subject to the best evidence rule. Consequently, where the appearance of a particular individual is sought to be established, the best evidence rule is not invoked.

X-rays. X-rays and x-ray films may invoke the operation of the best evidence rule. Where the object of proof is the physical condition of the person who has been x-rayed, the best evidence rule does not necessarily operate to prefer the X-ray over the testimony of the medical expert. The physical condition of the person in question is not a writing, recording or photograph. The testimony and the X-ray are both admissible to prove facts that are not within the scope of the Rule. Where, however, the X-ray is offered to establish a fact which may be derived only from the contents of the X-ray, the best evidence rule is invoked.

Original. The definition of an "original" is provided in Rule 1001(3). The Rule provides that an original writing or recording is the writing or recording itself and any counterpart intended by the person executing it or issuing it to be an original. Accordingly, a contract which is signed by the parties is an original even though the parties may not have initially distinguished that writing for execution. Multiple originals arise in the situation where, by virtue of intent, there is more than one original, for example, where parties to a bilateral contract intend that each should have an executed original.

Original of photograph. Rule 1001(3) provides that an original of a photograph is either "a negative or any print therefrom." In accordance with this Rule, either the negative or the print made from the negative is equally admissible in evidence as an original. The Rule also provides that any printout or other output readable by sight from a computer or electronic device is an original if the printout accurately reproduces the data that is stored. In addition to the printout, the computer data cards and magnetic tape should also be admissible as originals.

Duplicate. Rule 1001(4) provides a general definition of a duplicate that includes any counterpart that accurately reproduces the original. Accurate reproduction may be achieved by any of a variety of ways designated in the Rule, i.e., by the same impression, as in the case of a carbon copy; from the same matrix, as in the case of a published book; by means of photography, as in the case of photostats, enlargements, or reductions; by mechanical or electronic recording, as in the case of a tape recording; by chemical reproduction, as in the case of a thermofax copy; or by facsimile transmission or videotape; or by any equivalent techniques or means.

The rule refers to a counterpart; therefore handwritten copies will not qualify as counterparts under Rule 1001(4).

AUTHORITY

Weissenberger's Federal Evidence §§ 1001.1–.16

McCormick §§ 214, 229–31, 235

6 Weinstein 2d §§ 1001.01–.11

5 Mueller & Kirkpatrick §§ 551–566

3 Wigmore §§ 790, 792–98

4 Wigmore §§ 1173–80, 1230, 1232–41

Nance, *The Best Evidence Principle*, 73 Iowa L. Rev. 227 (1988)

Broun, *Authentication and the Contents of Writings*, 4 Ariz. St. L.J. 611 (1969)

Cleary & Strong, *The Best Evidence Rule: An Evaluation in Context*, 51 Iowa L. Rev. 383 (1952)

Cleary, *Evidence—Best Evidence Rule—Admissibility of a Carbon Copy as Primary Evidence*, 3 Vill. L. Rev. 217 (1958)

Levin, *Authentication and the Contents of Writings*, 10 Rutgers L. Rev. 632 (1956)

McMorrow, *Authentication and the Best Evidence Rule Under the Federal Rules of Evidence*, 16 Wayne L. Rev. 195 (1969)

Scott, *X-Ray Pictures as Evidence*, 44 Mich. L. Rev. 773 (1946)

Warton, *Duplicate Originals and the Best Evidence Rule*, 19 Ohio St. L.J. 520 (1958)

COMPARISON TO FEDERAL RULE

In substance, Colorado Rule 1001 is identical to Federal Rule 1001. However, on Dec. 1, 2011 Federal Rule 1001 was restyled. Please see Federal Rule 1001 in the appendix for comparison.

SIGNIFICANT CASES

Murray v. Just In Case Bus. Lighthouse, LLC, 374 P.3d 443 (Colo. 2016) ("under CRE 1006, trial courts abuse their discretion when they admit summary charts that characterize evidence in an argumentative fashion rather than simply organize it in a manner helpful to the trier of fact").

WRITINGS

Nesbitt v. Scott, 457 P.3d 134 (Colo. App. 2019) (when awarding attorney fees and costs, an "original" fee agreement is not required to prove the content of the writing, because not every motion for attorney fees and costs must be accompanied by a written fee agreement).

People v. Rieger, 436 P.3d 610 (Colo. App. 2019) (a digital image sent through a prison's electronic messaging system qualifies as physical evidence under Colorado's tampering with physical evidence statute (C.R.S. § 18-8-610), since persuasive authorities treat digital images as photographs and photographs are clearly "physical evidence" under the statute's unambiguous language).

Fasso v. Straten, 640 P.2d 272 (Colo. App. 1982) (court held photocopies of invoices and time records of contractor's work were admissible because duplicates are "generally admissible to the same extent as an original").

People v. Johnson, 613 P.2d 902 (Colo. App. 1980) (court held a recording of a conversation was admissible under the best evidence rule despite the fact that there were inaudible portions of the tape because these segments were not substantial enough to make the recording completely untrustworthy).

Chapter 1002

Rule 1002. Requirement of Original

Rule 1002 reads as follows:

To prove the content of a writing, recording, or photograph, the original writing, recording, or photograph is required, except as otherwise provided in these rules or by statute of the State of Colorado or of the United States.

ANALYSIS

Rule 1002 restates the traditional best evidence rule in modern terms. The Rule requires that in proving the contents of a writing, recording, or photograph, the original must be offered as evidence unless a foundation is established to justify its nonproduction. In addition, the Rule expressly provides that its application may be limited by statute or by other Rules of Evidence. It should be noted that the scope of Rule 1002 is in large part determined by the definition set forth in Rule 1001. *See* Analysis to Rule 1001.

In applying Rule 1002 it should be recognized that the Rule is only applicable where two conditions occur: (1) the evidence involves a writing, recording or photograph; and (2) the object of proof is the contents of that writing, recording or photograph. The first condition indicates that Rule 1002 is inapplicable in proving the nature of uninscribed physical objects or a fact which is subsequently memorialized in a writing. Consequently, the best evidence rule codified in Rule 1002 does not require that a confiscated substance be introduced into evidence to prove the nature, identity or status of the substance. The second condition for application of the best evidence rule provides that the Rule is only applicable where a party offering evidence seeks to prove the contents of that writing, recording, or photograph. A party is seeking to prove the contents of a writing, recording, or photograph only where the issue is what the writing or recording says or what the photograph depicts.

Illustration 1
Where the issue is whether a written contract obligates a party to perform in a certain way, the best evidence rule is triggered because the contract, being embodied in the writing, is established by proving the content of the writing.

Illustration 2

Where a motion picture is offered to prove an external fact, such as the mobility of the plaintiff, the best evidence rule is not implicated because the contents of the film are not at issue, only the mobility of the plaintiff.

STATUTES

The Rule provides for the continued application of any statutes that provide for the admissibility of copies. Specifically, the provision would preserve the Uniform Photographic Copies of Business and Public Records as Evidence Act under C.R.S. § 13-26-102, which permits copies of records kept in the regular course of business to be admissible as originals.

Statute reads as follows:

§ 13-26-102. Business and Public records as evidence

If any business, institution, or member of a profession or calling or any department or agency of government in the regular course of business or activities keeps or records any memorandum, writing, entry, print, or representation, or combination thereof, of any act, transaction, occurrence, or event and in the regular course of business has caused any of the same to be recorded, copied, or reproduced by any photographic, photostatic, microfilm, microcard, miniature photographic, optical disk or other form of mass storage, electronic imaging, electronic data processing, electronically transmitted facsimile, print out or other reproduction of electronically stored data or other process which accurately reproduces or forms a durable medium for reproducing the original, the original may be destroyed in the regular course of business unless held in a custodial or fiduciary capacity or unless its preservation is required by law. Such reproduction, when satisfactorily identified, is as admissible evidence as the original itself in any judicial or administrative proceeding whether the original is in existence or not, and an enlargement or facsimile of such reproduction is likewise admissible in evidence if the original reproduction is in existence and available for inspection under direction of the court. The introduction of a reproduced record, enlargement, or facsimile does not preclude admission of the original. The shall not be construed to exclude from evidence any document of copy thereof which is otherwise admissible under the rules of evidence.

AUTHORITY

WEISSENBERGER'S FEDERAL EVIDENCE §§1002.1–.4

McCORMICK §§229–33

6 WEINSTEIN 2d §§1002.01–.05

5 MUELLER & KIRKPATRICK §§567–571

4 WIGMORE §§1171–83

Nance, *The Best Evidence Principle*, 73 IOWA L. REV. 227 (1988)

Broun, *Authentication and Contents of Writings*, 4 ARIZ. ST. L.J. 611 (1969)

Cleary & Strong, *The Best Evidence Rule: An Evaluation in Context*, 51 IOWA L. REV. 825 (1966)

Levin, *Authentication and Content of Writings*, 10 RUTGERS L. REV. 632 (1956)

Comment, *Authentication and the Best Evidence Rule Under the Federal Rules of Evidence*, 16 WAYNE L.
REV. 195 (1969)

Note, *A Critical Appraisal of the Application of the Best Evidence Rule*, 21 RUTGERS L. REV. 526 (1967)

COMPARISON TO FEDERAL RULE

In substance, Colorado Rule 1002 is parallel to Federal Rule 1002. However, on Dec. 1, 2011
Federal Rule 1002 was restyled. Please see Federal Rule 1002 in the appendix for comparison.

SIGNIFICANT CASES

People v. Saiz, 32 P.3d 441 (Colo. 2001) (the best evidence rule did not require the admission of a
videotape of inconsistent statements from an interview of the defendant's son who testified, since no
rule or principle of evidence requires the admission of tape recordings either in addition to, or in place
of, testimony about events that are depicted in recordings).

People v. Robinson, 908 P.2d 1152 (Colo. App. 1995) (the defendant sought to exclude the testimony
regarding the contents of a surveillance videotape of the alleged crime, on the basis that testimony
about the contents of the videotape violated the best evidence rule; the trial court properly admitted the
testimony because rule 1002 does not prevent testimony regarding the subject of a videotape).

Airborne, Inc. v. Denver Air Ctr., Inc., 832 P.2d 1086 (Colo. App. 1992) (court held a summary of a
voluminous writing, a summary of revenue to prove a basis for damages did not violate the best
evidence rule).

People v. Wortham, 690 P.2d 876 (Colo. App. 1984) (trial court did not abuse its discretion by allowing
testimony about a "For Rent" sign as opposed to requiring the sign itself).

People v. Williams, 654 P.2d 319 (Colo. App. 1982) (introduction of photograph of chattel, rather than
chattel itself did not violate the best evidence rule because the contents of what was photographed was
not being proved).

WRITINGS

Chapter 1003

Rule 1003. Admissibility of Duplicates

Rule 1003 reads as follows:

> A duplicate is admissible to the same extent as an original unless (1) a genuine question is raised as to the authenticity of the original or (2) in the circumstances it would be unfair to admit the duplicate in lieu of the original.

ANALYSIS

Rule 1003 provides that duplicates are generally admissible as originals in all cases except where there is a genuine question of authenticity of the original, or where admission of the duplicate instead of the original would be unfair. The term "duplicate" is defined in Rule 1001(4). *See* Analysis to Rule 1001.

It should be noted that Rule 1003 does not create a "second best" evidence rule. In no case does it actually require the use of a duplicate. Nor does it create a hierarchy of secondary evidence in which a duplicate is preferred over some other type of secondary evidence. Rather, the Rule provides that a duplicate may be used interchangeably with an original, unless the opponent of the evidence challenges the use of the duplicate on one of the grounds specified in the Rule. Consequently, use of a duplicate does not require laying a foundation as to why the use of the original is excused. The duplicate is merely used in lieu of the original and will operate as the original unless appropriately challenged under the Rule.

Examples. Where there is a question as to whether the original was altered before the reproduction was made, whether accidentally, negligently or fraudulently, production of the original should be required where the opponent raises the appropriate objection under the Rule. Likewise, where a duplicating process fails to produce some of the most essential parts of an original, fairness may require production of the original.

It should also be observed that a duplicate, as defined by Rule 1001(4), may be used as "other evidence of the contents," even if Rule 1003 does not apply, so long as the requisites of Rule 1004 are met.

Statutes. A document determined not to be a duplicate under Rule 1003 could possibly be admissible as a copy under Rule 1004. Under C.R.S. § 13-26-102, copies made and kept in the ordinary course of business are treated as originals. Rule 1003 expands on this statute and permits copies in general to be treated as originals, without regard to whether they were prepared in the ordinary course of business.

AUTHORITY

WEISSENBERGER'S FEDERAL EVIDENCE §§ 1003.1–.3

McCORMICK §§ 229, 231, 235, 236

6 WEINSTEIN 2d §§ 1003.01–.05

5 MUELLER & KIRKPATRICK §§ 572–574

4–5 WIGMORE §§ 1177–80, 1190, 1198, 1229, 1232–41, 1249

Broun, *Authentication and the Contents of Writings*, 4 ARIZ. ST. L.J. 611 (1969)

Cleary & Strong, *The Best Evidence Rule: An Evaluation in Context*, 51 IOWA L. REV. 825 (1966)

Cleary, *Evidence—Best Evidence Rule— Admissibility of a Carbon Copy as Primary Evidence*, 3 VILL. L. REV. 217 (1958)

Note, *Authentication and the Best Evidence Rule Under the Federal Rules of Evidence*, 16 WAYNE L. REV. 195 (1969)

Comment, *The Best Evidence Rule—A Criticism*, 3 NEWARK L. REV. 200 (1938)

COMPARISON TO FEDERAL RULE

In substance, Colorado Rule 1003 is identical to Federal Rule 1003. However, on Dec. 1, 2011 Federal Rule 1003 was restyled. Please see Federal Rule 1003 in the appendix for comparison.

SIGNIFICANT CASES

People v. Huehn, 53 P.3d 733 (Colo. App. 2002) (mere speculation or supposition that an original document may have contained information that the duplicate did not, or vice versa, does not amount to a showing that it would be unfair to admit the duplicate, and thus does not preclude admission of the duplicate under CRE 1003).

In re Estate of Perry, 33 P.3d 1235 (Colo. App. 2001) (CRE 1003 and 1004 did not require the admission of a photocopy of a will to probate since CRE 1003 and 1004 do not provide the standards that control the admission of a will to probate).

People v. Chavez, 764 P.2d 371 (Colo. App. 1988) (trial court did not err by admitting a photocopy of defendant's declaration of ownership of a piece of jewelry).

People v. Weese, 753 P.2d 778 (Colo. App. 1987) (court held microfilm copies of driver's license was admissible as a duplicate).

Equico Lessors, Inc. v. Tak's Automotive Serv., 680 P.2d 854 (Colo. App. 1984) (trial court did not err by not admitting carbon duplicates when no genuine question was raised as to the authenticity of such duplicate).

People v. Wolfe, 662 P.2d 502 (Colo. App. 1983) (duplicates of bank records, check registers, and an admission by defendant with notations added to them were admissible because such duplicates with alterations are admissible "provided a full and satisfactory explanation of such alterations is made prior to their admission").

Fasso v. Straten, 640 P.2d 272 (Colo. App. 1982) (court held it was proper for trial court to admit duplicates of construction invoices and records of labor despite the fact that a party had such duplicates in their possession for eight months and knew of the original).

Chapter 1004

Rule 1004. Admissibility of Other Evidence of Contents

Rule 1004 reads as follows:

> The original is not required, and other evidence of the contents of a writing, recording, or photograph is admissible if:
>
> *(1) Originals lost or destroyed.* All originals are lost or have been destroyed, unless the proponent lost or destroyed them in bad faith; or
>
> *(2) Original not obtainable.* No original can be obtained by any available judicial process or procedure; or
>
> *(3) Original in possession of opponent.* At a time when an original was under the control of the party against whom offered, he was put on notice, by the pleadings or otherwise, that the contents would be a subject of proof at the hearing, and he does not produce the original at the hearing; or
>
> *(4) Collateral matters.* The writing, recording, or photograph is not closely related to a controlling issue.

ANALYSIS

Rule 1004 lists four general situations in which originals are not required to be produced and in which secondary evidence may be used to prove the contents of a writing, recording or photograph. If one of the Rule 1004 exceptions applies, a party may prove the contents of a writing, recording or photograph with any secondary evidence. Rule 1004 rejects the concept of degrees of secondary evidence, and the Rule allows any form of secondary evidence to be used to prove the contents of the original where an exception is satisfied.

Secondary evidence may consist of any of the following illustrations without ranking as to priority:

1. A duplicate original as defined in Rule 1001(4), even if Rule 1003 is not applicable.

2. A carbon or photocopy not otherwise admissible under Rule 1003.

3. Testimony of a witness who recalls the content of the writing, photograph, or recording.

4. Circumstantial evidence from which an inference could be made as to what the contents were.

It should be noted that Rule 1004 is superseded as far as public records are concerned by Rule 1005.

(1) Originals lost or destroyed

Rule 1004(1) codifies the principle that where an original is lost or destroyed, secondary evidence of the contents of the original is admissible providing the party offering the secondary evidence has not lost or destroyed the original in bad faith. Courts have traditionally placed the burden for proof of loss or destruction on the party offering the secondary evidence, and the party offering the secondary evidence must justify use of the secondary evidence by establishing a foundation satisfactory to the court to show that the original cannot be produced. Where the proponent is relying upon loss as a basis for nonproduction of the original, he or she must show that a reasonable or diligent search was undertaken. Destruction may be proven by direct or circumstantial evidence.

Rule 1004(1) does not absolutely bar a proponent from introducing secondary evidence to prove the contents of the original where the party lost or destroyed the original. The Rule only prohibits a party from introducing secondary evidence where the party has lost or destroyed the original in bad faith. While the Rule does not define bad faith, it is clear that the term applies to the destruction of an original with the intent of preventing its use as evidence or with the intent of perpetrating a fraud.

(2) Original not obtainable

Rule 1004(2) relieves the proponent from using the original to prove contents where the original is not obtainable by available judicial process. Although the Rule does not define the circumstances under which an original is unobtainable, case law generally provides that an original is unavailable where it is merely shown that the original is outside the court's jurisdiction. Rule 1004(2) is applicable where a third party within the jurisdiction refuses to produce a document, and where the object in question cannot be readily produced in the court, such as in the situation where the writing is inscribed on a tombstone.

Although no showing of an effort to produce the original is required where the original is outside the court's jurisdiction, such an effort must be shown where the original is within the jurisdiction. In essence, the effort required is that of serving a writ of subpoena duces tecum on the party possessing the original. Secondary evidence should be admitted where the possessor of the original refuses to obey the subpoena.

(3) Original in possession of opponent

Rule 1004(3) provides that if an adverse party (1) possesses or controls an original; (2) has received notice that the contents of the original will be an issue at the hearing; and (3) fails to produce the original, then secondary evidence of the original's contents will be admissible if offered by the opponent of the party in possession of the original. It should be noted that this Rule operates as a justification for the admission of secondary evidence. It does not have any compulsory force to produce the original. Also, it should be noted that satisfactory notice under the Rule may be effected through the pleading or through other means. The Rule does not require any formal notice.

Illustration

Q: Did you send a letter on or about July 10 to the defendant concerning the contract?

A: Yes.

Q:	Do you have the letter?
A:	No, the defendant has it.
Counsel:	Your Honor, the defendant was notified by pleadings in this case that the contents of this letter would be the subject of proof at this trial today and defendant has failed to bring the original to court, today.
Court:	Yes, counselor, you have met the requirements of Evidence Rule 1004(3). You may proceed.
Q:	Do you recall the contents of that letter?

(4) Collateral matters

Rule 1004(4) provides that proof of the contents of writings, recordings or photographs may be established by secondary evidence where the contents are not closely related to a central or controlling issue in the litigation. The trial court has wide discretion in determining whether proof of the contents is collateral to the matter at issue.

AUTHORITY

WEISSENBERGER'S FEDERAL EVIDENCE §§ 1004.1–.12

McCORMICK §§ 234–39

6 WEINSTEIN 2d §§ 1004.01–.41

5 MUELLER & KIRKPATRICK §§ 575–580

4 WIGMORE §§ 1188, 1189, 1192–1217, 1252–54, 1264–75

Levin, *Authentication and Contents of Writings*, 10 RUTGERS L. REV. 632 (1956)

Comment, *Evidence—Degrees of Secondary Evidence—Problems in Application of the So-Called "American Rule,"* 38 MICH. L. REV. 864 (1940)

Note, *Evidence—What Is Required to Establish a Lost Instrument*, 15 U. DET. L.J. 192 (1952)

Note, *Evidence—Documents—"Best Evidence" Rule Applied to Prevent Introduction of a Recording of a Destroyed Recording*, 64 HARV. L. REV. 1369 (1951)

COMPARISON TO FEDERAL RULE

In substance, Colorado Rule 1004 is identical to Federal Rule 1004. However, on Dec. 1, 2011 Federal Rule 1004 was restyled. Please see Federal Rule 1004 in the appendix for comparison.

SIGNIFICANT CASES

In re Estate of Perry, 33 P.3d 1235 (Colo. App. 2001) (CRE 1003 and 1004 did not require the admission of a photocopy of a will to probate since CRE 1003 and 1004 do not provide the standards that control the admission of a will to probate).

United Cable Television of Jeffco, Inc. v. Montgomery LC, Inc., 942 P.2d 1230 (Colo. App. 1996) (the plaintiff sought to introduce secondary evidence of the existence of an indemnification agreement between the parties because the original had been destroyed; the trial court improperly excluded the evidence since there was no showing that bad faith caused the loss or destruction of the original document).

People v. Banks, 655 P.2d 1384 (Colo. App. 1982) (where defendant's recorded statement on tape was erased and reused by a court reporter who transcribed defendant's statement from shorthand notes, the best evidence rule was not violated by the tape recording being erased. Tape recording as well as stenographic short hand notes were original evidence, but transcription prepared directly from shorthand notes which were illegible to jury served as best available evidence).

Chapter 1005

Rule 1005. Public Records

Rule 1005 reads as follows:

The contents of an official record, or of a document authorized to be recorded, or filed and actually recorded or filed, including data compilations in any form, if otherwise admissible, may be proved by copy, certified as correct in accordance with Rule 902 or testified to be correct by a witness who has compared it with the original. If a copy which complies with the foregoing cannot be obtained by the exercise of reasonable diligence, then other evidence of the contents may be given.

ANALYSIS

Rule 1005 provides that a copy of the public record may be used to prove contents of the original where the copy is certified as correct in accordance with Evidence Rule 902 or authenticated as correct by testimony from a witness who has compared the copy with the original. The Rule also provides that if a copy cannot be obtained by the exercise of reasonable diligence, "other evidence of the contents may be given."

Degrees of secondary evidence. By establishing a preference for certified copies or copies which are testified to be correct of official records and filed or recorded documents, Rule 1005 introduces into the Rules the concept of degrees of secondary evidence for documents within its purview. Copies of official records that are authenticated by the stipulated requirements are preferred to any other secondary evidence which might be offered to prove the contents of a public record.

Rule 1003 preempted. Accordingly, Rule 1005 preempts Rule 1003's general provision that duplicates are admissible as originals.

Rule 1004 preempted. In addition, the Rule supersedes Rule 1004 insofar as it allows the use of a copy certified or testified to be correct without any showing that the original is lost, destroyed, unobtainable, or pertinent to a collateral matter. It further supersedes Rule 1004 by creating a mandatory preference for the use of certified copies or copies testified to be correct over other types of secondary evidence.

Documents covered. It should be noted that Rule 1005 applies to public documents as well as to documents authorized to be filed or recorded and actually filed or recorded. It thereby authorizes the proof of the contents of such recorded documents as deeds, leases, or mortgages.

Secondary evidence. Rule 1005 provides that if, by the reasonable exercise of diligence, a copy that satisfies Rule 1005 cannot be obtained, other evidence of the contents of the public record may be admitted. Where this provision is satisfied, any otherwise admissible secondary evidence may be offered to prove the contents of the document. Secondary evidence might include, for example, an uncertified copy of the document, testimony by somebody familiar with the contents of the document, or other documentary evidence.

Obvious examples of the application of this rule would be:

1. Birth and death certificates, marriage records

2. Recorded deeds

3. Police records

4. Workers' compensation files

5. Rolls of the Supreme Court, Medical Board or other licensing agencies

6. Records of the Treasurer's and Auditor's office to show amount of taxes or assessments

7. U.S. Veterans' Bureau records

8. Statistical data

9. Court files

10. Reports or returns required by law to be filed with a government agency

Any report or document falling within this Rule must be otherwise admissible. This Rule only establishes the method by which the best evidence rule is satisfied.

AUTHORITY

WEISSENBERGER'S FEDERAL EVIDENCE §§ 1005.1–.4

MCCORMICK § 240

6 WEINSTEIN 2d §§ 1005.01–.06

5 MUELLER & KIRKPATRICK §§ 581–582

4 WIGMORE §§ 1215–18

Broun, *Authentication and Contents of Writings*, 4 ARIZ. ST. L.J. 611 (1969)

Cleary & Strong, *The Best Evidence Rule: An Evaluation in Context*, 51 IOWA L. REV. 825 (1966)

Levin, *Authentication and the Content of Writings*, 10 RUTGERS L. REV. 632 (1956)

Orfield, *Proof of Official Records in Federal Cases*, 22 MONT. L. REV. 137 (1961)

COMPARISON TO FEDERAL RULE

In substance, Colorado Rule 1005 is identical to Federal Rule 1005. However, on Dec. 1, 2011 Federal Rule 1005 was restyled. Please see Federal Rule 1005 in the appendix for comparison.

SIGNIFICANT CASES

People v. Weese, 753 P.2d 778 (Colo. App. 1987) (trial court's admission of microfilm copies of defendant's driver's license was not an abuse of discretion because a copy of a public record is admissible when an expert who has compared the copy to the original testifies to prove it is evidence of the original).

McClellan v. State, 731 P.2d 769 (Colo. App. 1986) (records of plaintiff's arrest for DUI, including copies of intoxilyzer test record, computer printouts of plaintiff's arrest, and car impound records, which were identified by arresting officer under oath, were properly admitted).

In re Marriage of Plummer, 709 P.2d 1388 (Colo. App. 1985) (court held that trial court's admission of photocopies pertaining to a wife's out of state property without proper authentication constituted error. The owner of the document testifying as to its authenticity may achieve Authentication of an official record).

People v. Johnson, 613 P.2d 902 (Colo. App. 1980) (a certified copy of a public record is properly authenticated, therefore a certified copy of defendant's New Mexico conviction is admissible to prove the defendant is a habitual criminal).

Chapter 1006

Rule 1006. Summaries

Rule 1006 reads as follows:

> The contents of voluminous writings, recordings, or photographs which cannot conveniently be examined in court may be presented in the form of a chart, summary, or calculation. The originals or duplicates, shall be made available for examination or copying, or both, by other parties at reasonable time and place. The court may order that they be produced in court.

ANALYSIS

Rule 1006 codifies an exception to the best evidence rule in providing that where writings are voluminous, summaries, abstracts, or schedules may be admitted into evidence. For a summary, calculation, or chart to be admissible under Rule 1006, three conditions must be satisfied. First, the writings, recordings or photographs must be voluminous. This is a question for the court. Second, a proper foundation must be established for the introduction of the summary. As part of this requirement, the originals must be admissible in order that the summaries, calculations or charts based on those originals be admissible. In addition, the charts, summaries or calculations may not include information not contained in or computed from the originals. Third, the originals or duplicates must be made available to all litigants for examination or copying at any reasonable time and place.

Illustration

Defendant has compiled a summary of all property transactions with regard to farm lands in the county within the past three years from records maintained by the county auditor's office and proposes to use the summary in lieu of specific records of the said auditor's office. Copies of all data are available for inspection or copying by the opposing party on request. The summary complies with Rule 1006.

The use of charts and summaries for illustrative purposes is governed by Rules 401–403 and 611, not by Rule 1006.

AUTHORITY

WEISSENBERGER'S FEDERAL EVIDENCE §§ 1006.1–.4

MCCORMICK § 240

6 WEINSTEIN 2d §§ 1006.01–.08

5 MUELLER & KIRKPATRICK §§ 583–585

4 WIGMORE § 1230

Broun, *Authentication and Contents of Writings*, 4 ARIZ. ST. L.J. 611 (1969)

Symposium on the Proposed Federal Rules of Evidence: Part II, 16 WAYNE L. REV. 195 (1969)

Dewey, *Best Evidence Rule—Use of Summaries of Voluminous Originals*, 37 MICH. L. REV. 499 (1939)

Comment, *Evidence: Best Evidence Rule: Admissibility of Secondary Evidence in Oklahoma*, 20 OKLA. L. REV. 56 (1967)

COMPARISON TO FEDERAL RULE

In substance, Colorado Rule 1006 is identical to Federal Rule 1006. However, on Dec. 1, 2011 Federal Rule 1006 was restyled. Please see Federal Rule 1006 in the appendix for comparison.

SIGNIFICANT CASES

United States Welding, Inc. v. B & C Steel, Inc., 261 P.3d 513 (Colo. App. 2011) (in breach of contract action it is proper for trial court to admit exhibit summarizing calculations of gross profits).

People v. McDonald, 15 P.3d 788 (Colo. App. 2000) (it was error to admit summaries of voluminous records pursuant to Rule 1006 where the proponent of the summaries failed to redact the records in accordance with patient confidentiality laws so that the records could be examined by the adverse party).

Airborne Inc. v. Denver Air Ctr., Inc., 832 P.2d 1086 (Colo. App. 1992) (summary of a company's revenues was properly admitted by trial court because the original documents had been given to defendants and proper foundation was laid by company president's testimony).

Pyles-Knutzen v. Bd. of Cnty. Comm'rs, 781 P.2d 164 (Colo. App. 1989) (summary of party's medical bills was admissible because party properly laid the foundation for the summary and party made the original bills available to opposing party by listing them in trial data certificate).

People v. Berger-Levy, 677 P.2d 351 (Colo. App. 1983) (court held "background information used by witness in making percentage calculations" which was presented to opposing party was admissible even though originals were not admitted into evidence).

Chapter 1007

Rule 1007. Testimony or Written Admission of Party

Rule 1007 reads as follows:

> Contents of writings, recordings, or photographs may be proved by the testimony or deposition of the party against whom offered or by his written admission, without accounting for the nonproduction of the original.

ANALYSIS

Rule 1007 shortcuts the best evidence requirement in certain cases where the opponent has admitted to the contents of the subject writing, photograph, or recording. In other words, the best evidence rule can be satisfied by offering an opponent's admission either in writing, or by testimony or deposition. Under Rule 1007 there is no necessity of accounting for the nonproduction of the original. The admission itself is sufficient to establish contents.

Therefore, the rule would not permit an out of court oral admission by an adversary to be sufficient to establish the contents of a writing. Since part of the basis for the original writings rule is centered around the idea that the exact wording of the writing may be essential, the danger of erroneous transmission of the oral admission would be substantial. This problem does not exist if the admission is at trial, in a deposition, or in writing.

It should be emphasized that the contents of the writing, recording or photograph sought to be proven through Rule 1007 need not have been prepared by the party whose admission is offered as a means of proof. For example, this exception to the best evidence rule may be used to prove the contents of a writing originally prepared by a person other than the party whose written or testimonial admission is used to prove contents.

Illustration

Action for slander. Defendant called to prove publication.

Q: *(To defendant by plaintiff's counsel)* Did you state in your deposition of September 24, that X had written a letter to you in which he acknowledged your telephone conversation with him?

A: Yes.

Q: And, did you also state that X said in his letter that he was surprised to hear you say in your telephone conversation with him that plaintiff was a liar and a cheat?

Objection: Best evidence and hearsay.

Court: Overruled.

The best evidence rule is satisfied because the testimony established that defendant admitted the contents of a writing (X's letter to D) in his deposition. The best evidence rule is satisfied under the provisions of Rule 1007 by such admission. Alternately the deposition could be read into evidence to establish the admission.

The letter of X is not offered to prove the truth of D's assertion but only to prove the slander was published by D to X. Therefore, the letter is not hearsay. *See* Rule 801.

AUTHORITY

WEISSENBERGER'S FEDERAL EVIDENCE §§ 1007.1–.3

McCORMICK § 242

6 WEINSTEIN 2d §§ 1007.01–.07

4 WIGMORE § 1255

Comment, *Evidence—Best Evidence Rule—Admissions of a Party as an Exception*, 17 TEX. L. REV. 371 (1939)

COMPARISON TO FEDERAL RULE

Colorado Rule 1007 is nearly identical to Federal Rule 1007. However, on Dec. 1, 2011 Federal Rule 1007 was restyled. Please see Federal Rule 1007 in the appendix for comparison.

Chapter 1008

Rule 1008. Functions of Court and Jury

Rule 1008 reads as follows:

When the admissibility of other evidence of contents of writings, recordings, or photographs under these rules depends upon the fulfillment of a condition of fact, the question whether the condition has been fulfilled is ordinarily for the court to determine in accordance with the provisions of Rule 104. However, when an issue is raised (a) whether the asserted writing ever existed, or (b) whether another writing, recording, or photograph produced at the trial is the original, or (c) whether other evidence of contents correctly reflects the contents, the issue is for the trier of fact to determine as in the case of other issues of fact.

ANALYSIS

Rule 1008 allocates responsibility for deciding preliminary questions of fact involving the admissibility of evidence other than originals to prove the contents of writings, records, or photographs. Factual questions otherwise respecting admissibility, which in reality are determinative issues in the case, and which generally turn on questions of credibility or the weight to be accorded certain evidence, are allocated to the trier of fact. Other preliminary questions of fact which relate to the admissibility of secondary evidence are within the province of the trial court.

Function of trial judge. Judges will decide if the original is lost or destroyed under Rule 1004(1); not required because it involves a collateral matter under Rule 1004(4); or when secondary evidence of public records or summaries is permissible under Rules 1005 and 1006. Under Rule 1008 the trial judge is not permitted to make a preliminary determination as to the appropriateness of secondary evidence and thereby exclude the secondary evidence based on a finding which embraces the conclusion that the original never existed, that some other writing, recording or photograph is the original, or that the offered secondary evidence is not a faithful reproduction of the original. These issues may not be taken from the trier of fact.

Function of trier of fact. This Rule implicitly allows the trier of fact to disregard evidence in which the conditional relevancy question is not adequately established. The trier of fact should place no probative value on evidence which it believes did not exist, which it believes was not the correct writing, or which it believes was inaccurate as to content. For example, the trier of fact may decline to attach probative value to a writing it believes was forged, or a writing or other evidence that it believes does not accurately reflect the contents of the original.

AUTHORITY

Weissenberger's Federal Evidence §§ 1008.1–.3

303

McCORMICK § 53 at 135–36

6 WEINSTEIN 2d §§ 1008.01–.05

5 MUELLER & KIRKPATRICK §§ 588–590

4 WIGMORE § 1192

Levin, *Authentication and Contents of Writings*, 10 RUTGERS L. REV. 632 (1956)

Comment, *Authentication and the Best Evidence Rule Under the Federal Rules of Evidence*, 16 WAYNE L. REV. 195 (1969)

Comment, *A Critical Appraisal of the Application of the Best Evidence Rule*, 21 RUTGERS L. REV. 526 (1967)

COMPARISON TO FEDERAL RULE

In substance, Colorado Rule 1008 is identical to Federal Rule 1008. However, on Dec. 1, 2011 Federal Rule 1008 was restyled. Please see Federal Rule 1008 in the appendix for comparison.

SIGNIFICANT CASES

United Cable Television of Jeffco, Inc. v. Montgomery LC, Inc., 942 P.2d 1230 (Colo. App. 1996) (where one party sought to admit into evidence the existence of a written document which was allegedly lost or destroyed, the court erred as a matter of law when it denied the admission of the evidence; admissibility of such evidence goes to its weight not the existence of the agreement which is a factual matter to be resolved by the trier of fact).

XI
MISCELLANEOUS RULES

MISC. FULES

Chapter 1101

Rule 1101. Applicability of Rules

Rule 1101 reads as follows:

(a) Courts. These rules apply to all courts in the State of Colorado.

(b) Proceedings generally. These rules apply generally to civil actions, to criminal proceedings, and to contempt proceedings, except those in which the court may act summarily.

(c) Rule of privilege. The rule with respect to privileges applies at all stages of all actions, cases, and proceedings.

(d) Rules inapplicable. The rules (other than with respect to privileges) do not apply in the following situations:

(1) Preliminary questions of fact. The determination of questions of fact preliminary to admissibility of evidence when the issue is to be determined by the court under Rule 104.

(2) Grand jury. Proceedings before grand juries.

(3) Miscellaneous proceedings. Proceedings for extradition or rendition; preliminary examinations in criminal cases; sentencing, or granting or revoking probation; issuance of warrants for arrest, criminal summonses, and search warrants; and proceedings with respect to release on bail or otherwise.

(e) Rules applicable in part. In any special statutory proceedings, these rules apply to the extent that matters of evidence are not provided for in the statutes which govern procedure therein.

ANALYSIS

Rule 1101 explains under what general circumstances the Colorado Rules of Evidence apply. The Colorado rule is derived from Rule 81 of the Colorado Rules of Civil Procedure and Rule 1101(e) of the Federal Rules of Evidence. The CRE apply to all Colorado courts in civil and criminal actions and in contempt proceedings under 1101(a) and (b).

Rule 1101(d) lists situations where the CRE are inapplicable. An example of such an exemption from the Rules is preliminary questions of fact under Rule 104.

Illustration

Evidence in deposition of deponent's whereabouts (which would excuse deponent's presence from trial because deponent is over 100 miles away from the court) need not be competent under CRE because it is a preliminary question of fact and therefore is not subject to the CRE.

Additionally, grand jury proceedings are exempted from the CRE under Rule 1101(d)(2). Rule 1101(d)(3) lists various instances where the CRE are inapplicable: extradition hearings, preliminary criminal hearings, sentencing, probation hearings, and other criminal proceedings including those to determine if warrants for arrest, summons, or search warrants may be issued, and hearings to determine whether bail should be granted.

Rule 1101(e) states that where the legislature has enacted a statutory scheme governing procedure of such a proceeding, the CRE do not apply. This exception to the rules of evidence has been used in workers' compensation hearings, as well as in products liability actions.

COMPARISON TO FEDERAL RULE

Colorado Rule 1101 is similar in substance to Federal Rule 1101. However, on Dec. 1, 2011 Federal Rule 1101 was restyled. Please see Federal Rule 1101 in the appendix for comparison.

SIGNIFICANT CASES

People v. Bowers, 801 P.2d 511 (Colo. 1990) ("a trial court is not bound by the formal rules of evidence in determining a preliminary question concerning the admissibility of evidence." Corroborative evidence establishing a child was sexually abused falls under the CRE 1101(d)(1). Also, where the legislature has created a statutory scheme with specific rules of evidence for certain cases, the trial court must follow that scheme under Rule 1101(e). The statute in this case creates an exception to the hearsay rule for a child's out of court statement and must be followed rather than the CRE).

Pruett v. Barry, 696 P.2d 789 (Colo. 1985) (while there is a tension in CRE 1101(d) and (e) concerning whether the rules of evidence are applicable or not for certain statutory proceedings, in an extradition trial a psychiatrist's report may be admissible because it is not directly related to the extradition itself).

People v. Pourat, 100 P.3d 503 (Colo. App. 2004) (although Colorado Rules of Evidence do not apply to sentencing hearings, it is an error for a court to rely "for sentencing purposes upon information and evidence not included within the presentence report or disclosed to defendant by some other means prior to the sentencing hearing") (not the final version and subject to revision upon final publication).

People v. McCoy, 939 P.2d 537 (Colo. App. 1997) (the rules of evidence do not apply to a quasi-judicial proceeding conducted under the Colorado Youthful Offender System, and therefore, the admission of hearsay evidence is permissible).

Donley v. State, 817 P.2d 629 (Colo. App. 1991) (evidence of a deponent being physically out of court's jurisdiction, deponent was more than 100 miles away, is a preliminary question of fact, and not subject to the rules of evidence).

Chambers v. CF&I Steel Corp., 757 P.2d 1171 (Colo. App. 1988) (in a workers' compensation hearing a counselor's testimony was wrongfully excluded under Rule 704 because a workers' compensation statute mandates the CRE apply in such hearings).

Chapter 1102

Rule 1102. *(No Colorado Rule Codified)*

Chapter 1103

Rule 1103. Title

Rule 1103 reads as follows:

These rules shall be known and cited as the Colorado Rules of Evidence, or CRE.